SHAPING COLLEGE FOOTBALL

Sports and Entertainment

Steven A. Riess, *Series Editor*

SHAPING
COLLEGE FOOTBALL

The Transformation of an American Sport, 1919–1930

RAYMOND SCHMIDT

SYRACUSE UNIVERSITY PRESS

First Edition 2007
07   08   09   10   11   12   6   5   4   3   2   1

A version of the chapter covering Haskell Indian Institute football previously appeared in the Fall
2001 issue of *NASSH Journal of Sport History*. Permission to reprint is gratefully acknowledged.

The paper used in this publication meets the minimum requirements of American National Standard
for Information Sciences—Permanence of Paper for Printed Library Materials, ANSI Z39.48–1984.∞™

For a listing of books published and distributed by Syracuse University Press, visit our Web site at
SyracuseUniversityPress.syr.edu.

ISBN-13: 978-0-8156-0886-8
ISBN-10: 0-8156-0886-1

Library of Congress Cataloging-in-Publication Data
Schmidt, Raymond.
    Shaping college football : the transformation of an American sport, 1919–1930 / Raymond Schmidt.
— 1st ed.
        p. cm.
    Includes bibliographical references and index.
    ISBN 978-0-8156-0886-8 (hardcover : alk. paper)
    1. Football—United States—History. 2. College sports—United States—History. I. Title.

GV950.S395 2007
796.332′630973—dc22   2007012397

Manufactured in the United States of America

For my good friends Bernie and Mark,

for reawakening my interest in the

history of college football years ago

and for their constant encouragement

RAYMOND SCHMIDT, a sport historian, is the author of two other books: *Two-eyed League* and *Football's Stars of Summer*. He has also authored articles for several reference collections, *Chicago History* magazine, and the *Journal of Sport History*. Schmidt is retired from a career of thirty-four years in software development for a major corporation based in Chicago and has served as editor of the *College Football Historical Society Journal* for nineteen years. He now lives in Ventura, California, with his daughter and granddaughter.

CONTENTS

ILLUSTRATIONS

PREFACE

The decade of the 1920s is traditionally referred to as the "golden age" of American athletic history—a time when many of the most charismatic and significant characters populated the world of sport. One of the most popular and meaningful games of the time for American culture was intercollegiate football.

Ranging from the return of normalcy in American collegiate sport in 1919 after World War I through the untimely passing of Notre Dame's Knute Rockne in early 1931, college football was peopled with colorful and outstanding players, teams, and coaches—many of whom will always be considered as among the sport's greatest of all time.

Yet this era of college football history more significantly represents a time of conversion or transformation of the sport into one that by 1931 very much contained all the foundation stones for the modern and commercialized game that today dominates our attention on autumn weekends. In looking at the events of college football's golden era, it was the many aspects of this transformation that intrigued me, as they combined with the gridiron game's inherent glamour and the freewheeling times of the post–World War I years to produce a sport that appealed to a very wide range of the still evolving landscape of American society.

To be sure, there have been any number of secondary sources on college football history that at some point eventually get around to mentioning the decade of the 1920s, but then usually only to skim the surface of the factors that shaped the intercollegiate game. A far more complete examination of the events of the time within the sport was possible only through an extensive use of sources such as newspaper and magazine articles from those years. Of invaluable assistance also was the considerable material that was unearthed in the archives of the universities visited, along with the student and alumni publications of the various schools.

During the approximately seven years required to research and write this history of college football's most significant era—hampered for the first few years by the requirements of my regular job—it was my privilege to visit sixteen university archives from coast to coast. A few other universities were far less than cooperative when contacted about a potential visit by a sport historian, but I prefer to recall the many archivists who did so much to make my research trips productive.

I would like to express my great appreciation to the archivists and their staffs at the following universities that were visited: Chicago, Georgetown, Illinois, Princeton, Notre Dame, St. Louis, Haskell Indian Nations, Missouri, Iowa, Ohio State, Fordham, Yale, Boston College, Detroit, Marquette, and St. Mary's of California. The reference staffs at the Harold Washington Public Library in Chicago and the Joliet (Illinois) Public Library were also extremely helpful in retrieving bound collections of old magazines from the dustiest and most remote of storage areas.

At this late date it is impossible to remember when the original concept for this work came to me. But after sketching out the initial list of topics to be researched and examined, I received significant encouragement to proceed from my two now departed friends and fellow football historians, Bernie McCarty and Mark Purcell. I am also very appreciative of the valuable comments and recommendations received about selected chapters from my friends and noted authors in the field of sport history, Professors Ronald A. Smith, Roger Saylor, and David Wiggins. In particular, I owe an immeasurable amount of gratitude to my friend and fellow historian Robert Pruter of Lewis University, who patiently and relentlessly read most of the manuscript during its development and offered many invaluable suggestions.

It is difficult to believe that the work on this project is now at last completed. I remember the many enjoyable hours of reading articles, poring through files of correspondence at various archives, and visiting the many schools where I was surrounded by such a sense of history, tradition, and learning. I loved every minute of it and would do it all again.

SHAPING COLLEGE FOOTBALL

INTRODUCTION

The decade of the 1920s has traditionally been referred to as the "golden age" of sports, although as the twentieth century was coming to a close it had become fashionable for the current-day media to decry the notion that an earlier era than theirs might have actually had some significance.

Yet extremely important those long-ago days of sport were, as the sweeping changes in American society and attitudes in the aftermath of World War I became driving forces in the transformation and definition of big-time commercialized sport that is so much a part of modern-day American culture. Providing the centerpiece for this defining era of sport was a cadre of colorful athletes such as Jack Dempsey, Gertrude Ederle, the Four Horsemen of Notre Dame, Red Grange, Bobby Jones, Suzanne Lenglen, Babe Ruth, Bill Tilden, Helen Wills, and others, performers who lent an aura of charisma and excitement that captivated the sports fans of that time—and who remain icons of American sport even into the twenty-first century.[1]

College football was one of those games that was at the center of America's craze for all things sporting during the 1920s. Through the expanded and improved attention given to the sport by the nation's newspapers and periodicals, college football of the 1920s, and all its surroundings, came to represent much of the reckless jazz-era culture of the Roaring Twenties for the general public. Beyond their exploits on the field, college football heroes—through writings and illustrations—were depicted as the epitome of young American masculinity, and the campus idols who usually attracted the willowy coeds. Although college football continued to be a predominantly male-oriented world during the 1920s, women on occasion appeared prominently in advertisements with a football setting in magazines and game programs, and at times even on game program covers. Often portrayed as avid followers of the gridiron sport, these illustrations of women were used to demonstrate the widespread popularity of college football while also lending social sophistication to the events. Periodicals in particular painted the collegiate game as the center of a glamorous, carefree world that included plenty of pep rallies, flappers, hip flasks, raccoon coats, and sophisticated football weekends.[2]

Although the intercollegiate gridiron game was already a half century old by the close of World War I, probably no other sport ever experienced such sweeping transformations as did college football during the 1920s. These transformations were significant changes that combined to migrate the game of college football from its semicloistered world of prewar days to one that by the end of the decade bore many of the characteristics of any late-twentieth-century American sport, or, in some cases, at least established the foundation stones for the completion of that migration in the following decades. Among those aspects of college football undergoing radical reshaping were the style of play, the stadia and locales in which the games unfolded, the financial significance and prestige possibilities available to the successful football schools, a recognition of football's importance and place within an increasingly urbanized and ethnically diverse American society, and even the very place of intercollegiate sport within the university community. By the dawning of the twenty-first century the sport of college football had moved through several notable eras, yet no period in its history other than the 1920s contained so many of those defining circumstances that ultimately resulted in the multimillion-dollar spectacles that can be witnessed today on fall Saturday afternoons.[3]

Prior to this era of the 1920s, college football was a sport that operated predominantly in a semiregionalized campus setting. Games were primarily played in relatively small stadia, with only Harvard (1903), Syracuse (1907), and Princeton (1914) having constructed steel and concrete stadia with relatively large seating capacities before World War I. There had been intersectional games dating back to college football's earliest days, such as the Michigan-Cornell matchups in the 1890s or Brown's visit to Chicago in 1899, but the truly long-distance intersectional game was not a consistent part of the college football scene until the Tournament of Roses games of 1916 and 1917. And dating from its earliest days, college football had been significantly influenced by the eastern universities, most notably the so-called Big Three of Harvard, Princeton, and Yale. Whether in the areas of rules making, style-of-play concepts, or in filling out the annual All-America selections, the eastern schools had wielded more than their fair share of clout.

The timetable for the other regions of the country beginning to play a larger role on the college football scene was delayed by several events. The greatest factor of all was the concern over the sport's ongoing level of violence. It was manifested in the Western Conference (later known as the Big Ten) in 1906 and 1907, when member schools were allowed to play football schedules of only five games, and thereafter were still required for many years to play annual schedules that were shorter than the calendars of major schools in other regions. On the Pacific Coast, schools such as Stanford (1906–1917), California (1906–1914), and Southern California (1911–1913) played rugby instead of American football, significantly retarding the development of technical playing skills on the West Coast.

With the onset of America's involvement in World War I, the impact on college football was significant. Because of manpower shortages, some schools such as Tennessee, Georgia, Cornell, Alabama, and Colgate dropped the sport for either one or both of the seasons 1917 and 1918. The Big Three of Harvard, Yale, and Princeton each fielded informal teams during those years and played only a limited number of games, all against military-related opponents.[4]

When World War I ended, the American servicemen flocked back to the States, and the country was about to become a much different place. Ahead were the days of Prohibition, the expansion of capitalism, and the booming stock market, along with the continuing issues of women's suffrage, racial conflict, and immigration. But the 1920s was also to be a time of release from the tensions and ordeals of the war. The youth of the United States had been very much changed by the European conflict, and what was about to follow was a revolution of manners and morals.[5]

In the aftermath of the war Americans were ready to partake in the continued evolution of a social structure based on capitalism, prosperity, and mass consumerism. This society was increasingly being driven by technology—a rapidly increasing ownership of automobiles during the 1920s being one example—and a growing middle class, one prepared to cast aside most of the puritanical restraints and provincial attitudes that had characterized much of prewar American culture. This embracing of a secular modern world—one that no longer relied on Old World values—also included a growing appreciation for higher education and its benefits. Between 1900 and 1930, the number of Americans between eighteen and twenty-one years of age who were enrolled in college increased from 4 percent in 1900 to 12.42 percent in 1930. Historian Stanley Coben has written that this trend was stimulated by a growing demand for professionalism in nearly every field, which "made academic degrees or professional credentials almost essential for advancement, if not employment," in postwar America.[6]

The world of college football was one of the significant beneficiaries of America's burgeoning interest in higher education, as the growing enrollments of colleges and universities provided a broader population base of potential athletes and ticket-buying fans. Historians Frank Freidel and Alan Brinkley have noted the changing attitudes of postwar collegians, writing that "an increasing number of students saw school as a place not just for academic training but for organized athletics, extracurricular activities . . . that is, as an institution that allowed them to define themselves less in terms of their families and more in terms of their peer group." Among the results was an onslaught of capable and exciting football teams and individual stars, which served to generate growing numbers of student and alumni fans, and in turn quickly outstripped the limited seating capacities available in the existing college football stadia. These factors all played significant roles during the era in the transformation of college football into the big-time commercialized sport upon which schools ultimately became so dependent. In 1919—the actual starting point for the gridiron sport's "golden era"—there was an attitude of change in the college football world, and significant was the spirit of entrepreneurship that pervaded the thinking of the major football universities and sport promoters from coast to coast. Ahead were twelve years of developments that would reshape the game of college football well beyond its prewar origins.[7]

When college football returned to normalcy in the 1919 season, the prevailing belief among many easterners was that the Big Three of Harvard, Princeton, and Yale would continue their leadership roles within the sport—both on and off the field of play. Although Walter Camp of Yale—credited with formulating so much of the American game's rules and techniques of play—was still alive and a member of the Football Rules Committee, the sport had already adopted a nationalized approach toward its governance in the years before World War I.[8] Thus, by 1919 the Big Three really no longer carried the political clout to any longer dictate the sport's administration. Even more significant was the fact that the wartime years had allowed the major universities of the Midwest and West Coast—soon joined by the South—to close the gap in technical playing skills between themselves and the eastern schools. Quickly, there was a noticeable shift in the balance of power away from the East on the field of play—evidenced in part by intersectional game results and All-America teams—as the gridiron game became truly "nationalized" in all respects.

Fueling the growing excitement surrounding college football during the early years of the era was the presence on the sidelines of many of the game's most legendary coaching names—including Amos Alonzo Stagg (Chicago), Fielding Yost (Michigan), Howard Jones (Iowa and Southern Cal), Glenn "Pop" Warner (Pittsburgh and Stanford), Knute Rockne (Notre Dame), Bob Zuppke (Illinois), Frank Cavanaugh (Boston College), Bill Alexander (Georgia Tech), Bill Roper (Princeton), and Ray Morrison (Southern Methodist)—and quickly many of these men were recognized as being the most important and influential personalities within the sport, a source of considerable discontent and controversy among the reform element. And to thrill gridiron fans around the country, the ranks of college football during the 1920s included such all-time stars as the Four Horsemen of Notre Dame, Red Grange of Illinois, Morley Drury of Southern California, Chris Cagle of Army, Johnny Mack Brown of Alabama, Brick Muller of California, Edgar Kaw of Cornell, Herb Joesting of Minnesota, Benny Friedman of Michigan, Gerry Mann of Southern Methodist, Ernie Nevers of Stanford, and Joel Hunt of Texas A&M.

None of these great coaches and players would have had quite the same impact in helping to fuel college football's transformation without two all-important publicity factors of the 1920s: the improvements in the newspapers' sport coverage and the development of radio as a viable commercial product. During the 1920s the major metropolitan newspapers progressively expanded the scope and quality of their college football coverage—featuring nationally recognized writers such as Allison Danzig and Grantland Rice—while bringing stories of every Saturday's major matchups from around the country to the eager followers of the gridiron game. It has become fashionable during the days of "revisionism" within sport history to belittle the frequently flowery prose—along with the often overglamor- izing of the period's star athletes—that typified a good deal of 1920s sportswriting, a case that completely overlooks the overwhelming majority of game coverage of that period, which was far superior and more comprehensive than any of the writ- ings of late-twentieth-century reporters. High-quality photos, along with articu- late columns of opinion and analysis, helped the newspapers to build enthusiasm for the collegiate sport.[9]

The first significant radio broadcasts of college football games took place in 1920 (Texas A&M–Texas) and 1921 (Pittsburgh–West Virginia), while the 1922 broadcast of the Princeton-Chicago meeting holds a place as the first game broad- cast to an intersectional audience. Sport radio and television historian Ronald Smith has noted the substantial interest generated in the East and Midwest by the broadcast of the 1922 Princeton-Chicago game and describes it as "probably the most important radio broadcast up to that point." The popularity and significance of radio in the spread of national interest in college football can be seen by January 1928, when officials of the National Broadcasting Company estimated a listening audience of twenty-five million for its coverage of the Rose Bowl game.[10]

These publicity vehicles for college football continued to fuel a national trend that began immediately after the war—sport fans now possessed the finances and the means (cars, trains, and improved highways) to attend the games themselves. Even before the war, athletic officials at many of the major football-playing uni- versities had noticed the limitations on their big box-office attractions because of inadequate seating capacities, and some had laid plans for the building of large stadia. As the 1920s dawned, many of these schools were progressing with their plans, and soon large football stadia were going up all around the country—a sig- nificant number of them designated as memorials to American military personnel lost in the war. Colleges and universities that could not justify seating capacities of fifty thousand or greater were not left out, though, as a class of medium-size stadia soon were under construction for these schools, providing a foundation for expansion in future years.

With the many outstanding players and teams populating American grid- irons, college football of the 1920s quickly adopted a far more open and exciting style of offensive play than had marked prewar efforts, including an increasing use of the forward pass as a true weapon of attack. Aided by the newspaper and radio coverage, more than ample interest was generated to keep the many new stadia filled for every football Saturday, and intercollegiate football soon turned into a moneymaking machine for the schools. By the 1929 season college football was believed to have an estimated drawing power of fifty million dollars a year, with well over 50 percent of that representing profit, which was sufficient to cover the expenses for all minor varsity sports teams at any of the schools and provide funding of the intramural programs for the general student populace. In 1928, Grantland Rice wrote, "There is no game even close to the average drawing power of the gridiron."[11]

Along with this ever increasing flow of monies into the athletic departments of the major football schools, and the ongoing clamor for good seats by overheated alumni and the general sporting public, there came the inevitable pressures to field winning football teams—oftentimes with the unstated directive "at any cost."[12]

The growing popularity of college football over the years had long been a sore spot for many in the academic branch of the collegiate community who questioned the increasing emphasis being placed on the intercollegiate sport and its potentially harmful effects upon the lives of the undergraduates and their pursuit of education. Adding more fuel was the belief that many had increasingly come to regard the image of a school itself as dependent upon the performance of its football team. In 1927, a commentary in the *New Republic* endorsed this view, as it stated, "The public values colleges according to prestige in football. . . . The public regards the provisions of football games as the chief function of local institutions of higher learning. . . . The players are coerced by loyalty to something higher than intellectual life. The faculty are constrained to become accomplices in the neglect of the legitimate business of college." The substantial hype and commercialization of college football during the 1920s, along with the many allegations of illegal recruiting and subsidizing of athletes, combined with these irritants to create a showdown between the academic and athletic sides of the universities. The decade would serve as a stage for the very peak of this battle over the place of athletics in the university community. Many of the transformations in college football between 1919 and 1930 would fundamentally revolve around this debate, which would culminate in the final days of 1929 with the issuance of the Carnegie Report.[13]

In the aftermath of the Carnegie Report it became clear that the reform element really had no realistic ideas for correcting college football's abuses of the so-called amateur ideals. Frustrated by the lack of specific action, President A. Lawrence Lowell of Harvard wrote to his counterpart at Yale—President James R. Angell—and proposed that the two prestigious universities take the initiative: "I believe that the intercollegiate contests should be reduced to the smallest number that would keep up the general interest in athletics. . . . I should like, if possible, to see only one intercollegiate football contest a year, and that with Yale; and as an approach towards that end, I should like to see the number of intercollegiate games diminished." Unfortunately for the reform element, by 1930 the universities had become very dependent on the monies being generated by intercollegiate football, and so Angell reluctantly replied that although he believed in such a reduction in gridiron schedules, he was unsure of Yale's Athletic Board, writing, "I suspect that I shall find myself somewhat alone in my views about the problem as a whole."[14] And so the gridiron sport would continue relatively unchecked on its way toward the multimillion-dollar spectacles and one hundred thousand–seat stadia that would eventually evolve by the close of the twentieth century. Yet along the way toward college football's survival of the reform efforts of the 1920s, the decade would also witness many other elements that would contribute toward the gridiron world's transformation.

Among these factors were the Catholic colleges' pursuit of football success as they sought to share the riches being garnered by Notre Dame, significant scandals and disputes that would bear testimony to the growing stakes within the gridiron game at the highest levels, black colleges of the East and South taking major strides toward a higher quality of intercollegiate football, and the Haskell Indian School teams—athletic successors to the legendary Carlisle Indian School of the prewar years—that would embody the continuing efforts to assimilate Native Americans into the new American society. Moreover, the universities would continue their longtime struggle against the slowly evolving game of professional football, an opposition contending that the play-for-pay brand of the sport threatened all the ideals of amateurism, sportsmanship, and character building supposedly represented by the college gridiron game.

Although intercollegiate football would experience struggles through the 1930s because of the economic hard times plaguing the country, the building blocks were all in place for the game's eventual resumption of growth toward unimagined riches and changes for American colleges and universities. Gigantic stadia stood ready to someday welcome back the major crowds that would be paying even higher ticket prices, while commercial media such as newspapers and radio would recognize the value of college football for their marketing efforts, and coverage of the sport would continue unabated toward the future riches of television.

By the end of the 1920s many forces had played a role in the shaping of intercollegiate football into an American sport of the people, while at the same time undeniably establishing the place of the gridiron game within the framework of university life. In 1928, John Tunis wrote that "football is more to the sports follower of the country than merely a game. It is at present a religion—sometimes it seems to be almost our national religion." Tunis later said of football in 1929, "Truly, this is the greatest of all seasons in the greatest of all American sports." The decade was truly a golden era for the sport and one that warrants a more careful consideration.[15]

1

SHAPING NATIONAL PARITY

In an era of college football history notable for its many transformations surrounding the sport, it should come as no surprise that there was a shift in the game's competitive structure and balance of power during the period. By 1919 a shifting of regional gridiron prominence away from the traditional Big Three schools of the East—a movement that had been gaining momentum since 1901—reached a state of affairs that could no longer be denied. This transformation of the competitive landscape of college football would continue throughout the 1920s, and by 1930 the intercollegiate gridiron sport was characterized by true regional parity on its national fields of play. This shifting of the game's competitive balance was one of the most significant aspects of change during the decade.

During the first decades of intercollegiate football history following the 1869 Princeton-Rutgers matchup, the colleges and universities of the East—and in particular the Big Three of Harvard, Princeton, and Yale—enjoyed a place of substantial prominence on the field of play. The proximity of eastern schools to the origin points of American football brought with it an early advantage in playing technique and skills, passed along and enhanced through the early coaching systems. The academic and social prestige of the Big Three, along with their pioneering and influential roles in shaping football's early playing technique and rules, soon had the trio of schools regarded as the sport's "elite," with the University of Pennsylvania making occasional inroads into football's upper echelon during the 1890s. During the last two decades of the nineteenth century, the Big Three's football teams were especially dominant, compiling twenty-two undefeated seasons.[1]

Yet with the dawn of the twentieth century there were already signs that challenges for the Big Three on the national gridiron scene were taking place in other regions, where improved coaching down to the high school level was beginning to produce substantially improved players and teams at the collegiate level. Amos Alonzo Stagg, a former Yale player, had been at the University of Chicago since 1892, and he was joined in the Western Conference (later known as the Big Ten) by Henry Williams at Minnesota (1900), Fielding Yost at Michigan (1901), and Walter McCornack, formerly with Dartmouth, at Northwestern in 1903. The South also began upgrading the quality of its football in 1904 with the hiring of Dan McGugin at Vanderbilt and John Heisman at Georgia Tech.

While the Midwest was the first region to begin regularly presenting serious challenges to the dominance of eastern football, the belief in the Big Three's athletic superiority was continued among newspaper writers and those people involved with intercollegiate football in the East. At the end of the nineteenth century the Midwest was still generally regarded as predominantly rural and backward when compared to the East, yet in a pair of postseason high school football games in 1902 and 1903, Chicago teams handed terrific beatings to their supposedly champion opponents from New York City. In the midst of the resulting debates over gridiron superiority between the two regions, Walter McCornack, who had coached in both sections, supported eastern football as he wrote, "In material, the East has more experienced and skilled men. Schools like Exeter, Andover and Lawrenceville have no equals in the country among preparatory schools who know football and can play it." Noting that the Western Conference schools had all hired professional coaches—"that is, the coaches receive compensation for their services"—McCornack advanced his belief that the alumni coaching method that "prevails in the East . . . is the ideal system." Yet it would be superior professional coaching in the Midwest and other regions that would prove to be the major factor in the eventual overthrow of eastern gridiron superiority.[2]

During the first several seasons after 1900 the Western Conference produced some of the sport's most memorable teams at Michigan and Chicago—squads that were virtually the equal of any of the Big Three of the East. Under the direction of Fielding Yost, Michigan went unbeaten for four consecutive seasons before being finally stopped by Chicago in 1905 in the final game of the Wolverines' bid for a fifth undefeated season. Walter Eckersall of Chicago, a three-time All-America, and Willie Heston of Michigan, a four-time All-America, are still considered to be among college football's greatest backfield men of all time. In 1904 Stagg said, "The West [is] so far ahead of the East in speed, variety and originality of attack, the game is much more open and dashing and interesting here."[3]

With the de-emphasis of football by the Western Conference from 1906 to 1908, the Big Three of the East continued to be regarded as the elite of college football until there was increasing evidence that outstanding teams and players were again being consistently developed elsewhere by 1914. Despite the improved competition, the Harvard-Princeton-Yale triumvirate continued to maintain its place atop the college football world in the minds of many noneastern observers, supported by the prominent coverage accorded the Big Three games by the wire services and New York newspapers.

When the Tournament of Roses Committee in California decided to resurrect its postseason football game at the close of the 1915 season, the invitations to oppose a

Pacific Coast opponent were automatically tendered first to the Big Three schools. Only when each of them had rejected offers did the Rose Bowl promoters settle for eastern also-rans Brown and Penn for the 1916 and 1917 games, apparently believing any team from the Atlantic seaboard was superior to the rest of the country. Harvard finally agreed to travel to California for the game at the close of the 1919 season, but the Presidents' Agreement among the Big Three would prevent any of them from ever again accepting.

THE SHIFTING FORTUNES CONTINUE

With intercollegiate football ready to begin its return to normalcy in 1919, the expectation among general followers of the game was that the Big Three would return to their place of prominence on the field of play. Yet Princeton and Yale each struggled to so-so records in 1919, while Harvard posted an undefeated season, although its reputation was tainted by a tie against Princeton and a generally weak schedule. Colgate, Dartmouth, and Penn State were generally considered the top teams in the East that season in a campaign notable for the number of surprising game results—a signal that gridiron parity, stimulated by the substantial numbers of returning servicemen-athletes, had arrived in the region. A postseason wrap-up article in the *New York Times* noted that "perhaps never before in the history of Eastern football have the so-called big elevens been so ruthlessly pushed into the background."[4]

Elsewhere around the country, the combination of excellent coaching and the growing numbers of well-trained high school athletes entering college began to show up in the number of top-flight teams being produced. In 1919, Knute Rockne and Notre Dame began a decadelong reign of terror in the world of college football with an undefeated season, while Illinois and Ohio State sat atop a competitive Big Ten Conference. In the West, Oregon and Washington shared the Pacific Coast Conference title—neither with particularly distinguished teams—yet Oregon nearly knocked off undefeated Harvard in the Rose Bowl game. Meanwhile, Coach Andy Smith was ready to launch a legitimate dynasty the following season at the University of California, and in Los Angeles the University of Southern California (USC) had hired a new football coach, Elmer Henderson, and was at last ready to start getting serious about the gridiron game.

The most telling indications that parity in college football had overtaken the Big Three came in several notable games during the first few seasons after the war. The team Yale fielded in 1919 was at best just average, but that did nothing to lessen the shock and outrage among the alumni when little Boston College handed the Bulldogs a stunning 5-3 defeat. Then in 1920, Boston College—under Coach Frank Cavanaugh who had compiled an impressive record as coach at Dartmouth from 1911 to 1916—handed Yale another defeat, and the Big Three school promptly dropped the upstart Catholic college from its future football schedules.[5]

The first loss to Boston College in 1919 had been enough to convince the Yale administration that changes were necessary in a football program that had basically been unimpressive since 1910. Although most of the demands for revisions in the operation of Yale's football program were publicly attributed to the "undergraduates," it was really alumni dissatisfaction that was forcing change. The *Yale Alumni Weekly* described the team's play of 1919 as "out-of-date football," and noted that there was a "new order of things on the football field, and Yale must accept the changes, however difficult it is for her mentors who have been brought up on the old system." Under considerable attack for his handling of the team, Yale's football coach and athletic director, Dr. Al Sharpe, yielded his coaching duties and brought T. A. D. "Tad" Jones back to head up the football program. Even more dramatic was the school's restructuring of its Graduate Football Committee, as three members were replaced because of "limited availability" owing to their business careers, including the patriarchal Walter Camp.[6]

Although Yale's losses to Boston College in 1919–1920 were shocking enough for followers of the Big Three teams, the defeats after all had come at the hands of an up-and-coming eastern team. Some believed they could be explained away as being no worse for the triumvirate's prestige than an occasional loss to a Brown or Colgate. Not so easily written off, though, was the 25-0 trouncing Princeton received in 1919 at the hands of West Virginia—never previously considered a major-level football program. It was the second consecutive Saturday that Princeton had gone down in defeat—Colgate notching a 7-0 victory the previous week—in games that the Big Three team normally regarded as "practice" affairs for its late-season matchups against Harvard and Yale. The sportswriter for the *New York Times* wrote that West Virginia's "husky mountaineers" thoroughly pounded the Tigers by a score "so decisive that not a shadow of a doubt remained as to which was the better team." The reporter also added that West Virginia had "a great team" and that the consecutive losses for Princeton "served to indicate that the old order is giving place to a new."[7]

Writer Donald Grant Herring attended the Princeton debacle in the company of Walter Camp, and he later commented, "Walter, with his historical perspective . . . must have had an inkling then of what so great a victory for a minor team foreshadowed, the beginning of the end of the reign of the Big Three." Herring added that "somehow this particular game has been accepted as the beginning of a period when other teams meeting the Big Three were given in advance an equal or better chance to win. This has come about not because the quality of Big Three football has declined . . . but only that the general level of football attainment has risen. If any date will serve to mark the end of a football era, November 1, 1919 is it." Harry von Kersburg, a former Harvard player and contemporary of the time, endorsed Herring's view of the decline of the Big Three as being attributable to the "rapid advancement" of the game in other regions rather than a "deterioration" on the part of the Ivies. He also pointed to 1919 as "the actual end of the long and glorious reign of the Big Three."[8]

The season of 1919 launched an ever increasing questioning of eastern football's automatic place atop the intercollegiate world. One of Camp's friends and correspondents was U.S. Representative Clifton N. McArthur from Oregon, an avid follower of football in the East and the Northwest. In late 1919 McArthur wrote to Camp, "After seeing the Navy-Georgetown, Penn-Pitt and Yale-Harvard games I am pretty well convinced that we are playing just as good, if not better, football on the Pacific Coast. . . . The teams in the east do not play with the dash and spirit that characterizes the Pacific Coast teams." Camp himself was impressed enough by the events of the 1919 season to write, "The fact remains that a high grade of football is played at many institutions hundreds and thousands of miles away from the northeast corner of this country. . . . Never has there been a season which has brought home the advisability of this wider outlook to anyone . . . as has the year 1919." Camp followed up on these comments by selecting two players from Centre College in Kentucky (Bo McMillin and Red Weaver) and fullback Ira Rodgers of West Virginia for his All-America First Team for 1919.[9]

In 1920 Yale's second consecutive defeat at the hands of Boston College was tempered somewhat, as Princeton and Harvard both posted undefeated records—including a 14-14 tie in their showdown. Some contemporary observers, still viewing the college football world through a Big Three prism, were prepared to advance Princeton as one of the top teams in the country despite the Tigers' schedule that contained no outstanding opposition—Harvard's schedule also being considered relatively weak. Pittsburgh, Penn State, and Boston College were also ranked at the top of the heap in the East after each posted undefeated seasons—the 0-0 tie game between Pitt and Penn State being considered one of the region's best games of the year. The *New York Times*, while naming Princeton the top team of the region, said that Pittsburgh "met more good teams this year than Harvard plays in two years." This issue of soft schedules among the Big Three schools would be magnified by the expansion of their Presidents' Agreement in 1923, and would become one of the significant factors in their diminished gridiron reputations as the years progressed.[10]

The 1921 season brought further evidence of the parity that was now becoming commonplace within college football, as both Harvard and Princeton suffered defeats against intersectional opponents, while Penn State, Lafayette, and Cornell were considered the top teams of the East. Princeton's loss came at the hands of a University of Chicago team that was not even the top outfit in the Big Ten, but

Centre's win over Harvard was the far greater surprise for football observers everywhere. Considering the Praying Colonels a "minor" opponent, Harvard opened the game with many of its first-team players on the bench, where they sat for much of the time until the second half, when a brilliant 32-yard touchdown run by quarterback Bo McMillin of Centre early in the third quarter produced the upset. Taking note of the intersectional defeats suffered by Princeton and Harvard on consecutive weekends, the Associated Press observed that "these defeats were accepted by followers of football with a national perspective as an indication that the gospel and the practice of the gridiron game were having a greater spread than ever before in sections removed from the scene of its origin and greatest development." For southern football observers, Centre's 6-0 victory over Harvard, and the rapidly improving teams being produced at Georgia Tech and Alabama, were symbolic of the region's steady movement toward national gridiron recognition.[11]

THE COLORFUL MIDWEST

During the seasons of 1920–1922 the balance of gridiron power continued its shift westward, despite whether the Big Three and the eastern sportswriters were prepared to recognize the fact. Although Illinois and Notre Dame had been impressive in 1919, by 1920 Rockne had the Catholic university team solidly entrenched as one of the top programs in the country—featuring a colorful All-America running back named George Gipp, who was easily as exciting as any of the Big Three's star players. Rockne once said, "Gipp was the greatest football player Notre Dame ever produced. He was unequalled in any game by anybody save, perhaps, by Jim Thorpe." Meanwhile, the Big Ten was becoming a conference noted for its competitive depth every football season. In 1920 Ohio State, which had replaced the legendary Chick Harley with yet another First Team All-America back in Pete Stinchcomb, barely edged out Wisconsin for the conference title. The two powerhouse teams, featuring a total of nine players who received All-America mention in 1920, each had to survive a trio of hard-fought conference games in addition to their showdown. Incredibly, E. C. Patterson of *Collier's* wrote that "Ohio State was represented by a team without any outstanding stars"—this statement about a squad with no fewer than six players who received All-America mention, Stinchcomb being a First Team consensus choice.[12]

Iowa, featuring All-Americans Fred "Duke" Slater, Aubrey Devine, and Gordon Locke, produced undefeated powerhouses in 1921 and 1922. After holding off excellent teams from Chicago and Ohio State for the 1921 Big Ten title, the Hawkeyes were forced to share the crown in 1922 with an undefeated Michigan team. The prominent sportswriter Lawrence Perry of the Consolidated Press Association tabbed Notre Dame and Iowa as the top teams in the country for 1921, although evidencing his lack of familiarity with the Pacific Coast when he failed to rate the great California team in his top five. The staid *New York Times* expressed concerns over the continuing sentiment for noneastern football in 1921, noting that "the pendulum has swung so far that the Western tradition is in danger of being overdone. . . . Assertions are blandly made that at least a half dozen of the teams out there are superior to the best eleven in the East. . . . These wonder teams and miracle men may really exist, but it is a question if the East has not been unduly neglected in the shuffle of this sweeping salaam to Western football."[13]

In 1922 Princeton fielded one of its most famous teams, its reputation in great part sealed by a 21-18 win on the road over Chicago. The *New York Times* cited Princeton's win over Chicago, along with a number of other intersectional victories for eastern teams, as evidence that "the football pendulum has swung back sharply toward the East." Among the games listed by the *Times* was Harvard's revenge win over little Centre College—the incongruity of claiming superiority in part because of a Big Three team's win over a so-called minor opponent apparently escaping the writer. Yet in the same article the writer did a complete reversal, giving small indication that the *New York Times* at long last may have recognized the nationalization of college football's playing skills, noting that "it would be futile and inaccurate to attach much importance to the victories of the East. . . . The truth is that football is too flexible, too fluid a game to be confined to one section. Football knowledge is too widespread to make sectional distinctions amount to much."[14]

Increasingly, there were indications that some sportswriters in the East were at last coming to recognize the changing college football landscape. After writing that Princeton was "generally regarded as the strongest in the East" for 1922, L. L. Little of *Outing* magazine took note of the growing numbers of strong teams around the country, adding, "Anyone who dares seriously to rank the teams in any section, for 1922, is a fit candidate for the nearest asylum." Albert Britt was another writer for *Outing* who recognized that the pendulum of gridiron power had in great part moved westward by the early 1920s, noting, "The story of football is no longer a story of a few teams in the East, nor even of the East." Meanwhile, an indication of the midwestern media's lowered regard for eastern football can be seen in a 1922 *Chicago Tribune* editorial that noted: "Football preeminence may be on the Pacific coast, but it certainly is not on the Atlantic, and it never will be again." The writer added that Yale "should be glad to get a place on any western schedule."[15]

Perhaps the greatest period for college football during the decade came in the seasons of 1924–1926, with Midwest teams continuing in the competitive forefront. The season of 1923 was one of considerably close-fought competition for top honors in every region, with one writer noting that "only in rare instances were the championship teams of any section definitely determined."[16] By 1924 many of the large new stadia were in place around the country, and college football began an annual parade of dazzling gridiron stars across the nation's sport pages. Recognized with All-America honors in 1923, Harold "Red" Grange of Illinois was superlative in 1924, and his renown was such that he came to symbolize college football of the 1920s for all time. His five-touchdown performance against Michigan in 1924, and an equally impressive performance against Penn in 1925, continue to this day as two of the most talked-about games in college football history.

The 1924 season also featured Notre Dame's "Four Horsemen" backfield—a quartet that had been around without a moniker in 1923 but was frustrated by a 14-7 defeat at the hands of Nebraska. After being given the nickname by sportswriter Grantland Rice—which became widely accepted after publication of a clever photo staged by student press assistant George Strickler—the soon-legendary foursome led Notre Dame to a 9-0-0 record for the 1924 regular season. Years later, prominent sportswriter Stanley Woodward took note of the group's enduring place in football lore: "It was considered strictly left-wing to write a football story for ten years after the Horsemen without referring to them five times." When Knute Rockne led his team to California on New Year's Day of 1925 and claimed the mythical national championship with a 27-10 win over an undefeated Stanford team—which had fought undefeated California to a dramatic 20-20 tie—the Rose Bowl's reputation as the stage for many of college football's elite teams was settled for the next twenty-five years.[17]

Grange was back for his senior season at Illinois in 1925, but the Big Ten also featured one of the best teams in conference history with the powerhouse at Michigan. In winning the Big Ten title for Coach Fielding Yost, the Wolverines shut out every opponent on their 1925 schedule with the exception of a 3-2 loss to Northwestern on a Soldier Field gridiron in Chicago that had been turned into a sea of mud by heavy rains. In 1926 Michigan returned with another strong team behind the passing combination of Benny Friedman and Bennie Oosterbaan, but the Wolverines were by no means the unquestioned leaders in the Midwest. Northwestern, under the direction of Coach Glenn Thistlethwaite, was a program on the rise, and the Purple earned a share of the Big Ten title with Michigan. Meanwhile, after a relatively disappointing record in 1925, Rockne had Notre Dame back in the national limelight for 1926 with a powerhouse that stopped Northwestern (6-0) and Army (7-0), with only a major upset at the hands of Carnegie Tech marring the season.

PACIFIC COAST FOOTBALL ARRIVES

The 1920 season ushered in Pacific Coast football as a serious challenger for annual national recognition, beginning with one of college football's great outfits—the "Wonder Teams" of the University of California. Technically, the title "Wonder

Teams"—coined by San Francisco sportswriter Brick Morse in 1920—applied to Coach Andy Smith's teams of 1920–1922. After the graduation of three-time All-America Harold "Brick" Muller and several other stars, the Golden Bears went on to notch two more undefeated seasons in 1923 and 1924. For the period of 1920–1924, California compiled an overall record of 44-0-4, captured four Pacific Coast Conference titles, and produced fourteen players who received All-America recognition.

San Francisco–area football observers quickly recognized the power of California's 1920 outfit, as the Golden Bears set about leveling all opposition. Just three weeks into the season the team was already being identified as the greatest in school history, and sportswriter Jack James wrote that "never was a football coach so blessed with capable material. . . . Don't let them tell you that all the real football played in these United States is centered in and around Cambridge, New Haven and Princeton—nor yet in Big Ten territory. It may have been once. But not now or hereafter."[18]

The California team's greatness initially went unrecognized outside the Bay Area. Walter Camp and Parke Davis (college football's first important statistician, a former head coach, and a selector of All-America teams) considered Cal a top-ten team of 1920—but just barely—while Albert Britt of *Outing* wrote that there was little to choose between Cal and Stanford, despite the Golden Bears having handed Stanford a 38-0 trouncing. Even on the West Coast some newspapers provided better coverage for the Big Three games than those in California. It all changed after the Rose Bowl game at the close of the 1920 campaign.

After Princeton rejected an invitation to meet Cal in the Rose Bowl, Ohio State, champion of the Big Ten, accepted a bid to come west on New Year's Day 1921. Oddsmakers installed Cal as an underdog—clearly an indication of the prevailing attitude of athletic superiority that existed east of the Mississippi River. Brick Morse would later write: "For years we had struggled to overcome the prejudice against Western athletes, this cringing of Californians to things Eastern. . . . Our fathers decided to leave the East and seek their fortunes in the West. . . . Only the strongest and bravest were able to endure. Are not the qualities those pioneers displayed just those qualities which enter into the makeup of a champion athlete?"[19]

The 1921 Rose Bowl game turned out to be a sensational platform for demonstrating the superiority of the California team, as the Golden Bears trounced an excellent Ohio State team by a score of 28-0. Football fans around the country marveled at the newspaper accounts of the beautiful scenery, the pageantry of the Tournament of Roses, and especially the exciting and wide-open Cal attack, led by All-American Brick Muller. This game represents one of the milestone events in college football history on a number of fronts, and prominent *Los Angeles Times* sportswriter Braven Dyer wrote that "until this battle, the rest of the nation had looked down a collective nose at Western football. . . . That day, January 1, 1921, truly ushered in the Golden Age of Sports in the West."[20]

With the core of the Wonder Team back in 1921, California rolled to nine straight wins in the regular season, no collegiate team coming within fourteen points of the Golden Bears. As the season was winding down, the Rose Bowl promoters were again rebuffed by the Big Three of the East, and so in late November an invitation to play Cal in the New Year's game was extended to Coach Howard Jones and his University of Iowa team, champions of the Big Ten. But permission to appear in the postseason game was denied by conference officials, and so the promoters looked elsewhere, finally settling on little Washington and Jefferson (W&J), an undefeated team from the East.

Cal was initially reluctant to agree to this matchup, as there were concerns over the academic standards adhered to by the eastern school, while West Coast sportswriters were not impressed by the little-known opponent from Pennsylvania. Unfortunately, southern California was pelted with a considerable amount of rain in the days leading up to the Rose Bowl game, and on the day of the matchup the field was very muddy and in terrible condition, according to several sportswriters. The combination of an extremely wet field and a rugged W&J defense ground Cal's high-powered attack to a halt, and the teams settled for a 0-0 tie.[21]

The Pacific Coast gridiron wars escalated with the arrival of Glenn "Pop" Warner at Stanford in 1924 and Howard Jones at Southern California in 1925. Weary of the dominance imposed by archrival California, Stanford went out and hired a football coach who could fill the mammoth stadium built earlier in the decade. Warner, with a long record of success at Carlisle and Pittsburgh, paid immediate dividends, as he had Stanford in the Rose Bowl at the close of the 1924 season. Only a loss to Washington kept Warner's crew from returning to Pasadena at the end of the 1925 campaign.

The University of Southern California had also decided to develop a big-time football program in the immediate aftermath of the war. The school had hired Elmer "Gus" Henderson to take over the program in 1919, and football fortunes seemed to be on the rise, as USC garnered a win in the 1923 Rose Bowl game over Penn State when California declined to make another appearance on New Year's Day. Yet despite notching winning records against improved schedules, Henderson had been unable to produce the desperately sought victory over the University of California. Athletic officials and alumni were also embarrassed over the 1924 disclosures of player eligibility and subsidization concerns at USC that had resulted in Stanford and Cal terminating athletic relations with the Los Angeles school. So in early 1925 USC officials began a serious effort to lure Knute Rockne to Los Angeles as the West Coast school's new football coach.

1. Coach Howard Jones of Southern California. After coaching stops at a number of schools, he moved west and quickly built a gridiron giant at USC in the 1920s. Courtesy of the Amateur Athletic Foundation of Los Angeles.

By mid-January USC's comptroller, Warren Bovard, who was leading the effort to land Rockne, wired that he had obtained approvals for all of the Notre Dame coach's conditions. To clear the way for a new coach and to satisfy Rockne's concerns, Bovard secretly paid off Henderson for the two years remaining on his contract, along with a bonus, the total coming to $16,100. But by late January 1925, any chances of Rockne leaving for USC had gone by the boards after details of the offer to the prominent coach had been leaked to Los Angeles sportswriters, and Notre Dame officials had insisted that he would be held to his contract at the Indiana school.[22]

After the debacle with Rockne, USC athletic officials managed to sign Howard Jones as the school's new football coach for 1925. Jones, a coach with football ties back to Yale, had headed up a number of programs, and his most recent success had come at Iowa where he fielded Big Ten powerhouses in 1921 and 1922. By the 1926 season Jones had the USC football program ready to challenge Stanford and Cal for Pacific Coast superiority.

That season, with standout players such as All-America halfback Mort Kaer, Manuel Laranetta, and Don Williams, Jones delivered the long-awaited win over

Cal, and then his Trojans faced off against Warner and his Stanford powerhouse at the Los Angeles Coliseum in a showdown that produced one of the greatest battles in West Coast gridiron history. Stanford held on for a 13-12 win that catapulted Warner's team back to the Rose Bowl and recognition as the mythical national champion. In 1927 USC and Stanford battled to a 13-13 deadlock that earned Jones and his team a share of the Pacific Coast Conference championship—the first in school history—and shifted the balance of power in the West to the Los Angeles school. USC would garner conference titles in four of the next five seasons—including mythical national championships in 1928 and 1931—as Jones perfected his "Thundering Herd" running attack.[23]

SOUTHERN FOOTBALL GAINS RECOGNITION

The most significant development of the 1924–1926 period within college football was the spread of playing parity to the South and Southwest, although the substantially improved style of play was still not recognized by eastern sportswriters. Behind such highly respected coaches as Matty Bell at Texas Christian, Dana X. Bible at Texas A&M, John Heisman at Rice, and Ray Morrison at Southern Methodist, the Southwest Conference was ready to begin producing some top-flight football teams, beginning with the three-year struggle (1925–1927) for supremacy between Southern Methodist and Texas A&M.

In the South the season of 1925 became a landmark within the region's intercollegiate football history, as Alabama managed to get past Georgia Tech on the way to an undefeated season, capped off with an invitation to play Washington in the Rose Bowl. Alabama, featuring running backs Pooley Hubert and Johnny Mack Brown (a future cowboy movie star), and Washington, led by All-America tailback George "Wildcat" Wilson, staged one of the most thrilling duels in Rose Bowl history. Another undefeated season for Alabama in 1926, with basically a new cast of players, earned Coach Wallace Wade and his Crimson Tide squad another invitation to the Rose Bowl. There the football world was stunned when Alabama fought Stanford, the mythical national champions, to a 7-7 tie. The South would go on to provide one of the teams for the New Year's Day spectacular five times during the games of 1926–1932.

Southern schools had struggled to attain some measure of equality on the national landscape of intercollegiate football since its earliest years. Although Vanderbilt had fielded some good teams prior to the war—a 0-0 tie with Yale in 1910 causing major reverberations through the region—and Georgia Tech had been regarded as one of the top teams around in 1917, southern football generally suffered from an inferiority complex until the early 1920s, much like the region's general culture. On the eve of Tulane's visit to Michigan for an intersectional matchup in

2. Johnny Mack Brown of Alabama, sweeping end against Washington in the 1926 Rose Bowl thriller. Brown would later return to Hollywood and become a movie star. Courtesy of the Amateur Athletic Foundation of Los Angeles.

1920, Adolph "Germany" Schulz, a former star at Michigan and then the athletic director at Tulane, took note of the general lack of recognition accorded the South's developing football fortunes: "The people [in the South] have not been educated to the gridiron game because they have never seen any really great teams in action. . . . Some great elevens have been developed in the south, but unfortunately they have never met teams of note. . . . A well known northern eleven would furnish the necessary attraction to interest the public in football. There is a great future for football in the south."[24]

In the early 1920s the South was gaining recognition for its emerging urbanization and commerce, yet to a great extent the region was still commonly perceived elsewhere in the United States as a rural and agricultural society. Within this cultural dilemma, many southern academic leaders, civic officials, and newspaper sportswriters came to view the region's intercollegiate football as a symbol of the modernization of southern society and the rapid strides being made toward the respect that many believed had been absent since the days of Reconstruction.

Throughout much of the 1920s, southern sportswriters filled their articles on intersectional football games involving the region's teams with all manner of militaristic symbolism that harkened back to the Civil War conflict. Southern gridiron squads were pointed to as representatives of Dixie and the "Lost Cause." Indeed, when Alabama appeared in the Rose Bowl at the close of the 1925 and 1926 seasons, there was a substantial increase in regional fervor throughout the South, and there was a widely expressed view that the Crimson Tide football team was not so much representing the University of Alabama as the heritage, spirit, and values of the South itself. Historian Andrew Doyle has written that events surrounding the two bowl games indicate the extent to which southerners viewed intersectional football play "as a recapitulation of the Civil War" and that Alabama's play in the 1926 Rose Bowl game "instantly transcended the game of football and became symbolic vindication of southern honor." In considering the 1926 Rose Bowl, sportswriter Zipp Newman commented that "no game ever meant so much for the rise of football in the south," while *Nashville Banner* writer Fred Russell added that "what really focused the national spotlight on the South . . . was Alabama's second straight trip to the Rose Bowl" in January 1927.[25]

Historian Keith Dunnavant has noted that football in the South "quickly assumed greater importance in the region than in other parts of the country. . . . With few outlets for organized recreation, college football teams provided a powerful unifying force for a physically scattered population." In considering the South's struggle between urbanization and agriculture in the 1920s, Doyle has added that "a region beset by these fundamental conflicts used college football as a symbolic reconciliation of progress and tradition."[26]

ALL-AMERICA PARITY ARRIVES

Further demonstration of the shift of power toward other regions of the country than the East can be seen in a brief review of the All-America team selections for the period 1919–1931. For that period the first- and second-team choices named by three major selectors each year are examined—always including Walter Camp's eastern-biased teams until his passing in 1925.[27]

For the 1919 season, the first year of football's return to normalcy after the war, we find the East garnering forty of the sixty-six spots available from the three selectors (two teams of eleven players from each of three All-America selectors), including nine players from the Big Three alone, with the Midwest receiving fourteen, the South eleven, and the Pacific Coast just one. However, by 1921 midwestern universities were making major inroads into the previous dominance of eastern schools, and the annual All-America selections reflect this fact. For 1921 the East collected twenty-six of the sixty-six available spots from the three selectors, but for the first time another region had attained more of the coveted places on the mythical elevens, as thirty players were selected from the Midwest, while the Pacific Coast and South garnered five places each.

In the 1922 and 1923 postseason selections Camp tilted the advantage on the mythical elevens substantially back to eastern schools, naming thirteen eastern players in 1922, while Walter Eckersall and Lawrence Perry named ten and seven, respectively. In 1923 Camp awarded sixteen of his twenty-two spots to eastern players, while Eckersall and the International News Service named just ten and nine, respectively.

After Camp's passing, the All-America selections began to more closely reflect the shifting balance of power that was playing out on the gridiron. In 1925—with Grantland Rice replacing Camp in this survey—the East and the Midwest dominated the available sixty-six places, garnering twenty-eight and twenty-six, respectively. By 1927 the Pacific Coast and the South were receiving greatly increased recognition in the postseason selections, and in 1928 this trend continued, as the East received nineteen places, the Midwest seventeen, Pacific Coast fifteen, and the South twelve. Thereafter, the Midwest began to dominate the mythical elevens each season through the end of the survey, as the postseason mythical elevens continued giving clear testimony to the shifting balance of power on the field.[28]

THE SHARING OF GRIDIRON POWER

In 1924 Yale had been generally recognized as one of the top-ten teams in the country, but from 1925 onward there was no longer any question that the best football in the country was being played outside the Big Three. In the future, members of the Harvard-Princeton-Yale triumvirate of old would only occasionally break into the top ten of nationally rated teams. Instead, eastern football came to feature a revolving list of schools, including Dartmouth, Pittsburgh, Army, Navy, Penn, and Fordham. In 1925, Dartmouth, featuring All-America tailback Swede Oberlander, was regarded by many to be the top team in the country, while Colgate was also considered among the nation's top ten. In 1926 the top level of eastern teams comprised Navy, Lafayette, Army, and Brown. The Naval Academy, led by All-Americans Tom Hamilton at halfback and Frank Wickhorst at tackle, was regarded as a serious challenger to Stanford in the battle for the mythical national title. Indeed, one of the top games in college football history was contested in 1926 between Army and Navy, as the two service academies fought to a 21-21 tie before an estimated 110,000 fans at Chicago's Soldier Field.[29]

The last few years of the 1920s presented wide-open races for conference and national team honors around the country, with the leading contenders changing from season to season. The South featured no fewer than four top-flight teams in 1927 alone (Georgia, Georgia Tech, Tennessee, and Vanderbilt), while Southern California was ready to head up Pacific Coast football with the first of Howard Jones's "Thundering Herd" backfields, and many gridiron observers considered

Illinois to be the top team in the land for the season. In 1928 the Pacific Coast and South were again singled out as the top football regions in the country, and Fred Russell has written, "Southern football had progressed to such an extent by 1928 that it was generally believed that the section's top three or four teams might be on a par with the best in any area." In 1929 Bob Zuppke of Illinois was declaring the Big Ten to be "the anchor of American football," and by the 1929–1930 seasons Knute Rockne had Notre Dame back in the limelight with two of the greatest teams in school history.[30]

When college football's "golden era" came to a close after the 1930 season, there was little question that national parity characterized the sport's action on the gridiron and that outstanding teams and players could be found in every region of the land—with a slight edge in power to be found in the Midwest and South. The importance of having a high-quality football coach had become an unquestioned precept for any university seeking to field a competitive gridiron program, and the many talented and innovative coaches active in the game as the decade progressed were the preeminent stimuli to the shift in the balance of power. Coach Charles Crowley of Columbia had acknowledged this fact in 1927, when he stated that "the cause of national equality in power is the result of Eastern coaches going West and South, Western coaches going East . . . and the general exchange of ideas here and there wherever football is played." Fielding Yost endorsed this contention in 1928 when he wrote that the "interchange of ideas and coaches has spread the game's knowledge to every corner."[31]

Despite the Big Three's declining football fortunes on the national stage—assisted in great part by the restrictions imposed by their "Triple Agreement," which was expanded several times during the early years of the 1920s—the students and alumni of the Harvard-Princeton-Yale trio did not easily concede their lost prestige within the intercollegiate gridiron world. In 1926, while discussing the Princeton-Yale game, Hugh MacNair Kahler wrote, "Smart-aleck comment by outsiders will never in the least affect Princeton's conviction that victory over Yale, year in and year out, stands as the ultimate achievement in college football. There is nothing mythical or sentimental about the championship that belongs to any team that can beat a Yale eleven." The sense of denial on the Princeton campus is further seen in 1927 after the Tigers defeated Ohio State 20-0, when the *Daily Princetonian* pointed to the victory as evidence that the current team was the school's "best one since the war," not only forgetting about Princeton's outstanding 1922 outfit but also apparently losing sight of the fact that Ohio State was at best just a fair team that finished with a 4-4-0 record in 1927.[32]

There was somewhat more realism on the campuses of Harvard and Yale as the gridiron struggles continued. After Harvard suffered a shocking defeat in its 1926 season opener against little Geneva College, the *Harvard Alumni Bulletin* acknowledged that "there are scores of colleges which now have as good material and coaching as the half dozen institutions in the Northeastern part of the country that used to fear no opponent except one another. . . . Almost any team which is on the Harvard schedule in these modern times . . . is likely to be victorious over the Crimson."[33]

At Yale, mediocre seasons in 1925 and 1926 had many students and alumni questioning the handling of the team by Coach Tad Jones. An article in the *New York Times* mentioned that many Yale observers were "aghast at the victories of Brown and Army" over the Bulldogs in 1926, while the *Yale Alumni Weekly* called for "an investigation of a number of features of the present football season" after the Bulldogs suffered three consecutive shutout defeats that year. Demonstrating that there was a limit to manners even in the Big Three, Jones fired back: "Those yellow bellies are not going to crucify me. . . . This criticism is coming from shyster lawyers, poor doctors and dentists, and eighteen-dollar-a-week clerks who think they know more football." The *Yale Daily News* leaped to the defense of the beleaguered coach, describing the system he had implemented to be "as fine as Yale wanted . . . and that nothing represented the Yale ideal more nearly than Tad Jones and the present Yale team." A season-ending win over a poor Harvard team in 1926 was enough to temporarily hold off the critics, but Jones eventually tendered his resignation, effective at the end of the 1927 season.[34]

By the end of the decade the gridiron battles among the Harvard-Princeton-Yale trio had become more recognized as prestigious social events than athletic contests of wide-ranging consequence, and historian Preston Slosson could write that "the old dynasties of the East had given place to a turbulent democracy of sport." Before a Harvard-Yale game with no national or even regional significance late in the 1920s, one eastern writer noted that "the Western elevens look on with a bored smile." James Isaminger of the *Philadelphia Inquirer,* on the eve of another Harvard-Yale game, remarked that the two teams "are certainly no longer the giants they were in the old days . . . but their annual clinch remains as big a coonskin coat success as ever. It is still the biggest and zippiest private football war seen on the football lawns." Yet a win over one of the Big Three could still carry significance for many football people, such as when Georgia's victory over Yale in 1930 prompted longtime southern coach Dan McGugin to state, "Because of Yale's great traditions . . . a victory over her is still one of the great prizes of the gridiron."[35]

The balance of gridiron power had been tilted away from the traditional old-line teams of the East by many factors among the football programs of other regions: superior coaching, innovative styles of offensive play, supportive school administrations, the recruiting of athletes, and the significantly rising enrollments at public universities that produced more outstanding athletes and a greater depth of manpower. Yet the transformation of college football's competitive balance was also brought about in part because of changes within the social and university landscapes of the United States.

As the decade had progressed, the place of football within university life increasingly came into question on many campuses—especially in the Northeast—and some of the developments within the sport during the 1920s were in part the result of a declining interest in big-time football. In 1929, prominent sportswriter John Tunis described the lifecycle of enthusiasm on campuses for intercollegiate football as consisting of the rah-rah period, the big-business period, and the stadium period and beyond. He believed that eastern football had merely preceded the other regions in moving through these cycles. According to Tunis, no longer was the fate of the university's football team at the core of student life at the eastern schools, but rather "the emphasis is now distinctly on the cultural side of college life. . . . [The student's] mind has matured; he takes far less interest in the spectacular side of collegiate games."[36] This general lessening of interest in big-time sport on the part of the students at many schools could not help but contribute toward the diminishing results of the football programs.

The spreading and sharing of prestige within the world of intercollegiate football during the 1920s were also partially the result of the assimilation that many ethnic and cultural groups were then successfully achieving within American society, along with the movement toward a more middle-class, democratic society. Taking note of the ethnic aspect of football's transformation during the decade, historian Michael Parrish has written that "the center of gravity in the college sport shifted from the old-stock Americans of the Ivy League schools to second-generation Irish, Italians, and Slavs who played for universities, many of them public, in the Midwest and on the Pacific Coast."[37] By the 1930s many college football lineups around the country were heavily populated with ethnic-related names that had never appeared on campus gridirons in previous decades.

The establishment of regional parity within college football proved to be the fundamental building block that stimulated many of the other transformations that took place within the gridiron sport during the decade of the 1920s and beyond. On the field of play, the sport of intercollegiate football had left behind its New England roots and been transformed forever into a national sport.

2

RISE OF THE INTERSECTIONALS

Another of the significant transforming agents for college football during the 1920s was the phenomenal growth of intersectional games, which included the nationalization and greatly expanded popularity of the annual Tournament of Roses game on the West Coast, along with the use of neutral-site big-city stadia. Building on football's rapidly growing influence on the American sporting scene—facilitated by the arrival of competitive parity among the various regions—the increasing role of intersectional play was a natural outgrowth of the gridiron game's ever increasing visibility within the popular media of the day.

The seasons prior to the onset of World War I had been characterized by the occasional playing of what were true intersectional games. The decades of the 1880s and 1890s had been notable for the number of intersectional games that included one of the Big Three schools (Harvard, Princeton, and Yale), although they tangled only with Michigan and touring teams from the Chicago Athletic Club—except for Yale's 1899 matchup with Wisconsin and Princeton's game with North Carolina that same season. A key aspect of the Big Three's participation in these games was that the opponent team was always required to travel to the eastern site for the game. After the turn of the century intersectional games that included one of the Big Three schools were severely curtailed, and a proviso in their Presidents' Agreement of 1916 was aimed at eliminating such affairs by the three universities.

Cornell, Michigan, Penn, and Chicago were among the most active in taking on intersectional foes prior to World War I. Michigan, in addition to its 1906–1917 series against Penn, also played an intersectional series against Cornell from 1911 to 1917. Amos Alonzo Stagg scheduled his Chicago teams against a variety of intersectional foes before the war—highlighted by a bizarre trip to the West Coast in 1894 to play Stanford. Among schools elsewhere around the country there was considerably less intersectional play, although the University of Texas and Vanderbilt did pursue some of these type games before the war.[1]

In the years immediately after the war the Tournament of Roses game in Pasadena, California, featured two potentially attractive intersectional matchups. After the 1919 season Harvard met Oregon in the postseason game, the Big Three team being allowed to make the trip as part of an endowment fund-raising program for the university. But although the eastern team was one of the great names of college football and potentially held great appeal for the fans, the game was the type of low-scoring slugfest typical of old-school football.

In marked contrast was the 1921 game that pitted California's "Wonder Team" against the open-style offense of Ohio State from the Western Conference, one of the most significant games in college football history. This Rose Bowl matchup launched the annual postseason game on its way toward becoming an immensely popular and prominent American sporting tradition and was also the stimulus for the ever widening popularity of big-time intersectional football that evolved during the decade.[2] Football fans around the country were thrilled by the images that were conjured up in newspaper stories of the game between Ohio State and California. Soon they were clamoring for excitement and change on the annual schedules as one of the prerequisites for filling the giant new stadia—no longer being willing to accept the usual inferior opponents that were traditionally used to fill the nonconference dates.[3]

Even before the 1921 Rose Bowl game there had been evidence of a growing support for expanding the amount of intersectional play and the distance that teams were willing to travel. The 1920 season had included Michigan-Tulane, Notre Dame–Army, Georgia Tech–Pittsburgh, Harvard-Centre, Dartmouth traveling to Seattle to play the University of Washington, and the University of Nebraska, unquestionably a vigorous advocate of intersectional games, taking on Penn State, Washington State, and Rutgers that season. The Nebraska-Rutgers matchup was played at New York's Polo Grounds, as was the annual Army-Navy game, a signal that big-city promoters were ready to expand their staging of college football games in the neutral, noncampus, and—most disconcerting of all to many university officials—"professionalized" environments of the large metropolitan stadia or ballparks.

For college football fans and most newspaper sportswriters it was all good news. Walter Eckersall of the *Chicago Tribune* noted that "important intersectional games will be one of the many features of future football seasons," while the *New York Times*, in its review of the recently concluded 1920 season, commented on the popularity of intersectional play and added that "interest never was greater. . . . There was considerable intersectional competition, which is growing yearly and must prove highly beneficial to the sport." Another writer described intersectional play as "one of the healthiest movements noted in the history of football. . . . A beginning has been made, and the public is evidently eager for more of these intersectional games." Promoters also came forward in 1920 and advanced a proposal for a college football "intersectional Saturday every fall" that anticipated by seventy years the interconference commercialized circuses staged by college basketball. The idea was that on this one autumn afternoon, "four of the big eastern teams will go west for a game, and four of the best middle-western teams will come east to do battle." The rationale for this proposal was that "a more definite line may be had on the relative strength of the teams . . . and to a certain extent there will be satisfaction in knowing who are the really leading teams."[4]

The promoters of such intersectional games at big-city sites were motivated solely by financial considerations, and justifying such large-scale commercialization of the collegiate game as a means of identifying the top teams was a false facade aimed at stirring up interest among the ticket-buying public. By 1919 talk about the need for a college football national championship playoff had begun to circulate around the sporting world, prompting Walter Camp to respond that "football is not a game where a great national championship is possible or desirable. The very nature of the sport would forbid anything like such a series of contests as are played in baseball." Later in the decade, Stagg, having no problem with intersectional play that did not detract from the studies of the players, saw no purpose in the debate over regional superiority as a justification for such games, viewing college football as a cyclical venture in which "no one section of the country is superior in football. Whenever a section has a great group of men it produces a great team."[5]

Just as late-twentieth-century media members would be swept along by those individuals advocating a college football playoff, so too did talk about the need to determine the merits of the football as played in the various regions continue in the 1920s media. Eckersall of the *Chicago Tribune,* in discussing the Princeton-Chicago series scheduled to begin in 1921, wrote that "the series . . . will attract no end of attention from the football world. The results will be watched with interest . . . as the games will be representative of the brand of football played in the two sections of the country. . . . It is east against west, with each team striving to uphold the caliber of football as it is played in its respective section." The media focus on regional comparisons eventually progressed to the point where the Associated Press began tracking and publishing a seasonal by-region breakdown of the won-lost records resulting from intersectional play among each of the four regions.[6]

With intersectional games becoming an accepted part of college football as the decade progressed, some media writers, as part of their ongoing discussion of the relative merits of each region's teams, sought to explain the difficulties teams from the East and Midwest frequently encountered in making the long trip to the Pacific Coast for games. Although admitting that the gridiron balance of power had moved westward by late in the decade, among the frequently advanced explanations for Pacific Coast superiority in many of the intersectional games was the radical differences in climates, the impact on player training and conditioning, especially for postseason games, and the always-popular "transcontinental train ride alibi." The long overland trip seemed a valid point until the 1928 season when the teams from Stanford and Oregon State made the journey across country to New

York City, where they proceeded to handily defeat Army and New York University, respectively. The future of college football, when such issues of travel would no longer be relevant, could be glimpsed in 1929 when Yale chartered a fleet of nineteen passenger planes to fly people from New York City down to the University of Georgia to follow the Bulldog team. *New York Times* sportswriter John Kieran predicted an increasing amount of intersectional games in the future, when "the teams will be scooting across the country and back in big passenger planes. . . . It is bound to come, the way football and aviation are growing."[7]

Intersectional play continued to expand through the early seasons of the decade, and teams from the East were among the most active. In 1921 Dartmouth followed up on its trip of the previous season to Washington with games against Tennessee and Georgia, while that same season Penn State met Georgia Tech and then made the long trip to Seattle to play Washington. And even the stately Big Three, defenders of the Victorian-age principles of intercollegiate sport, were active in playing intersectional opponents. In 1921 Harvard played Indiana, Georgia, and Centre, while in 1922 the Crimson hosted Centre and Florida. Yale played the University of North Carolina in 1921 and 1922, while Iowa also came east to play the Bulldogs in the latter season. Along with Princeton's 1921 matchup against the University of Chicago, all of these games were played on the campuses of the Big Three schools and so theoretically posed no threat to the spirit of amateurism imbued within the Presidents' Agreement of 1916 among the trio of schools.

But it all changed in October 1922 when Princeton traveled to Chicago for the rematch with the Maroons at Stagg Field. The game was preceded by significant publicity, and the demand for tickets far exceeded the available thirty-two thousand–seat capacity of Chicago's small stadium, Eckersall telling readers that "at least four times that number would be glad to pay any price to get through the gates." The *New York Times* noted, "Never in the history of football at Princeton has an early season game created so much interest among students and townspeople," while Eckersall added that the approaching game was "one of the great intersectional struggles in history." Adding to the growing hysteria surrounding the game was the large number of Princeton fans converging on Chicago—the eastern school having received an allotment of eight thousand tickets for the game—which prompted sportswriter Hugh Fullerton to describe the tremendous invasion of Princeton alumni as "the greatest gathering of Princeton men ever held outside of the shaded gates at Nassau."[8]

After Princeton staged a fourth-quarter rally for an exciting 21-18 win, not only was there a good deal of celebrating by the Tigers' fans in Chicago but back at Princeton the students also started several bonfires around the campus and hundreds staged a parade down Nassau Street while the bell in the belfry of old Nassau Hall began to toll. The Princeton football team having traveled so far had been a significant break from Big Three tradition, but here was a greater encroachment onto sacred tradition by the growing hysteria and commercialism of intercollegiate football—the tolling of the old bell at Princeton for winning any game other than against archrivals Harvard and Yale. The *New York Times* remarked that "never has [the bell] been known to ring for an early season victory before . . . [and] all agreed that never in football history has a game, outside of the Big Three, created so much fierce interest."[9]

With the forces of academe already beginning to challenge the growing importance of football within the university community, here was substantial evidence of athletic overemphasis and commercialism as threats to the old-school ideals of cloistered intercollegiate amateurism. There was no question that a Big Three university's football team traveling to what some considered an unofficial championship game was completely in opposition to the spirit and intent of the Presidents' Agreement. The events related to the game at Chicago had only confirmed a situation that Big Three officials had previously seen approaching, and before the 1922 season the presidents of Harvard, Princeton, and Yale had met and agreed that there would be no further traveling to intersectional football games. Accordingly, in September 1922 the football committee at Princeton announced that its two-year home-and-home contract with Chicago would not be renewed.[10]

Princeton's share of the gate receipts from the 1922 Chicago game had come in at more than forty-four thousand dollars, so the nonrenewal of the contract with the Midwest university came at a cost. Of course, teams from other schools were welcome to make the trip east for a game, but there could be no return visit by the Big Three team. After their game of 1922, athletic officials of the University of Iowa reached an agreement with their counterparts at Yale for a home-and-home football series in 1923–1924, yet when President W. A. Jessup of Iowa wrote to President James Angell of Yale to obtain final approval for the agreement, he was rebuffed. Angell wrote: "Our present agreement with Princeton and Harvard prevents our entering into any definite arrangement which would take the team to Iowa. We shall cordially welcome Iowa here." Apparently, the Iowa officials did not intend to continue the one-sided athletic agreements that the Big Three schools believed they were still in a position to command, and so no further games were scheduled between the two universities.[11]

Stagg had been very interested in continuing the series with Princeton, and in fact was receiving considerable unofficial encouragement to pursue a renewal of the series from both Princeton officials and alumni of both schools. But the Chicago coach was finding his efforts at scheduling intersectional games hampered by Big Ten officials. In June 1922, the faculty committee of the conference had adopted a resolution that essentially prohibited member schools from scheduling "intersectional contests involving long trips and prolonged absences."[12]

The Chicago coach had pushed his university's officials into breaking an earlier agreement among the conference schools regarding intersectional play when the Princeton series was scheduled in 1920. Regardless of whether the latest conference resolution was mandatory, it was a virtual certainty that Stagg would not receive permission for a renewal. In any event, it was all irrelevant, as Princeton's administration had no intention of allowing its football team to leave the immediate region in pursuit of commercialized games. In letters on the subject, Stagg took to attributing partial responsibility for the demise of the series on the demands of the other Big Ten Conference schools for games with his Maroons. He wrote: "The Conference resolution is really the crystallization of a sentiment on the part of certain Conference Universities who wish to get on Chicago's schedule. . . . All kinds of pressure will be put upon me by the other Conference Universities to schedule games with them."[13]

As soon as 1924 the Big Ten Conference revised its resolution on intersectional games again and adopted a more liberal position, although continuing its opposition to postseason play such as the Rose Bowl. This decision put the conference schools in position to capitalize on the booming popularity of football and the demand for attractive matchups that was being fueled by the many new stadia coming on line around the country by the middle of the decade. The Big Three schools of the East continued limited intersectional play under their terms until Harvard and Princeton severed athletic relations in 1926, an event that forced those schools to consider intersectional games every season.[14]

By the mid-1920s intersectional games had become a significant feature of every college football season for the sporting public, and the *New York Times* began to run a preseason listing of such games by 1926. The season of 1926 also witnessed two notable intersectional games that demonstrated just how far the commercialized appeal of college football had progressed: the launching of the long-running Notre Dame–Southern California series and the playing of the Army-Navy game in Chicago. The annual spectacle between the two service academies was usually played in either Philadelphia or New York City, although the 1924 game had been awarded to Baltimore. These three cities joined Chicago in a bidding war for the right to host the 1926 game. Chicago promoters pledged to raise $100,000 to cover all expenses for the two schools, while Yankee Stadium owners in New York were arranging to increase their seating capacity to nearly 80,000 for football to produce a larger gate. None of the cities hesitated to roll out all the political support they could muster.

The 1926 Army-Navy game was eventually awarded to Chicago, and game officials were swamped with more than 600,000 applications for tickets, with only 40,000 seats actually being available for sale at prices of $15 and $10 each. On November 27, 1926, an estimated crowd of 110,000 fans flocked to Soldier Field to see what proved to be one of college football's most memorable games. Afterward, it was revealed that the sale of tickets to the game had brought approximately $800,000 into the bank for the Chicago game promoter. The cost of transporting the teams and student bodies of both service academies to Chicago, along with feeding and housing them for two days, and other game-related expenses, had amounted to a staggering $600,000. But this still left a nice payday of a little more than $100,000 for each school, along with all the economic benefits that had been realized by the businesses of Chicago.[15]

The possibility of a Notre Dame–Southern Cal matchup had been a topic of discussion as early as 1924, with the Tournament of Roses Committee originally announcing that the two schools would be meeting in the Rose Bowl on New Year's Day 1925. It was the season of Notre Dame's "Four Horsemen" team, and all arrangements had supposedly been completed to bring Rockne's popular outfit to the West Coast to meet the Trojans. Rockne told reporters that the game had indeed been arranged by telephone, and he believed that the Notre Dame Athletic Board would give permission to make the trip.

Notre Dame's acceptance of the offer to play in the Rose Bowl game was conditioned upon the event's organizing committee "selecting an opponent that met with the approval of Coach Knute Rockne and other members of the local board," according to the Reverend Matthew Walsh, president of Notre Dame. Walsh said that no invitation had yet been extended to Southern Cal, contrary to announcements, and there were rumors circulating around Notre Dame that the Los Angeles school was not considered a satisfactory opponent, as the Trojans had lost two games. There were also concerns over the subsidizing charges against USC in 1924 that had caused Stanford and California to sever athletic relations with the Trojans. A wire-service dispatch reported, "It is generally accepted that Notre Dame would refuse to play anyone on the Coast but California or Stanford, with a decided preference for the latter."[16]

Notre Dame eventually did play Stanford in the 1925 Rose Bowl game, but later that year athletic officials at the South Bend school and Southern Cal recognized the big box-office potential available to them now that both schools had access to major metropolitan stadia—the Los Angeles Coliseum and Soldier Field in Chicago—and so the two schools scheduled the first meeting of their long-running intersectional series for the fall of 1926. In a letter to a friend in the coaching ranks, Rockne commented that "the Southern California officials came to South Bend and offered the authorities such a flattering guarantee that they could not turn it down. It seems as though money makes a big difference now days." More than 75,000 fans attended the 1926 game in Los Angeles, while reported crowds of more than 115,000 each witnessed the 1927 and 1929 games at Soldier Field. Conservative estimates placed the gate receipts for the 1927 game in excess of $350,000, which after expenses produced a profit figure approaching nearly $150,000 for each school. The first five games of the Notre Dame–Southern Cal series (1926–1930) drew a total of 453,889 fans—an average of more than 90,000 per game. The potential significance of these and other six-figure profit days to a school can be seen when considering Notre Dame's 1929 plans to build a new on-campus football stadium at an estimated cost of $750,000 and a new $350,000 law school building, or Ohio State's 1928 announcement of a program to construct five new athletic-related buildings at an average cost of $350,000 each.[17]

CHALLENGES IN SCHEDULING

In the early years of the decade the possible participants for the Rose Bowl game and other postseason intersectional contests always provided a source of continuous speculation in the newspaper sport sections. Until it became clear that the Harvard-Princeton-Yale trio was committed to maintaining their ban on traveling to intersectional games, the Big Three was always in the forefront of speculation about possible Rose Bowl participants. Yet not every school was opposed to appearing in the newly popular Rose Bowl game early in the 1920s. One of the most colorful college football teams of the 1921 season was the Centre College Praying Colonels from Kentucky, and the little school intended to take advantage of every opportunity offered. Accordingly, the Colonels accepted an offer to travel to San Diego for a postseason game being sponsored by the city's Chamber of Commerce on December 26. Meanwhile, the Rose Bowl committee had been continuing its pursuit of an eastern team to play on New Year's Day 1922, and, after being rejected by several other schools, a bid was extended to Centre College in late November. The Praying Colonels, in New Orleans to play Tulane, promptly announced their acceptance of the offer.

The University of California, already scheduled for the Rose Bowl on New Year's Day 1922, had earlier declined an invitation to play Centre College in San Diego in December; the statement from university officials included the comment that the Golden Bears "would not care to accept a game with a third-rate team." There were already rumors circulating about the academic credentials of some members of the Praying Colonels, and their widely traveled schedule for 1921 had created an image of something other than true amateur sportsmen. For California athletic officials—waiting to learn if Yale would agree to travel west to play their team—an opportunity to play Centre College did not hold the same artistic and cultural appeal for the socially and academically upper-class Pacific Coast university. When Rose Bowl officials learned of Centre's scheduled appearance in San Diego on December 26 and Cal's opposition to such a matchup, the Colonels were quickly dropped from further consideration, and Pasadena game officials publicly denied ever having issued an invitation. Finally, in early December 1921, Notre Dame accepted terms for a game against the Praying Colonels in San Diego—only to be rejected when Centre decided it would play only a Pacific Coast school. What eventually took place is that Centre played the University of Arizona in the San Diego game and then stopped in Dallas on the way home for a game against Texas A&M. Meanwhile, California had to settle for a 1922 Rose Bowl matchup against little Washington and Jefferson.[18]

Such tribulations in scheduling intersectional postseason games were a common occurrence during the early 1920s, leading one sportswriter to note that the Rose Bowl committee "is hard at work trying to break down the faculty and conference barriers that are always interposed when an eastern eleven is invited to come west."[19] One positive aspect from the annual scheduling hassles was the eventual nationalization of the Rose Bowl matchup by the middle of the 1920s, which also signaled the final acknowledgment that championship-level college football had indeed spread far beyond the boundaries of the old-line Big Three schools of the East. Tournament of Roses officials had grown weary of entreating the traditionally elite eastern and midwestern football schools to consider a winter-time trip to the Pacific Coast. Having noticed the top-flight football being demonstrated during intersectional play by teams from the Deep South, the Rose Bowl committee decided in late 1925 to expand the scope of its talent search.

The relatively small-scale pursuit of intersectional play by southern teams before 1920 had done much to fuel an image of regional gridiron inferiority, yet many of the South's major universities were ready to more aggressively pursue national football reputations as the 1920s began. Interest in expanding the scope of southern college football was part of a general change in regional attitudes during the decade. Historian George Tindall has observed that for southerners, the "experience of war had in many ways altered and enlarged their perspectives. . . . Sectionalism had retreated before nationalism. . . . For most Southerners the over-riding theme of the 1920s was, very simply, expansion." Building on that view, sport historians such as Michael Oriard and Andrew Doyle link the fortunes of southern intercollegiate football teams with attitudes of regional pride and aspirations during this period. Oriard has described intersectional play as a key strategy in potentially escalating the institutional and commercial prestige of many southern universities and locales.[20]

In the early 1920s southern universities began an escalation of the overall quality of play within the region, propelled by a willingness to adopt the open offensive strategies that included the forward pass and an aggressive attitude toward the subsidizing of athletes. Alabama's thrilling win over Washington in the 1926 Rose Bowl was the major breakthrough game for Dixie football, and southern university football teams would appear in the Rose Bowl game five times in the period 1926–1932.

The national attention focused on the Southern California region by the Rose Bowl game soon inspired the Deep South to consider sponsoring such postseason intersectional games, with Florida promoters seeking to begin an annual game as early as 1925, while city officials in New Orleans were petitioning the Southern Conference in early 1930 for assistance in staging an annual postseason football matchup.[21]

The scheduling of regular-season intersectional games was conducted in a more orderly manner, but there was a definite hierarchy of schools that figured heavily in the scheduling of such games. With the sport of football having been transformed into a big-business activity among the major universities by the mid-1920s, the scheduling of attractive opponents was essential. Of even greater significance was that games outside one's usual circle of schools (or conference) should be scheduled only in accordance with institutional prestige and goals. According to writer Francis Wallace, "The man who schedules the games . . . is the man who really runs the football business," while Charles L. Bruce, graduate manager of athletics at the University of Detroit in 1923, noted that "schedule making . . . is probably considered the most important duty of the athletic officials."[22]

In 1929 Wallace remarked, "Schedule makers are planning five years ahead, signing contracts for attractive intersectional games, based no longer on national rivalry or academic interest . . . but upon their ability to guard or increase prestige while also filling the stadium. . . . It is simply an algebraic problem the correct solution of which is required by good business." Wallace defined three levels within college football's hierarchy that were carefully adhered to in setting up intersectional games:

1. The autocrats—the old families of education who fathered football and fostered it;

2. The middle group—including the leaders in all sections of the country;

3. The climbers.[23]

The autocratic universities were typified as having recognized the "commercial possibilities" offered by 1920s college football, "even though falling behind the times in the development of technic." This definition clearly encompassed the Harvard-Princeton-Yale triumvirate, along with certain other schools such as Pennsylvania, Cornell, and Stanford. Even though the balance of competitive power in college football had moved westward by the late 1920s, the names of these schools still carried a cachet of old-school tradition, academic prestige, and athletic dignity. Wallace pointed out that the Big Three universities did not have to travel in order to obtain favorable games, and when they did venture out, "it is a reasonable conclusion that they receive far more generous financial inducements than are offered other squads of . . . less prestige."[24]

The middle group of football-playing schools, primarily made up of state universities, was defined as those institutions "who took up football early . . .

[and] who have kept pace and sometimes pioneered in its technical advancement, and who have profited normally by its commercial growth." At this level could be found schools such as Illinois, Michigan, Nebraska, Notre Dame, Ohio State, Alabama, Georgia Tech, Texas, California, and Southern California. Members of this group were further described as "always trying to break into the circle just above but refuse to be paid off mostly in prestige, as they are not in dire need of this intangible return." Wallace also noted that the scheduling of games for this level of football-playing schools was an extremely important endeavor, as "prestige in this group is even more jealously guarded than among the autocrats," and they "must avoid the catastrophe of a fellow lower down the ladder climbing at [their] expense."[25]

The class of football "climbers" was defined as including "those who have consciously and comparatively recently . . . installed football on a grand scale and gone out after the business advantage of prestige, money and publicity." Schools considered to be at this level by the late 1920s included Iowa, Missouri, Penn State, Southern Methodist, Carnegie Tech, and just about every Catholic university that was pursuing a major-level football schedule. Football teams from the "climber" category could expect to travel a good deal in order to secure the attractive matchups that offered the opportunity for financial reward, but more significantly the increased prestige associated with competition against their athletic and academic superiors. There are numerous examples throughout the decade of the prodigious distances that some teams were willing to travel in search of lucrative games; for example, during the 1921 season the Penn State football team traveled approximately eighty-five hundred miles.[26] If the "climber" made the mistake of defeating the school from the higher stratum, it could expect to be dropped from future schedules as quickly as possible, as when Yale dropped Boston College after suffering defeats in 1919 and 1920 and Princeton dropped West Virginia after a loss in 1919.

As the decade headed toward its close, the number of intersectional games played and the distances traveled by teams seemed only to increase in spite of the vocal opposition from some of the game's leaders. Teams from the West Coast were consistently among the most aggressive travelers—for example, the ten teams of the Pacific Coast Conference traveled nearly sixty-four thousand miles during the 1928 season, which included Oregon State and Stanford each traveling to New York City, while Oregon ended its season in Hawaii. In 1929 that same conference of teams traveled nearly seventy-three thousand miles, or, as the Associated Press pointed out, "a distance almost equal to three times around the world." The major intersectional matchups of 1929 included California at Penn, Oregon at Florida, Army at Stanford, Harvard at Michigan, Carnegie Tech at Southern Cal, and Yale at Georgia. This slate led Grantland Rice to state, "There have been intersectional tests before, but nothing that will compare . . . with the current season." Yet, in 1930, St. Mary's of California and Fordham of New York City would launch one of the most bizarre cross-country intersectional rivalries in football history.[27]

Many football coaches and promoters sought to justify the considerable traveling with the claim that the experience broadened the educations of the young athletes. But sportswriter Norman Brown argued that the real value from intersectional games accrued to the universities themselves, both from "the best form of publicity" and "because they help materially to pay the freight of the other athletic activities." Here was the basic defense of major college football's transformation into the big-business endeavor it had become in the 1920s.[28]

On the other side of the debate over extensive intersectional play were some prominent coaches and administrators of the time. Fielding Yost of Michigan was solidly opposed to postseason games, commenting that "if intersectional games are to be played at all, they should be scheduled for the regular season so as not to prolong the training period of the players . . . [I]n general, intersectional games that require much time away from classes are unwise." Bob Zuppke of Illinois was an opponent of extensive intersectional play, calling the practice "barnstorming." Differing from Yost, the Illinois coach saw "no great evil in intersectional battle as a classic once a year, for it may cement national friendship and wholesome rivalry, but it should not be at the expense of much classwork." Zuppke described the extensive traveling of some schools as a "dangerous practice . . . not in keeping with the general principles of the game." In announcing plans to construct a new football stadium on the Notre Dame campus, the Reverend Charles L. O'Donnell, president of the university, lamented the fact that the school's team would be forced to play its complete 1929 schedule on the road, adding that "it is not sound academically to have a roving set of collegians."[29]

The intent of transforming intercollegiate football into a "national as opposed to sectional sport" through the medium of intersectional matchups had been espoused as early as 1920, one writer recognizing that "such contests . . . go for the establishment of better friendship and understanding between sections." Coach John Heisman in 1922 defended the expansion of intersectional play on that basis: "I think that these games are among the greatest boosters that football has. I think that they tend to make the interest national instead of sectional, and that such a state of affairs is very good for the sport." By 1929 John Kieran of the *New York Times* was able to note that "the intersectional idea is not only firmly rooted but flourishing mightily. . . . Where before football was sectional, it is now broadly intersectional, which means national." Michael Oriard has examined the cultural significance of college football's nationalization, contending that intersectional games allowed teams to become active participants within this growing sporting culture while still maintaining their regional identities.[30]

As the new decade of the 1930s dawned there was no question that wide-spread intersectional play had become an integral part of college football's financial and cultural fiber. The rise of intersectional football had served to stimulate spectator interest, engendered regional school loyalties, and encouraged an overall improved level of play—meaningless early-season games being dropped from the schedules of major teams in response to the increasing need to generate sizable box-office receipts. Meanwhile, the nationalization of the annual Rose Bowl game had also been a key factor in the growing fan mania for intersectional play, while also setting the stage for an ever growing number of such postseason games in the future.

During the 1920s college football unquestionably capitalized on the evolution of regional competitive parity while integrating intersectional play as a key component of the sport, and these dual transforming agents made possible the days of stadium building and big business during the decade and beyond. Nothing approaching the 1920s transformation of college football into a true "national" sport would occur on this scale again until the final two decades of the century.

3

STADIUM BUILDING AND
THE DAYS OF BIG BUSINESS

Perhaps the most defining and long-lasting legacy of 1920s college football was the conversion of the sport into an unquestioned big-business venture for the schools as a by-product of the wave of stadium building that swept across the universities during the decade. Building on the continuing evolution of national competitive parity and the rising popularity of intersectional play, there soon was a growing demand for game tickets at the major football schools that easily exceeded the capacity of most of the old-style stadia. Quickly, many athletic officials moved ahead with plans to build massive stadia to house their football teams and to capitalize on the potentially great financial rewards. The stadium-building mania throughout the 1920s set college football on a path of transformation toward wide-ranging commercialism and professionalism, from which there would be no turning back without the dismantling of the sport.[1]

Already anticipating the approaching battle between the academic and athletic factions over the growing emphasis on college football, athletic directors and coaches presented stadium building to their university administrations as an opportunity to generate much-needed funding for the construction of more campus buildings and facilities that would benefit the entire student body. With the initial designs for many of the stadia including some type of memorial to the dead of World War I, along with considerable architectural grandeur, the athletic officials represented their new football stadia as monuments to patriotism and culture.

Before World War I the building of stadia for college football had a sketchy history at best, as primarily modest arenas were built on college campuses, few resembling the mammoth structures that would rise in the postwar years. Many universities had erected relatively small wooden grandstands with an enclosing fence around the field in the 1890s, but a considerable number of schools had continued to play on an open field where the spectators stood along the sidelines or behind the end zones. Credit for building the first true college football stadium is given to the University of Pennsylvania. Penn's Franklin Field, opened in 1895, soon proved to have inadequate seating for the big games, and it was replaced in 1903 with a permanent horseshoe-shaped stadium.

In 1903 Harvard built the first steel-reinforced football stadium in the country, an architecturally attractive structure that featured two classic tiers of Roman arches and piers, with a seating capacity for nearly 40,000 spectators. In 1908 Syracuse University built the next large stadium, also with a seating capacity of nearly 40,000. Except for these schools, general football stadium construction prior to 1914 was more typified by schools such as Northwestern, which built a wooden structure in 1905 with seating for approximately 10,000, or the University of Illinois, which enlarged the capacity of its wooden grandstands from 300 to 4,000 in 1905.[2]

In 1914 Princeton and Yale opened their own modern-style stadia, thereby establishing the framework for the building boom that would begin in 1920. Princeton opened its 45,725-seat Palmer Stadium on October 24, 1914, with a game against Dartmouth. It was a U-shaped structure that also included a running track, a feature making the stadium a multisport facility—an obligation in the 1920s in order to demonstrate that the athletic department was really furthering the muscular development and fitness of the university student body and not just building a monument to the great football god. Of far greater significance for the future was the construction of the massive Yale Bowl in New Haven. Although the permanent seating capacity of 64,025, with temporary seats that carried the capacity to 70,657, was staggering enough, of particular significance was the bowl shape of the stadium, featuring a single tier and sloped grandstand, which would become the standard design for the largest seating-capacity structures of the 1920s.[3]

Although many universities had been considering plans for new football stadia before World War I—in emulation of the ones built by the eastern Big Three—all those plans were put on hold during the country's involvement in the war. In the aftermath of the great performance by the nation's military forces, a considerable wave of patriotism swept across the country's population, which of course included the universities of the land that were in theory responsible for the physical well-being and muscular development of the nation's elite youth.

When the more aggressive athletic administrations began planning the construction of their new football stadia at the dawn of the 1920s, the fervor of patriotism provided one justification for the projects. Historian Patrick Miller has described this rationale well: "Vast memorial stadiums became the foremost patriotic symbols of the twenties, solidly establishing the bonds between muscular and martial values, cementing the relationship between the war effort and the academy, Mars and Minerva." Many schools announced that their stadia would serve as memorials to the men who had so ably served their nation, and a number of the new stadia built before 1925 would in fact be called "Memorial Stadium."[4]

After the war, the country's enthusiasm for having a good time and casting off the last vestiges of its restrictive Victorian principles would be one of the driving forces in the escalation of college football's popularity during the 1920s. In a nation still on a high from its performance in the war, football provided an opportunity to peacefully continue experiencing that excitement. Percy Haughton, a former coach at Harvard who had served in France during the war, wrote that football's appeal could be found in its combining of "physical skill and strength with an intellectual side closely resembling that brought out in modern warfare, in something like a complicated game of human chess." College football was viewed by some writers as part of the "cooling off" process for the country after the war, and the significantly growing interest in the sport that resulted provided another justification for "a well-defined movement among all colleges and universities for the expansion of sports fields and stadiums."[5]

There were other substantive issues that fueled the sport's growing popularity and translated into the stadium-building boom. Foremost among them would be the major improvements in the country's highway systems, along with the physical improvements in automobiles and the widespread ownership of these vehicles, which had been increasing at a rapid pace since before the war. Prior to World War I, the traveling of any significant distance by automobile was a chancy business at best given the relatively great amount of unpaved roadways, while during the uncertainties of autumn weather traveling in an open auto often produced an uncomfortable experience. All these factors began to change as the number of registered cars in the United States increased from less than 2.5 million in 1915 to nearly 20 million by 1925, while the number of autos manufactured with interiors enclosed against the weather increased from just 2 percent in 1916 to 72 percent by 1926.

Meanwhile, the states had embarked upon major road-building and paving projects after the war, spurred along by major funding from the federal government beginning in 1921. The state of Missouri was typical of this effort, engaging in a $60 million road-building program that when completed would place Columbia, home of the state university, within five hours by auto of every corner of the state. The result of the various improvements relative to automobile travel was that driving any distance became something other than a miserable experience, while the football stadia of the universities were brought into range for a substantial amount of the general population that did not live convenient to efficient train transportation. Thus was created a potentially vast audience for college football games.[6]

The stadium-building phenomenon that took place during the 1920s was in keeping with the general prosperity in the nation's construction business. With the economy growing again in the aftermath of a short-lived depression in 1921, along with the increasing populations in urbanized areas, there was a substantial demand for the construction of new office buildings, apartment buildings, and real estate developments. The demand produced a construction boom that would reach its peak in 1925 with an estimated $5 billion in building revenues, gradually tapering off to approximately $3 billion by 1929—a trend line that was also characteristic of the building of college football stadia.[7]

Architecturally, the stadia that would rise on many of the nation's campuses reflected a transition in design concepts that was taking place in the general construction business. In the aftermath of the war many architects were moving to a modern style of geometrically severe and utilitarian design concepts that seemed more appropriate for the commercialized culture of the 1920s. These same design principles that stressed functionality became essential in the construction of the stadia, as the universities sought to maximize the purposes for which the structures would be used while providing the greatest possible seating capacity and some degree of convenience for the spectators—and all theoretically at a cost that was within the school's economic capability.[8]

What resulted among the major stadia constructed was a considerable variance in such aspects of design as the slope of the grandstand, the distance from the field to the first row of seats, and the elevation of the seats from the field surface itself. Many of the new stadia were influenced to some degree by the arenas that had been built in ancient times by the Greeks and Romans—especially in areas such as the use of some type of ellipse-shaped design, the methods for controlling spectators, and the appearance of the outside walls.

The avowed intent was to build stadia that "provide advantageous seats for spectators at football games," or as architect James H. Forsythe of the University of Minnesota explained: "A stadium has for its principal purpose the provision of seats to which a small or a large number of spectators may find ready access and egress under absolute control and from which each individual may secure the best possible view of the action taking place in the arena." The shape of the stadium (U-shaped versus bowl-shaped) would ultimately determine how successful the university was in giving the fans good seats for the game, evidenced by the proportion of seats that were located along the sidelines and between the goal lines. Some examples from stadia built in the 1920s include Cornell with about 65 percent of the seats along the sidelines, Illinois with 72 percent, and Brown with about 83 percent, standing in contrast to the Yale Bowl that has only about 35 percent of its seats between the goal lines, while the maximum length of view existing in the famous stadium is a whopping 600 feet.[9]

Regardless of whether all the ticket-buying fans were going to get that first-class seat, the fact remained that the growth in student enrollments and general population counts were pushing the universities toward providing larger stadia than had previously existed. Figures from the Big Ten Conference are typical for illustrating the substantial growth in potential ticket buyers. Between 1890 and 1920, the general population of the seven states in which conference schools were located had experienced a 57 percent increase, while the population of the towns in which the universities were located had increased 169 percent during the same period. Considering that total student enrollments at the Big Ten schools were nearly four times larger in 1925 as compared to 1900, there was no reason to be surprised at the increasing clamor for football tickets.[10]

At some schools the need to proceed with plans for a new football stadium did not meet with immediate acceptance, much to the frustration of the athletic officials and coaches. At Notre Dame the need for a larger stadium had been a topic of discussion almost since the arrival of Knute Rockne as head coach in 1918; a 1919 editorial in the *Notre Dame Scholastic* raised the issue in the immediate aftermath of the war. Attendance for home games at the school's Cartier Field, with an eventual seating capacity of approximately 27,000 by 1927, was relatively small, and the inadequate paydays for visiting teams made it a difficult proposition to lure big-name schools to South Bend.[11]

Through Rockne's promotional efforts, Notre Dame had been able to draw occasional overflow crowds to Cartier Field in the years after 1920, while also drawing well at away games, all being made possible by the outstanding teams that were by then representing the school. A 1923 editorial in the *South Bend News-Times* entreated the university to build the new football stadium that the prestige of Rockne's teams deserved and that the vast numbers clamoring for tickets made essential. The editorial suggested the potential benefits possible for any university that used football as a vehicle for maintaining close ties and school loyalties among its alumni, while also noting that the university needed to recognize that "Notre Dame is a part of South Bend . . . and the large contribution which it makes to the permanent prosperity and good fame of the city."[12]

In 1924 the student body of Notre Dame sent a petition on behalf of a new stadium to Father Matthew Walsh, the university president, but the Notre Dame officials continued to move slowly on the issue, much to Rockne's annoyance. In mid-November 1927, the university's board of lay trustees met and formed committees to investigate the feasibility of building a new football stadium, which the newspapers construed as the project being given the go-ahead. A short story in the *Chicago Herald and Examiner* was headlined "Trustees Move to Rush Stadium," while the *New York Times* reported the item and specified that the stadium would be built at a cost of $800,000 with a seating capacity of 50,000. But the new stadium had not yet been approved, and in his frustration over the school's internal politics involving the athletic program, Rockne submitted his resignation as football coach right after the 1927 season ended. Glenn "Pop" Warner had used a similar tactic at the University of Pittsburgh after the 1919 season, when he linked his signing of a new contract as head coach to the school's promise to build a new football stadium, which ultimately led to the opening of Pitt Stadium in 1925.[13]

Rockne had used the threat of leaving Notre Dame too many times prior to 1927, though, so Father Walsh simply did not accept the coach's resignation, and the committees went on with their studies. Rockne continued to fume, telling an architect, "This all seems very nonsensical and silly but you have to understand the intricate workings of an organization of this sort in order to have the proper patience." Finally, in a speech at a Notre Dame Club of New York luncheon in February 1929, Father Charles L. O'Donnell, now the university president, outlined the school's ten-year building program that included the announcement that work would begin on the new football stadium later that spring, with completion expected in time for the 1930 season.[14]

Amos Alonzo Stagg of the University of Chicago was another of college football's prominent coaches who experienced considerable difficulty in his attempts to get a new football stadium built on campus. Stagg's teams had been playing their home games since 1893 at Marshall Field, renamed Stagg Field in 1913 in conjunction with the addition of a large new grandstand that greatly expanded the total seating capacity. For years Stagg had been proposing a new stadium in order to capitalize on the popularity of college football in the city. By 1922 Stagg had completed detailed studies on changes that could be made to the existing stadium to increase capacity without embarking on major construction work, coming up with a figure of 3,462 seats that could be added, which in Stagg's mind was a stop-gap measure at best. And so, during a meeting that fall with the Trustees Committee, Stagg advanced a proposal for the building of a new football stadium on university property a few blocks to the south of the current stadium, with a seating capacity of approximately 100,000. In a letter afterward Stagg remarked, "I didn't hesitate . . . and nobody made any objections to my comments."[15]

But the temper of the times toward intercollegiate football was already beginning to change on the campus of the University of Chicago. A short time later the president of the university, Harry Pratt Judson, announced that the cost of building such a gigantic stadium would be far too expensive and that the school had pressing educational needs that were far more important. Finally, in 1924 plans were approved by the university's Board of Trustees that called for a major construction project on the current Stagg Field, which was expected to increase its seating capacity to between 60,000 and 70,000, the actual work not being completed until 1926. The frustration in not being able to fully capitalize financially on the excellent teams Stagg fielded from 1921 to 1924 is reflected in a letter his son wrote in 1927 to a Harvard athletic official: "We have had great difficulty for many years in filling applications [for tickets] but it is mainly because of a shortsighted policy of the University by not allowing suitable accommodations to be built."[16]

The Building Begins

Despite those universities that were taking a cautious approach toward the stadium-building issue, the predominant situation among the larger schools was to proceed as quickly as possible toward the anticipated box-office bonanzas. Stanford was one of the leaders out of the gate, as the Palo Alto, California, university opened its new 65,000-seat stadium in 1921, just six months after the project had been approved. In the aftermath of the war Stanford had looked with envy at the gridiron success experienced by archrival California, and Stanford officials considered the building of a new stadium before Cal to be a vehicle for not only obtaining its share of the financial gains available but more significantly ensuring that Stanford was viewed as an academic and social equal of the Berkeley university.[17]

In short order over the next three seasons came the opening of several more stadia with seating capacities that had previously been achieved only at Yale and Princeton. The first wave of giant structures included the University of Pennsylvania's expansion of Franklin Field to a capacity of 61,000 in 1922, Ohio Stadium on the campus of Ohio State in 1922 with 63,000 seats, California's Memorial Stadium in 1923 with 73,000 seats, and Memorial Stadium on the campus of the University of Illinois in 1924 with a capacity of approximately 67,000.[18]

In the face of such large seating structures, many universities elected to build what came to be regarded as midsize stadia in the new construction environment, with seating capacities of approximately 40,000–50,000. Examples from this group were schools such as Minnesota (1924), Northwestern (1926), and Missouri (1926). As mentioned earlier, universities such as Chicago and Pennsylvania chose to expand their existing stadia, and these schools were joined by the University of Michigan, which expanded its old Ferry Field from 21,000 to 46,000 in 1921—which soon proved to be inadequate and led to the construction of Michigan Stadium in 1927 with a capacity of 84,401.

Not all schools were prepared to yield to the clamor for more and more seats, though, the most notable being Yale University, which already had one of the great football bowls in the country with a capacity of more than 70,000. But with the Big Three of the East still considered to be among the nation's football elite, some believed that an addition to the stadium that had been constructed only in 1914 could be justified. In 1921 a proposal was made to expand the Yale Bowl with 42,000 additional seats, which would bring the capacity to 117,000, far beyond any stadium being considered at the time.

Architecturally, the idea to expand the Yale Bowl was feasible, and the original designer of the stadium, Charles A. Ferry, already had prepared plans for a concrete and steel upper deck to effect the increased seating. But Professor C. W. Mendell, chairman of Yale's Athletic Board of Control, called the proposal a "pipe dream" and said such a project would never be undertaken while he was there. "It would spoil the beauty of the bowl, as well as a large number of seats under the proposed gallery," said Mendell. "The more you add to the seating capacity the more will the law of diminishing returns apply; the cost of maintenance would eat up the extra profits."[19]

The idea was back, though, in late 1923 at the near height of the building boom, with Ferry ready with plans for an expansion to 125,000 seats, again with the addition of a second deck to the bowl. Architecturally, these proposed expansions of the Yale Bowl were feasible without adding a second deck, as an engineering study showed that a single deck in such a football stadium could be expanded to hold seating for about 150,000—130,000 if the field was to be enclosed by a running track—all without creating a view any farther from the action than the most distant view already existing. But this proposal was in the immediate aftermath of the extended provisions for athletic reform made to the Big Three's Triple Agreement by the presidents of the universities, and any plan to expand the Yale Bowl was seen as contrary to the spirit of the new agreement and "not for the best interests of college athletics."[20]

The box-office potential to be realized from college football had also been recognized by metropolitan areas that were strategically located and aspired to begin promoting collegiate gridiron spectaculars. The Polo Grounds in New York City was among the first to get in on the football craze, adding new grandstands in 1920 that would increase the seating capacity for gridiron dates to more than 40,000.[21]

Major new metropolitan stadia with college football in mind were also constructed—two of them originally built in anticipation of also luring the Olympic Games—including the Tournament of Roses Stadium in Pasadena, California (later renamed the Rose Bowl), in 1922, a horseshoe-shaped arena with an initial seating capacity of 57,000 that was expanded to 76,000 in 1928; the Los Angeles Coliseum in 1923, with a capacity of approximately 75,000; and Grant Park Stadium in Chicago (later renamed Soldier Field) in 1924, with a seating capacity of approximately 60,000, which would be expanded to more than 100,000 within two short years. That the general sporting public was coming to believe that no seating capacity was apparently too large can be seen in a short piece that appeared in the *New York Times* in 1927, in which the writer reports that plans were in place to raise the seating capacity of Chicago's Soldier Field to 165,000.[22]

The media of the time delighted in contrasting the mammoth stadium building of the U.S. universities with the classical amphitheaters of ancient Greek and

Roman times. One typical article pointed out that "many of the American structures are far larger than anything in the ancient world" and that the number of large new stadia built in the United States was more than double the number that had populated the Roman Empire—and it was 1922, before the building boom really took off. The atmosphere at a college football game in the large new stadia was characterized by the same writer as one of "almost regal pomp," with the interest in American football probably exceeding even the ancient Romans' interest in the one hundred–day games that had opened the famous Coliseum in A.D. 80. The writer also linked the grandeurs and excitement of ancient sport to intercollegiate football: "He who thrills at reading of a gladiatorial contest can get the same thrill, experience the same 'mob psychology,' by attending a football game at one of the new American stadiums."[23]

Not everyone in the university communities was pleased with all the talk of large-scale arenas. For example, when the plans were being laid out for the new stadium at Ohio State in 1921, Dr. T. C. Mendenhall, the sole surviving member of the school's original faculty of 1873 and an influential trustee, insisted that a maximum seating capacity of 35,000 was more than enough to handle ticket demands. Yet far more publicly visible were opinions of men such as Walter Camp, who in 1922 replied to those individuals who were questioning the need for the large seating capacities being constructed, stating that the numbers of ticket-buying fans packing the new stadia "put to rout the idea that institutions were building too largely to accommodate the spectators of the popular fall sport." Later, James L. Knox of Harvard would also defend the stadium building as nothing more than what the sporting public was clamoring for: "Stadia have been built simply because of the known demand for seats. The seats are in demand because football comes nearer crystallizing the underlying traits of human nature than any other game evolved." Or as another writer described it, "All this means that the game of football has taken its place among the great popular spectacles of history."[24]

Justifying the Mania

With the considerable number of new football stadia being built on college and university campuses, the school presidents who had given final approval for the building of these giant arenas, and their athletic officials, sought to rationalize the obvious contradiction to the concerns about overemphasis in their athletic departments by the academic communities. It became essential that these new stadia be represented as a fundamental component of the school's physical facilities. The stadium complexes also had to be defined as significant to the physical development and well-being of the entire student population, while also serving as a symbol of the school's progress and prestige in the eyes of its alumni.

The idea that the football stadium was an essential element in maintaining the muscular virility of the country's youth was advanced by Dr. J. W. Wilce of Ohio State: "The Stadium is not a monument, however, in its largest interpretation; it is a living stimulation toward the maintenance of strong, virile, clean, active elements in the broad field of education." Dean William McClellan of Penn asserted that the universities had a major responsibility in helping to maintain a satisfactory state of physical preparedness among the nation's young people and that the now worldly aware population of the 1920s would demand adequate athletic facilities that allowed the participation of many, rather than merely the muscular elite.[25]

Typical of the efforts made to represent the new stadia as vehicles for providing athletics for the masses, or intramurals, was the statement made on the University of Missouri's stadium subscription-pledge form: "It should be emphasized that the Stadium is not merely bleachers for the football season, but that it will house recreational facilities for every student in the University and will be the center of a larger development in physical education than it has heretofore been possible to make." The claim that the new stadia would make available substantial space underneath the grandstands that could be used for other sports was a common one, and one that often could not be realized for financial reasons. Among those institutions making such promises were Chicago, Minnesota, Illinois, and Ohio State. Interestingly, in later years Ohio State would convert space under the grandstands into student living quarters in response to the growing on-campus housing shortages.[26]

The new stadia were also increasingly represented as symbols and advertisements for the universities and a key link in maintaining alumni sentiment and its fund-raising potential. A *New York Times* writer noted that the enjoyment of athletic contests in such stadia was "part of a desirable college life which may produce memories to be treasured," while a San Francisco sportswriter described Stanford's new stadium "as a lasting testimonial of Stanford spirit and enterprise." Amos Alonzo Stagg envisioned some of the same nostalgia for Chicago alumni: "Sitting in the stadium with a view of some of the campus buildings will bring back old memories to the graduates and will stir sentiment for their Alma Mater." Stagg was also constantly aware of the fund-raising potential a new stadium might hold among the general public, noting that "greatly increased seating capacity would develop thousands of additional friends of the University" and that "tying the public to us will mean future students and no telling how many hundreds of thousands of dollars in gifts."[27]

Many alumni also endorsed the importance of a new stadium to a university's future, such as one former University of Chicago student who described "the advantages of a stadium in the way of advertising . . . and stimulation of public interest as too obvious to need discussion." Some were just as enthusiastic in their belief that athletics had an equal partnership role in the overall life, curriculum, and prestige of the university. In 1922, Ernest Quantrell, president of the University of Chicago's alumni association of New York, told Stagg, "In my judgement a stadium is becoming just as much a requisite of up-to-date University equipment as a gymnasium or physics laboratory." When Notre Dame's new stadium opened in 1930, the university's alumni magazine noted the public belief in the importance of a school's athletic prestige, commenting that finally "Knute Rockne's teams, the royalty of football, now are housed in a manner to which public opinion has forced them to become accustomed."[28]

Another approach taken in justifying the new stadia was to suggest that they might provide a venue for all types of civic, sporting, and cultural functions for the general populace of the local area, in addition to enhancing the prestige of the region surrounding the university. Ohio State was one of the first to link a sparkling new football stadium to the general perception of a geographic region, noting in its fund-raising booklet that "the Stadium will be for all Ohio . . . [A]s an architectural triumph, it will lend prestige to the city of Columbus and the State." In describing its plans for the Baker Field athletic facility in New York City, which included the new football stadium, Columbia officials noted that it was the university's intention to offer the use of its new layout to "all amateur athletes of this city . . . making Baker Field an athletic playground not only for Columbia but for the whole city." With Baker Field being constructed near the edge of the Hudson River on the north end of Manhattan, the plan was to build a boat landing as part of the facility so that the stadium could be used as "a reception place for noted guests of New York City." When the University of Detroit, a Catholic school, was building its new on-campus stadium in 1921, an article in the student newspaper explained, "The erection of the stadium means not only glory to the University but to the city at large. It means that Detroit will have facilities to take care of the national A.A.U. and collegiate games. . . . It might even mean the World Olympic games for Detroit."[29]

Yet not all students were in favor of these athletic-building projects. A 1922 editorial in the University of Chicago's *Daily Maroon* declared that the students and faculty did not want a new stadium built, and the writer added that the school did not need to build a football stadium in order to maintain a relationship with the surrounding city, railing over the idea that the need to provide more seats for the general public should even enter into any debate over the proposed new arena. The editorial further asserted that "the university—all of it—feels that it is not an integral part of the city." It was not exactly a position to be taken by a university that might need construction-zoning favors and permits in the near future, and the school's president, Harry Pratt Judson, quickly stepped in and stated that "while

3. Stadium at the University of Detroit. This overhead view shows a typical midsize football stadium built in the 1920s. The site is now a parking lot. Courtesy of the University of Detroit Mercy Archives, Marine Historical Collection.

it is true that the university is not legally related to the city, it feels itself none the less really a part of Chicago and the university regards it as a duty to make every contribution it can to the life of the city."[30]

Then there was President David Kinley of the University of Illinois, who in the early 1920s contemplated the plans for his school's new Memorial Stadium, which he envisioned as a cultural beacon for the university populace. The stadium design called for an extremely classical exterior that would include Greek-style columns and facades, along with an open-air theater, an Italian garden, and even a fountain outside the entrance. President Kinley, who believed that the grandiose new stadium would "provide a link between American culture and the classical Greek civilization upon which modern education was based," wrote in the fundraising booklet: "Perhaps my greatest interest in the Stadium is the cultural effect. Our Stadium will bring a touch of Greek glory to the prairie. Young men and women spending four years of their lives in the vicinity of such an edifice cannot help absorbing some of its lofty inspiration."[31] Unfortunately, as happened with the proposed extras for so many of the new stadia, escalating costs and unfulfilled subscription pledges forced the elimination of virtually all the classical trappings before the stadium at Illinois was finally completed.

Paying the Bills

The raising of the necessary money to build a new stadium, with virtually no government-provided funding, basically came down to subscription pledges that were tied into ticket-buying privileges, or the issuance of some type of interest-bearing bonds by the university to the general public.

Yale University served as the model for subscription plans that were tied into ticket-purchasing privileges, the eastern school having used such a plan in its construction of the Yale Bowl in 1914. A 1912 article in the *Yale Alumni Weekly* stated the basic premise: "It is believed that the amount of money requisite for building and equipping a Coliseum can be secured by the issuance of certificates to carry no other privilege or dividend than the right for fifteen years to secure tickets for the important game each year." The key to loosening the wallets of the football followers was to build in a scaled purchasing plan that tied the number of tickets you might purchase to the size of your subscription. Yale's stated principle was the following: "It is manifest that some relationship between subscriptions of varying amounts and the ticket privilege attached thereto should be established."[32]

In application during the 1920s, the universities building new stadia used a number of variations based on the Yale formula. Generally, the promise was only to allow the subscriber to purchase "choice seats" for the season's home games during the period of years stated. For example, for each $100 pledged the University of Illinois issued an option on "one good seat" for ten years, and each additional $100 pledged brought an option on another ticket; each $100 pledged to the Stanford drive brought the right to purchase two choice seats at a $1 per-seat discount; Ohio State's system was scaled from pledges of $100–$199, which would bring an option on two seats for ten years, up to the "Founders" contribution category of $5,000 or more that carried the prestige of having a box of seats named in your honor, along with the option to purchase tickets for as many of those seats as you desired. The University of Iowa issued bonds in 1929 to raise the needed money for its new stadium, with the purchasers entitled to obtain two seats for each $1,000 of par value of bonds owned. Notre Dame was one of the schools that pegged the amount subscribed to relatively specific seat locations, offering that a pledge of "$3,000 for 10 years" would bring title to six seats in a box between the 45-yard lines—between the 35- and 45-yard lines required $2,500—scaling down to seats between the goal line and the 15-yard line for $1,250. The University of Michigan's fund-raising plan offered a similar option, as holders of its interest-bearing $500 bonds were entitled to purchase season tickets for ten years, the seats guaranteed to be between the 30-yard lines.[33]

Predictably, many of those individuals signing up for stadium subscription pledges failed to always come through on schedule with their payments, causing embarrassing cash-flow problems for the university athletic departments that had signed contracts and started construction. At Ohio State the subscription drive had raised just over $1 million in pledges by January 1921, and so university officials signed a contract with the E. H. Latham Company of Columbus, and ground for the new stadium was broken in August 1921. But by January 1922, the Stadium Executive Committee learned that approximately $175,000 in pledge payments was already overdue, with the figure expected to increase with the next installment being due that month. A considerable portion of the delinquent amount was due from students, and in frustration President William O. Thompson wrote a letter to them in which he stated: "As a man of longer experience let me suggest that an unpaid obligation to a fund of this sort is an annoyance. . . . One never feels quite right in the company of other men who have met their obligations while conscious of the fact that there is an unpaid pledge awaiting his attention." Ohio Stadium opened on schedule in 1922, but ultimately the university would have to take out bank loans of $378,740 to make up for the shortfalls in subscription payments and construction-cost overruns.[34]

This situation contrasts with Notre Dame, which was able to raise all the funding and payments for its subscription drive despite the Depression (charging 6 percent interest on late payments), while a school with smaller football aspirations—the University of North Carolina—had a less stressful route, as it was able to build its new stadium in 1926 with seating for 24,000 after a gift of $275,000 was received from William Rand Kenan Jr., whose parents the stadium is still named after.[35]

Other universities ran into funding difficulties for their stadium construction as a result of general economic factors. Originally, the University of Nebraska's Memorial Stadium was going to be funded by the state legislature, but a major agricultural slump around the state during the early 1920s forced the cancellation of that promise, and the school had to instead use a subscription program. The University of Iowa issued $500,000 of ten-year 5 percent stadium bonds in 1929, but the onset of the Depression hit the state particularly hard, and the resulting decrease in revenues to the university created major problems in making the annual interest payments on the debt. The school was finally forced to default on interest payments, not resuming payments to investors until 1938, and the bonds were not retired until 1946. The University of Michigan also found itself unable to maintain the redemption and interest payments on its bonds once the Depression began, going delinquent on the bonds for six years, and the university was unable to retire the issue until 1947.[36]

4. Main entrance of Ohio Stadium at Ohio State. Dedicated in 1922, this stadium is typical of the large arenas built during college football's first building boom. Author's collection.

The University of Missouri was another school that was hit hard financially by the economics of the early 1930s. The popularity of athletics through the 1920s at Missouri had convinced the university of the need for a new football stadium and field house, with the stadium being constructed in 1926 at an approximate cost of $365,000. The major sources of funding for the football stadium came from subscription pledges and the issuance of $200,000 of ten-year 6 percent interest-bearing bonds, and by January 1931 one-half of the bonds had been redeemed. But the onset of the Depression basically shut off all payments on the subscription pledges, only about one-third of the payments having been made at that point. When combined with major declines in football attendance and the continuing principal and interest payments on the bonds, the Missouri athletic department was soon losing money at a rapid rate. After defaulting on the bonds' principal and interest payments for two years, Missouri arranged for the issuance of new bonds in lieu of the defaulted ones, with a more conservative payment structure.[37]

The decade of the 1920s witnessed a great transformation of college football's physical landscape—many large seating-capacity stadia having risen in every region of the country as testimony to the American commitment to capitalism. These giant structures also signaled the eventual defeat of the old-school university ideals of amateur athletic competition and served as beacons toward the future of the sport—to a time when commercialism and overemphasis in college football would exceed anything imagined in the 1920s. Yet even before the 1920s came to a close, the stadium-building boom had catapulted college football into another realm of significant and long-lasting change.

COLLEGE FOOTBALL GOES BIG BUSINESS

One of the most dominant themes to emerge in college football during the 1920s was the sport's rapid ascension into the realm of big business. Fueled by the tremendous surge in football's popularity after the war—combined with the many new stadia, the surging enrollments at American universities, and the significant expansion of intersectional football—an escalating flow of money was soon pouring into athletic department coffers in the 1920s. This transformation of college football into a big-business endeavor would soon create a financial dependency that the schools would be able to escape only by returning the sport to its earliest days as a small-scale amateur affair.[38]

Schools from the Western Conference (Big Ten) were among the leaders in generating revenue from football throughout the decade, the string of record years for attendance and receipts beginning immediately after the war, and by 1922 it was being noted that "football in the mid-west is rapidly assuming the proportions of an industry—a very successful industry." Despite the record football paydays that prompted that observation, university officials within the conference were eagerly awaiting the completion of their new stadia, as in 1922 it was estimated that more than 500,000 ticket-buying fans had to be turned away because of inadequate seating capacities.[39]

As the new stadia began coming on line within the Big Ten, attendance at games rose significantly, and the total receipts generated by football within the conference increased from a total of $1.32 million in 1923 to $2.71 million by 1929. During this period Michigan, Illinois, and Chicago were generally the conference leaders in football receipts, Michigan increasing its annual figure from $194,000 in 1923 to nearly $509,000 by 1929, while the football revenues at the University of Illinois grew from more than $182,000 in 1923 to nearly $352,000 by 1929.[40]

Growing attendance and revenue figures were also being realized on a national basis, and for the 1924 season it was reported that college football had drawn more than 10 million fans. While the Big Ten Conference was regarded as the national attendance leader by 1924, the continuing value and appeal of combining mammoth stadia and traditional rivalries were demonstrated that season by the approximately 623,000 fans who attended the ten highest-drawing eastern games that season. For the 1924 season the University of Michigan was identified as the national attendance leader with a total of 340,000 fans, while the University of Pennsylvania was tabbed as the best drawing card in the East with a total of 320,000. In 1925 the estimated total national attendance rose to 12 million, while the Big Ten Conference reported a profit of $1.28 million. Always conscious of the opponents of commercialism, the Big Ten's press release hastened to add that this gain had been accomplished with coaching staffs that were being paid an average salary of just $2,500 per individual.[41]

Despite the substantial growth in stadium capacities through the early years of the 1920s, for many of the attractive dates each season the schools were still unable to satisfy the ever increasing demand for tickets. In 1923 an eastern sportswriter noted, "Despite the enlargement of many stadiums, desirable tickets for the big games are almost unattainable unless one happens to be an alumnus of one of the universities participating"—his comments coming in the aftermath of the announcement that there would be no public sale of tickets for the Army-Navy game. The noted sportswriter Allison Danzig of the *New York Times* observed that "for the general public there is no longer any chance for it to get into the amphitheater when ancient rivals meet . . . [S]ome of the colleges have raised the price [of tickets] in order to keep out the general public and make the games solely for the undergraduates and alumni."[42]

When the mammoth Yale Bowl had been built in 1914, with a capacity of 70,000, it was believed that sufficient space would be available for the most attractive of games in New Haven. Yet in 1923 it was reported that Yale ticket officials were swamped with several hundred thousand applications for seats for the Army game, whereas in 1924 approximately 165,000 applications for tickets were received in New Haven for that season's Yale-Princeton matchup. When Ohio State dedicated its new 63,000-seat stadium in 1922, more than 72,000 fans jammed into the arena, and many thousands were turned away. The overdemand for football tickets at many of the large Big Ten universities led to a situation where athletic officials were taking out paid newspaper advertisements to inform the public that seats were not available for approaching games. Danzig observed, "Each year finds the interest in football growing more widespread, and greater numbers being turned away from the classic games of the season. . . . As large as they build the stadiums, they are never large enough to meet the growing need." In the face of the overwhelming ticket demand for the most attractive games, it was no surprise that the scalping of tickets became a widespread and thriving business on college campuses.[43]

Ticket prices throughout the decade did relatively little to discourage the large-scale demand for seats at the games. In 1920 Ohio State was still using its old

Ohio Field, and the reserved seats were scaled from a top of $3 for the Michigan game to $2.50 for the Purdue and Wisconsin games and $2 for matchups against small college foes. When the new Ohio Stadium was opened in 1922, the same scale remained in effect for a time. Meanwhile, in 1922 Princeton was charging $3 for a ticket for its home game with Yale, and only $1 each for games against all its so-called minor foes. Harvard and the University of Chicago were each charging a top of $3 dollars when they hosted Princeton in 1922 games.[44]

By the middle of the 1920s ticket prices remained comparable for most grid-iron dates: Northwestern charged $2.50 and $2 each for reserved seats in 1925, with Penn pricing every seat in Franklin Field at $3 for its game with Chicago in 1926. A notable exception to reasonable pricing were the tariffs of $15 and $10 each for those precious few reserved seats available at Chicago's Soldier Field for the 1926 Army-Navy clash—when dinner at the beautiful Empire Room of the city's Palmer House Hotel ran just $2.50. By 1929 Princeton was charging a top of $4 dollars each for tickets to its games against Navy and Chicago, while Harvard priced tickets for its home game against Yale at $5 dollars each. That same season Yale priced reserved tickets for its home game against Princeton at $5, cutting back to $4 each for the Army and Dartmouth games at a time when single rooms with bath at New York's Hotel Governor Clinton or the Hotel Lincoln started at $3 nightly. And in 1930 Notre Dame opened its new stadium with reserved seats priced on a scale of $5 and $3 each.[45]

The increasing attendance and revenue figures being recorded every season quickly gave rise to extensive discussion over the growing commercialism of college football. Walter Camp, a defender of college football and a vigorous advocate of physical fitness, firmly believed that the increased revenues from football should be used to help fund improved athletic facilities and programs for the benefit of the entire student body and not just the gridiron heroes, contending that "wisely directed commercialism and exploitation can give sport in the next few years the greatest boom it has ever known." But by 1923 Camp saw university officials using the increased income from football to finance "elaborate and expensive coaching staffs," instead of funding the minor sports and intramural programs. Camp then wrote, "Commercialism will be an evil if the premium is all on development of a few stars and winners at any cost."[46]

On the other side of the debate, E. K. Hall, chairman of the Rules Committee, discounted the criticisms of college football's gigantic ticket revenues: "Let us . . . be proud of a game which is so wholesome and so rare a sport that the friends of the colleges and of the game are anxious to deposit at the gates . . . an amount of money which literally is supporting practically every other branch of athletic activity in the college." Danzig supported Hall's claims of football's financial be-nevolence, as he wrote in the *New York Times* that football "is the one college sport that pays, and pays well . . . [and it] usually foots the bill for everything." Meanwhile, Ohio State athletic director L. W. St. John described football as "the father of the University's complete recreation program," while Big Ten commissioner John Griffith declared that "in the conference colleges the Department of Intercollegiate Athletics is not only self-supporting but also to a large extent furnishes the money for carrying on the physical education work." Throughout the 1920s university athletic officials made certain that the newspapers received annual dispatches dealing with the extent of football's assistance to the rest of the programs. A typical example is Cornell University reporting that its 1928 football team had covered losses from the other varsity sports totaling $89,225 for the 1928–1929 school year and was still left with a surplus of $50,212.[47]

Athletic officials were also on relatively safe ground in pointing to the fact that football's large revenues were also making possible the expansion of on-campus facilities that were supposedly available to all students participating in physical education activities. By 1927 Fielding Yost, athletic director at Michigan, could state that profits from the university's football program since 1921 had made possible the addition of more than $2 million worth of physical facilities that included such things as more than thirty acres of land, separate field houses for men and women athletics, an intramural sports building, a skating rink, and tennis courts. Yost wrote, "What has been done at Michigan has been accomplished at virtually all the other schools," and he added that his university was "providing opportunity for recreation for all members of the student body. If this is commercialism in sport . . . I am glad to be numbered among those who have some part in its development." By 1928 Ohio State was able to announce that over a period of seven years the university's football profits had paid off a debt of $1.75 million on the new stadium and that athletic officials were looking ahead to raising a comparable amount over the next ten years to pay for the expense of five new athletic-related buildings on campus. Various levels of building programs such as these examples were being realized as a by-product of football revenues at campuses across the country by the late 1920s, and sportswriter Francis Wallace pointed out that "the money is used for worthy purposes which outweigh any wounds which amateur ideals may experience; and as the culmination of such worthy purposes does not damage prestige, the business goes on."[48]

Not everyone, though, subscribed to the contention that sufficient profits from the college football programs were being used to provide athletic and physical education opportunities for the entire student body—intramural sports specifically. In a 1924 report to the National Collegiate Athletic Association (NCAA), Professor Thomas E. French, athletic board chairman at Ohio State, stated that his school was spending only $13,000 that year in support of intramural sports, or 4.7 percent of the football receipts. A year earlier, in his comments on the state of athletics at Ohio State, St. John had provided a breakdown of the number of participants competing in each of seven intramural sports at his school, ranging from 347 in swimming to 2,089 for indoor track, with a total of 7,395 participants. Allowing for the fact that there certainly were some students playing more than one sport and that intramurals are generally an inexpensive activity, St. John's figures indicating that at least 60 percent to 70 percent of the university enrollment was participating would seem to demonstrate that Ohio State was generally failing to adequately fund its intramural programs.[49]

Professor French's report went on to itemize similar relatively small contributions that were being made by other schools around the conference—citing Minnesota with $14,000 and Michigan at $10,000, while others were providing as little as $7,500–$8,000 per year. That same year, from its football receipts of $194,000, Stanford spent just $7,500 on intramural programs. The well-known sportswriter John Tunis noted that these examples were typical of the support provided by major schools across the country and that when considering the magnitude of the funding going to varsity programs, "it might appear that intramural athletics would be likely to receive less than their share." Tunis contended that football was in reality doing less to promote widespread athletic participation among the general student population than it was publicly taking credit for.[50]

As college football moved into the second half of the 1920s, record attendance figures continued to pile up at schools around the country. For the 1926 season the estimated total national attendance figure for college football was reported to be 15 million, up 25 percent from 1925, with receipts of approximately $30 million. The Associated Press described college football's burgeoning attendance marks as being part of the decade's "unprecedented development of public interest in all major branches of sport."[51]

Intersectional games had established a firm foothold within the college gridiron world by 1926 and were contributing greatly to the record box-office figures being realized, yet university officials were growing increasingly concerned over the flagrant commercialism attendant to so many of the major games. And the "professional" atmosphere surrounding games played at big-city stadia was far from keeping with the campus-oriented traditions of college football. San Francisco sportswriter Curley Grieve covered a college game at New York's Polo Grounds and then observed: "There's an utter lack of color and atmosphere at the football encounters. It's almost a professional background, with rooting sections obscured behind the goal posts; the cheer leaders like so many wooden soldiers. . . . College football is handicapped under these conditions."[52]

The substantial attendance figures had also generated such problems for university officials as widespread gambling, drinking, and the scalping of tickets at games among the fans. These issues had become increasingly significant problems at college games around the country and were definitely not a situation unique to off-campus games either. In 1922 Big Ten athletic directors had reported on the "alarming" amount of betting that had been taking place for years at conference stadia, yet efforts to curtail the practice produced no improvements in the situation. Then in 1926 the conference athletic directors announced a crackdown on the drinking in Big Ten stadia—describing the current state of affairs at conference arenas as a "mass violation of the prohibition law."[53]

HEADING FOR THE FALL

Even with all the pieces in place to support college football's continued gathering of riches, no one was prepared for the tremendous surge in attendance figures during the 1927 and 1928 seasons. College football officials estimated the total national attendance for *each* of those two seasons to be somewhere between 25 and 30 million—far exceeding any previous seasonal figures. Conservative estimates placed the gate receipts at approximately $50 million for the 1927 season. One sportswriter took note of the millions of additional fans who followed the big games by radio and described the total college football audience as of "unprecedented proportions in any season for any sport."[54]

The Big Ten Conference realized an increase of more than $500,000 in total football receipts in 1927 in comparison to the previous season, and this record figure of approximately $2.7 million would continue in each of the following seasons of 1928 and 1929. A university such as Yale, which had the advantage of a large-capacity football stadium, obliterated all its previous football receipt records in 1927, as it took in just over $1 million that season, and then followed it up with another $1 million season in 1928. A popular independent team such as Notre Dame, even with a poor season on the field by its standards, still attracted a new school attendance record of 419,705 in 1928, helped greatly by an estimated audience of 120,000 for the Navy game at Soldier Field in Chicago. An editorial in the *New York World* commented that "football . . . can now dictate to the American university about a great many things . . . and our university officials had better do some hard thinking as to whether they want this state of affairs to continue."[55]

The craze for college football that was being convincingly demonstrated at the box office continued right through the 1929 season, with hardly a noticeable ripple from the major stock market crash in October of the year. But college football's box-office boom days were about to abate as a by-product of the Depression, and the prominent sportswriter Stanley Woodward would later note that "with the collapse of business, the Golden Era of football . . . was definitely over. The sag had commenced, though the big teams continued to draw full houses."[56]

Attendance figures for college football in 1930 reflected the country's economic woes, as gate receipts began to tumble everywhere. In a later study of college football attendance trends conducted by the University of Chicago, it was estimated that total attendance for the 1930 football season was approximately 10.3 million, with receipts of $21.5 million—both figures representing substantial declines from previous seasons. Noting that the survey had included a large number of the most prominent football-playing universities, the report closed with the rather obvious conclusion that the available evidence indicated that there was "good reason to assume that hard times rather than declining interest is responsible" for the substantially lower attendance figures.[57]

The impact on university athletic programs was swift and severe, as by the close of the 1930 gridiron season announcements were already being issued about the forced need to economize in the various minor sports that football gate receipts had previously subsidized. Purdue was typical of the schools in an economic crunch, as after the 1930 season its football program came up approximately $97,000 short of estimated gate receipts. Faced with a $40,000 athletic department deficit for the fiscal year, Purdue officials responded with tentative plans to eliminate as many as ten varsity sports. The Carnegie Foundation, in its *Report Number 26* which was issued in 1931, contended that "four out of five institutions" had been forced to make adjustments to their minor sports programs. Of even more serious consequence in the minds of many university officials was the financial crisis being created while attempting to repay the major debts schools had incurred in the building of their new football stadia.[58]

The financial struggles of the athletic departments helped to renew the forces opposed to the large-scale commercialized sport college football had become. The *Yale News* again raised the issue of reducing the number of games played each season, whereas other foes believed that the abolishment of football gate receipts would move the sport a long way back toward its ancient origins of real amateur sport. John Kieran of the *New York Times* contended that the universities could satisfactorily fund their athletic programs through the collection of a modest annual fee from all the students—$100 was the figure suggested—along with an athletic association dues fee from the alumni in exchange for free game tickets, and the games would be played strictly for the university communities. Another writer, George Trevor, added, "After all . . . colleges are not in the business of purveying public entertainment."[59]

In fact, by 1930 college football had moved well beyond the point of being able to seriously consider such notions. Rather than downgrading the efforts to financially capitalize on college football's great popularity, many athletic officials believed that the universities needed to take the opposite approach—which is what Knute Rockne meant at a late 1930 banquet when he said that college football was "not commercialized enough." An article by Douglas Haikell of the *New Republic* made the case that "should the undergraduates . . . by some miracle demand that college football be made a game for its own sake . . . presidents and trustees could not, for financial reasons, turn it over to them. . . . The real force of this money lies in the fact that large groups within the institution have come to depend on it."[60]

Intercollegiate football was solidly entrenched in the American sporting psyche by the close of the 1920s, or as one columnist wrote: "Football has come to be a fashion and a passion."[61] The decade had generated an economic transformation of the college football landscape that left the sport undeniably linked with the forces of commercialism—and there was the very root of the opposition to intercollegiate athletics. Although the onset of the Depression brought immediate and significant financial difficulties that would continue through much of the 1930s, most athletic officials realized that college football was unquestionably a reliable source of major revenues, one that would eventually return to heights that exceeded even the giddy days of the late 1920s.

No matter whether they wished to publicly say as much, university administrations recognized that the full benefits of maintaining a major football program transcended the immediate gate receipts, providing what sportswriter Francis Wallace described as "prestige, which attracts students, bolsters morale and keeps wealthy alumni close to the old school." Only with the sacrificing of considerable alumni loyalties, physical facilities, and the other athletic programs that provided physical training to the general student populace could a return of college football to the days of old-school amateurism be realized. The transformation of college football into the world of big business was irreversible and would remain as one of the most significant legacies of the golden era of the 1920s.[62]

4

OPPOSING ORGANIZED
PRO FOOTBALL

One of the enduring themes in the world of college football throughout the 1920s was the intense opposition to all forms of organized professional football—generally represented by the fledgling National Football League (NFL), or the American Professional Football Association, as it was first called—by virtually everyone associated with the campus brand of the sport. The 1920s was a time when most college football coaches and officials were, incredibly, still publicly advocating the Victorian Age principles of gentlemanly amateur sport, where playing the game was reward enough in itself. It was widely held that a "college man" would never besmirch himself by association with pro football, and so the university world regarded the struggling professional gridiron sport as a major adversary.

For a time after World War I there was a widely held belief that the college teams played a better brand of football, but the animosity toward organized professional football was really fueled by the elitist class prejudices of the academic and athletic leaderships of the universities. With most of pro football's origins tracing back to the independent teams of the industrialized or smaller blue-collar towns, collegiate officials considered the play-for-pay game to be a haven for gamblers and the rank dishonesty of local "get rich quick" promoters.

Within a few years after World War I it was already clear that college football was in the midst of substantial transformations that were bringing new shape to the sport. Many universities were building large new football stadia or had plans to do so, big-time intersectional games and the use of large metropolitan stadia were on the rise, head football coaches at many universities were often achieving celebrity status as their salaries increased, and on the field of play college football was moving toward national competitive parity—all forces that were reshaping the sport into a big-business, moneymaking venture for the universities. Yet despite all these factors being obvious to everyone, much of college football's leadership appeared to see no contradictions between the changing world of their sport and their attitudes toward the organized professional game.

Professionalism was a term that had been around college football for many years by the 1920s, and it was almost always used in a context that referred to such things as the illegal recruiting of players, bestowing of monetary or other benefits upon the athletes, or an overemphasis on football beyond its perceived place in the academic community. These issues would continue to resonate within college football throughout the decade, but the campaign of words and actions against organized pro football that we will discuss involved none of these issues. Rather, it was an attack on those individuals who sought to use their athletic skills for financial gain after college or to earn a living playing a version of the game where football itself and who won or lost were all that really mattered. It was an attempt to continue guiding the lives of the athletes even beyond their days of eligibility.

University officials believed that they were preparing their upper- and upper-middle-class students for their rightful places as the nation's industrial, political, and military leaders of the future. Organized professional football was considered a moral threat to the collegiate athlete—a distracting force in the training of the country's elite youth. Major John Griffith, the Big Ten commissioner, wrote of professional football's potential corrupting influence on college men: "Is it not a very questionable benefit to a young college man to make it possible for him to receive large fees and salaries for short terms and comparatively easy work?" Some called pro football a "parasitical growth" on the intercollegiate game, one that sought to profit from the popularity of the collegiate sport and its star players.[1]

Most of all, professional football was considered a threat to the finest elements of intercollegiate football—a force that would very likely fuel the problems of "professionalism" within the college game, a force that posed a very real danger to the spirit of university traditions and the so-called code of amateur athleticism. It was against this backdrop of emotions that the collegiate forces waged a campaign of both words and actions against organized professional football throughout the 1920s. Yet the sporting public, growing numbers of the players, and even some of the coaches would eventually come to recognize the inconsistencies between the realities of big-time college football and the attacks on the organized professional game, and so the outcome of this struggle would prove to be another of the more significant transformations within the intercollegiate sport during the 1920s.

Origins of Conflict

Professional football can trace its roots back to the early 1890s, originating in the game as played by athletic-club and town teams. This brand of football was played by adults outside the realm of the organized college game, and it provided an opportunity for the expression of physical prowess and the excitement of serious athletic competition. Pro football is generally believed to have started with a reported five hundred dollars that was paid to Yale's legendary William "Pudge" Heffelfinger in 1892 by the Allegheny Athletic Association of Pittsburgh, one of many so-called independent teams. Town teams played a game of football that became a form of serious entertainment for the local populace, with the games generally being played on Sundays in deference to the primarily industrial locales where the sport fans were required to work the other six days of the week. These town football teams became extremely popular and helped to publicize their locale's growing industrialization and civility as the twentieth century dawned.[2]

The intercollegiate community had not widely opposed the evolution of professional football in its early years, despite the widespread signing of former college stars. The issue of "professionalism" within intercollegiate sport had been receiving plenty of attention all along in the media of the day from the two leading voices, Walter Camp and Casper Whitney. But, as mentioned earlier, with the term *professionalism* the two writers really were addressing the many abuses plaguing the college sport, such as the recruiting of athletes, illegal scholarships, excessive involvement of alumni, and the tramp athlete—all themes that would predominate throughout the 1920s.

Yet by 1916 the leaders of intercollegiate football, concerned over the growing atmosphere of gambling and the increasing salaries that were luring ever greater numbers of college men to professional football, decided it was time to begin dissociating the college version of the sport from the play-for-pay game. In June 1916, the presidents of the Big Three schools of the East—Harvard, Princeton, and Yale—adopted the first version of their Triple Agreement. One of the key planks of the agreement outlawed participation in professional sports, stating, "With a view to keeping the spirit and the associations of professionalism out of college sports . . . no man who has ever received any pecuniary reward or its equivalent by reason of his connection with athletics—whether for playing, coaching, or acting as teacher in any branch of sport—shall represent his university in any athletic team."[3]

The attacks against organized professional sport began to escalate from the 1916 issuance of the Triple Agreement, but there was evidence that not all collegiate and amateur athletic officials were in agreement on the issue. At the annual meeting of the Amateur Athletic Union (AAU) in November 1916, an attempt was made to revise the union constitution and by-laws so as to bar any individual previously associated with professional sport from serving as an AAU official. Surprisingly, one of the opponents of the new by-law was Gustavus T. Kirby of the Intercollegiate Association of Amateur Athletes of America, who stated: "I believe the time is here when we should recognize the honesty, integrity and bigness of the men who are professionals." The delegates finally defeated the proposed new rule after considerable debate, but the lines of battle had been drawn.[4]

Into the Fray

In 1919 professional football succeeded in organizing a formal league of teams—the American Professional Football Association (APFA)—with the intent of introducing regular schedules and, most significantly, to regain control of the escalating player salaries being paid to former collegians. Yet by this time the play-for-pay game was under attack from an expanding universe of opponents.

After the Big Three agreement of 1916, the Big Ten Conference stepped in when its faculty representatives met in December 1916. Driven by the relentless opposition to professional sport by the University of Chicago's Amos Alonzo Stagg, the professors ultimately adopted a three-part program clearly aimed at cutting off the flow of college athletes into professional football: "That participation as players or officials in a professional football game shall disqualify [them] for all employment in connection with conference athletics. . . . That all employees of athletic departments who take part in professional football games, shall be thereby suspended from their employment. . . . That letters of men won in college be revoked if they play professional football after their collegiate careers have ended." Professional football's chances at promoting its game in big-city venues also received a blow in October 1919, when New York's corporate counsel, William Burr, ruled that playing football on Sundays within the city would be illegal. This pronouncement caused the immediate cancellation of a series of games that had been planned for the Polo Grounds, featuring former Harvard All-America Charlie Brickley and his Giants team.[5]

By 1920, Stagg had clearly moved to the forefront in college football's opposition to professional football. In an exchange of letters with the Rules Committee chairman, E. K. Hall, Stagg advocated that the committee take a strong stand against professional football. Then in December 1920, at the Big Ten Conference meeting, the faculty representatives adopted a rule barring pro football game officials from working in Big Ten contests. Meanwhile, the ranks of college coaches opposed to professional football were also expanding. In December 1921, when the American Football Coaches Association (AFCA) was organized in New York, one of the first orders of business was taking a stand against the professionals. The meeting, attended by about one hundred coaches, adopted a resolution stating that professional football was "detrimental" to the best interests of American football "and that the football coaches lend their influence to discourage the professional game." The new AFCA also decided to admit only college coaches to its membership.[6]

By the early 1920s professional football did manage to achieve some support from men with influential college backgrounds. In late 1920, Walter Camp came out in favor of professional football, stating, "I am practically satisfied that professional

5. Coach Amos Alonzo Stagg of Chicago. Already known as the "Old Man" by the 1920s, he was a major advocate of amateurism and strongly opposed professional football. Courtesy of the Chicago Historical Society [SDN-062948].

football will be a success. . . . We must define its position and place in the athletic curriculum of the nation. . . . I have studied the professional football situation and am convinced it is with us to stay." In this same article Camp also described the intention of revoking athletes' letters after college as "silly." Former collegiate star lineman and referee Bob Maxwell, still referring to professional football as "independent football," wrote a November 1921 newspaper article that received wide national syndication after he defended the play-for-pay game and said that it was "flourishing." After paying homage to the collegiate game, Maxwell wrote, "There is no reason why a college athlete, after receiving his degree, should not continue to play football if he wants to. . . . They are too young to retire from active sport." After putting in a plug for the high quality of play by the professionals, Maxwell made a statement that, although referring to the organized APFA league, would soon backfire: "One of the reasons for the success of the independent game is that no effort is being made to lure college players away from their teams. In fact the college athletes are being discouraged every time they apply for a job."[7]

By January 1922, both professional and independent football—anything that was not college football—were under severe scrutiny for the very thing Maxwell had said was no longer happening: the use of current college players under assumed names before their graduation. The first case involved the organized APFA professional league, yet the potential scandal was handled with great dispatch, which helped to contain any large-scale outcry against the league. The *Chicago Tribune* had written an article on the affairs of the Green Bay Packers team, in the process of which it had been revealed that the professional team used three Notre Dame players in its final game of the 1921 season in Milwaukee. The three players—Hunk Anderson, Ojay Larson, and Hec Garvey—were all declared ineligible for further athletic competition at Notre Dame, and their letters were taken back. At a special meeting, the APFA quickly revoked Green Bay's franchise within the league and also adopted a rule that required a one thousand–dollar bond from each member team as a guarantee for adhering to the rule against using college players. Several days later it was also disclosed that star halfback Johnny Mohardt of Notre Dame had played for the Racine American Legion team against the Packers in the December 1921 game at Milwaukee, but he had since left school after completing his studies, and so no action was taken.[8]

The scandal that came to light at about the same time in January 1922 involved independent town football teams, but predictably college football authorities took it as another indictment of professional football and its encroachments into the arena of amateurism. In January 1922, the Associated Press broke a story detailing a semiprofessional football game that had been played on November 27, 1921, in Illinois between the teams representing the towns of Taylorville and Carlinville. The initial stories claimed that approximately thirty thousand dollars had been bet on the game, the figure eventually growing to one hundred thousand dollars, but that was not what was causing all the commotion. Evidence had also been brought out disclosing that nine players from the University of Illinois had played for Taylorville, while eight players from Notre Dame had filled the lineup for the Carlinville team.

Illinois acted quickly and ruled all nine men ineligible to participate in future Illini athletics, while Notre Dame took an additional five days before announcing that all eight of their athletes had been formally disqualified. The damage control began almost immediately, as the Illinois athletes maintained that they had received no money for their services. It was alleged that the Illini players, when approached by Taylorville people, had been told that the game was an American Legion benefit, and so they had agreed to appear—apparently forgetting for the moment that their playing would still be in violation of university rules. The investigation by the Notre Dame faculty board had corroborated their players' claim to having received no money, other than travel expenses.

The recruitment of star college players to appear in semiprofessional or professional games under assumed names was a problem that intercollegiate football had been contending with since the 1890s. The play-for-pay team officials were often brazen in their approaches to the college players. In December 1916, the president of the Fort Wayne Friars club wrote to the captain of the Rose Poly Institute football team about recruiting players for the following season. In the letter it was stated that the Friars team had featured a number of "big stars who played under fictitious names" during the 1916 season. In a February 1921 letter to a University of Chicago player, one professional manager claimed to already have signed contracts with some of the best college players in the country, and included the question: "Do you realize the amount of money you can earn playing football Sunday afternoons in the professional game?"[9]

Word of the Taylorville-Carlinville affair had become common knowledge in sporting circles within days of the game, raising the question as to exactly when the head football coaches of the two schools had first heard talk of it. Many were prepared to believe that Coach Bob Zuppke of Illinois probably had not learned of the affair until late January, although he had irritated Big Ten athletic officials by stating that he was not sure if the players were actually ineligible to continue participating in collegiate sports since this had been a postseason game.

Knute Rockne of Notre Dame was another story, given his close association with the players and his active presence on the university campus, along with his own personal record of playing for various professional football teams after his graduation. Grover Hoover, manager of the Taylorville team, was reported to have stated that Rockne knew about his players' participation within a few days of the game. The Notre Dame coach immediately responded by announcing that he was filing a libel suit against Hoover, and called the Taylorville team official "a liar." Within a day, though, Rockne dropped his threatened suit when the semipro official placed a telephone call to the college coach and said that he had made no such statement. Hoover's denial was just one of the many that were issued by various officials associated with the semipro game, and taken in total the denied statements account for a substantial portion of the alleged facts that were presented in the first couple days of the scandal. Yet historian Murray Sperber has written that "Rockne's claims of ignorance and innocence strain credibility," whereas writer Michael Steele has stated that Rockne knew nothing of the semipro game "until it was too late." Both writers have contended that Rockne's team was dropped from consideration for the January 1922 Rose Bowl game because of the specter of professionalism surrounding Notre Dame, which could have happened only if knowledge of the semipro game was widely spread through the intercollegiate community by December 1921.[10]

One of the enduring controversies of the Taylorville-Carlinville scandal concerns whether any money was paid to the players, despite their denials to the contrary. An Associated Press story in the *New York Times* stated that according to backers of the Carlinville team, the Notre Dame players were initially offered two hundred dollars each plus expenses, the total coming to twenty-seven hundred dollars. Rivers Anderson, business manager of the Carlinville team, was quoted as saying that he had "hired and paid Notre Dame university men to play for Carlinville," although he declined to state how much money had been involved. The following day Hunk Anderson issued a denial of that statement, saying that the Notre Dame players had not even gone to the game and that he did not know who the players appearing for Carlinville that day were. Hoover of the Taylorville team was said to have told the game umpires that it had cost less than five hundred dollars to get the Illinois players, whereas a local area newspaper story years later stated that no more than thirteen hundred dollars had been spent getting the Notre Dame players and that Taylorville had paid the Illinois players only forty-five dollars each. Such examples of claims and denials were common through the scandal and make it difficult to construct the true story, while also casting an unfavorable light on the integrity of all the participants.[11]

Although organized professional football had not been involved, the Taylorville-Carlinville scandal had cast a long shadow over anyone associated with the play-for-pay version of the sport. It was clear that opposition to professional football was only going to increase, after Stagg announced that as president of the Big Ten Athletic Directors Association he intended to "forcibly bring the menace of the professional game before them." Even as the two universities involved were trying to sort out the truth in the Taylorville-Carlinville affair, quickly widening accusations and rumors of athletic wrongdoings continued to circulate about many of the conference schools in what the newspapers referred to as "the Big Ten Scandal." No one disagreed when Stagg added, "The time for common action is at hand."[12]

The Battle Is Joined

The Big Ten Conference did indeed believe the time was at hand for more vigorous action in defense of intercollegiate football and the spirit of amateurism. With Stagg, Fielding Yost of Michigan, and L. W. St. John of Ohio State leading the way, in the spring of 1922 the conference embarked upon a search for its first athletic commissioner. The man they ultimately hired that July was Major John Griffith, a widely experienced athletic administrator who had most recently been working on George Huff's staff at Illinois while also teaching physical education courses. In the press release announcing Griffith's appointment, T. E. Jones, Wisconsin's athletic director, noted that "professional promoters have been permitted free reign with little opposition" and that it had been made clear to Griffith that he would "devote the greater part of his time to an educational campaign for amateur athletics."[13]

Griffith would prove to be a prodigious generator of correspondence, and the new commissioner got off to a quick start with a lengthy paper titled "Professionalism in Collegiate Athletics." In this essay Griffith endorsed the Victorian beliefs and ideals of the universities for intercollegiate or amateur sport, stating that "the influence of athletic professionalism is detrimental to a college man. It tends to make him dissatisfied to play the game for its own sake and makes of his athletic powers a marketable commodity. . . . The game is robbed of the exhilarating in-spiration of achievement merely for achievement's sake, and many of the very important character building qualities which form a part of collegiate athletics are lost the moment the incentive of personal gain is introduced."[14]

Even with a conference commissioner, Stagg continued his aggressive public stands against professional football. In late 1923, the Chicago coach publicly re-leased a letter titled "To All Friends of College Football" in which he wrote that professional football, "under the guise of fair play but contenancing [sic] rank dishonesty in playing men under assumed names . . . was another serious men-ace possibly greater than all others. . . . To patronize Sunday professional football games is to cooperate with forces which are destructive of the finest elements of interscholastic and intercollegiate football." Stagg's letter appeared in newspapers nationally, while also being quoted extensively in college newspaper editorials, and it soon served as the drumbeat of intercollegiate opposition to professional football. At this same time the Big Ten athletic directors sent a press release to their respective student newspapers in which they declared: "It is not desirable that their men shall engage in professional football either before or after graduation" and that "the boy who now plays on a professional football team . . . sells not only his ability but also the name of the college he formally represented."[15]

Many newspaper and magazine writers also targeted pro football throughout much of the 1920s as part of the widespread media bias in favor of the intercol-legiate game. For example, Herbert Reed of *Outlook* wrote, "Professional football will never do as a substitute for real lovers of the game, even those who are sup-posed to be unable to get tickets to the big college games. . . . I have talked with hundreds of employers who look to the colleges to recruit their business forces. The answer is unanimous. 'I want no professional football player in my employ.' Professional football cannot survive."[16]

Stagg was not satisfied with the increasing public attacks against professional football—he also placed himself in the position of moral conscience for Univer-sity of Chicago athletes, either past or present. In November 1923, Stagg called three former Chicago gridmen in to see him individually concerning their current involvement with professional football, and the coach attempted to intimidate each of them out of their associations with professional sport. Each of the three had finished college; two of the them were playing professionally to make finan-cial ends meet. The third, R. T. Halladay, said that he was playing in order to save money to buy a home for himself and his wife, although Stagg's notes make it clear that he believed Halladay "could get along nicely on his income without playing professionally." Stagg's attitude and comments in all three of the visits are typical of a condescending inquisitor who is hearing the confessions of the athletes. With all three men Stagg attempted to leave them with a sense of guilt over their involvement with professional football, and when one of his former players exhibited no remorse and indicated he had no intention of dropping out of professional football and basketball, the coach made clear his total lack of respect for the athlete. So far the battle over professional football had been a completely one-sided affair.[17]

Football for the Masses

With Stagg temporarily distracted while Chicago was winning its last Big Ten football championship in 1924—and with the collegiate brand of the game reaching new heights in popularity with gridiron stars such as Red Grange, the Four Horsemen of Notre Dame, and Ernie Nevers of Stanford—the attacks on professional football eased off a little. Yet the popularity of the play-for-pay game had not grown to any extent, given the relative lack of attention from the newspapers and the chaotic scheduling that still characterized the pro game. Michael Oriard has written that in 1925, "professional football was less than important in the United States; it was felt by the majority of fans to corrupt the sport's essential spirit. . . . [P]rofessional football continued to be perceived as the dark underside of the college game."[18]

There were signs that professional football, wishing only for a peaceful coexistence with the collegiate game, was beginning to gain some supporters among the popular magazine writers of the time. The theme that would become the battle cry for the Sunday game was that professional football was a sport for the masses—not one that was staged for the educated elite of the country. Writing of the controversy over Red Grange's entry into professional football in the mid-1920s, biographer John Carroll asserted that Grange was "the victim of a class bias against pro football shared by many associated with the collegiate game." Pro football historian Keith McClellan has also taken note of the class polarization of the play-for-pay game's audience, commenting that "workers could relate better to professional players than to many of the upper-middle class and well-to-do college players." A *Chicago Tribune* editorial in 1925 said, "The men who oppose professional football are among the elect who can see the [college] games, and they don't care whether any one else gets the same fun."[19]

Professional and semiprofessional football had become popular wherever there were few football-playing colleges nearby or the colleges in the area played the gridiron game on a big-time basis with few tickets available to the general public for the most popular and important games. Universities such as Fordham, Georgetown, New York University, and Boston College, which were located in big metropolitan areas, generally played their games at major league baseball stadia, and because they were representing universities smaller than the state universities, they were able to satisfy most of the ticket demands from the general public. Even with the great improvements in the country's highway and transportation systems that made previously isolated universities easily accessible, and with the large new stadia that were springing up everywhere, the football teams of the elite universities were still playing before audiences that substantially consisted of alumni and students. Grantland Rice took note of the ticket-buying issue and the pro game's belief: "There is now a widespread public interest which can't be properly fed because at the important games only the alumni and their friends have any chance for a seat."[20]

The growing national popularity of football among the ticket-buying sporting public was being fueled by the college game and the sensational publicity it was usually given in the newspapers. Yet unable to obtain tickets for the prestigious college games that were played on Saturdays, and with much of the workforce still locked into the six-day workweek, the football fans among the unwashed masses were increasingly turning to professional football on Sundays for an outlet from the daily pressures that plagued the middle- and lower-class workers. An indication that pro football owners recognized this situation is seen in a 1925 newspaper article, when Chris O'Brien of the Chicago Cardinals commented that "college football never need fear any inroads from professional sport. . . . The professional game belongs in another field in the commercial world, where the workers want to get away from their daily grind." A *New York World* article of the time declared, "Today in the hinterlands 'goose-grease' kings and 'ladle' princes fit out and finance professional football teams. . . . Professional football is a natural result of an exuberant democracy."[21] Professional football was increasingly coming to represent an autumn rallying point for the common man within the American sporting hierarchy.

RED GRANGE AND THE END OF MYTHOLOGY

No individual player represents the image of college football more vividly that Harold "Red" Grange of the University of Illinois. Today, more than eighty years after his career ended, the "Galloping Ghost" is still revered as an icon of college football history, a symbol of the spirit of 1920s intercollegiate sport. But that spirit turned out not to be the stately, traditional, academic view of amateur sport, where competition and love of school were ends in themselves.

Grange's football career was the event that sounded the beginning of the end for the old-school beliefs, including the idea that the universities were entitled to continue influencing the athletes' lives even after their student days. The Illinois star also gave initial shape to the concept of professional football as a large scale moneymaking venture, while also foretelling the future attitudes of the superstar intercollegiate athletes toward their college days, a future that would eventually see the universities converted to mere way stations on the path to careers in professional sport. Although Grange's college and early professional football days have been chronicled to exhaustion, a look at some of the events will help to see the launching of those transformations.

Grange had been a sensational high school athlete in Wheaton, Illinois, before moving on to the University of Illinois. There he made an immediate impact in the 1923 football season, his sophomore year, being named an All-America after leading the Illini to an 8-0-0 record. The 1924 game against Michigan, in which he scored on four sensational touchdown runs in the first quarter alone, is the event that catapulted Grange into the pantheon of 1920s sporting heroes. Any doubts the eastern media might have had about Grange's abilities were laid to rest on October 31, 1925, in the mud and rain in Philadelphia, as the Galloping Ghost—a nickname given him by Warren Brown of the *Chicago Herald and Examiner*—romped up and down the treacherous field for three dazzling touchdowns, as Illinois hammered a good Penn team, 24-2.

With the end of Grange's college football career just weeks away in 1925, rumors began to circulate that the star running back was being approached with offers to play professional football. Certainly, it was already common knowledge that Grange had been offered contracts to appear in motion pictures and to write for a newspaper syndicate, but for the player who now symbolized college football to play professionally was unthinkable to athletic authorities. Major Griffith, the Big Ten commissioner, was quoted as saying that he hoped Grange would refuse to play professionally, "no matter what he was offered." Considering the relatively modest economic background of Grange's upbringing, and the considerable amounts of money that were being mentioned for playing professionally, a comment such as Griffith's clearly demonstrated the naive and unrealistic attitudes that still pervaded the intercollegiate sport of the 1920s. The rumors became so widespread in the week before Grange's final college game that University of Illinois athletic officials began investigating claims that the gridiron star had been negotiating with a local Champaign, Illinois, promoter named C. C. Pyle. Grange was called in by Coach Bob Zuppke and quizzed on the stories, but the player denied he had done anything to jeopardize his amateur standing.[22]

Stories claiming that Grange's turning professional was already settled continued circulating among Big Ten football writers, and it was said that the University of Illinois was desperately attempting to convince college football's most publicized player of all time to remain in school. In a memorandum to his father, Amos Alonzo Stagg, Amos Jr. provided details he had learned from Joe Foley, the sports editor of the *Chicago Evening-Journal* newspaper, about Grange's agreement to play for the Chicago Bears on the Thursday after the season finale for Illinois on November 21—including a description of some of the financial arrangements for the first three games of the Bears' tour that would follow.

Stagg Jr. described discussions with other Chicago newspaper writers, including Warren Brown of the *Herald and Examiner,* who confirmed that Grange intended to immediately turn professional and that Brown had offered the player a position as a sportswriter for his paper "when he finished college." Stagg Jr. also wrote of having dinner on November 18 with Bill Morganstern, a sportswriter for the *Herald and Examiner,* who elaborated on the efforts to hire Grange as a newspaperman.

Morganstern said that in October, when Grange's plans to turn pro and leave school had been learned, President David Kinley of the University of Illinois and the school's athletic director, George Huff, had approached Brown about helping to get the athlete to sever his connections with Pyle. Brown and Morganstern had driven out to the Grange family home in Wheaton on the afternoon of November 18, with Brown carrying a check for five thousand dollars and a contract offering the player a job with the *Herald and Examiner,* "with the understanding that he was to continue his college work." Grange was to be paid his full salary from November 1925 onward "but would not have to really start work until next September." The sportswriter said that his paper was also prepared to get Grange's father a political job and would give the player's brother, Garland, a job at seventy-five dollars a week. Morganstern also said that once Grange was a sportswriter, the *Herald and Examiner* would not restrict him from playing professional football—making it clear that all that was really important was not having a star college athlete quit school as soon as his eligibility was used up. But the newspapermen had been unable to meet with Grange that afternoon to make the offers, as the athlete had hastily gone out the back door after their arrival and had never returned.[23]

All this maneuvering became academic after the game against Ohio State on the afternoon of November 21, 1925. Within five minutes of the game's ending, Grange made the announcement that he was immediately turning professional and would make his first appearance with the Chicago Bears on Thanksgiving Day in Chicago. Although specific contract details were not announced, the story given out was that Grange had decided to play professional football in order to repay his father and to also help provide for his brother's education. In his statement the star running back said, "I believe the public will be better satisfied with my honesty and good motives if I turn my efforts to that field in which I have been most useful." Grange added that he might return to school in the second semester, to which Bob Zuppke replied that his former running back "will no more graduate from Illinois than will the Kaiser return to power in Germany."[24]

6. Harold "Red" Grange of Illinois. A three-time consensus First Team All-America running back, his signing of a professional football contract immediately after his last college game stirred a national controversy. Courtesy of the Chicago Historical Society [SDN-065675].

Grange's immediate turning away from school for the big money and the commercialized world of professional sport represented a tremendous blow to the Victorian principles of the American universities, which regarded higher education, along with hard work, discipline, and patience, as the only sure and traditional path to success in life. Historian Michael Parrish has written that, "as Grange's career illustrated only too well, colleges and universities risked becoming mere sub-assembly plants for the larger professional football factories."[25] The outcry, both in support and in opposition, over Grange's decision was immediate, emotional, and widespread.

Many alleged that Grange's sole purpose for attending college had been to play football and that he had exploited both the sport and the University of Illinois. Writers across the land charged that professional football had now broken down the honor of the college player, while J. D. McKee of the *Cleveland Plain Dealer* noted that in quitting school Grange had "undoubtedly harmed college football and done a disservice to the institution which he has represented on the athletic field." An editorial in the Boston College student newspaper was one of many making the charge that Grange attended college only to play football, adding that all the publicity and overemphasis placed on the Illinois star had given him "a false set of values." Grange and the Illini coach, Bob Zuppke, remained friends for life, and although he acknowledged Grange's right to play professional football, Zuppke continued to disapprove of collegiate players moving into the play-for-pay game. Zuppke, who typified the attitudes of college coaches who adhered to the old university ideals of sport and true amateurism, in spite of the forces that had already transformed major college football into a big business, believed, "We must have an amateur ideal. If a man plays for himself alone he can't be happy. If he plays for the spirit of the school in a true sense, nothing can make him more truly a man."[26]

There was also considerable commentary from writers who believed that Grange had been perfectly justified in leaving school after the collegiate season. An unsigned article in *Outlook* noted, "It is no more disgraceful for an athlete to be a professional than for an athlete to be an amateur. Whatever disgrace or credit there may be depends solely upon the way in which the athlete . . . conducts his business or his sport." The writer even suggested that the Grange case could be a positive event for intercollegiate football, believing that a rise in the national popularity of pro football might eventually lead to the college game losing much of its overemphasis and thus returning to its on-campus origins—"quite as thrilling as ever to undergraduates and graduates, but less and less a matter of national concern." The idea of professional football's potential growth in popularity being a vehicle for returning college football back to a "strictly sport basis" was also advanced about the same time by the *Harvard Crimson* newspaper, while a column in the *New York Herald Tribune* said the colleges might regain "a sense of proportion as to the value of athletic prestige."[27]

It was Grange personally who produced some of the sharpest attacks on the universities' traditionalist beliefs. The former Illini star said that he had "early found out after entering college that an arts degree isn't worth a dime in business," and also said, "I'm not ashamed of a thing I've done. I think I showed plain common sense in cashing in on an asset after I have given everything I had to my university. . . . I don't owe the University a cent." Later, Grange also took a swipe at the concept of school spirit, when he said that "a good football team plays for the coach rather than for the dear old alma mater" and that "the institution was impersonal and remote in the affections of the team, whereas Zuppke was real to us." Sportswriter W. O. McGeehan attempted to put a positive spin on the affair when he wrote an article suggesting that a college man like Grange might potentially uplift the image of professional football. And in spite of Grange's comments about the value of education, there was still a growing social awareness of the value of college, evidenced by an editorial in the *Chicago Herald and Examiner* asserting that Grange's success would inspire thousands of young boys to attend college where they would "become better, more capable men solely because they longed to emulate Grange's athletic prowess."[28]

There was no escaping the fact that 1925 had produced the first large-scale national interest in professional football.[29]

Continuing the Struggle

With the prestige of college football reeling from the shock to its traditions and beliefs, university athletic authorities sought to return to the attack against professional football. Yet even these efforts received setbacks when two of college football's top officials began to modify their positions. Major Griffith of the Big Ten predicted the eventual financial decline of college football if the professional sport "is encouraged too much," but then said he did not blame Grange for turning professional and believed that many of those individuals censuring the former Illinois star would take the money if given the chance. If that was not bad enough, E. K. Hall, chairman of the prestigious Rules Committee and an official with strong ties to traditional eastern football beliefs, commented that he had no quarrel with professional football—provided that the promoters would not invade the college sport, as in the Grange case, and that the play-for-pay game would do nothing to tarnish the image of college football, that is, via gambling. Then Hall, who had once been described as the "strongest and most active" opponent of professional football "and practically the successor to Walter Camp," said further that he had no quarrel with the college player who, after graduating, went on to play professional football.[30]

In the midst of all this turmoil, the case for opposing professional football found new life when it was disclosed that four players from Chicago's Englewood High School had played for the Milwaukee Badgers in a game against the Chicago Cardinals on December 10, 1925. Rumors that the St. Louis pro team had used a college player when it took on Grange and the Bears was another in a series of events that had marred the close of the 1925 NFL season, but the Milwaukee Badgers scandal was far worse.

The Cardinals' owner, Chris O'Brien, was concerned that the Milwaukee team would not be able to get together enough players for the quickly scheduled game, and he mentioned it to his quarterback, Art Folz. The Cardinal player had been a prep star at Chicago's Englewood High School, and he was able to round up four players from the current Englewood football team to play with the Milwaukee club—allegedly telling the high school boys that it was just a practice scrimmage to be played with no spectators and no money involved. Despite smearing mud on their faces, the four were recognized by people at the game, and the matter was reported to high school officials—the scandal exploding across the sports pages.

As school board officials pressed their investigations, O'Brien was initially quoted as saying that he knew "absolutely nothing about the make up of the Milwaukee team," a statement that he would soon retract. Here was probably the worst possible scenario for the National Football League: a professional player, under false pretenses, luring four supposedly innocent high school boys into playing with a pro team. James Crusinberry of the *Chicago Tribune* wrote, "Professional football, which rose to the heights of public favor . . . with the acquisition of Red Grange to its membership, yesterday sunk into a mire of scandal," and the newspapers regularly described how the vile professionals had lured the high school youths into trouble with lies and deception. The four Englewood players were eventually ruled to be professionals and were barred permanently from further prep and college athletic competition, while for the NFL the decision stood as an indictment against the entire structure of professional football.[31]

Apparently finding new energy in this latest pro football scandal, representatives to the NCAA convention in December 1925 devoted a considerable portion of their meetings to the perils posed by professional football. In a resolution prepared for the convention, it was recommended once again that the colleges refuse to employ, or continue to employ, any coach, trainer, official, or others who "in any capacity give service to or aid in the promotion of professional football." Later, under pressure from the various intercollegiate conferences, the banning of pro football game officials would be made an option that was left to the discretion of the individual schools. The NCAA resolution of 1925 also noted that college football's great popularity was seriously affecting the chief educational purposes of the universities, a situation that would soon set in motion the investigations for the Carnegie Report of 1929.[32]

Others were also busy attacking the professionals. At its December 1925 meeting in New York, the American Football Coaches Association passed a resolution declaring any person associating in any capacity with professional football after September 1, 1926, to be ineligible for membership in the AFCA. Believing that the collegiate coaches wielded considerable political clout within their sport, an article in the *New York Times* called this decision "the most drastic action yet taken against the professional game." There was also some resistance to pro football among the media at this time. The managing editor of the *New York Sun*, "feeling that professional football is a menace," closed the *Sun*'s sports pages in the fall of 1926 to any pregame publicity about approaching pro games, the only New York City paper to do so. The editor wrote that the *Sun* was "anxious to do something positive towards suppressing the wave of commercialism which is now threatening college football" and even suggested that "a pledge be exacted" from each football player, "binding him not to play professional football until a year shall have elapsed following graduation of his class." This proposal was too radical for even the educational elite of the eastern Big Three schools.[33]

At their annual meeting on January 25, 1926, in Detroit, NFL owners attempted to defuse the embarrassments that had taken place in late 1925 when they adopted a rule prohibiting any member club from signing a college player to a contract before his college class graduated. The owners believed that the adoption of the rule—referred to as the "Grange Rule"—"would eliminate the chief objections to the professional game" and that the rule was essential in protecting the progress the league had made in gaining widespread acceptance among football fans.[34]

The year 1926 also brought the formation of a new pro football circuit, the American Professional Football League (APFL). The new league, formed with Grange and C. C. Pyle as its leading promoters, named "Big" Bill Edwards, a figure famous in Princeton football annals, as its first president. Edwards announced that the "high college standards of football will be the aim of the professional league" and that he had accepted the job as league president because he wanted to "help preserve high-class football as it is played at the colleges." After reporting that the APFL would adhere to the NFL rule banning college players until after their classes graduated, Edwards mentioned the growing availability of top-flight pro football to those fans who were unable to obtain tickets for the big-time college games, thus seeking to link the APFL to the football fans of America's growing middle class.[35]

As the decade of the 1920s proceeded toward a close it was apparent that professional football was going to remain a fixture on the American sporting scene. The liberal *New Republic,* considered the voice of progressivism on societal issues, published an article in 1926 by Glenn Hoover, a college professor, that took a favorable position on the issue of professional football. Hoover described the emotional opposition to professional football as "mere campus idiocy" and predicted that the Sunday game would someday grow to "a grand scale" where "immense profits will be made from it." He continued on to say that "a big [pro] football team in every large city would do for college football what [professional baseball] has done for college baseball, to wit, remove it from the spotlight. . . . When football is as frankly professional as is baseball, the world may forget the colleges entirely, but in any event, they will not be known for their teams."[36]

In the late 1920s, college football authorities continued to describe the technical quality of play within the professional game as inferior to the college brand of the sport. This opinion spread widely among the media of the day; for example, a column in *Outlook* magazine said, "To state it flatly and frankly, the professional game is not worth watching if there is a college game even among small institutions under way within a distance of twenty miles."[37] Although leading college coaches such as Stagg and Rockne characterized the professional teams as being not very well trained, the predominant theme of the attacks on pro football's style of play was that the play-for-pay sport could never incorporate the same spirit and commitment as the amateur collegiate sport.

Typical of these critics was Coach Bill Roper of Princeton, who wrote in 1927 that "the professional game lacks the flame, the spirit, that keeps the college game going upward and onward . . . as a hard, bristling sport" and that pro football "will be first, last and always, of minor importance to the intercollegiate game." In

1928 Bob Zuppke of Illinois added, "All cynics to the contrary, the college athlete fights to the last drop for his alma mater. . . . Therein lies the success of the college game and the failure of the pro game. . . . [T]he pro is willing to 'lie down' every so often for he no longer has the same incentive. Professionals have vainly attempted to transform the college background, spirit, color and drama that is distinctly collegiate. . . . Professional football is the imitator of the college game, and the imitator can never be the master." The idea that professional players were not always performing at full speed was frequently carried to the further suggestion that the pro game was very much involved with gambling interests, and therefore not honest. In an article for *Outing* magazine, Herbert Reed noted that "the profession [pro football] has broken down the honor of the college player, a thing intolerable. I doubt if any games have been 'sold' yet, but that will come when the wreckage of the college player's ideals is complete."[38]

A belief in the importance of the collegiate athletic spirit was also still heavily entrenched within media circles, an example being seen in comments from famed sportswriter Grantland Rice in 1926: "Pro football may get over well . . . but will mere technique ever take the place of the spirit and the flame of the college game where it is a matter of service and sacrifice and not a matter of money?" Rice, unable to anticipate the immense popularity of professional football that would grow from the mid-1960s onward, wrote further, "Tradition is no small part. . . . Professional football lacks the elements which feature the college game, and it will never approach the interest now given the college side." Many of the student newspapers around the country were dutifully issuing the same critiques of professional football. Typical was an editorial at Boston College that said, "Football is essentially and fundamentally a college game. . . . It is a far cry to the day when games between professional aggregations will . . . arouse enthusiasm to an extent in any way comparable to . . . the spirit aroused by college football."[39]

College football had plenty of its own problems from within by 1926, and gradually the attention of the athletic officials was turned away from professional football, while the attempts to maintain the original class separations between the two versions of the gridiron sport were eventually proving unsuccessful. Bill Roper was one who continued to believe in the social superiority of the college man, writing, "My contention is that if the professional promoters get the majority of their players from the industrial groups they can do more with them in the way of training. . . . The college player . . . has his education to fall back on and his memories of stirring contests . . . which make the professional game seem dull and flat and cheap." Yet ultimately, the increasing distribution of wealth throughout the economic good times of the 1920s, and the resulting escalation of college and university enrollments, served to bring about the democratization of American collegiate life and a resulting acceptance of professional football.[40]

The launching of Red Grange's professional football career had not only shown the economic possibilities for both players and professional team owners but also vigorously asserted the increasingly middle-class makeup and beliefs of the undergraduate population where a view toward economic security and commercial opportunities would come to hold an equal place with institutional traditions and school spirit. The diverse campaign of words and actions against organized professional football during the 1920s had been waged in spite of the obvious contradictions represented by the transformations that were already under way within the collegiate sport by early in the decade. As such, the campaigns by college officials would seem to have been motivated in great part by a continuance of the elitist class prejudices that predated World War I within the academic world, along with a desire to remain the dominant influence in guiding the athletes toward their perceived destinies.

Despite these factors, by the end of the 1920s organized pro football was becoming an increasingly acceptable pursuit for college players after graduation. Whether realized or not, college football was already moving along in a gradual transformation of attitudes that by the late twentieth century would make the intercollegiate game at the major universities primarily a training ground, or minor league, for professional football. The opening up of professional football as an increasingly viable option would also place premiums on state-of-the-art gridiron skills for college athletes, such as the forward pass, and so contributed to another area of transformation during the 1920s and beyond, which we will next examine. There would remain some hard-core opponents of professional football well into the 1930s, but soon enough the national acceptance and popularity of pro football—with no real harm to the college brand of the sport—would bring to a temporary close the struggle that had stretched across nearly three decades.[41]

5

ADVANCES ON THE GRIDIRON

Significant transformations in the style of play on college gridirons evolved through the 1920s, creating a more open offensive attack—one that held greater appeal and excitement for the ticket-buying fans. These transformations were the result of advances in the application of the running game and an ever growing use of the forward pass. With some origins in pre–World War I days, the major innovations being incorporated by ever more aggressive coaches were producing offensive theories that continued to move the game away from the traditional conservatism of the eastern universities—but not without controversy.

The crisis days of 1905–1906 for college football had brought about the legalization of the forward pass. A major feature of the rules changes installed at that time, the forward pass was intended to be a vehicle for opening up the offensive game and reducing football's violence and serious injuries. But the many restrictions placed on the use of the forward pass initially inhibited all but the most innovative coaches from exploring its full offensive possibilities. Yet fans and sportswriters still found excitement in the new play, and modern-day historian John Watterson has written that between 1906 and 1909, "The public quickly warmed to the pass for the simple reason that it added zest to the game. . . . Spectators found the forward pass a breathtaking innovation that transcended its purpose of creating open-field play."[1]

The rules revisions of 1906 had not fully eliminated mass plays from college football's offensive arsenal, as linemen were still allowed to assist the ball carrier by either pushing or pulling after the back had reached the line of scrimmage. Watterson has noted that "the new football in 1908 began to look like the old grinding, pushing and pulling game again—especially in the east, where coaches preferred running plays to the forward pass." No less an authority than Coach Percy Haughton of Harvard described the new system of mass plays as being "as deadly as its predecessors." By 1909 the number of serious football-related injuries and deaths was again on the rise, and in February 1910 the joint Rules Committee of the Inter Collegiate Athletic Association began debating proposed rules revisions. With Haughton and Coach Bill Roper of Princeton among the leaders, the majority sought to expand the use of the forward pass, along with outlawing the pushing and pulling of ball carriers and the flying tackle. However, Walter Camp and Yale continued to oppose any further opening up of the offensive game, and the committee meetings were bitterly contested through the spring until the group that included Haughton and Roper succeeded in finally adopting their major reforms in May 1910.[2]

CONTRASTS IN OFFENSIVE THEORY

And so the game of football was ready to begin moving toward its modern era. The period 1910–1918 witnessed significant innovations in the style of play on collegiate gridirons, the running attack still being the offense of choice for most major programs. But increasingly, the offenses sought to exploit the flanks of the opposing defenses rather than just continue the pounding of the interior lines, and the forward pass continued its progress toward being widely recognized for its full possibilities.

The progress in opening up the game's style of play was such that in the annual Rules Committee report for 1920, Chairman E. K. Hall wrote: "The season of 1920 just closed simply adds one more year of evidence in support of the statement made in our last report—that a good all-round open game has at last been fairly established." By 1921 Amos Alonzo Stagg, recognized as one of the leading offensive innovators since the turn of the century, had come to believe that the game had fully explored the major offensive possibilities allowed by the current rules, but he was also leaving the door open for the future: "I do not think the inventive possibilities of the game are nearly exhausted and yet there are not likely to be any startling developments of new systems of attack and defense. The game itself, I believe, is established. I think there will be no important changes in it. I do not myself see any ahead." Even Walter Camp noted in 1921, "It was possible to note last year more real progress in the scientific development of the game than any season in the last decade. We now see a far better rounded-out attack."[3]

Yet the enthusiasm for football's evolution into a more wide-open game was not finding acceptance among the traditional football powers of the East, most notably the Big Three of Harvard, Princeton, and Yale. When these schools met in their annual gridiron struggles, there was still a tendency to revert to a more conservative, close-to-the-vest style of offense—which meant not much passing. In the games of 1919 Yale attempted very few forward passes against Princeton and Harvard (Yale losing both contests), prompting sportswriters to criticize the Bulldogs for trying to win games with an offense that was more suited to pre-1906 days.

The writers affixed responsibility for the overly conservative offenses on coaching staffs of the East, where "it is no secret that some of these men actually believe that the type of football which they played is superior to the present game." The more open style of attack—whether in the running or passing game—did require more skills, athleticism, and teamwork from the players, concepts not quickly accepted in a region where the size and strength of the players had long been the major prerequisite for success. Writer Donald Herring was one who recognized this fact, pointing out in 1919, "Don't forget that the type of game Yale played this fall was the type most easily grasped by the material at hand." That the offensive philosophy of the East remained rooted in conservative prewar theory, believing in a battle of field position while waiting for an opposition mistake, can be seen in the comments made in 1922 by an eastern coach who told Walter Camp that "he did not regard the offense of his team of such essential importance so long as he had good kickers because he could keep himself out of difficulty."[4]

Charles Daly, prominent head coach at West Point and a former All-America quarterback at Harvard, was an eastern coach who recognized the potential rewards from the forward pass but still leaned toward the safer running game. Daly believed that "a well-rounded attack should have eight running plays, a kick, three passes, and one or two standard deceptions, one of which is the fake kick." The Army coach saw the forward pass as a weapon "reserved in general for use in the opponent's half of the field when the normal methods of attack have failed." Given his military experience, it was no surprise that Daly saw football as "a war game," where "superiority is directly analogous to fire superiority in war." Consequently, though believing that "a good team is skilled in all methods of attack," Daly favored the power running game and adhered to principles that called for focusing the attack on the line behind aggressive blocking, with any attempts at deception by sending men away from the point of attack weakening the chances for success. In 1921 Daly's offensive philosophy was summed up by his statement that "the direct and simple assault . . . has been the only form of attack that has yielded consistent success in football."[5]

A conservative approach to the offensive attack would continue to typify eastern college football through the early years of the 1920s, although in late 1922 Camp saw movement toward a more open game: "There were indications that the balance was turning a little in favor of the attack where teams had perfected a combination of the running game with forward passing." By late 1923, after watching Yale switch to an open attack in the second half of a win over Army and its "traditional close-formation attack," Camp declared, "Old-fashioned football was definitely buried." The legendary member of the Rules Committee recognized that it was offensive daring and innovation that were carrying teams from other regions past the eastern elite, and he reluctantly conceded that the "past history of football shows that progress has been made only by a venturesome coach adopting new tactics and staking his all on the venture . . . [and] that the older conservative institutions were slipping back in the football world, and the younger, more aggressive and venturesome teams were going to come to the front."[6]

As the decade progressed it was clear that the on-field balance of power was shifting away from the East, as teams in the other regions were far more willing to risk the more wide-open style of attack. In a 1924 article written by newspaperman William Abbott, comparing the two halves of the country, he stated, "The chief difference in the style of play between the two sections is the nature of the offense. Compared to the eastern teams the elevens of the western conference and colleges along the Pacific coast are faster and smarter. . . . The eastern style is more cramped and still revolves around the old power plays, or inside football, as some prefer to call it. . . . If eastern coaches expect to recover their former prestige they will have to forsake the old-style game for more speed and more deception on offense."[7]

Right there was much of the explanation for the rift in offensive philosophy—the coaches. Abbott, referring to Percy Haughton of Harvard and Columbia as "one of the few originally progressive coaches in the east," recognized that virtually all the game's progressive offensive minds were coaching somewhere other than the East by the middle of the 1920s. Herbert Reed of *Outlook* magazine credited the spread of progressivism in football to coaches such as Knute Rockne of Notre Dame, Bob Zuppke of Illinois, Glenn Warner (by 1924 he was at Stanford), and Dr. John Wilce of Ohio State, along with the numerous summer coaching schools that many of these innovative offensive minds conducted each year. Stagg also endorsed the importance of coaching schools in spreading the gospel of open football: "Coaching schools have spread knowledge . . . so that now the systems of offense and defense have become more and more standardized." Reed noted that "in general the more radical of the coaches had their way and their reward."[8]

Although many coaches had long recognized the capabilities of the forward pass, it was speed and deception that became the defining characteristics of their offensive ideas. In his review of the 1925 season, Reed noted that there was a "general acceptance of the theory that the game must be fought out on the flanks," and he pointed to the "shift plays" as a major contributor to that concept. Reed also pointed out that "the shift plays have become more valuable because of the suddenness of the combined power and deception that can be brought to bear on the outside defense." The importance of team speed in the modern offense was endorsed by noted sportswriter Grantland Rice: "Rockne long ago discovered the value of speed, more speed and still more speed. . . . You see no big, powerful, lumbering guards or tackles in a Notre Dame battalion. . . . [T]hey are all cavalry." Camp added that "the day of the lumbering lineman is gone, for now; in addition to possessing the power to withstand an attack, he must be fast enough to come out of the line to join the interference."[9]

Warner—one of the game's leading coaches after his years at eastern schools such as Carlisle, Cornell, and Pittsburgh—became one of the most outspoken advocates of western football after his move to Stanford in 1924. By 1925 Warner was pointing out that Pacific Coast teams were "developing a dashing and brilliant style of play, more daring" than that played in the East. He also contended that "Pacific Coast teams tend to open, fast plays, with plenty of forward passing, but not too much to over-balance the game."[10]

After two more seasons at Stanford, Warner emphatically believed that the East was now behind in football, primarily "because the majority of coaches in that part of the country are not as progressive and anxious to improve the game as the football mentors of the West and South are. . . . [T]oo many of the coaches there feel that they know their stuff and that they have nothing to learn." As Warner now saw it, when noneastern schools combined superior player talent and coaching capable of using that resource, the result was that "many old traditions and methods and axioms of the game were rendered obsolete [and] the West and South have forged to the front, adapting themselves to the new conditions much more quickly than in the conservative East."[11]

The concept of utilizing speed, deception, and players intelligent enough to execute the more wide-open offenses had clearly been accepted on a wide-scale basis by the middle of the decade. Although size and strength would always be valuable commodities, the modern game of 1920s college football now required quick-thinking athletes with the ability to digest ever growing playbooks. Robert Edgren of the *New York Evening World* wrote that "brain and speed have discounted beef," while Fielding Yost of Michigan said that "the opening up of the game . . . has added interest for the player because wits and quick thinking, and not only power, are the requirements."[12]

Coach Bill Roper of Princeton was one eastern coach who recognized this need for intelligent athletes in executing the wide-open attack. Roper wrote, "The successive changes which the game of football has been undergoing have made it a very different affair for the player," adding that his 1922 team had been "selected, trained and developed to meet the changed requirements of the modern game," and the result had been an undefeated season. The respected Princeton coach noted that "today the fastest, the brainiest and best conditioned players make up the eleven. . . . Roughly speaking, the thinking team wins football games from the team which can't or won't think."[13]

Even with the widespread acceptance and recognition of the open game, there was still a continuing effort to balance the attack with the threat of power formations that sought to outnumber the defense at the point of attack. By 1929 Stagg would identify the four predominant systems of football then in general use as the Notre Dame Shift, the single wing, the short punt formation, and the double wing. Warner is widely identified as the creator of the double-wing formation, the last major offensive innovation of the decade, as he had been experimenting with it to a limited extent prior to World War I at the University of Pittsburgh. Arriving at Stanford in 1924, Warner soon incorporated the double-wing formation as his primary system of attack.

The double-wing formation aimed at deception and power, revolving around a series of reverses, double reverses, fakes, and pass plays, always striving to keep the ball hidden from view of the opposition until the ball carrier reached the hole in the defensive line. Stagg described the double wing as "an attempt to make safe and sure yardage with little or no gamble . . . never forgetting the fact at all times that he practically has a nine man line operating against a five man line of defense, and therefore always a direct and immediate and powerful weapon for massed purpose." Stanford's impressive display of the double wing in a 26-0 win over Army in 1928 at New York's Polo Grounds stimulated a widespread adoption of the formation by eastern universities. Eventually, the double wing would be abandoned by many teams because of its complexities, writer Stanley Woodward remarking that "the timing is so delicate and the assignments so intricate that many coaches who have attempted to teach the method superficially have given up in despair."[14]

Howard Jones of Southern California was another of the innovative coaches who believed in the use of a power running attack in order to capitalize on the defense having been spread out by the threat of the more open attack: "Pressure and deception are the two main elements of offensive football. . . . All the best systems are similar in that they attempt to employ formations from which the line driving, end running and passing games can be used with equal facility." By the end of the 1920s the USC coach had incorporated a series of complex and deceptive spinner plays into his offense. After Jones's Trojans destroyed Warner's Stanford team by a score of 41-12 in 1930, a *San Francisco Examiner* reporter described how USC's speedy running backs, Orv Mohler and Marshall Duffield, executed the spinner: "A complete whirl with the ball outstretched and faking reverse shots, [they] struck quickly way round end, inside end, on either side of tackle, or cut back through the center."[15] With a consistent influx of talented running backs into the USC program, Jones would continue the expansion of his ground-attack theories well into the 1930s.

By the late 1920s Coach Lou Young of the University of Pennsylvania had incorporated a variety of hidden-ball plays that attracted considerable attention, the practice quickly spreading to many teams in other regions. The hidden-ball plays of the 1920s were not the crude efforts of the early game where the football was slipped under a player's jersey, but rather were plays based on the clever faking of handoffs and passes, bearing a resemblance to the option attack of later-twentieth-century football. The attempts at incorporating ever more deception and trickery into their offenses soon became a passion for coaches everywhere. One sportswriter covering southern football wrote, "Dixie teams have added reverse plays, lateral passes and swift-moving formations to their repertoire this season to form a more colorful and exciting panorama. Almost every member of the Southern conference is offering a different type of formation for dazzling aerial attacks or a new method of spinning off runs." A prominent football referee of the 1920s, Tom Thorp, called the "hidden ball" offense the most advanced running attack developed in years.[16]

A belief in the merits of a diversified and open attack eventually came to be recognized in every region of the country by the end of the decade, although the best college football was no longer being played by the once powerful teams of the East. By the end of the 1920s college football's offensive theories had been transformed into a style of play that provided an exciting product to keep the large new stadia filled, while also creating a gridiron product with many similarities to late-twentieth-century college football.

THE SHIFT FORMATION

One of the most controversial offensive tactics of the decade was the shift formation—usually referred to during this period as the "Notre Dame Shift."

Specific credit for developing the concept of shift formations during the first decade of the 1900s is usually attributed to Amos Alonzo Stagg and Dr. Henry Williams of Minnesota. However, the fact remains that the idea of building and focusing the offensive power of the running game by the movement or motion of the backfield players before the ball was snapped was a fundamental precept of the "momentum" or "wedge" plays that plagued college football in the 1890s. The many post-1900 variations of shift formations were merely applications of momentum-play concepts within the rules of the day.[17]

The system of shift formations for a time experienced great popularity and wide-spread use—especially among Catholic college teams in the 1920s. Dr. Eddie Anderson, a former Notre Dame player who went on to coach at Holy Cross and Iowa, wrote that "the purpose of the shift, in short, is deception and concentrated power. The idea is . . . to throw the opposing players, the line especially, off balance."[18] Yet by the second half of the 1920s the use of shift formations had accumulated considerable opposition among leading coaches who viewed the concept as unsportsmanlike in its borderline adherence to the rules. What followed were rule revisions that eventually removed most of the advantages of deception and momentum from the shift formations, which substantially reduced their popularity and usage.

While the "Minnesota Shift" of the prewar years had been widely known in college football circles—mentioned often by sportswriters in their game coverage—it was with Notre Dame's explosion onto the national scene immediately following World War I that the general football public truly became aware of shift formations. Knute Rockne pointed to his predecessor, Jesse Harper, as the coach who had first installed shift formations at Notre Dame during the seasons of 1913–1914. Harper had been exposed to the shift while playing for Stagg at the University of Chicago. The Maroons' plays included shifting a tackle to create an unbalanced line, whereas Harper and Rockne would run their formations from lines that were usually balanced. Stagg wrote that the strategy of the Notre Dame system was based on "a quick backfield shift with different timing for passing [snapping] the ball, which . . . furnishes the background of deception for quick thrusts through the line and off-tackle plays and end runs."[19] But just as the Minnesota Shift and its variations had led to controversy and change in 1910, so too did the Notre Dame Shift in the 1920s.

By 1921, innovators such as Stagg had incorporated all variety of movement into their offensive formations, much to the dismay of opposing defenses. After Chicago's 9-0 win over Princeton in 1921, Robert Kelly of the *New York Evening Post* wrote that Stagg "employed a shift that brought what appeared to be almost half his team into the interference in every play, sending the runner off tackle behind a veritable cloud of his own men."[20] With Rockne turning out powerhouses immediately after the war, many coaches began to question the competitive fairness of shift formations. One of the first to loudly raise the issue was West Point's influential coach, Charles Daly, in 1921, in the aftermath of his team's third consecutive defeat since the war at the hands of Notre Dame.

By now recognized as one of the country's top college coaches, Rockne no longer believed that it was necessary to capitulate to every complaint from the eastern schools. In early November 1921, newspaper stories began appearing with the suggestion that Notre Dame was no longer interested in continuing its series with Army. Daly immediately wrote to Rockne, expressing Army's desire to continue the rivalry and inquiring about the stories, while also doing an about-face on the issue of Notre Dame's shift formations: "My objection to your formation on certain plays I trust has not been too aggravating. . . . At any rate since the game was played I have come to the conclusion that shift plays are a necessary and valuable part of the game of football and that restrictive legislation should not be effected."[21]

Yet increasingly, coaches believed that the current rules covering players in motion created too much confusion for the game officials, hence the debatable legality of many of the shift formations. In a letter to Stagg, Bob Zuppke of Illinois wrote, "We know that it is very difficult for an official to decide some times whether or not men are illegally in motion when shifting. The recent rule which allows one man to be in motion towards his own goal complicates the situation. . . . It seems to me that it would be better not to allow anyone to be in motion."[22]

The response of the Rules Committee was to revise the man-in-motion provisions by requiring the offensive players to come to a full stop before the ball was snapped. For the 1923 season the rule book specified that "on all shift plays the man who has moved from one position to another before the ball is put in play, must come to a stop with both feet stationary so that when he starts he will go from a standstill." Although appearing to make it easier for the officials to catch offensive players in motion when the ball was snapped, the revised rule still left it to the officials' judgment as to whether the players in motion had indeed come to a stationary point before the snap. Coaches such as Rockne, along with many of his former players who had spread across the country into coaching jobs, quickly revised their offenses to test the new legal limits of man-in-motion. There were frequent game reports of teams, usually coached by former Notre Dame men, being flagged for numerous illegal motion penalties, while the head coaches claimed that the officials were misinterpreting the concept of "stationary."[23]

Despite the ongoing controversy over shift formations, the offensive concept continued to be widely used and studied. Of course, Notre Dame's use of the shift was of particular interest, although its formations had become less complicated by 1924, the season of the school's mythical national championship with its Four Horsemen team. Opposition to the strategy of shift formations continued, as coaches and officials still battled over what constituted a backfield man becoming stationary. This disagreement resulted in another revision of the man-in-motion rule after the 1924 season, this version requiring that the "players must come to an absolute stop and remain stationary in their new position sufficiently long so that there is no doubt in the mind of the officials as to the legality of the play."[24]

This latest legislation did nothing to slow down the use of the shift formation and any number of its variations. Georgia Tech traveled to New York's Yankee Stadium in 1925 and handed Penn State a defeat with an offense that consisted almost exclusively of shift formations. At the University of Illinois, Zuppke had installed formations off a shift that had "only the barest hesitation" before the ball was snapped. The Illini coach had his backfield men lining up in a more spread-out alignment than previously, while also eliminating the direct pass from center. Instead, the ball carriers received a lateral from the quarterback as they approached the line of scrimmage at full speed, thus allowing the runner to get through openings created in the defensive line before they could be closed up.[25]

Despite his success with the shift formation, Zuppke became one of its most outspoken opponents after the 1926 season. Announcing his intention to fight for the elimination of shift plays at the approaching Rules Committee meeting in New York, Zuppke declared that there was "too great an advantage to the offensive team employing the shift . . . that the momentum gained in the shift . . . places the defensive team distinctly at a disadvantage." The 1926 Army-Yale game was

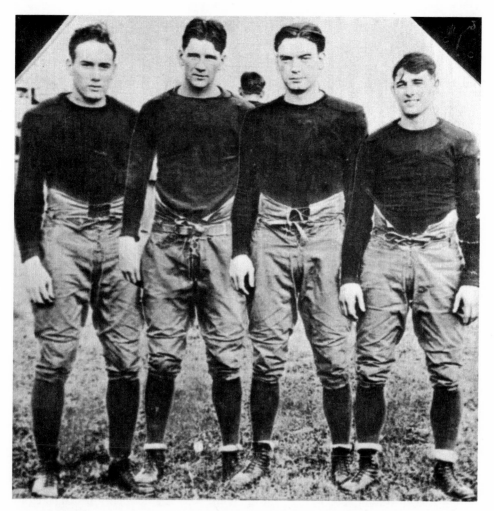

7. Four Horsemen backfield of Notre Dame. The legendary 1924 backfield that executed Coach Knute Rockne's shift formations to perfection included *(left to right)* Don Miller, Elmer Layden, Jim Crowley, and Harry Stuhldreher. Courtesy of the Amateur Athletic Foundation of Los Angeles.

cited as a major example of the difficulty of enforcing the rule, as Army's coach, Biff Jones, had openly admitted that he was using shift plays as Notre Dame did, "that is with the passing of the ball while the shift was still being made." It was said that Jones "discovered that to evade the rule successfully with the shift once, more than offset being caught and penalized four or five times" at 5 yards each, as Army crushed Yale 33-0. Stagg and Fielding Yost of Michigan were aligned with Zuppke in opposition to shift formations, Yost contending that a shift play had no value to an offense if the officials would correctly and "rigidly enforce" the existing rules.[26]

Notre Dame had continued to build successful seasons behind its use of shift formations, and Rockne considered the Big Ten coaches' attacks on the offensive concept as a direct assault on his gridiron program, and himself personally. Rockne believed that Stagg and Yost were hypocritical in many of their demands, including their calls for athletic reforms, and that much of Yost's opposition was attributable to a personal jealousy of the Notre Dame coach. Rockne pointed to the "pageantry of shift plays and the thrill of the forward pass" as primarily responsible for the great popularity of college football. Zuppke responded that "the new restrictions have not worked out successfully. If the rule should be changed to make the back field halt two seconds, the officials would have something definite upon which to base their decisions."[27]

There was no dissuading the growing opposition to the rule that still allowed for too much subjective interpretation by the game officials. At the Big Ten's annual scheduling meeting in late November 1926, the athletic directors voted to enforce a two-second stop by the players before the ball was snapped on all shift plays in conference games. Predictably, Zuppke was the leading sponsor of the new rule that was seen as virtually eliminating the use of shift formations, as all advantage to the offensive team would be lost with its momentum gone and the defense having sufficient time to react to the movement. The Big Ten resolution also indicated that nonconference opponents would be expected to adhere to the "two-second rule," and one of the coaches declared the revised rule "the most radical step since the forward pass."[28]

In the aftermath of the action taken by the Big Ten, the Eastern Association of Football Officials held its annual meeting on December 27, 1926, at New York's Hotel Astor. Among the changes the meeting recommended to the Rules Committee was the effective abolishment of shift plays, calling for a stop of three full seconds by the moving players. "The shift must go," said one official. "We have found that 99 out of every 100 shift plays are direct violations of the rules." Two days later the American Football Coaches Association met, and during an early session a resolution was adopted that called for the "two-second" stop rule on players in motion.[29]

In the face of these growing efforts to legislate the shift formations out of existence, Rockne responded by lobbying directly with the head of the Rules Committee, E. K. Hall. Although the Notre Dame coach still believed these efforts were really attacks on himself and the Catholic university, he now recognized that some sort of a beefed-up rule was inevitable. In a February 1927 letter to Hall, Rockne suggested a one-second stop after the shift—calling a two-second stop "purely ridiculous"—along with a 15-yard penalty for the shifting team that fails to set for the required time. The Notre Dame coach added: "I do not believe that the good gentlemen who have in their hands the destiny of the American game of football wish to abolish the shift. . . . If you abolish the shift I am afraid we will have to go back to the rough football . . . and we will suffer as a result as we will be called harsh names."[30]

Hall replied to Rockne: "I should be very much surprised if the Rules Committee comes to the conclusion that it is necessary to abolish the shift. . . . The real problem is this: What can be done to retain all the legitimate advantages and strategy which the shift affords and at the same time find some way to correct its continued and unfair abuse." When the Rules Committee met in March the rule book was revised exactly as Rockne had proposed—a one-second stop after the shift, and a penalty of 15 yards for noncompliance. In his 1927 report on the rules meeting, Hall wrote: "The Committee felt that it would be a distinct loss to the game to lose the shift and the strategic possibilities it affords. . . . The illegal shift has disappeared and the danger of any return to momentum plays through this device has apparently been eliminated."[31]

Rockne expressed satisfaction with the revised ruling, and then set about to change his football teams in response to the one-second stop. With most of the advantages previously realized through deception and speed of execution now legislated away, Rockne began incorporating heavier and stronger players both on the line and in the backfield. Notre Dame's running attack became dependent on the straight-ahead power blocking of the larger linemen to create holes for ball carriers, with spinner plays in the backfield adding a degree of deception. Rockne would never really accept the efforts to curtail the use of the shift formations, even when he was fielding national championship powerhouses in 1929 and 1930. The Notre Dame coach continued to believe that the opponents of the shift were "against success and Notre Dame in particular." To the very end of his coaching days Rockne never ceased to work for the elimination of the "timed" stop, regularly encouraging his many former players who had moved into coaching to continue using the shift. In his opposition to a "timed" stop, the Notre Dame coach always maintained the position that a "shift should stop long enough to eliminate momentum but not long enough for a stupid team to spot your formation." Rockne cited military history as a case for the greater use of offensive flanking maneuvers, which he related to the shift formations.[32]

In 1930, during the final season of his coaching career, Rockne told reporters that "Notre Dame can get along without the shift. We can stop 10 minutes on every play if necessary. . . . We can win without the shift but we won't draw the crowds. The color will be gone. . . . There's nothing unsportsmanlike about the shift. It merely gives little men of ability and speed a chance. . . . It adds speed and grace to football."[33] With Rockne's untimely passing there was no longer a prominent college coach to carry on the battle, and so the controversial shift formations eventually fell into disuse, ending the long struggle over their place in offensive football.

TAKING TO THE AIR

In an era of college football history that is remembered for the many legacies it passed on toward modern football, one of the most significant for the sport was the expansion and complete integration of the forward pass into the offensive theories of the game.

Many casual sport historians remain unaware of the real evolution of the forward pass in college football, preferring to accept Notre Dame's Hollywood-promoted mythology that attributes the first serious use of the forward pass to Knute Rockne and Gus Dorais in 1913. Others subscribe to the old Southwest Conference's story that Southern Methodist taught the country's collegiate teams how to play the open style of offense with the advent of its "aerial circus" of the 1920s.

The fact is that the serious use of the forward pass and the exploration of its offensive possibilities began in 1906, the first season of its legalization. Although its use prior to World War I—and even for a period afterward by the more conservative eastern coaches—was usually more of an offensive strategy to deceive the defenses, there was a definite recognition and application of the pass play's potential. In the aftermath of the war years there was a growing willingness to use the forward pass as a key component of a truly balanced offense, with occasional outbreaks of wild passing games throughout the decade.

With the game's rapidly expanding popularity through the early years of the 1920s, it was absolutely essential that college football maintain an "on the field" product that would keep the fans satisfied and the increasing number of large new stadia filled. The successful use of the forward pass became essential for any team that wanted to remain competitive, as supporters of college football increasingly demanded winning teams as a prerequisite for continuing the revenue from large ticket sales and other sources upon which many of the universities had become so dependent. The end result was that by the close of the 1920s, college football had developed the use of the forward pass to a level that resembled the so-called passing revolution of the late 1930s, when the sport's administrators and publicists became more aware of statistics.[34]

Early Evolution of the Forward Pass

The legalization of the forward pass in 1906 came about with other reforms at the time in an attempt to open up the offensive style of play in response to the persistent violence that had continued to plague college football since its origins. However, with Walter Camp among the opponents of the forward pass, the new offensive tactic was initially burdened with a number of restrictions that were intended to discourage its use. Among the restrictions placed on the forward pass in its initial 1906 version were such things as the ball had to cross the line of scrimmage 5 yards outside where the ball was received from center, with a violation of the provision creating a turnover; the forward pass could not cross the goal line—if it did the ball was awarded to the defensive team; and incomplete passes were treated as a turnover and the ball awarded to the defensive team.[35]

Yet there were innovative college coaches who saw the strategic potential of the forward pass, and so proceeded to develop its usage within the current rules. The most aggressive coaches in the application of the forward pass during its first years were Stagg of Chicago, Eddie Cochems of St. Louis University, and Warner at Carlisle. Materials from his coaching files show that in 1906 Stagg had already conceived and diagramed nine different play variations for the forward pass, from which he had generated sixty-four different pass patterns. Ranging from quarterback sprint outs before the pass to play-action passes, Stagg had envisioned virtually the entire array of late-twentieth-century approaches to using the forward pass.

In 1906 Stagg was not just fantasizing about potential uses of the forward pass but was ready to apply it in game situations. After bad weather frustrated Stagg's plan to spring the forward pass on Minnesota in 1906, the following week Chicago unleashed its new weapon, and the Maroon crushed Illinois by a score of 63-0. In 1907 Stagg expanded his use of the aerial attack, and, under the direction of halfback Walter Steffen, the Maroons played a wide-open brand of football all season, including two touchdown passes in the big win over Minnesota.[36]

Meanwhile, Cochems had also installed the forward pass as a key part of his offense at St. Louis in 1906 and 1907. With a capable passing combination in halfback Bradbury Robinson and end Jack Schneider, St. Louis used the forward pass to great advantage in piling up 407 points and an 11-0-0 record in the 1906 season, including wins over Kansas and Iowa. The following season the Billikins crushed an excellent Nebraska team on the way to another successful record that again featured the forward pass. John E. Wray, sports editor of the *St. Louis Globe-Democrat* during the Cochems era at St. Louis University, writing in 1927, described the well-rounded offensive attack that Cochems built around a variety of pass plays: "Opponents . . . were hopelessly confused by the alternation of long and short forward passes and line bucks. . . . It is doubtful if today there is any more intelligent use of the weapon made than when Cochems baffled his opponents."[37]

The third coach generally recognized as one of the earliest proponents of the forward pass was Warner, who had returned to the Carlisle Indian School in 1907. Unlike some teams that passed the football in an end-over-end manner, Carlisle teams were using the spiral pass as early as 1907. That season Warner took his Carlisle team on a trip to the Midwest to meet the University of Chicago, and before the showdown Warner told reporters that his team was generally considered "the best exponents of the new game in the east." The Carlisle coach continued: "The reason that other teams were not using the forward pass in the east was that they have not realized as yet the possibilities of it." After Carlisle had scored on a long touchdown pass while knocking off the powerful Chicago outfit, the writer from the *Chicago Tribune* told readers that the Indians "showed themselves masters of modern football and gave such an exhibition of its possibilities as will not be forgotten by anyone."[38]

Yet years later prominent football historian Parke Davis wrote an article in the annual *Football Guide* in which he made the statement that in 1906, "notwithstanding the great opportunities offered by this new device [the forward pass], the players . . . treated this new weapon lightly and made little use of its possibilities." In writing of the 1907 season, Davis said there was "no conspicuous example of the play" to be found until late in the season when Yale used forward passes to rally for an exciting win over Princeton. Obviously, Davis had not seen games outside of the East in 1906–1907, which would explain his lack of familiarity with developments elsewhere, except for the fact that he wrote his article twenty years later (1927), by which time the early innovations of the forward pass had become well known. Certainly, his comments had some validity for the Big Three's use of the forward pass in 1906–1907, although the outcomes of the Princeton-Yale and Harvard-Yale games of 1906 both revolved around late pass plays.[39]

Former Princeton player Neilson Poe described the Big Three's general execution of the passing game at this time as being "of the hit-or-miss order without much accuracy in execution," and that "the play acted as a boomerang [an interception] in too many instances, and the teams were consequently unwilling to take chances with it except in desperate situations." Such commentary certainly did not apply in 1906–1907 to some of the leading advocates of the forward pass. Years later, Stagg, Knute Rockne, William Sprackling (a former Brown University great), and Bob Zuppke would all describe the Midwest as having been far and away the early leader in the development of the aerial attack's potential under the rules of the time.[40]

Despite the success being demonstrated with the use of the forward pass by these innovative coaches, the restrictions on its use imposed by the rule book were inhibiting the realization of its full possibilities. In the rule meetings of 1910 a group of delegates came in looking for revisions to eliminate the last vestiges of mass plays that had evolved from the 1906 rule revisions, along with the removal of some of the restrictions on passing, but instead found an organized effort led by Camp and Yale to eliminate the aerial game. After a lengthy battle that stretched across the spring of 1910, the reformers succeeded in retaining the forward pass without all of the previous restrictions, while also codifying other rule changes that helped to launch college football toward its modern era.[41]

In the seasons before the war, following the 1910 rule revisions, general use of the forward pass increased in popularity. One of the more significant games of this period came in 1910 when Michigan stunned a previously undefeated Minnesota team with a fourth-quarter touchdown that was set up by two long pass completions. Covering the game for the *Chicago Tribune*, sportswriter Walter Eckersall told his readers, "Michigan's success must be attributed to its thorough mastery of the forward pass. . . . Minnesota relied upon old football . . . and it is no wonder it went down in defeat. . . . [S]uccess cannot be obtained by using plays which have outlived their usefulness."[42]

Another notable prewar game took place during the 1913 season when Notre Dame caught Army unprepared to defend the passing game, and so the Irish handed Army a surprising 35-13 defeat. This game would eventually assume a mythical reputation after Rockne (a player in the game) became one of the nation's most prominent coaches during the 1920s. The eventual story line went that the little Notre Dame team had taught the entire country the merits of the forward pass that day as the combination of Gus Dorais and Rockne passed the Army team silly and so triggered a revolution in college football. The *New York Times* account of the 1913 game noted that "the Westerners flashed the most sensational football that has been seen in the East this year" and reported that "the yellow leather egg [the football] was in the air half the time." No less an authority than game official Bill Roper, a former and future coach at Princeton, was quoted as saying "he had always believed that such playing was possible under the new rules, but that he had never seen the forward pass developed to such a state of perfection." If Roper in fact made such a comment, it indicates a complete unawareness of the innovations that had been developed in other areas since 1906. Notre Dame sport historian Murray Sperber has commented that this game "did not revolutionize football" and pointed out, "Notre Dame football has sparked many legends and the first victory over Army generated more than most."[43]

By the 1914 season the forward pass had been accepted as an integral part of the offensive attack at many universities, and Herbert Reed of *Outing* magazine wrote: "The season proved that the free-passing game is with us to stay." Reed went on to note that "many prominent coaches set out frankly and openly . . . to put on a passing-game that had all the appearance of radicalism run wild. It was a case, however, not of revolution, but of evolution. . . . The new passing was put on not merely as a desperate chance at a scoring play but as a resuscitated form of attack that might safely be built into the system." Yet eastern coaches continued to evince an attitude that the pass play was merely one of desperation. Their continued adherence to an old-style, run-oriented offense is typified by a remark in an *Outing* article at the close of the 1916 season: "The experience of Yale demonstrated the value of fundamental football. The attack was simple and contained few plays." But there was a growing number of nationally well-publicized games that refuted this antipassing sentiment, and it became increasingly difficult to ignore this exciting offensive weapon.[44]

By the 1919 season Princeton, under Coach Bill Roper, was demonstrating a growing willingness to use the forward pass in the most critical of its games. Meanwhile, George Gipp of Notre Dame was garnering plenty of attention with his aerial exploits in the 1919 and 1920 seasons. But the game at the time that drew the greatest national attention for its use of the forward pass was the 1921 Rose Bowl game between California and Ohio State. The Big Ten team, under the direction of Coach John Wilce, was widely known for its passing attack, and the powerful Buckeyes completed eleven of twenty-four passes for 133 yards, while California notched 102 yards passing in the highly publicized game. The play that stunned Ohio State, and caught the imagination of football fans around the country, was a touchdown pass thrown by Harold "Brick" Muller of Cal that traveled 53 yards through the air.[45]

Against a background of growing attention given to the Rose Bowl game by the newspapers, along with the attractive matchup that Ohio State and California's "Wonder Team" had provided, Muller's pass became representative of the excitement and color that could be provided by a wide-open collegiate passing attack. As mammoth new football stadia soon began rising on university campuses around the country, the forward pass and the open style of offense would play major roles in the exciting spectacle needed to keep ticket-buying fans in the seats. Neilson Poe wrote, "A forward pass is one of the prettiest plays in the game. . . . [T]he open game is what develops the thrilling plays in football . . . that are remembered and looked forward to when the teams of the great American universities meet."[46]

Forward Passing Escalates

It was no longer possible to ignore the aerial game, and even Camp, while continuing to remain an enemy of the forward pass, reluctantly had to admit after the 1919 season that "today it is a part of the offensive of every first-class team. . . . It is evident that this forward pass is needed for there has been no great amount of progress in the ordinary running offense." Another prominent college football personality, Robert "Tiny" Maxwell, commented in 1921 that "coaches seem to have suddenly realized the effectiveness of the play and included it in their regular attack instead of holding it back for a last desperate chance when everything else failed. . . . The forward pass is the play around which modern football is built." A New York sportswriter added that "the possibilities of the forward pass were proved to be almost limitless."[47]

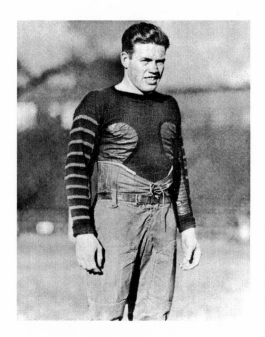

8. Harold "Brick" Muller of California. A three-time All-America, his gigantic forward pass in the 1921 Rose Bowl electrified college football. Courtesy of the Amateur Athletic Foundation of Los Angeles.

After Princeton used its passing attack to defeat Chicago in a sensational intersectional battle in 1922, the *Princeton Alumni Weekly* noted: "If this game proved anything at all it proved that a fine forward-passing game can defeat a fine line-plunging game." Roper had installed a passing attack that played a more important role within Princeton's total offense than either Harvard or Yale had yet been willing to attempt, and the consensus of opinion clearly placed the midwestern collegiate teams far ahead of the East in the effective use of the forward pass. A *New York Times* article noted that the western schools "realized more fully on the possibilities of the play as a threat . . . opening up new fields of strategy for the already belabored defense to wander through."[48]

Despite the inroads on eastern football's offensive thinking, there was still evidence that many of the region's college coaches held a skeptical opinion of the forward pass. In his 1922 book, *Football and How to Watch It*, Percy Haughton acknowledged that "the pass added a substantial measure of offensive variety to the old single idea of power superiority." But the prominent eastern coach then went on to add that, in his opinion, on average just one of four pass attempts could be completed for a gain of only 10 yards, while one of those four passes would also be intercepted by the defense, certainly not favorable statistically for any team. Coach Daly of Army added, "Given a strong defense, the chances are two to one against the success of the forward pass." And Camp was never really going to drop his battle against the aerial game, noting in his review of the 1922 season that two prominent coaches had told him that their defenses could intercept three or four of every dozen passes thrown against them and then return them for more total yardage than the completed attempts would produce. Camp stated: "If these assertions are true . . . the enormous growth of forward passing may find its own limitations in the danger attending it."[49]

As the football seasons of 1923–1926 unfolded, it appeared that the conservatism of many of the eastern coaches would be swept away by the rush to capitalize on the excitement provided by the forward pass. Sports pages around the country were increasingly reflecting the fact that more passes per game were being attempted, while a growing number of games were being decided by an effective and well-balanced use of the aerial attack. Yet coaches had finally started to develop effective defensive strategies to counter the passing game, and no longer was it possible to just drop straight back and throw the ball well down the field and hope for the best. Defenses were also being devised with the flexibility to respond to either the run or the pass, instead of attempting to outguess the offense, and so coaches were being required to devise pass plays that incorporated as much deception as possible into the backfield's ballhandling and the pass routes of the potential receivers.[50]

Princeton's aerial attack was still the most aggressive of the Big Three teams during this period, and the Tigers were willing to use passes with some regularity against their ancient rivals. In 1925 Princeton received considerable attention in eastern football circles after completing twelve of twenty-five passes for 162 yards in a crushing win over Harvard. Meanwhile, the Harvard offense was coming under considerable criticism for its conservatism, especially after Holy Cross passed its way to a stunning upset of the Crimson in 1926. Evidence that a wide-open passing attack still held wonder for some eastern sportswriters can be found in Robert Kelley's naive-sounding remarks concerning this game: "Toward the close the Harvard backs were running in circles chasing a football that had become a sort of flying phantom."[51]

Navy was one eastern team that consistently used the passing game, but none of its outings drew as much attention as the matchup against Washington in the 1924 Rose Bowl game. In an exciting affair that ended in a 14-14 tie, Navy completed sixteen of twenty pass attempts for 175 yards, which included connecting on its first fourteen passes. One of the most advanced eastern passing attacks developed during this period belonged to Dartmouth, under the direction of Coach Jesse Hawley. The Dartmouth aerial attack reached its peak on the arm of Swede Oberlander in 1925, stampeding to an 8-0-0 record with possibly the top passing game in the country. Late in the season Dartmouth crushed a good Cornell team, as Oberlander passed for 161 yards in the first half alone, prompting writer Grantland Rice to note afterward that "this Dartmouth attack took its place among the greatest in football history." The following weekend Hawley took his charges west, and Dartmouth used four touchdown passes to knock off

Chicago, inspiring Allison Danzig of the *New York Times* to describe Hawley's offense as "the most dazzling forward passing attack that probably was ever projected on a football field."[52]

During this period teams in the Big Ten continued to be among the leading advocates of the aerial attack, as in 1923 when teams such as Iowa, Purdue, and Minnesota occasionally attempted twenty or more passes a game. On its way to the Big Ten championship that season, Illinois pulled out a key win over Iowa when Red Grange made four pass receptions for a total of 79 yards on the winning touchdown drive. But previous Big Ten passing attacks faded into the background with the arrival of Benny Friedman at Michigan in 1924, as he hooked up with All-America end Bennie Oosterbann to fill the air with passes through the 1925 and 1926 seasons—highlighted by Friedman's five scoring passes against Indiana in 1925.[53]

The Big Ten was not the only midwestern venue where an aggressive use of the forward pass could be found in the period 1923–1926. As usual, Notre Dame had a good aerial attack, and Rockne's great Four Horsemen team of 1924 made masterful use of the open game—demonstrated while connecting on fifteen of nineteen pass attempts, including twelve straight completions, in a win over Carnegie Tech. Just as Rockne's former players among the coaching ranks were installing his shift formations, so too had they adopted the use of the forward pass in their offenses. Edward "Slip" Madigan's St. Mary's teams on the West Coast and Loyola in Chicago were just two examples of Rockne's influence, one writer describing the latter's offense after a typical game: "Loyola displayed one of the cleverest forward passing attacks that has been seen in St. Louis in years."[54]

The Missouri Valley Conference included some teams that had always been willing to go to the aerial game, and the University of Missouri was generally the conference's leading advocate of the forward pass in the mid-1920s. Examples of Missouri's willingness to take to the air fifteen to twenty times a game can be found from 1920 onward, but it was with the arrival of Coach Gwinn Henry in 1923 that the Tigers really developed the passing game as an integral part of their offense. Missouri was willing to use the forward pass in the most important of its games—an example being the seventeen attempts that produced 112 yards in the 1924 showdown against Nebraska—as the Tigers won the Missouri Valley Conference championship in 1924 and 1925. Missouri was considered one of the top passing teams of 1926, and with the combination of Abe Stuber and Bert Clark leading the way, the Tigers averaged 116 passing yards per game across their five key outings that season, including sixteen of twenty-two for 204 yards against Oklahoma.[55]

In the Deep South there were plenty of teams that turned to the forward pass as a key part of the offense, and 1925 appears to have been the big breakthrough season for the passing game among southern teams. Georgia, Florida, Auburn, and Georgia Tech all demonstrated a willingness to regularly throw the football, often logging fifteen to twenty aerials a game. Vanderbilt also had a budding passing attack that would finally burst forth in the 1927 season on the arm of Bill Spears.[56]

Myth of the Southwest Aerial Circus

The southwestern region produced some of the leading passing teams of the decade, yet, unfortunately, an enduring legacy of the now disbanded Southwest Conference (SWC) results from its role in one of the mythologies concerning the national popularization of the forward-passing attack. Revisionist efforts by south-west-region sportswriters have given widespread circulation to the claim that Southern Methodist University (SMU) teams—coached by Ray Morrison—taught not only the rest of the southwest region but also the rest of the country the advantages of the passing game throughout the 1920s.

The earliest origins of the Southern Methodist "aerial circus" date to 1923 when Morrison guided the Mustangs, and his so-called Immortal Ten of SWC lore, to an impressive 9-0-0 record. SMU that season did not possess much physical size, which contributed significantly to Morrison's installation of a more wide-open style of offense under the direction of his tailback, Logan Stollenwerck. One writer has advanced the proposition that instead of "juggernauting in the muck of the line," SMU "getting offensively wild was to beat the heat and humidity" that has always plagued the region's football seasons. Interestingly, a review of the region's 1923 season that was written by a Dallas sportswriter for the annual *Football Guide* most likely provides a true description of SMU's offensive strategy: "smash a line, circle ends, execute the forward pass successfully"—in other words, nothing out of the ordinary for any open-attack team by 1923.[57]

By 1924 the popularity of the aerial game could certainly be seen everywhere in the country, and after the season Camp wrote that "teams have turned to a greater use of the forward pass as a real attacking weapon." As early as 1914 Oklahoma teams had been using the forward pass with great success, and in the Southwest in 1924 there were ample sports-section headlines that trumpeted the success of the aerial game around the conference—teams such as Arkansas, Texas Christian, and Texas showing a growing willingness to consistently use the forward pass in their offenses. Demonstrating a bent toward conservatism when faced with an important game, SMU attempted just thirteen passes for a total of 30 yards in its show-down with eventual conference champion Baylor in 1924 on a day that featured perfect weather conditions. That same season Sewanee College journeyed from Tennessee and used its passing attack to push Texas A&M to the limit before dropping a 7-0 decision. Interestingly, considering that SMU was said to be already using its "aerial circus" offense, William Ruggles of the *Dallas Morning News* wrote that "Sewanee dazzled the Texas spectators with an aerial attack never equaled in point of consistency of use on a Southwestern gridiron."[58]

From 1925 through 1927 the SWC featured a running battle between SMU and Texas A&M for the conference title. Each team was led through these three seasons by a brilliant all-around tailback, Gerry Mann for SMU and Joel Hunt for the Aggies. Mann was considered the better forward passer, whereas Hunt, also a good passer, was the superior all-around player. Texas A&M won the conference championship in 1925 and 1927, and SMU did not display a particularly dazzling passing attack or offense in 1925, despite the presence of Mann. In fact, the Mustangs were shut out in four consecutive games during that season.

But in 1926 SMU put together an excellent season that included considerable success with the forward pass as part of a balanced offense that favored the running attack, a fact proved by the statistics developed by sport historian James Mark Purcell. In writing of the SMU offense, Purcell noted, "What is striking about Gerry Mann and SMU in 1926 is not the total number of yards they made, but how they did it; their integration of the pass with the run." That season SMU made a trip north to take on Missouri and its vaunted passing attack, and in a relatively wide-open offensive show the rival passing attacks played to a virtual statistical standoff in the 7-7 tie. Later, in the major showdown of the 1926 SWC season, Hunt and Texas A&M outpassed SMU by a wide margin.[59]

The Southwest Conference season of 1926 again was highlighted by the passing attacks of a number of the other teams. After Texas handed Texas A&M a surprising 14-5 defeat, one headline declared: "Longhorns Use Aerial Attack to Win Battle," while Baylor was also consistently noted for its use of the forward pass. The growing attention to the forward pass continued into 1927, highlighted by the march to the SWC title by Texas A&M. Hunt again passed well all season for the Aggies, and after the game against Texas, Milt Saul of the *Dallas Morning News* reported that "so many passes were hurled it seemed more like a glorified game of basketball than anything." But on a national scale, the 1927 season was more noted for the passing accomplishments of Spears and his Vanderbilt teammates, as they *averaged* 148 passing yards per game.[60]

It is clear from the above review that teams of the Southwest Conference—and not just Southern Methodist—were certainly exploring the full use of the forward pass during this period, but comparable evidence is also found among the midwestern and southern teams for at least the same level of the aerial game. The origins of the claims that Southern Methodist taught the nation's teams the value of the passing attack stems from the 1928 season when the Mustangs traveled to West Point for a game against Army. There SMU attempted thirty passes, completing sixteen, while giving up three interceptions on the way to a 14-13 loss to the

Cadets. Danzig of the *New York Times* wrote that the game was "one of the biggest extravaganzas of forward passing . . . ever put on" and featured "bewildering and spectacular aerial pyrotechnics."[61]

This 1928 game against Army represented a more than usual number of passing attempts for SMU, based on the available statistics. Most eastern sportswriters—usually subjected to the conservative approach to passing in their region—rarely traveled to games in other sections of the country. Such intersectional exposure would have allowed them to realize that a substantial number of the major teams in other regions were fully using the forward pass, and that this contest was not a normal game for SMU. Eastern writers apparently did not read newspaper game accounts from other regions of the country or even notice many major games in their own region, because they should have known that the forward pass was already being widely used. In mid-November 1928, Missouri brought its outstanding aerial attack to New York City, and, before many of the same writers, the Tigers completed fourteen of twenty-seven passes for 153 yards in a romp over New York University. Besides which, Fordham University, located in New York City and playing major college football, *averaged* nineteen pass attempts and 107 aerial yards per game that season.[62]

The erroneous claims concerning the extent of SMU's influence on the use of the forward pass nationally, which today are still given wide circulation, were fueled by the later comments of several writers. In the 1948 book *Sport's Golden Age,* speaking of SMU's 1928 game against Army, Weldon Hart, an Austin, Texas, sportswriter, quoted an Associated Press statement: "Passes such as Eastern football never saw before flew from the hand of Redman Hume [an SMU player], a Texas version of what Red Grange should have been." After writing that "the elite East and the hard-bitten North hadn't paid much mind to Southwest football" prior to the 1928 game, Hart added that Ray Morrison was "the first coach in the Southwest, and one of the first in the land to use the forward pass as a basic weapon of attack."[63] Hart clearly had no awareness of football history even by 1948.

Adding to the regionally generated confusion, Kern Tips, a Texas sportscaster, in his book *Football—Texas Style* wrote that "Morrison's tactical concept of the forward pass . . . developed into a sectional kind of hurly-burly. . . . This dipsy doodle sent teams from other sections of the country back to the drawing boards." The most inexcusable and confusing endorsement of all comes from Allison Danzig, the prominent *New York Times* writer, who from the safety of 1956 certainly should have been better informed. In his *History of American Football,* Danzig stated: "It was Morrison who made the Southwest pass conscious as it never has been before and thereby sold the rest of the country on the pass." One page later we find Danzig discussing the serious passing attacks being used at Michigan, Dartmouth, and Alabama by 1925, including this statement by Michigan's Benny Friedman: "We brought the forward pass in 1925 to a point that hadn't been developed up to that time."[64] Apparently, Danzig must have believed that the coaches at these schools developed extremely effective passing attacks almost overnight.

Although it can certainly be said that the Southwest Conference of the 1920s ranked as one of the top three regions in the development of the aerial game, there is ample evidence from 1906 onward to refute any claims that Morrison's SMU teams first made everyone aware of how to use the forward pass or were solely responsible for its popularity around the country.

The Opposition Returns

Forward passing's widespread acceptance as part of a balanced, open-style collegiate offense was the topic of numerous articles throughout the 1920s, such as a 1924 piece in *Literary Digest* that noted, "The game has been a beautifully open one of clean, hard-running, hard-tackling sport." Herbert Reed of *Outlook* concurred: "Modern football has reached new heights of open play. . . . The demands of the huge crowds . . . were met by spectacular passing and by wide running." And that same year William Abbott commented, "Football strategy is turning more to the aerial attack. . . . Never before has forward passing been so extensively used."[65]

Yet not everyone was enthralled with the increased role of the forward pass in football's offensive theory, and by 1921 there had already been hints that the opposition was returning. An article in *Literary Digest* warned: "To such an extent has the forward pass featured some of the season's games that experts are beginning to suggest that this form of play be curbed to prevent development of present-day football into a game more nearly resembling a combination of baseball and basketball." By late 1924 a small group of eastern coaches was characterizing the forward pass as an "evil," and with the annual Rules Committee meeting approaching in December 1924, the idea was being advanced that some form of restrictions on forward passing—such as awarding only three points for a touchdown pass, penalties for incomplete pass attempts, limiting the number of attempts allowed, or eliminating running with the ball after the catch was made—was needed to maintain a balance between offensive and defensive play.[66]

Sportswriter W. V. Morgenstern of the *Chicago Herald and Examiner* counterattacked by attributing the calls for restrictions on the pass to its generally limited use in the East: "Down East the forward pass is not a regular weapon of offense; rather it is something to be used in desperation, and usually without a great amount of skill . . . and the coaches of that section tacitly admit the fact by clamoring for revision of the rules." Finally, two of the game's most influential coaches, Rockne and Zuppke, came out in opposition to "tinkering" with the forward pass—Rockne declaring that "he was opposed to any rule that would hinder the open game and that he believed a rule against the forward pass would be the first step toward killing football"—and ultimately nothing came of the revision attempts in 1924.[67]

By early 1926 the proponents of a more conservative offensive game were back again in force, and at the Rules Committee meeting they succeeded in adopting a rule revision that imposed a penalty of 5 yards for each incomplete pass after the first during the same series of downs. According to E. K. Hall, chairman of the committee, this revision was "intended to discourage and minimize the indiscriminate heaving of forward passes which marred the fourth quarter of so many games." Hall recognized that "it is to the forward pass that we are indebted in a very substantial degree for the greatly increased and widely diversified strategy of the modern game," yet he was also aware that from some critics, "the argument is made that the pass is not football, that it is a feature of basketball . . . and that it has become too much of a ground-gaining play." Sportswriter W. O. McGeehan represented the typical eastern view, which held that "the forward pass is a gamble, but a gamble for which there has been no penalty."[68]

Stagg, a member of the committee, did not see the new rule making any significant change in how often teams would use the forward pass, and in fact he believed that the perfection of pass plays and the development of players' technical skills would be encouraged. Bill Alexander, Georgia Tech's coach, agreed with Stagg and wrote that he was "of the opinion that the rule would not make any radical change in the way forward passes are used or in the number used." Fielding Yost of Michigan felt otherwise, believing that since the forward pass had been legalized in 1906, "it was used too little and not too much . . . [and that] beyond any question the penalty will restrain the use of the forward pass to some extent and will not encourage its use." At separate meetings of the Big Ten coaches and the Eastern Association of Football Officials after one season of using the new rule, most of the attendees were convinced that it had failed to reduce the number of indiscriminate passes and, as several coaches pointed out, "made no great difference in the general playing of teams." Soon there would be an unsuccessful movement to increase the harshness of the rule's penalty, since the 5-yard provision was not producing the desired result. Eventually, most coaches nationally came to oppose the rule, and in 1934 the Rules Committee would finally revoke the 5-yard-penalty provision.[69]

During the final seasons of the decade the number of teams using the forward pass as a consistent part of the offense continued to grow. The Big Ten continued to feature many of the country's leading passing teams, including Michigan, Ohio State, and Illinois. In the East, Bill Roper of Princeton had become a leading supporter of the passing game, even stating, "I have always believed the pass was a safe play." And in 1929, Harvard stunned everyone by completing fifteen of twenty-six pass attempts for 172 yards in a thrilling struggle with Michigan. Yet many in the East were still just coming to realize the potential of the aerial game, as can be seen in a December 1928 article by Herbert Reed. While discussing Roper's passing theory, Reed wrote that it "seemed to be that the passes were there to be mixed in as much as possible—literally built into the attack—which all modern coaches worth their salt henceforth will proceed to do."[70]

With the close of the 1920s, the forward pass was firmly entrenched within the legitimate offensive philosophies of college football. The aerial game had been an integral part of college football's great success and growth during the 1920s, as it appealed to and stimulated a ticket-buying public that had the expectations of an era of American society that was typified by ongoing excitement. One writer noted that the passing game "produces action, and that is what is wanted. . . . [T]he game is now the property of the masses—the masses who seek thrills and individual feats of prowess."[71]

By the end of the era the progressive coaching minds of the game had convincingly succeeded in overcoming the old-school offensive beliefs of eastern football and its efforts to curb the use of the forward pass in particular. Significantly, the effective blending of open-style running plays with an aggressive use of the forward pass had served to transform college football into an offensively oriented game that was radically different from the defensive-minded philosophies that had dominated the sport in prewar days. By 1930 the forward passing game had matured into a form that would be recognized by any late-century follower of college football, while the potential had also been demonstrated and the groundwork established for an even more aggressive style of aerial game. The 1920s had defined the pathway toward the use of the forward pass in a manner that would eventually come to again transform offensive football by the end of the century.

6

SEARCHING FOR THE
NOTRE DAME EXPERIENCE

In an era notable for its many legacies within the sport of intercollegiate football, one of the most significant developments of the period is today virtually forgotten. In a time when the sports pages of the nation's newspapers regularly trumpeted the exploits of the latest gridiron heroes, while the athletic departments of the large public universities were seemingly minting money at the ticket windows, there existed another segment of American colleges that sought some of the same adulation and riches—the Catholic schools.

Spurred on by the growing prestige and popularity garnered by the football program of one of their own (Notre Dame) in the years immediately prior to America's involvement in World War I, many Catholic colleges and universities sought to emulate some degree of that success. Ready to pursue the expansion of their own gridiron programs when college football returned to normalcy in 1919, many Catholic schools were encouraged to pattern their football programs after the successful approaches employed by Knute Rockne and his Notre Dame squads.

For most Catholic schools, this quest involved becoming part of an unofficial Notre Dame "network" that included hiring substantial numbers of former Rockne players as coaches, adopting the same techniques of offensive play, and, in some instances, being prepared to join the Notre Dame football program in opposing public universities. Yet on the field of play, Rockne and his successors would always take care to maintain a separation between themselves and the other Catholic football programs, Notre Dame being unwilling to share its prestige as the college football team of the nation's Roman Catholics.

EARLY HISTORY

Although it is well known that Notre Dame was playing football schedules consisting almost exclusively of college opponents by the late 1890s, many other Catholic schools had also fielded their own gridiron squads prior to 1900. Only four Jesuit schools from the East (Boston College, Fordham, Georgetown, and Holy Cross) played primarily college opposition prior to 1900, and during the period 1902–1910 they would begin to substantially upgrade the quality of their schedules. Meanwhile, during the first decade of the new century their ranks were joined by football-playing parochial colleges such as Detroit, Marquette, St. Louis, and Villanova. On the Pacific Coast, St. Mary's and Santa Clara had fielded minor teams in the late 1890s, but both of the small Bay Area schools switched to rugby in 1909, St. Mary's returning to American football in 1915 and Santa Clara in 1919.[1]

St. Louis University fielded outstanding teams in 1906–1907 and achieved major victories over public universities such as Iowa, Kansas, and Nebraska, while Notre Dame began to attract attention after notching significant victories over Pittsburgh and Michigan in 1909. Notre Dame had played its first Catholic college opponent in 1897 (St. Viator), and then added Marquette to its schedule for the football seasons of 1908–1912. The Fighting Irish played a total of four Catholic opponents in 1911 and three in 1912, yet it all changed after Notre Dame's great upset win over Army in 1913.

Notre Dame's surprising win over Army was witnessed and reported on by a sportswriter from the *New York Times,* this coverage giving the Notre Dame football program more widespread recognition than any of its previous efforts, and the effects began to show up on its schedules in subsequent seasons.[2] Notre Dame's 1913 schedule had included Christian Brothers College, another parochial school, but no other Catholic schools appeared on its football schedules until Marquette reappeared in 1921. Instead, with Coach Jesse Harper moving to capitalize on the newfound publicity, Notre Dame schedules through 1917 began to include more upscale opponents such as Yale, Syracuse, Nebraska, Texas, Army, and Wisconsin.

Meanwhile, the other Catholic universities had not failed to notice the upgrading of Notre Dame's recognition factor, and so, before the war, many of these schools resolved to also pursue more aggressive gridiron programs. The eastern Jesuit universities, most notably Georgetown and Holy Cross, were among the leaders in this effort, but the movement toward a greater emphasis on football was widespread among the Catholic universities that had already taken up the sport. And there would be no escaping the fact that these other Catholic football teams, like the schools themselves, were perceived as symbols of Roman Catholicism, and therefore subject to many of the current attitudes of mainstream American culture.

FOOTBALL, RELIGION, AND THE PUBLIC

By the 1920s, Roman Catholics represented a sizable minority within the American landscape, constituting approximately 16 percent of the total U.S. population by 1926. American Catholics were considered different from the so-called host culture; they were members of "a culture within a culture," and therefore the target of various suspicions and attitudes that would be publicly manifested throughout the decade—most notably by the Ku Klux Klan and by what historian Charles Morris has described as an "outpouring of anti-Catholic hysteria that met Al Smith's nomination" for president by the Democratic Party in 1928. The rank-and-file Catholic population looked to the organized church in the United States for the spiritual reinforcement, moral guidance, and bonding influence that would provide a sense of belonging. Yet it was essential that Catholics be assimilated into the mainstream secular culture if they were to achieve the positions of prominence and influence that were important for escaping their minority image.[3]

Historian Gerald Gems has noted the "concerted efforts" of church officials toward these assimilation efforts during the 1920s and has written that sporting practices in the decades following the war provided critical assistance in resolving issues concerning Catholic assimilation. The Catholic population of the 1920s comprised many ethnic factions, described by historian Mark Massa as "representing a dynamic, flexible social mechanism," and football proved to be a significant vehicle for combining these Catholic ethnic factions into a unified stance, creating a shared pride in the accomplishments of "their" football teams. Catholic universities provided not only the higher education needed for a place within the professional workforce but also the organized sporting activities (primarily football) that could place individuals in the public spotlight.[4]

There was a widespread sentiment among the Catholic schools that intercollegiate football was a positive force for higher education. Typical was the sentiment echoed by T. Semmes Walmsley of the athletic council at Loyola of New Orleans in 1922, when he noted that "by introducing athletics . . . we are doing something for the young man who goes to school. We are likewise building up, not tearing down. Athletics are essential to the success of every university." In 1925 the president of Marquette University, Father Albert C. Fox, S.J., commented, "Sport is an integral branch of the university and we want our indulgence in sport to be signal, to stand out, just as we are not satisfied with mediocrity in any branch of our work here." And in 1929, Father Charles H. Cloud, S.J., president of St. Louis University, noted that "the highest type of student body was developed through participation in athletics."[5]

Emphasizing the importance of football to many Catholic colleges, Brother Gregory, the president of St. Mary's, told a reporter in 1920 that he was "frank to admit that the college or university that does not appear on the sporting pages of the newspapers is out of the running. The boy coming to college selects his school largely because of its athletic prowess." In 1922, the presidents of St. Mary's and Santa Clara noted that "today a school is judged by its 'team,' rather than by its faculty and its power. . . . We are compelled, therefore, to combat these evil times by meeting the situation squarely and advertising our institutions by sports . . . as a means, the only one which will enable us to exist at all in efficient competition with the large non-sectarian institutions."[6] The idea that highly visible athletics could make a college's fortune was particularly relevant to the many Catholic institutions that were interested in building their enrollments and physical facilities to even modest proportions in the 1920s.

The Church also regarded the Catholic universities as a component in spreading the messages of morality and decency within American society. The "Catholic spirit" of upper education was described by an editorial in the St. Louis University student newspaper as "a spirit that is essentially Catholic in tone and Catholic in its ideals, its aspirations and its practical manifestations. . . . It must be rooted in and spring naturally from a group of men devoted to . . . becoming not merely educated men but genuine Catholic gentlemen." Many of the parochial colleges took steps toward building a long-term relationship with the surrounding Roman Catholic communities, as in 1922 when Santa Clara and St. Mary's enlisted the help of the local parishes in the San Francisco Bay area. The presidents of the two colleges joined in sending a letter to every pastor in the diocese, asking for their support in promoting the two schools and Catholic education among their parish communities. The letter closed by asking the priests to also mention the approaching St. Mary's–Santa Clara football game—being played "as a means of showing a none too friendly world that Catholics are ready and willing to support even football games for the greater honor and glory."[7]

This concept of high morality manifested itself in a belief among the general Catholic public that the football programs of their parochial universities were operated on a basis of purity and integrity. Historian Murray Sperber has described Notre Dame football of the 1920s as representing a "triumph of Catholicism" in the United States for many, but one that brought with it pressures to rise above cheating either on or off the field.[8] These same beliefs in athletic integrity were applied to Catholic universities everywhere, yet events at Notre Dame and some of the other schools during the decade would give lie to these ideals.

Outwardly, there was usually every sign of mutual respect between the Catholic football programs and the general public, and the Catholic schools always sought ways to establish close ties with their urban neighbors as part of their mission as ambassadors for the Church. The Catholic universities were often a source of pride for the general community, as in 1915 when an article in the *Boston Saturday Evening Transcript* referred to Boston College as "Chestnut Hill's Touch of Oxford . . . [and] one of the sights of Boston."[9] This comment and the overall tone of the article, coming from a publication generally considered to be the official voice of Yankee Boston, attracted a considerable amount of favorable attention to the Catholic university that had first opened its doors in 1864 on Boston's South

End. Many of the Catholic universities located in large metropolitan areas had been leasing professionally owned arenas for their games since relatively early in their football histories. Although the leasing of public stadia was motivated by the intention of maximizing the school's financial benefits from football, there was also an underlying goal of generating a fan base among the general public of the locale surrounding the college.

Disappointingly, these off-campus games usually drew smaller-than-antici-pated crowds with the exception of matchups against a major rival, such as the Boston College–Holy Cross games of 1920–1925, which all drew in excess of forty thousand fans to Boston's Braves Field, or Fordham's games against New York University, which usually drew decent crowds to Yankee Stadium throughout the decade.[10] All too often the gate receipts generated were insufficient to cover the rental requirements, and many of the Catholic universities faced a losing proposi-tion in the leasing of professional stadia. By 1921 Georgetown and Detroit were proceeding with plans for the construction of on-campus football stadia, and other Catholic universities would do the same as the decade progressed.[11]

After the opening of their new on-campus stadia, most Catholic universi-ties continued to seek and encourage a close relationship with the public and in particular the ethnic groups that composed a sizable percentage of the Catholic population of the surrounding areas. One example is seen in a 1926 *Marquette Tri-bune* article that declared, "Marquette's athletic events are Milwaukee's, and if big games are to be brought to Milwaukee, not only Marquette but Milwaukee must support them. And support must come from the Milwaukee newspapers." Oc-casionally, the schools would lend their stadia out for public functions, such as Marquette's stadium being used for Milwaukee's Archdiocese Jubilee celebration in 1925 or Detroit's field being used in 1926 to stage a gigantic pageant in celebra-tion of the anniversary of the 1776 American Revolution.[12] Generally, the Catholic universities took every opportunity to emphasize the bond between the schools and the cities surrounding them.

Yet there definitely existed hostile feelings toward some of the Catholic univer-sities during the 1920s. The University of Detroit had started moving its campus from the original downtown location to farmland west of the city by the mid-1920s, and in 1923 the school's new football stadium was the first structure on the campus with the exception of a chapel, which had been set up in an old farmhouse on the property. The Ku Klux Klan—very active in Michigan—harassed Father John McNichols, the school's president, throughout much of the decade. The more serious challenges came during the summer of 1925 when the Klansmen paraded out to the small campus every Saturday night and then set fire to a cross along the passing road, being prevented from burning down the buildings and the stadium only by the presence of McNichols and armed deputies every weekend.[13]

Notre Dame was another of the Catholic schools that attracted a good deal of apparently religious-motivated animosity, much of it no doubt generated by the success of its football teams after 1913. Gerald Gems has described this period in the aftermath of Notre Dame's win over Army as typifying a "sense of Catholic separation and anti-Catholic sentiments [that] reached national proportions with the success of the . . . Notre Dame football team." In 1914 Notre Dame sought to use the University of Chicago's Stagg Field in order to boost the gate receipts from a game against the still-exotic Carlisle Indians, but the request was refused by the Chicago trustees. The trustees' statement indicated that they did not consider it desirable to have their athletic facilities used for "games of this sort," an action that many interpreted as reflecting a hostile attitude toward the Catholic university. During the 1920s Rockne frequently complained of a perceived anti-Catholic bias against his school with respect to issues such as recruiting and his beloved shift formation. One event that seemed to clearly reflect an anti–Notre Dame bias came in 1930, when Northwestern and Notre Dame, two of the nation's best football teams, sought to capitalize on a great demand for tickets to their game by requesting permission of the Big Ten to move the game to the much larger Soldier Field in Chicago—even offering to donate the extra gate receipts (estimated at one hundred thousand dollars) to the relief funds for the poor. Yet the Big Ten faculty representatives denied the request on the basis of a rule that prohibited the transfer of games within one hundred miles of another conference school—in this case the University of Chicago—despite the fact that Chicago's team would be playing at Michigan that day.[14]

Equally as disconcerting for Notre Dame officials, and many of the other Catholic universities, were the physical threats, attempts at intimidation, and taunting often directed toward the Indiana school and its football team. In the early 1920s the Ku Klux Klan regularly sought ways to harass the small Catholic university, and in the spring of 1924 the Klan held a major gathering in South Bend amid considerable tensions and threatened hostilities. Fortunately, bad weather forced a cancellation of many of the Klan's outdoor events. More politically threatening to Notre Dame was the election in 1924 of a Klan sympathizer, Edward Jackson, as governor of Indiana and his subsequent continuous support of anti-Catholic legislation.

Notre Dame and Nebraska had launched a very competitive and profitable football series in 1915, yet as the hotly contested series continued, the attitudes of the fans attending the games in Lincoln, Nebraska, began to gradually evolve into outright hostility toward the Catholic football team. Despite Rockne's attempts to downplay this anti-Catholic attitude because he valued the nice paydays for his football team, by 1925 the insults from fans, students, and the local newspapers in Lincoln had reached an intensity that the Notre Dame administration could no longer ignore. After the 1925 game was marked by the fans chanting an ongoing variety of anti-Catholic insults, along with a halftime show by Nebraska's student pep organization that the Notre Dame party found to be in very questionable taste, the Catholic school's athletic board decided to terminate the annual series. In 1928 Rockne attempted to resurrect the series with Nebraska, only to have Notre Dame officials reject the idea of again playing in such an anti-Catholic area.[15]

The scheduling of football games reflected a more subtle form of hostility toward the Catholic universities, as it became increasingly difficult to find a place on the annual slates of major nonparochial schools in their regions—particularly if the Catholic school was fielding good teams. Two of the more significant games in college football history were Boston College's wins over Yale in 1919 and 1920, but thereafter the Catholic school could never find a place on the gridiron schedules of the prestigious Big Three. In 1923 an editorial in the Boston College newspaper expressed the school's frustration over the situation, but noted that someday "athletic Boston College will force recognition from those who today, timorous of their unsustained reputations, fear honest defeat." Other examples of scheduling difficulties can be found in the University of Wisconsin's avoidance of Marquette football teams from 1920 through 1931, despite numerous attempts by the Catholic school to schedule a game, while St. Louis was dropped from the schedules of the University of Missouri from 1924 until 1930. In late 1926, Marquette athletic officials actually traveled to the Big Ten meetings in Chicago in an attempt to personally meet with Wisconsin officials concerning a proposed football date for 1927, but they were once again refused.[16]

Another variation of anti-Catholic sentiment in athletic relations can be found in early 1930, in the aftermath of the slush fund scandal at the University of Iowa. Commissioner John Griffith of the Big Ten was accused of suggesting that pro-Catholic sentiments among some Iowa alumni had motivated their desire to see Gus Dorais (a former Notre Damer) hired as the school's new football coach. Griffith, though not denying that he had written to a university official on the possible hiring of Dorais, quickly attempted to separate himself from the controversy, as he wrote to Iowa's faculty representative, "I have never felt that a man's religion should be scrutinized relative to the selection of coaches or the makeup of university teams."[17]

Although that statement may have served in general as the public posture toward Catholic universities and their football teams during the 1920s, the underlying truth is that there was a significant correlation between Catholic-university football teams and organized Roman Catholicism in the United States in the minds of many on both sides. This association gave rise to Roman Catholics feeling a "presence" or a "coming of age" within American society through the success of Catholic football teams, whereas for many in the public sector it was a stimulation for attitudes of resentment and hostility toward a subculture that would not be totally accepted until well beyond the 1920s.[18]

THE JESUIT CONFERENCE

Catholic universities did not band together into any formally organized, competitive athletic conference, although many of the schools went to great lengths to ensure that they were conforming to athletic regulations similar to the rules followed by surrounding major public universities. They did so to eliminate a potential roadblock to being given a place on the secular universities' schedules, but also to avoid being labeled as "outlaw" schools—a charge that often plagued Notre Dame.

In the 1920s the four prominent eastern Jesuit schools (Boston College, Fordham, Georgetown, and Holy Cross) did band together into an unofficial organization that was called "the Jesuit Conference." This arrangement was intended to keep the four universities operating under the same athletic regulations, deemed essential because of the amount of competition among the four schools in various sports, yet also significant as an example to the smaller Jesuit universities that sought to operate acceptable athletic programs. The graduate managers and faculty directors for athletics from the four schools held annual meetings, during which they reviewed items such as specific eligibility issues, their dealings with secular athletic administrations (particularly the Big Three of the East), and any new regulations being considered by the major athletic conferences.[19]

Although the sole intent of the Jesuit Conference was to facilitate consistent athletic administration, the students and the news media instead predictably focused on the sporting competition among the four universities, tallying conference standings and selecting all-Jesuit teams. Since 1913, when Boston College had joined Fordham and Holy Cross in playing at least two of its Jesuit archrivals each football season, there had been talk each autumn about the so-called Catholic champion of the East, and maintaining unofficial conference standings intensified the debate over the mythical Catholic champion. Whenever the four Jesuit teams were matched up in a pair of games on the same Saturday, New York newspapers frequently ran the stories of the two games side by side and highlighted their importance to the eastern Catholic title race. Giving further appearance of a formal football grouping was the selection by some of the student newspapers of all–Jesuit Conference teams throughout the decade, which usually received wide publication in the East.[20]

The growing attention to the football rivalries among the four Jesuit schools solidified the importance of their games on the respective campuses, as noted by a Fordham newspaper article: "The rivalry that exists between these Jesuit colleges is intense and the coaches of the respective teams regard the games with the other Jesuit colleges as the main objective of every football campaign." An article in the Boston College student newspaper declared that "success in any branch of athletics at Boston College is measured by the showing made against . . . Holy Cross. . . . When success crowns our efforts after an epic struggle with Holy Cross all else is blotted out." Yet by the early 1920s intercollegiate football was a business venture for the Catholic universities also, and in 1923 when Georgetown and Boston College became involved in a dispute over the visiting-team guarantees each was offering the other, the football series between the two was dropped for three seasons.[21]

In the immediate aftermath of the October 1929 release of the Carnegie Report, there was a significant cutback by the student newspapers in publicizing the mythical Jesuit Conference, yet the intensities of the football rivalries among the eastern Jesuit universities continued. The Jesuit Conference played a valuable role in publicizing top-flight Catholic-university football during the 1920s, but, more important, it also served as a model for athletic administrative policies for any Catholic universities that sought to build athletic relationships with other parochial schools and the secular universities in their regions.[22]

JESUIT FOOTBALL IN THE MIDWEST

The growing football popularity being garnered by the eastern Jesuit universities and Notre Dame at the start of the 1920s served to encourage the athletic efforts of many other Catholic schools around the country—most of them Jesuit institutions. Among the more aggressive in building their football programs were schools such as Marquette, Detroit, and St. Louis.

Marquette, a Jesuit school located in downtown Milwaukee, fielded its first football team in 1892, although the annual gridiron schedules were not considered to be primarily on an intercollegiate level until 1902. After Frank Murray was promoted to the head coach position in 1922, the Marquette football program began to grow quickly, the Milwaukee team going undefeated in 1923 with wins over Catholic rivals Boston College and Detroit. For years Marquette teams had played their home games on a field near the original campus, but in 1924 a new stadium was dedicated on Milwaukee's West Side. The stadium began to pay immediate dividends, as beginning with the 1925 season Marquette was able to attract to Milwaukee such teams as Kansas A&M, Oklahoma A&M, Oregon State, Kansas, and Holy Cross. Meanwhile, Marquette's schedules had also been upgraded with away games at schools such as Auburn, Army, and Navy.[23]

Marquette had long sought dates with the prestigious Catholic football program from Holy Cross, and finally, for the 1927 season, the Crusaders agreed to travel to Milwaukee. As the date of the game approached, the Marquette student newspaper described the event as "the most important game on the year's sched-ule, and one of the most important in the history of Marquette . . . and it marks the beginning of a new era in Marquette athletics."[24] That season Marquette would also meet the prestigious and powerful Army football team, yet the Holy Cross date carried far greater athletic and political significance for the Milwaukee school, as Marquette sought to establish an ongoing football rivalry with the eastern Jesuit school as a vehicle for joining Catholic football's inner circle of prominence.

Marquette fielded several excellent football teams during the latter part of the 1920s, its student newspaper noting in 1928 that "from a mere spec [sic] upon the American gridiron horizon, Marquette has advanced steadily . . . until to-day she stands as a recognized power." Marquette and Holy Cross did play a three-game series (1927–1929), and the Milwaukee school resumed its series with Boston College in 1929. Yet although every season would feature some Catho-lic opponents, Marquette increasingly upgraded its schedules through the 1930s with rugged secular university teams, and the school was regarded as having one of the country's outstanding Catholic football programs until World War II.[25]

The University of Detroit, another Jesuit school, fielded its first football team in 1896, although its gridiron schedules were predominantly of a small college nature until the end of World War I. By 1920 school officials had begun upgrading their football program under the direction of Coach James Duffy, and Detroit's schedules began to include other Catholic schools such as Marquette, St. Louis, Fordham, Holy Cross, Georgetown, and Duquesne. From 1920 onward, the Detroit football schedules also included an increasing number of major gridiron schools such as Army, Carnegie Tech, and West Virginia.[26]

Detroit alumni and school officials demonstrated the extent of their interest in the gridiron sport by building a football stadium on the new campus in 1922, even before classroom buildings were constructed. The school took a major step in 1925 when it managed to entice Charles "Gus" Dorais away from Gonzaga to take over as its new football coach and athletic director. The former Notre Dame star wasted no time installing Rockne's shift formation, and by 1927 the presence of Dorais produced the long-sought game with Rockne's Catholic powerhouse.

In 1927 Dorais, having managed to recruit some of Michigan's top high school stars, had the nucleus of one of Catholic-university football's greatest teams. That season the Titans made a big impression on eastern sportswriters with a win over Carnegie Tech in Pittsburgh, being compared favorably to the outstanding teams at Nebraska and Pitt. Everything came together in 1928 for Dorais, as Detroit, paced by two dazzling backfield men in Tom "Cowboy" Connell and Lloyd Brazil, stormed to a 9-0-0 record and strong consideration as the top team of the Midwest. The highlight of the season was a November trip to New York City where the Ti-tans thrashed Fordham, again before the influential eastern media, which assured

9. Lloyd Brazil of Detroit. One of the outstanding tailbacks of the 1920s, he was an All-America selection in 1928 and 1929. Courtesy of the University of Detroit Mercy Archives, Marine Historical Collection.

Brazil of receiving All-America recognition in the postseason. Dorais remained at Detroit until 1942, and although he consistently fielded competitive teams, the Titans would never quite equal their stature of the 1927–1929 period.[27]

St. Louis University was another Jesuit school that sought to join the ranks of the top Catholic football programs during the 1920s. St. Louis fielded its first football team in 1899, and in the 1906–1907 seasons its teams gained national attention, as Coach Eddie Cochems was one of the first to capitalize on the offensive capabilities of the newly legalized forward pass. The school played football schedules that included several major public university opponents each season from 1907 through 1913, before returning to primarily midlevel schools through the first years after World War I.[28]

As the 1920s dawned, St. Louis was giving every indication that it wished to upgrade its gridiron fortunes. After arranging for the use of the city's major league stadium, Sportsman's Park, for its home games and practices, school officials turned to an experienced coach named Steve O'Rourke to head up the football program in 1921. The school yearbook declared 1921 to be a turning point in St. Louis athletic history, bringing both a new coach and a commitment to upgrading the football schedules. Although Missouri was the only true major on the 1921 schedule inherited by O'Rourke, the 1922 slate included five major opponents—highlighted by the first of two games against Notre Dame. O'Rourke described Notre Dame as being six years ahead of any other midwestern team in terms of football strategy, but believed his Billikins would gain considerably from such an experience.[29]

By 1923 O'Rourke had become the school's athletic director, and the football team had a new coach in Daniel Savage, a successful St. Louis high school coach. The schedule had again been upgraded, highlighted by a visit from Notre Dame on Thanksgiving Day, but after posting two seasons of winning records St. Louis tumbled to a 2-6-1 mark in 1925, and Savage was dismissed. In 1926 the university lured Robert Mathews away from the University of Idaho to become both athletic director and football coach. Mathews, a former Notre Dame player, came in expecting to build a winner within three years but quickly learned that a lack of manpower and tough schedules were not going to be easily overcome. After just two seasons he resigned to go into private business.[30]

The answer for St. Louis in 1928 was to turn to another Notre Dame man—this time Hartley "Hunk" Anderson, who declared that in two years he would field winning football teams. But after struggling through two seasons against schedules that had been considerably downgraded, Anderson gave up after the 1929 campaign and went back to Notre Dame as an assistant coach. There was more stability after Anderson's departure, beginning with Charles "Chile" Walsh, another Notre Dame man, hired in 1930. Yet St. Louis settled into the lower middle class of college football after 1929, along with membership in the Missouri Valley Conference for a time, and the school never achieved its dreams of joining the elite of Catholic college football before the sport was discontinued in 1949.[31]

THE NOTRE DAME OF THE WEST

Of the many Catholic colleges that sought to share the football success realized by Notre Dame after World War I, there were really only two that approached anywhere near that level of national recognition: Fordham and St. Mary's of California. St. Mary's College, a tiny Christian Brothers institution founded in the San Francisco Bay area, fielded its first football team in 1894. But its early seasons were plagued by minimal numbers of games, and after embarrassing losses to California and Santa Clara in 1898, the sport was dropped until 1908 when the school began to field rugby teams through the 1914 season. When football was revived in 1915 at St. Mary's, the following seasons reflected a mixture of college, military, and club-team opposition until 1919.[32]

In 1920 the St. Mary's football team was under the direction of Coach Billy Hollander, a former Georgetown player, when the Saints were handed a 127-0 trouncing in the third game of the season by the great University of California team. Amid the embarrassment and alumni discontent, it came out that since the beginning of the season Hollander had been embroiled in a dispute with the school's athletic moderator, Brother Vantasian, over football styles of play. The result of all the turmoil in the aftermath of the Cal game was that the coach was fired and the

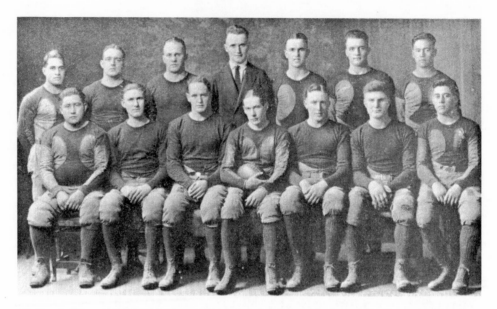

10. Coach Edward "Slip" Madigan of St. Mary's. Shown *(back row, fourth from left)* with one of his first teams at St. Mary's, he developed gridiron powerhouses that became known as the "Notre Dame of the West." Courtesy of the Archives Collection of St. Mary's College of California.

balance of the 1920 schedule canceled—player injuries being the official explanation. Yet believing that a successful football program could do much to help attract students to the struggling little Catholic college, the St. Mary's administration then searched for a former Notre Dame man to solve its gridiron problems. In early January 1921, the school announced the hiring of Edward "Slip" Madigan away from Columbia College in Portland, Oregon.[33]

Madigan, a former player under Rockne before the war, wasted no time in demonstrating his intentions of building a football powerhouse in emulation of his gridiron mentor in South Bend. When Madigan arrived at St. Mary's he was accompanied by two former collegiate players from Oregon, who were reported to be "crack" gridmen. When spring practice opened in April 1921, Madigan conducted all the drills in secret except for one day a week, stating that he had "concluded that privacy makes for a greater degree of efficiency in football." Actually, what he was doing was installing the Notre Dame Shift into the St. Mary's offense, and he intended to brook no interference from the administration or the alumni.[34]

To demonstrate further that a new football era was about to unfold, Madigan announced an eight-game schedule for 1921 that opened with matchups against California and Stanford and closed with a Christmas Day visit from no less than Notre Dame. Rockne would soon decide to cancel the game, but the obvious intention to upgrade the football program, along with the training-table

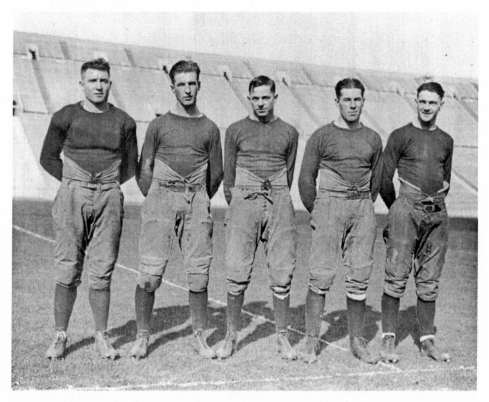

11. 1924 St. Mary's backfield, the outfit that produced a 14-10 upset of Southern California and launched the little Oakland school toward big-time college football. Norman "Red" Strader *(far left)* received All-America mention in 1924 and would later serve as a St. Mary's head coach. Courtesy of the Archives Collection of St. Mary's College of California.

arrangement that greeted the players in the fall, struck a responsive chord with the alumni. Three days before the 1921 opener, an enthusiastic throng of five hundred alumni joined Madigan at a San Francisco restaurant for a luncheon to kick off the new season.[35]

St. Mary's posted a 4-3-0 record in 1921, and Madigan continued to upgrade the football schedules throughout the decade, including a resumption of the annual game against nearby Catholic archrival Santa Clara. St. Mary's got its big break in 1924 when Stanford and Southern California canceled their matchup at the last minute in a controversy over the eligibility of certain players, and Madigan's Gaels were hastily recruited to face USC in the Los Angeles Coliseum. St. Mary's shocking 14-10 upset win over the Trojans catapulted Madigan's program along the path toward Catholic football's national elite, and the peak period of his reign at the little school came during the seasons of 1929–1932.

By the late 1920s St. Mary's football schedules each season included several Pacific Coast Conference opponents (highlighted by the popular California series), but the rivalry that cast Madigan and his Gaels into the national spotlight was the Fordham series that began in 1930. Each autumn Madigan would lead his team, and a trainload of alumni, on an odyssey across the country to tangle with Fordham in New York City before the nation's prominent sportswriters. The two schools clearly recognized the financial potential for their cross-country rivalry, as in late 1929 J. F. Coffey of Fordham offered St. Mary's a "twelve thousand dollars guarantee with option of fifty percent of net receipts" to initiate the series—and this proposal six weeks after the stock market crash.

Although the initial guarantee offered by Fordham would prove to be valuable to any football program during the lean years of the Great Depression, the relatively small amount of $12,000 pales in comparison to many of the guarantees that were available during the 1920s. For example, after opening its new stadium in 1922, Ohio State paid out an average of $25,870 in guarantees to each of five opponents that season. In 1927 Southern Methodist made an unsuccessful offer of a $100,000 guarantee to Notre Dame for a game, and in 1929 the University of Georgia received a guarantee of $50,000 for appearing in a game in New York City. Yet the relatively small offer by 1920s standards was important to St. Mary's both financially and in terms of the national publicity the game would produce for the school. Later, it would be learned that Madigan had a part interest in the travel agency that arranged the cross-country tours, and his coaching contract provided for his receiving a percentage of the game profits going to St. Mary's. The series with Fordham was played until 1946, but Madigan left St. Mary's in 1939 because of a financial dispute with school officials. St. Mary's would continue as one of the nation's Catholic football elite, including trips to the 1939 Cotton Bowl and the 1946 Sugar Bowl, until the late 1940s.[36]

THE NOTRE DAME NETWORK

By 1920 many Catholic colleges and universities around the country had made a commitment to upgrade their football programs, and increasingly they turned to Notre Dame as a source of coaches who were familiar with a "system" that was proving successful in competition against all levels of opposition. Yet soon the desire to have a former Notre Dame football player came to be a reflection of more than just gridiron technique and philosophy.

As the decade progressed the aura of Rockne and his football teams grew to near mystical proportions among Catholics, whether fans or not, and it was written that the South Bend coach "offers a magic name, a legend of invincibility, [and] gridiron legerdemain." From 1919 through 1930, Rockne's Fighting Irish would compile five undefeated seasons, garner three national championships, suffer only one defeat in each of five seasons, and produce no fewer than forty-six players who received All-America selections.[37]

Historian Mark Massa has written that during the 1920s Notre Dame symbolized "a resolutely masculine, athlete culture and . . . set a tone of manly spirituality that would become every Midwestern Catholic schoolboy's dream . . . a macho image of good boys becoming good men." Notre Dame's supporters believed that the school's consistent success was generated by "a manliness and ruggedness off the football field that inculcates in the minds of the entire student body the non-stop aggression that tramples heralded bulwarks of defense . . . and that every man at the school breathes an atmosphere tinged with the pungency of pigskin." In the immediate years after the war the Notre Dame football team was considered a "defender of American Catholicism's honor," and for any Catholic college or university lusting to join that crusade, the quickest road seemed to begin with the hiring of Rockne's former players.[38]

When the growing demand for Notre Dame men was combined with Rockne's aggressiveness in placing his former players in coaching jobs, there soon developed a "network" of former Notre Dame players across the country. Rockne's collected letters contain numerous examples of requests from schools, Catholic and secular, that sought his recommendations for coaching candidates, and his word carried considerable weight with everyone involved. In late 1924 the University of Detroit believed it had Gus Dorais hired away from Gonzaga when the former Notre Damer began to yield to the pressures to stay in Spokane. Detroit officials responded by informing Dorais that he was dealing a "terrific setback to Detroit and humiliation to all concerned," and then mentioned that they were prepared "to top any figure possible from there." They also telephoned Rockne to seek his intercession, and Dorais soon ended up at Detroit. By 1926 the director of the Notre Dame alumni association reported that sixty-eight former players from the school were employed as college head coaches or assistants, which did not include the many teaching and coaching at the high school level.[39]

The former Notre Dame men placed at schools around the country owed an unspoken allegiance to Rockne, and their dedication to the South Bend coach was reflected in their immediate installation of Rockne's offensive shift system and other techniques and the hiring of even more former Notre Dame players as assistant coaches. Rockne, for his part, looked to exploit this network in a number of ways, including as a recruiting tool with athletes who hoped to someday coach. He took great care to nurture his unofficial organization, occasionally holding off-season get-togethers during which he stressed the bond of the "Notre Dame coaches." The former Notre Dame players basked in the glow of their association with Rockne and the South Bend school, often letting everyone know of their football pedigree.[40]

When Hunk Anderson was hired as the head coach at St. Louis University in 1928, one of his first public comments was the following: "We're going to have a

12. Coach Charles "Gus" Dorais of Gonzaga and Detroit. As a player at Notre Dame, he played a major role in the popularization of the forward pass. As a head coach at Gonzaga and Detroit, he always made sure that people knew of his close ties to Knute Rockne. Courtesy of the University of Detroit Mercy Archives, Marine Historical Collection.

different brand of football and that's Rockne's brand, which naturally I know better than any other." But this self-promotion could also backfire if the results on the field were not Rockne-like. When Dorais arrived at Detroit he often referred to his days as a player at Notre Dame, but some of the school's underpaid professors described him as "an insignificant sap who boasts at the slightest provocation that he played football with the late genius Knute Rockne! As if there were not nine others just as good." A member of the alumni wrote that Dorais was "a mere bungler who boasts to be a second Knute Rockne because he happened to play football on the same squad."[41]

Many of Rockne's coaching disciples believed that they had an inside track for obtaining games against Notre Dame, but soon learned that the South Bend coach did not wish to play other Catholic schools, whether coached by one of his former players or not. After 1913 the prestige of Notre Dame's football teams among America's population began to escalate through the years before World War I, and then exploded into another dimension with the coming of Rockne's powerhouse teams. The religious and laity populations—especially in heavily ethnic urban areas with substantial Catholic populations—could not seem to get enough of the Fighting Irish. Stories of nuns leading their schoolchildren in prayers for Notre Dame in the week before a big football game were common. Combined with other factors, it all amounted to a tremendous advantage in reputation and prestige for Notre Dame in comparison with any other Catholic colleges—even in the home cities of the other schools—and paid off in particular in the recruiting of even more outstanding players for Notre Dame. Even though most of his Notre Dame teams would have been heavily favored to beat any other Catholic squad during the 1920s, Rockne had no intention of risking any portion of his school's prestige and its benefits among American Catholics. Throughout his coaching tenure, Rockne's Notre Dame teams played only five games against Catholic-school opponents—and then only after receiving considerable pressure to do so.[42]

It was certainly not for a lack of potential opponents that Notre Dame seldom played Catholic gridiron foes, as Rockne regularly received requests for games from other Catholic universities. In the summer of 1920, a missionary priest, Father M. Matties, visited Rockne and proposed a game against the University of Detroit, with all proceeds going to the mission fund. As he usually did, Rockne expressed great enthusiasm for the proposal, but this matchup never came about. Efforts by Detroit to schedule a regular season date with Notre Dame also came to naught. Repeated rejections by Rockne caused Charles L. Bruce, Detroit's graduate manager of athletics, to write, "Some day we may be able to overcome their mysterious objections, but that will only be when we have the good fortune to find out its raison d'etre." Many of the attempts to obtain a football date with Notre Dame went to extraordinary lengths. In 1924, Loyola of New Orleans offered Rockne his choice of a ten thousand–dollar guarantee or 50 percent of the net proceeds, along with a commitment to pay the full expenses of the Notre Dame football party for an entire week in New Orleans. Georgetown became the most frustrated of potential Notre Dame opponents, despite the relentless pursuit of Rockne by Coach Lou Little of the Washington, D.C., school in the quest for a gridiron matchup. Rockne, for his part, often held out the hope of a future game to Little, but invariably offered the excuse of other commitments for his football team. Yet when it was announced in 1929 that Little was moving to Columbia, Rockne was right there asking the frustrated Georgetown coach if he would hire a former Notre Dame player as an assistant in New York.[43]

Historian Murray Sperber has written that the other Catholic schools "did not observe regular intercollegiate athletic rules," as a partial explanation for Notre Dame's ban on football games with the other parochial schools. The fact is that Notre Dame's major Catholic rivals—such as Georgetown, Holy Cross, Boston College, St. Mary's, and Fordham—endeavored to assure Rockne of their conformity to a high level of athletic policies. In a 1927 letter to Notre Dame, the eastern Jesuit Conference schools contended that they were "working under a code of rules as strict as those governing any group of colleges in the country." Yet they still could not find a place on Rockne's football schedules.[44]

Considering Notre Dame's immense popularity by the mid-1920s, as reflected in the media publicity for its football program, the attendance figures attracted to its games, and the substantial recruiting advantage Rockne already held among

Catholic high school athletes, the refusal to share any part of the wealth by playing other Catholic schools is an indication of the Notre Dame coach's exploitation
of the Catholic "network" for his own gains. And exploitation was the bottom
line for the Notre Dame network that Rockne carefully nurtured throughout the
1920s. Along with a far-ranging alumni network, Rockne was able to use many
of his former Notre Dame players now in coaching as a recruiting vehicle. He
also attempted to maintain a unified front of Catholic-school coaches in football
matters that were frequently opposed by their secular-university counterparts.
That this unofficial organization was meant to continue on can be seen in the
first season after Rockne's death when his successor, Hunk Anderson, secretly
exchanged films and scouting reports with Slip Madigan of St. Mary's. Although
none of it seems terribly grave, the fact is that Rockne did little in return for the
other Catholic colleges.[45]

CATHOLIC FOOTBALL AND ISSUES OF AMATEURISM

Throughout the 1920s there was a growing clamor against the excesses of intercollegiate football, and in the years immediately after the war there quickly were
signs that the gridiron programs at many Catholic universities were capable of
harboring some of the same abuses against amateur athletic ideals that plagued
the secular schools.

In 1919 administration of the struggling athletic program at Fordham was
turned over to an alumni committee of three members, and soon there were stories
of paid athletes who seldom attended classes. In late 1921 the university decided
it needed to reform its athletic programs, and so school officials appointed Father
Charles Deane as faculty moderator in charge of athletics, along with a new football coach and graduate manager of athletics, Frank Gargan. Within the first year
the pair quickly installed changes at Fordham, including the "One Year Rule" that
effectively eliminated tramp athletes, while also requiring all athletes to attend
classes and maintain satisfactory grade levels and discouraging the use of graduate students on varsity teams. The school would, however, offer the athletes partial
help with their tuition, room, and board expenses.

Notre Dame was rocked in January 1922 by the news of a scandal involving a
number of its football players who had accepted money to play for a semipro town
team in Illinois in November 1921, and many observers also suspected Rockne of
arranging illegal incentives for some of his players. In December 1921 the University of California was named as one of the teams to appear in the 1922 Rose Bowl
game, but the West Coast school had a proscribed list of three institutions it refused
to play, and Notre Dame was one of them. Rumors circulated that the reason for this
ban on the Catholic school was because of the professionalism of some of Rockne's

players. And in 1922 the faculty moderator of athletics at Santa Clara, Father Edward Ryan, wrote to his counterpart at St. Mary's and described the difficulties he regularly encountered over athletic matters with the alumni: "They are the people that give the most trouble, tho they do little for me in getting fellows to come to the school. And yet I feel that it is a dangerous thing to oppose them."[46]

Recruiting, subsidizing of athletes, and eligibility questions were all seen as major problems within college football during the period, and Catholic schools were participants in these abuses against the amateur ideal. There exists substantial evidence at Notre Dame that Rockne was effectively orchestrating his alumni network to assist in procuring football players. In one example, former Notre Dame standout end Roger Kiley was actively assisting Rockne in the recruiting of three Chicago-area prep athletes in 1929. Concerning one of the athletes, Kiley wired the Notre Dame coach and inquired if the recruit "will be fixed up as I was." In a letter to Kiley, Rockne directs that another recruit be verbally informed of the arrangements for his college expenses, wishing nothing to be put into writing, and then specifies that the athlete should send his high school academic records directly to the coach. While arranging with Kiley for a visit to Notre Dame by two high school athletes, Rockne lamented the state of affairs in recruiting: "It isn't like it used to be—it requires a lot of the old time chiseling."[47]

In 1925 the presidents of Boston College and Holy Cross were locked in a dispute over the recruiting of athletes from area parochial high schools. That summer it came to light that Holy Cross had registered a football player from Boston College High School, which brought an immediate response from Father William Devlin, S.J., the president of Boston College. In a letter to his Holy Cross counterpart, Father Joseph Dinand, S.J., Devlin stated, "I cannot permit this to happen as it would be a very bad precedent. The High School is still the High School of Boston College, and no boy must be prevailed upon to go to others of our colleges, without consulting us." In the same letter, Devlin disclosed that the athlete in question had been partially subsidized by a local monsignor, with the intention that the boy would eventually attend Boston College, while he also lamented the loss of a local public high school athlete who decided to attend Holy Cross "with all expenses paid."[48]

Father Dinand responded at once, indicating that Holy Cross had been unaware that the prep student had been subsidized by an influential Boston-area monsignor. Dinand, very aware of church politics, added, "We shall not do anything whatever to influence McCabe [the athlete] to come here and . . . you can rest assured that we shall be the last in the world to do anything to thwart [the monsignor's] desires." That being said, Dinand then launched into an attack on the concept that Catholic high school students were subject to territorial ownership claims: "I do not see your point that students of Boston College High School are not free to be approached about attending any college other than Boston

College. I do not think that your view would be accepted generally. . . . Greater Boston is an open field and I do not think that there can ever be any question of making it a special preserve for any college . . . and I do not imagine that Boston College should be consulted in case there is desirable material there." Father Devlin, at the end of his presidency at Boston, replied that there should be some form of territorial rights; failing that, he proposed that the athletic moderators from the two schools should meet each year to divide up the prospective prep recruits.[49] Devlin's retirement soon afterward brought a close to the debate, with no agreement over recruiting rights.

The Carnegie Report, released in October 1929, closely examined the recruiting of athletes for intercollegiate competition. In the report there were two references to Georgetown University as being among those schools that "frankly and unequivocally award athletic scholarships" or other types of financial assistance to varsity players. The school's football coach and director of athletics, Lou Little, emphatically denied these allegations: "There is no such thing as an athletic scholarship at Georgetown . . . and there is no reason for classifying us in the group which subsidizes teams." Yet on May 4, 1929, Little had written a letter to the president of Georgetown, Father W. Coleman Nevils, S.J., in which the coach specifically requested "the number of men that we may have here next year on scholarship for athletics." The priest wrote the number "95" in the margin next to the request, then reconsidered, scratching out the "95" and raising it to "100."[50]

The Carnegie Report statements were damaging to Georgetown's reputation, and proved to be the last straw in settling Little's fate in the minds of the school's administration. For more than a year the coach had been pursuing the Georgetown administration for a new contract, along with the payment of his 10 percent share of the 1928 football profits, an arrangement that had been put in place in a June 1926 memorandum from the school's faculty director of athletics. There had been rumors since January of Little receiving offers from other schools, but as late as December 3, 1929, Little was still denying that he had been approached about leaving Georgetown. Yet within days of his latest public denial, Little accepted an offer of a reported eighteen thousand dollars annually from Columbia and left Georgetown, still contending that the Catholic school owed him a substantial amount of money. In a history of the Georgetown football program it was stated that the university could not afford the bidding war over Little's services and that he "was lured away from the Hilltop with the jingle of filthy lucre." This point of view conveniently overlooks the fact that Little had become an embarrassment to the school as a representation of the fact that Georgetown was really just another school that subsidized its athletes.[51]

All this history is not to suggest that there did not exist a reform element within the ranks of Catholic college football. The University of Detroit developed one of the most successful football programs among Catholic institutions during the period, and the school's president, Father McNichols, once stated that no institution he headed would ever become the mere background for a varsity eleven. Consequently, in response to growing unrest expressed by its faculty members and a concern for the school's image, the administration took steps to clearly define sport's place within the university framework. In 1930 McNichols announced that the administration of Detroit's athletic affairs was being transferred from an Alumni Board of Control to a newly formed Athletic Board of Control. The new committee would consist of five faculty members, one coach, and three alumni, thus ensuring a major voice in athletics for the academic community.[52]

Far more radical was the action taken at Loyola University of Chicago on December 4, 1930, when President Robert M. Kelley, S.J., announced the discontinuance of the school's intercollegiate football program. Loyola, a Jesuit institution with an enrollment of approximately seven thousand students, had just completed the most ambitious gridiron schedule in its history, after building a twelve thousand–seat on-campus stadium with lights in 1928. The shocked student body responded with mass protests and threats of a classroom strike but failed to overturn the decision. Father Kelley stated, "It is our belief that the interest and appeal of these spectacular football games are getting away from the colleges and universities and are being centered on the public. . . . The present prominence and emphasis placed on football is endangering the true ideals and right purposes in education. The university has no hostility to football as a sport but considers that it has been overemphasized to the detriment of both the game and the school."[53]

Summary

Catholic-college football in the 1920s clearly went beyond Notre Dame, although there was a far-ranging network that linked many of these other institutions closely to the Indiana school. Seeking to emulate the fortunes of Rockne's program and the major secular universities, many Catholic colleges made serious attempts to establish a permanent place within the ranks of intercollegiate football's middle class. As such, non–Notre Dame parochial-college football was another agent of transformation within the sport during the 1920s, establishing the foundation for an interesting and significant part of intercollegiate football history over the next three decades. Schools such as Fordham, St. Mary's, Detroit, Marquette, Boston College, Santa Clara, and Georgetown succeeded in fielding competitive and visible gridiron programs into the World War II years and even beyond. But ultimately, the financial costs of maintaining a big-time college football program in a world of increasingly large public universities proved the undoing of virtually all the Catholic schools.

During Catholic-college football's glory days of the 1920s and 1930s, the parochial schools' gridiron programs incorporated most of the aspects of the period's
big-time football, such as stadium building, subsidizing of athletes, intersectional play, and classic rivalries—just on a smaller scale. In the early 1930s, Robert
Hutchins, the president of the University of Chicago, in reference to intercollegiate
athletics and professional scholarship, said that Catholic colleges "imitated the
worst features of secular education and ignored most of the good ones."[54] Yet the
undeniable fact is that the greatly increased popularity of Catholic-college football
teams, well beyond the Notre Dame experience, contributed greatly to an expansion of the personal and religious pride of the general Roman Catholic population,
in an America still capable of demonstrating substantial antireligious attitudes.

7

BLACK COLLEGE FOOTBALL
A Separate Gridiron World

While most of the sporting world of the 1920s was avidly following the football played by the mainstream, predominantly white, universities and colleges of the United States, there existed another realm of the gridiron sport. Operating in a very separate though similar universe, almost completely unknown or ignored by the mainstream sporting culture, was the game of intercollegiate football as played by America's historically black colleges, or Negro colleges, as they were then called. Just as the game of college football at the predominantly white schools underwent significant transformations during the 1920s, so too did the gridiron world of the Negro colleges. The effects of the transformations that began within black college football during the 1920s would resonate throughout the gridiron sport for the rest of the twentieth century and beyond.

Consisting mainly of schools from the Atlantic seaboard and southern states, with some representation of colleges from the Southwest and the Midwest, the black colleges entered the post–World War I era in a loosely organized fashion. Yet as the decade of the 1920s progressed, these schools systematically continued their organization into formal conferences, a practice that most notably had begun in 1912 with the Colored Intercollegiate Athletic Association. As many black colleges began providing their players with better equipment and more knowledgeable coaching and even generated funding for the building of modest-sized football stadia, the overall state of black college football was substantially transformed during the 1920s into a more structured and disciplined sport.

In many respects black college football of the 1920s emulated the gridiron sport as played by the mainstream American universities, as black educators sought to measure their educational and athletic products against the standards of white collegiate society. Historian Michael Oriard has pointed to Edwin B. Henderson of the 1920s as the first important black intellectual who took sport seriously enough to advocate that the mastery of various "white men's games" could serve to prepare young black men for the rigors of American culture. Oriard adds that "in the absence of an alternative football or broader sporting tradition within black culture, there was only one standard, a 'white' one, against which to assess black performance in football." Yet any belief in sport as a powerful force in American race relations faced an uphill battle in the 1920s.[1]

Before the war there had been indications of movements aimed at improving the social and cultural lot of blacks. The National Association for the Advancement of Colored People (NAACP) had been founded in New York in 1909, followed a year later by the organization of the National Urban League, which intended to work toward improving employment and industrial opportunities for blacks. Advocating alternatives for blacks other than an integration into mainstream white American culture was Marcus Garvey, who founded the Universal Negro Improvement Association in 1914, a movement that would soon garner many enemies for its leader by virtue of his radical beliefs. In 1910 *Crisis* magazine published its first issue, and by 1920 its circulation had grown to one hundred thousand, while the metropolitan black newspapers began a long-running improvement in the breadth and quality of their coverage of news with particular significance for blacks. And similar to the substantial growth within the mainstream universities, the period between 1917 and 1927 witnessed a doubling of the number of black colleges in the United States, along with a growth of enrollments of more than 600 percent. In 1926 W. E. B. DuBois of *Crisis* wrote, "Nothing illustrates the revolution through which the American Negro is passing better than the increasing demand on his part for college training."[2]

Yet despite these efforts at expanding black society's role in American culture, there was no denying the hatred toward blacks that still existed in many areas of the country after World War I. Evidence of these hostile feelings could be seen in major race riots in East St. Louis, Chicago, and Tulsa between 1917 and 1921, and national Ku Klux Klan membership was estimated to approximate four million by 1925. Against this backdrop of potential violence, the black colleges proceeded in their efforts at expanding the academic and athletic programs of their institutions throughout the 1920s.[3]

PREWAR BLACK FOOTBALL

The first intercollegiate football game between two black schools is generally considered to be the matchup between Biddle University (now Johnson C. Smith) and Livingstone College on December 27, 1892. The football program at Howard University in Washington, D.C., was organized by Professor Charles C. Cook, and the school's first game is recorded as a 40-6 win over the Washington YMCA in 1893. In 1894 Lincoln University (Pennsylvania), in the first year it fielded a football team, played Howard in the initial matchup of what for many years was regarded as black college football's "classic" rivalry. Atlanta University and the Tuskegee Institute also fielded their first teams in 1894. A number of other schools also launched their gridiron programs by 1900.[4]

In addition to games against other black football-playing schools, the early black intercollegiate schedules also included outings against YMCA, military, high school, and town teams. Town and military opponents would sporadically appear on black college schedules well into the 1920s. After the turn of the century, every year witnessed additional black colleges, some only two-year schools at that point, launching their football programs. Coverage in even the black newspapers was very sparse, while the enforcement of eligibility standards and other athletic regulations was being handled by each school's administration.

More structure became evident in black intercollegiate sport, football in particular, with the organization of the first two conferences in the years just before World War I. After a meeting on February 2, 1912, at Hampton Institute in Virginia, the Colored (now Central) Intercollegiate Athletic Association (CIAA) was formed with members that included Hampton, Howard, Lincoln, Shaw, and Virginia Union. On December 30, 1913, representatives of eleven black schools met at Morehouse College in Atlanta and organized the Southeastern (now Southern) Intercollegiate Athletic Conference.[5]

Through the years preceding World War I the quality of football played at the black colleges slowly improved, as some of the teams sought to incorporate innovations that were also being adopted by the mainstream white schools, including the more open style of offensive play and the use of the forward pass. Yet even with the improvements realized in the style of play through better coached teams, black college football continued to operate with a general degree of nonstandardization until the years after the war.[6]

Just as intercollegiate football at the predominantly white colleges was widely impacted by the days of World War I, so too was the gridiron sport at the black colleges that had fielded teams prior to the United States entering the conflict. Some black schools fielded Student Army Training Corps teams in 1918—a practice also resorted to by many white schools. Many black college men entered the military and served with distinction, yet not all returned to their campuses after the war. Those students that did return to their football teams were more mature and physically stronger, which laid the foundation for the sport's substantial improvement in the quality of play at the black schools.

For the 1919 season, most of the prewar football programs at the black colleges were back in action. Lincoln University featured a prominent football name with Fritz Pollard as its head coach, and the Pennsylvania school was so confident in the prospects for its gridiron program that it leased Shibe Park in Philadelphia, a major league stadium, for its 1919 game against archrival Howard.

Black college football still displayed occasional evidences of a sport that was not completely disciplined, though, as in November 1919, when the Tuskegee team walked off the field at Atlanta and forfeited its game against Morehouse College in a dispute over a referee's decision. Despite such incidents that continued with disturbing frequency through much of the 1920s, black intercollegiate football soon came to embody and emulate many of the significant features that typified the sport at the predominantly white colleges—black football operating in a similar, though never totally equal, sporting world for both students and black society.[7]

ANOTHER FOOTBALL WORLD

Major black intercollegiate football games had often served as an excuse for social events that surrounded the gridiron matchups. Such events offered black society an opportunity to demonstrate its culture and sophistication in emulation of the social trappings that had long surrounded the games of the prestigious white universities of the East. The social festivities, the media's descriptions of the pregame excitement, and the staging of significant gridiron matchups in metropolitan stadia were all features of black college football that had close resemblance to the world of mainstream intercollegiate football. For a short time on the day of a game, black society and black college students could share a cultural experience with their white counterparts, without the bias and occasional threats of violence that still existed in mainstream American society of the 1920s. The growing pride during the decade through participation in the world of black intercollegiate football was part of a much larger movement, described by W. E. B. DuBois in 1920: "Above all comes the New Spirit: from a bewildered, almost listless, creeping sense of impotence and despair have come a new vigor, hopefulness and feeling of power."[8]

Social events surrounding the major black college games included dances, luncheons, recitals, lectures, concerts, and parades. For example, when Hampton traveled to Philadelphia to play Lincoln in 1924, the southern school brought along its glee club, which performed in concert the night before the game, while an alumni breakfast dance and another dance in the evening were scheduled for the day of the game. With Morehouse scheduled to play the Bluefield Institute in a 1928 Thanksgiving Day game at Columbus, Ohio, a reporter described "a week's attack on drab living as the gay social world begins to make whoopee." That week's festivities included a Mardi Gras party, a dinner in honor of the two teams at the Crystal Slipper—"with fifty of the prettiest local debutantes as hostesses"—and the Shrine Ball at the Columbus Auditorium.[9]

The football team from highly respected Howard University often served as a social beacon during its travels. As early as 1916, when Howard traveled to Nashville, Tennessee, for a game against Fisk University, its visit was the centerpiece for a number of high-class events. The entertainment provided by the city's black society was said to have portrayed Nashville as "the Athens of the South." The festivities were particularly notable in the 1920s when Howard and Lincoln met each year on Thanksgiving Day for what was described by many sportswriters as "the football classic of the Negro educational world." In 1924 one writer called the grid-iron matchup of the two eastern schools "the outstanding athletic and social event for Negroes in America" and described the game as having the same significance for blacks as the Harvard-Yale and Army-Navy games had for white Americans. Indeed, the annual game became the centerpiece of a social competition between the black populace of Washington, D.C., and Philadelphia, or what one reporter described as a struggle to determine "the social center of the Negro universe." The descriptions of bonfires, snake dances, and the many visitors pouring into town for the games could just as easily have been the reports of the scenes surrounding any major football game between two predominantly white universities.[10]

Beyond those social aspects that typically surrounded major football games, there were other indications that black college football was operating in a simi-lar though separate gridiron world—black All-America teams, mythical national champions, and controversies between the schools. And in writing of teams and personalities in black football, sportswriters regularly used references that clearly symbolized the desire to emulate and "belong" to the mainstream intercollegiate football world—whether admitted to or not. For example, running back Franz "Jazz" Byrd of Lincoln was frequently called "the black Red Grange," and Coach Cleveland Abbott of Tuskegee was commonly referred to as "the Knute Rockne of our schools."[11]

In the 1920s, the Big Three universities of Harvard, Princeton, and Yale still symbolized the elite of American education and intercollegiate football for many observers, and the black media frequently associated some of the best features of black football with the trio. For example, as early as 1924 sportswriter W. Rollo Wil-son referred to the Hampton, Howard, Lincoln trio as the Big Three of black foot-ball, and in 1926 William Nunn declared that the field-goal kicking by Ed Ritchie of Wilberforce was "a reminder of the great Ted Coy [of Yale] at the zenith of his gridiron career."[12] Using the gridiron world of the predominantly white universi-ties as a reference point for black college football would continue for many years.

CONTROVERSIES

The history of intercollegiate football has been marked by controversies from its earliest days, and the gridiron sport of the black colleges was no different. By the 1920s an increasing amount of discipline and organization within black college football had greatly reduced the seriousness of such controversies; however, there remained a sufficient-enough number during the decade that the matter should not be overlooked.

Disputes with game officials constituted an ongoing potential embarrass-ment for black college administrators. Even after World War I, much too often these incidents resulted in one team walking off the field and taking a forfeit loss, or, worse yet, fans or players physically attacking the officials. For example, on Thanksgiving Day 1920, after a game that was described as having been clean and hard fought, the Hampton team walked off the field in the fourth quarter and forfeited to Virginia Union over a disputed decision by an official on a crucial touchdown play. The many spectators who surged onto the field and "became unmanageable" while the argument ensued only compounded the tensions. In its 1921 game against Virginia Union, the Lincoln team, incensed over an official's call that deprived them of a fumble recovery, quit the field with four minutes left in the game. In 1927, Wilberforce forfeited its game with Howard University after a long argument with the officials over a touchdown scored by a Howard player in the game's final minutes. It was the second serious football controversy in three years between the two schools.[13]

Far more serious were events such as the 1926 game at Greensboro between Virginia Union and North Carolina A&T, when a group of spectators attacked referee L. U. Gibson at the close of the game before players of the A&T team rescued the beleaguered official. The attackers were primarily nonstudents, but A&T officials did suspend two students who were involved and pledged the future safety of both players and officials to avoid being banned from competition by the CIAA. The game between Simmons College and Kentucky State in 1926 was marked by constant arguments between the Simmons team and the officials, and referee W. Lawrence Campbell later reported that he had been offered money by Simmons fans to throw the game and that "weapons" had been displayed to intimidate him.[14]

After the game between Clark College and Alabama State Normal in Montgomery in 1927, fans of the latter school attacked the visiting team. With a mob in pursuit, the Atlanta collegians made it onto a streetcar, and the conductor alertly got the vehicle in motion ahead of the Alabama State fans. Meanwhile, back on the football field, another group surrounded and threatened Sam Taylor, coach of the Clark team, and the Atlanta school's president until the Alabama State president escorted the two men off the field to safety. These types of incidents were facilitated by the difficulty of maintaining crowd control because of the relatively small grandstands at the black colleges that required many fans to stand around the field itself.[15]

Throughout the decade the sports sections of the prominent black newspapers gave ample space to coverage of the controversies that often plagued the black college game. Although many of the incidents received just straight reporting, throughout the period Frank Young of the *Chicago Defender* frequently authored outspoken articles and editorials on the embarrassing situations and the damage they were bringing to the black intercollegiate game, situations that had been basically eliminated long before in the land of mainstream college football. Yet as the decade progressed many observers took note of the improving sportsmanship that was gradually surrounding black college football games. Much of the improvement in sportsmanship in the late 1920s was attributed to threatened sanctions from the organized conferences. By 1928 Young could note: "We are glad to report that the conduct of both fans and players has improved about 100 per cent in most places. We are gradually learning 'how to lose' and do it graciously."[16]

Although the forfeiting of games and the physical attacks on game participants might be on the decline, the questioning of the competence of football officials used by black colleges continued consistently throughout the decade. In 1921 an editorial in the *Chicago Defender* pointed to the importance of having competent game officials and cited the tendency of the host schools to hire personal friends or those officials who could be obtained for the cheapest possible fees. The writer declared that first-class officials should be paid between twenty-five and forty dollars per game and that "a list of competent officials should be sent out by a committee organized for such purpose. The officials not showing the proper class should be blacklisted." Young of the *Defender* reflected the view of many critics who contended that decisions made in error because of an obvious lack of background in the rules, and the resulting disputes that often led to forfeits, were doing a disservice to the fans and contributing to the declining attendance figures within black intercollegiate football.[17]

Yet the officiating controversies continued, the high-profile 1925 Wilberforce-Howard game producing a major disagreement over some calls made by the officials that triggered a debate that continued for weeks in the black newspapers. By late 1928 Young and others were ready to suggest that white football officials should be used on occasion by the black colleges. Young made note of the many white game officials interested in working black college football—despite the fact that they "would refuse to eat at the same table or in the same room." He also reported that white officials were asking four times the amount being paid to black football officials, which ensured that the proposal would not gain acceptance. Controversies involving game officials would continue to plague black college football well beyond the decade of the 1920s.[18]

THE FOOTBALL CRISIS AT HOWARD UNIVERSITY

Some of the most prominent controversies of black intercollegiate sport in the 1920s involved the Howard University football team. The school's gridiron squads were considered to be among the elite programs of black football, and their success had included winning or sharing the mythical national black football championship three times between 1920 and 1926. Yet there were signs that all was not well within the Howard program midway through the 1920s, as Dr. Edward P. Davis, chairman of the school's Board of Athletic Control, found it necessary in 1924 to publicly assure alumni and other school officials that steps were being taken to place intercollegiate sport at Howard on a firm financial footing.[19]

In the early 1920s Howard University was under the direction of a white president, J. Stanley Durkee, who had come into conflict with many of the black alumni and professors of the school as he aggressively pursued programs aimed at expanding the academic prestige of the Washington, D.C., school. Concerns over football's role within university life were being considered by some of the more prominent black schools by the mid-1920s, and it was inevitable that Durkee's emphasis on moving Howard into the highest academic levels would bring an eventual debate over football.[20]

Controversy at Howard began to surface in late 1924, when a dispute over the eligibility of a football player named Robert Miller—who had played the season before at Virginia Union—caused an organizational crisis for the school's intercollegiate athletic programs. Though meeting nonconference opponents presented no difficulty, when the CIAA football schedule began each of the opposing teams protested Howard's use of Miller in 1924 on the basis of a conference rule that decreed he sit out for one year. But the Howard coaches and athletic officials refused to hold Miller out—contending that since he was officially only a freshman at the Washington school, the rule did not pertain.

With the big Thanksgiving Day game against Lincoln approaching—with Dr. Davis counting on a large crowd for the matchup at Washington's major league stadium—the Pennsylvania university notified Howard officials that unless Miller was held out, there would be no "classic" gridiron matchup between the two schools in 1924. After some attempts to maintain their position, the Howard athletic officials backed down. Yet the Washington school continued to declare the righteousness of its position and stated that it was giving in because "she was unwilling to accept the responsibility of disappointing the thousands of persons who had arranged at great expense to attend the game"—which really meant that Howard did not want to refund the money already collected.[21]

A blow such as this one to the traditional football prestige of Howard apparently could not long be tolerated, and the school's Board of Athletic Control voted unanimously to withdraw from the CIAA, an action that was accepted by the other colleges at the conference meeting in December 1924. The secretary-treasurer of the conference wrote Dr. Davis, "The C.I.A.A. in meeting assembled, regrets deeply that Howard University has found it necessary to withdraw from our Association. . . . [We] cannot in justice of our ideal of true sportsmanship arrange athletic contests under conditions which destroy the integrity of the Association." The CIAA schools agreed that as long as Howard remained outside the conference, no member of the CIAA would compete in any branch of athletics with the Washington university.[22]

Yielding its membership in the prestigious CIAA in a trivial dispute over athletic eligibility was an embarrassment to the alumni, faculty, and students of Howard University, and the focus of the resulting anger was directed at President Durkee for allowing the athletic board to resign the school's position in the conference. Historian Patrick Miller has written, "Combined with numerous other actions that outraged the black community, the controversy over sports helped forge an alliance that challenged the entire educational administration."[23] Despite Durkee's many efforts at elevating Howard University's institutional prestige, dropping out of the CIAA, and what doing so said about the relative importance of athletics within the Howard University community, was more than could be accepted by the alumni and faculty. After a year of turmoil Durkee was forced to resign his presidency at Howard in 1926.

With a vacancy in the leadership at one of the most important black colleges in the United States, it seemed appropriate for Mordecai W. Johnson to become Howard's first black president after Durkee's departure. A strong advocate of academic excellence and its role in university life, Johnson soon turned his attention to the school's athletic programs.

Before Durkee's reign ended there had been additional signs of serious problems within Howard's football world. Soon after the 1925 season it came to light that there had been considerable dissension between Coach Louis Watson and his young assistant, Charles West. The claim was also made that the fraternity allegiances of the players were resulting in favoritism toward their fraternity brothers when it came to lineup decisions and play selection. In the aftermath of the embarrassment over dropping out of the CIAA, these problems were further public displays that did little to enhance the school's overall reputation to outside observers. Howard fielded another outstanding football team in 1926—being named mythical national cochampions with Tuskegee—but again the accomplishments on the gridiron were forced to the background by the continued arrogance of the athletic board.[24]

In October 1926 Charles H. Williams, secretary-treasurer of the CIAA, was directed to write to both Howard and Lincoln and propose a meeting for the purpose of bringing the two schools back into the conference—Lincoln having been suspended in early 1925. Williams apparently regarded Dr. Davis at Howard as a hard-liner in the school's decision to quit the conference, and so the CIAA's letter was directed to Coach Watson in his position as the director of physical education. But Watson turned the letter over to Dr. Davis, and the chairman of Howard's Board of Athletic Control responded with a vicious broadside that brooked of no wrongdoing by the school. After repeating Howard's contentions for using Miller back in 1924, Davis demanded that the CIAA schools rescind their boycott of athletic competition with Howard "as a preliminary to any resumption of relations." Davis took his arrogance a step further and declared, "We shall probably in any event not renew membership in the C.I.A.A.," and then tendered an invitation for the CIAA schools to disband and join Howard in forming a new conference to be titled the American Collegiate Athletic Association.[25]

These events represented yet another embarrassment for the university and probably settled the ultimate fate of its football program. The blow came on September 30, 1927, the day before Howard's game against the Bluefield Institute, when the members of the football team were informed that all scholarship assistance was canceled and that the training table and the training quarters for the team were no longer available. Amid reports of team members having spent the night out with no place to sleep, many players were said to be considering not playing against Bluefield or—worse yet—deliberately losing the game "to teach the university authorities a lesson." What followed was a lackluster affair that produced an 18-7 defeat for Howard.[26]

University officials disclosed that game receipts and student athletic fees covered less than one-half of the expense of fielding intercollegiate teams at Howard and that the action was taken in response to a twenty thousand–dollar deficit by the school's athletic programs. Although the matter could have been handled better, it was not a complete surprise. President Johnson had first advised the football players of his contemplated action the previous spring, and when they had reported for practice on September 15 a proposal was made that they begin paying the same amount for tuition, room, and board as the other students as of October 1. The players did not intend to pay these fees, and when classes began efforts were made to raise funds to subsidize the team but had proved insufficient.

The response of the forty-five football players was to go on strike as of October 4, prompting Johnson to request on October 7 that twenty-two men come out for football under the new arrangement or else the Board of Athletic Control was prepared to begin canceling blocks of games by the following evening. Twenty-four players reported for practice the next afternoon—only six of them varsity men—but the full squad was soon back in uniform after a temporary agreement was reached whereby the expenses for board and lodging for players would be covered until the end of the season.[27]

By 1928 the scholarships for football players at Howard University had been eliminated, the school instead providing free board and lodging for the players only during the two weeks of training camp before the start of classes. Now committed to an athletic policy that included adhering to strict eligibility rules, Howard returned to membership in the CIAA in December 1928. The impact of eliminating scholarships was felt almost immediately, as the 1929 Howard football team tumbled to a record of 0-7-2.[28]

This sudden drop from gridiron prominence did not sit well with Howard's alumni and students, and the school administration was made the focus of their criticisms. An article in the *Amsterdam News* of New York City noted, "President Johnson alone is to be blamed for the miserable football team that represents Howard University. . . . The miserable showing of his mediocre team has created a spirit of sullen indifference among the students and sour indignation among the alumni." The gridiron fortunes of Howard University beyond 1930 rebounded slightly but seldom progressed beyond average-to-dismal seasons, and it would be more than thirty years before the school would again field an outstanding team.[29]

Far more significant than a future filled with mediocre football seasons was the damage to the prestige of Howard University. Despite what academic reformers of the 1920s believed, just as in the world of the primarily white universities, there was a definite correlation in the public consciousness between athletic performance and institutional prestige. A writer in the *Amsterdam News* pointed out, "The public expects the best in everything from Howard, the best scholarship, the best sportsmanship, and the best athletic competitions. Why not? Is not Howard the capstone of Negro education?"[30]

BLACK FOOTBALL WRITERS

The view toward an emulation of the white collegiate world was also increasingly evident in the style of sportswriting through the decade by the black media. The coverage of black college football by the black newspapers had been very substandard in the years prior to 1920, certainly far behind the writing style and layout work that had evolved in the mainstream media for its coverage of football at the predominantly white colleges. While the mainstream newspapers and magazines would make significant improvements in their sports coverage during the 1920s, the black newspapers also made considerable progress in the quality of their football reporting during the period.

In the years before World War I the black sports pages had carried only occasional college football coverage—certainly not adequate to follow any of the teams or conferences with any degree of completeness throughout the seasons. Only occasionally were sportswriters actually sent to cover the games on site. The majority of articles on black college football were provided by correspondents at the schools, which meant that there were frequent factual errors and exaggerations, and the game articles were often slanted toward one of the teams.

As the 1920s progressed, black newspapers, recognizing the value of the sports page in building circulation figures, began to devote considerably more space to college football. By 1925, Edwin Henderson, taking note of the increased readership of black newspapers, could write in the *Messenger*, "Many men and boys to whom our newspapers were unknown now read the sports sheets, and take interest in various local, national and international affairs. The athletic page is a good advertising method for news of more serious import."[31] Systematically, the papers revised the layout of their sports pages to more closely resemble the styles of the mainstream newspapers, and many assigned a writer to full-time coverage of black college football during the season. Starting from basically straight reporting of the games' action, by the middle of the 1920s the black sportswriters had adopted a good deal of the flowery style that typified much of the mainstream sports coverage of the period.

Although many of the football articles each week continued to originate with correspondents at the schools—often the coaches—the coverage also increasingly consisted of dispatches and game reports from professional writers who served as regional correspondents. The football writers from the major black newspapers—such as Young and Eric Roberts of the *Chicago Defender,* along with Chester Washington, Nunn, and Wilson of the *Pittsburgh Courier*—soon became national celebrities within the world of black intercollegiate sports, and their appearance to cover a game was often treated as a major event. In 1928 Young described his typical season of covering black college football: "We have traveled about ten thousand miles through 12 states, went without meals, sat up all night, changed trains at 3 A.M., all to give our readers what we believe is a first-hand report on college football." The combination of regional and full-time football writers produced an increased and improved amount of coverage for the black college gridiron world.[32]

Yet despite the growing professionalism and prestige of the black sportswriters within the sporting world they reported on, such was not always the case when they ventured into the major arenas of mainstream intercollegiate sport. In 1927 Young and three other black writers were in Atlanta to cover a Thanksgiving Day game, and with a Saturday free they were provided sideline passes by the athletic department of Georgia Tech for the day's gridiron showdown between Tech and the University of Georgia. From the moment the black writers arrived on the field they were harassed and insulted by fans and nearby bystanders. With fans yelling and swearing at the four men, an Atlanta police lieutenant informed them that their sideline passes from Georgia Tech—the host school—"warn't no good" on his say-so, and rather than enter the grandstands the black writers left the stadium. Young wrote, "They do some funny things down there—those people with white skins. We couldn't call them white people because they aren't." He then contrasted his experience with the "well ordered" crowd in attendance at the black college game in Atlanta's Spiller Park.[33]

Examples of such treatment also surfaced occasionally at the large metropolitan stadia leased for major black college matchups. In 1929 the Polo Grounds in New York City was the site of the Hampton Institute–Lincoln game. Wilson of the *Pittsburgh Courier* declared, "At last the flatland under Coogan's Bluff has gone colored," and he reported that thirty thousand fans were expected for the first football contest in New York between "major Negro colleges." But on the day of the game the conditions in the press box were less than ideal for Wilson. The prominent black sportswriter reported that initially the "attache" (attendant) refused to allow him entry into the Polo Grounds press box, despite his credentials. After a heated argument, Wilson was reluctantly given a seat in the "Jim Crow part of the section"—meaning the most undesirable location possible for viewing the game. Incredibly, Wilson took note of three black reporters from the New York daily newspapers who had been given seats in the front row. Wilson bitterly wrote, "I have sat in better press boxes than the make-shift one used for football at the Polo Grounds, and it is the first time I ever experienced such a discrimination."[34]

Despite such incidents, black writers generally did much to advance the awareness and appreciation for black college athletics during the 1920s—even if only among the readers of the black newspapers. These men recognized that the world of black college football did not measure up to the environment of the predominantly white schools in terms of financial resources, public interest, overall quality of play, organization and discipline, or athletic prestige, yet they covered black football in an interesting and professional manner that cast the sport in a generally favorable light. And black writers could not resist the occasional comparisons to the sporting culture of mainstream intercollegiate football. Historian Michael Oriard has written that "the black sportswriters who judged black football by white standards did not betray their race but acknowledged its plight, savoring its triumphs without minimizing its obstacles."[35]

The black newspapers systematically improved and expanded the scope of their football coverage, objectively reported such events as the Howard University crisis, and treated the social aura surrounding the traditional black college football rivalries with the same dignity and respect accorded to the classic matchups of white college football. Black sportswriters proved to be a key component in the transformation of black football into an organized intercollegiate sport by the 1930s.

BIG-CITY GAMES

The playing of games at prominent neutral sites grew in popularity during the 1920s for mainstream college football, and the black colleges were soon emulating this promotional tactic. One of the notable games of the 1921 season was played in Chicago between Wilberforce University and Roger Williams College, and the *Chicago Defender* described it as the first time "two universities of the Race" had ever met for a football game in the midwestern city.

By 1920 Chicago had become one of the major centers of black society in the United States, and the city's heavily black-populated South Side had become recognized for its many clubs and other night spots that featured some of the best black jazz musicians and orchestras in the country. A football game in the city between two church-related black colleges—especially with one from the South—seemed a natural, given the significant numbers of residents who still had close ties to other regions.

After more than four thousand spectators turned out at Schorling's Park to watch Wilberforce triumph by a score of 20-0, Young of the *Defender* chided those black fans who had instead attended the nearby University of Chicago's game, noting, "It was their privilege to go where they chose, but we do not want to hear from any of them that did go . . . and never patronize anything only what is fostered by the other races." An indication of the mainstream media's regard for black intercollegiate sport can be seen in the *Chicago Tribune*, which errone-ously declared Roger Williams as the winner in the headline for its one-sentence clip that described the game as the first "between teams of colleges owned and directed by Negroes."[36]

This 1921 game in Chicago was just one of the many major intersectional matchups that were played during the decade at neutral metropolitan sites by prominent black college teams. Though some of these were considered postsea-son games, most were regular-season meetings. State Fair Week in Dallas, Texas, provided the occasion for the matchup between Wiley and Langston Colleges on several occasions, with Wiley meeting Prairie View there in 1929, which prompted regional reporter Bert Lewis of the *Defender* to write that "never before in the his-tory of football has the little New York of Texas witnessed such interest."[37] New Orleans and Marshall, Texas, were other popular sites for games tied in with county or state fairs.

These neutral-site games often attracted a sizable number of white football fans, with separate sections of seating being provided for the white spectators—particularly advertised in Texas and Louisiana. Pregame ticket locations were also segregated in the southern cities, such as in Dallas in 1925, when whites were to obtain their tickets at the Santa Fe Drug Store, whereas "negro patrons" were to purchase theirs at McMillan's Cafe. Considering the prevailing social climate in the Deep South in the 1920s, it is surprising to find the following pregame plug for black college football in the mainstream *New Orleans Times-Picayune*: "Those who have never seen negro teams in action have something in store for them; it is the brand of football that old-timers say passed in the days of Sullivan and Corbett. Less aerial work and more line-bucking is the rule." Although the southern writer meant well, the comment reflects an unfamiliarity with the technical advances in the style of play that were taking place at many black colleges in other regions. Within a year these advances would be a regular topic in the sporting sections of black newspapers and magazines.[38]

The most prominent neutral-site games of the 1920s were usually to be found in cities of the North. The matchup between Wilberforce and the West Virginia Institute was usually played each season at Neil Park in Columbus, Ohio, and the Thanksgiving Day game served as the focal point for major social events among the city's black society. The popularity of this event in the central-Ohio city prompted one reporter to note in 1925 that "it will soon outrank any event of its kind in the country." When the two schools moved their intersectional game to Cleveland for one year in 1928, the promoters at Columbus quickly slotted in a Thanksgiving game between the Bluefield Institute and Morehouse College. Chicago was a site for major black football in 1929—now playing at mammoth Soldier Field—with a much publicized game between Tuskegee and Wilberforce.[39]

The most prestigious game throughout the 1920s was usually the annual matchup between Howard and Lincoln. First played in 1894, the game became the counterpart to the Harvard-Yale matchups of mainline intercollegiate football. By the 1920s the Thanksgiving Day game had reached a level of popularity that moved both schools to lease the major league stadia in Philadelphia and Washington in alternate years as the site of the matchup. In 1921 the *Chicago Defender* presented a "little brown jug" to be retained each year by the game's winning school—in undisguised emulation of the trophy played for annually by Michigan and Minnesota.

In 1922 Young of the *Defender* described Howard versus Lincoln as "the game of all games" and predicted that "the two social affairs which follow the game will even outrank those given at either New Haven or Cambridge." The anticipated attendance for the 1922 game in Washington was so great that the schools took out an insurance policy against rain, to be paid in case of inclement weather even if the game was not canceled. The game's popularity continued throughout most of the decade—including Howard's moving of the Washington-site games to its new on-campus stadium in 1926—yet the declining gridiron fortunes of the two schools after 1926 brought about a gradual lessening of the game's national significance for black college football. In 1929 the game played at Philadelphia's Municipal Stadium (with ticket prices ranging from two to three dollars) attracted barely ten thousand spectators.[40]

ON THE FIELD

The black college football world of the 1920s was particularly notable for the many improvements in the technical style and quality of play among its teams. That some of the schools intended to upgrade the quality of play in the immediate years after the war is evidenced by Lincoln University's hiring of Fritz Pollard as its football coach in 1919 and 1920. Unfortunately for Lincoln, Pollard's agreement allowed him to frequently absent himself on weekends to play professional football for Akron—a source of agitation for students and alumni.[41] It seemed clear that many expected college football as played by the black schools to improve significantly while becoming more disciplined in its administration, one indication coming when the *Pittsburgh Courier* began to select an annual mythical national gridiron champion for the black colleges as of the 1920 season, with Howard sharing the title that year with Talladega College of Alabama.

Virginia Union was named the mythical black national champion in 1923, but an article that season about southern football made mention of the improving fortunes of the Tuskegee Institute under its new football coach, Cleveland Abbott. Beginning with the 1924 season, Tuskegee became one of the preeminent gridiron powers in black college football, winning or sharing the mythical national championship on six occasions through the 1930 season. The Golden Tigers compiled forty-six consecutive victories, along with five ties, in the seasons of 1923–1928 and, even more impressively, tallied a record of 79-1-8 from 1923 through 1931. Along with Coach Abbott, the common denominator throughout the period was a sensational tailback named Ben Stevenson.

While a student at Tuskegee's prep school in 1923, Stevenson began to play with the college varsity, and he continued his football career as a college student through the 1930 campaign—a total of eight seasons of intercollegiate football. There was no denying the greatness of this triple-threat tailback. By 1925 Stevenson was named a black First Team All-America by the *Chicago Defender,* which called him "the terror of the South." That season Coach Abbott described his star backfield man as "the outstanding player of the year," as Tuskegee went 8-0-1 and was never really tested by any opponent. Much of Tuskegee's consistent gridiron success resulted from the waves of capable reserves that Abbott had available to use in wearing down the opposition in the hot southern autumns.[42]

Before the 1927 season at Tuskegee there had been serious concerns that Stevenson was all set to attend Lincoln University, but unfortunately for the Pennsylvania school he did not have enough credits to begin college work and so remained in Alabama. Just as Red Grange had demonstrated his greatness to eastern sportswriters in Philadelphia against Penn in 1925, so too did Stevenson with a trip to the Quaker city in 1927 when Tuskegee trounced Lincoln 30-0. A black southern football writer, Eric Roberts, commented that "Tuskegee today is one of the greatest teams that America has ever seen"—not indicating if he was referring only to black college football.[43]

By the middle of the 1920s the advances in the quality of play among most black college football teams was obvious to onlookers. After the 1925 season, writer Paul W. L. Jones of *Crisis* magazine attributed the continuing improvements in the quality of black college football to such factors as the larger numbers of players at each school, a "keener" system of coaching and administration, the increasing popularity of conference affiliation, an increased and more effective use of the forward passing game, and the presence of abundant numbers of outstanding athletes at the skill positions. After the 1926 season Coach Abbott of Tuskegee took note of the fact that the public was developing a greater degree of interest in the football games staged by the black schools, adding that more students were coming out for the teams, many schools were improving and expanding their football facilities, and the teams were being taught sound fundamentals. Typical of the fine black coaches coming into the game was Brice Taylor, a former Southern California star, who was the head coach at Claflin College in 1927 before he moved to Southern University in 1928. Yet there could be plenty of pitfalls for black coaches, just as at the predominantly white football schools: Lincoln summarily fired its head coach, William E. Morrison, during the 1928 season because of the team's poor records under his direction.[44]

Black football featured other outstanding backfield men during the 1920s. Lincoln was led by a dazzling open-field running back named Franz Byrd through 1924. Also, for several seasons the football fortunes of Wilberforce were shaped by a dazzling halfback named Harry Wu Fang Ward, a black athlete with Chinese relatives. When the all-around athlete played his final football game for Wilberforce in 1928, J. B. Simms of the *Chicago Defender* described him as "that scintillating, marvelous, non-eccentric idol of all Wilberforce and alumni . . . the greatest athlete that Wilberforce has ever produced." The Bluefield Institute was named the mythical national cochampion for the seasons of 1927 and 1928, under the direction of Coach Harry Jefferson, and the Big Blue were led both seasons by their All-America quarterback, Herbert Cain. The 1928 Bluefield gridmen featured a high-powered offense on their way to a 7-0-1 record that was marred by only a scoreless tie with Howard. They were to have played Wiley College at Marshall, Texas, in a postseason game to settle the national championship, but a last-minute disagreement over financial arrangements caused the game's cancellation.[45]

Despite the many improvements within black college football during the 1920s it still remained a dangerous game, caused by the often poor equipment for the players, along with the continued presence of inexperienced men at some of the schools—problems that plagued the black gridiron programs throughout the decade. During a hard-hitting game in 1928, Herbert Cain of Bluefield suffered a broken leg, while Jack Young of Howard came away with a fractured kneecap—yet these incidents were minor compared to some of the other injuries.[46]

At Savannah, Georgia, on December 3, 1921, Lynwood Scott, a fullback for Claflin College, was knocked unconscious while attempting to make a tackle on an end sweep by the Georgia State backfield. Efforts by the fire department to revive

13. Franz "Jazz" Byrd of Lincoln University. Often called "the Black Red Grange," here he sets off on an 85-yard touchdown run against Howard University in 1922. Courtesy of Lincoln University of Pennsylvania, Langston Hughes Memorial Library Archives.

the player were unsuccessful, and he died on the sidelines with the game still in progress. In 1924 Haywood Johnson, an end for Howard, was fatally injured during the school's first game of the season, and in 1927 Samuel Carline of Straight College of New Orleans suffered a broken neck during a practice tackling drill and was left paralyzed. It would be a number of years beyond the 1920s before all black college football teams would be uniformly outfitted with state-of-the-art protective equipment.[47]

THE BLACK ATHLETE AND MAINSTREAM COLLEGE FOOTBALL

While the football world of the black colleges provided ample opportunities for athletes throughout the 1920s and beyond, there was an alternative experience available to those black athletes willing to endure the hardships involved in playing for varsity teams at the mainstream white universities. Examples of black athletes playing football at the primarily white universities can be found back to the earliest days of the sport in the late nineteenth century, and frequently these pioneering black athletes were the focus of considerable controversy.

George Jewett at the University of Michigan was one of the earliest in 1890 and 1892, while the first prominently regarded black gridman was William H. "Bill" Lewis. Playing throughout his undergraduate days at Amherst College, Lewis was named the football captain for 1891, his senior season. Then, while attending law school at Harvard, Lewis continued his football career for three years as a member of the Crimson varsity. He was named the All-America center by Casper Whitney for the seasons of 1892 and 1893, and years later Walter Camp would include Lewis on the All-Time All-America squad he named for *Independent* magazine.[48]

One of the most publicized running backs in the East immediately before World War I was a black athlete named Frederick "Fritz" Pollard at Brown University. Pollard came into his own during the 1916 season, as he led Brown to a berth in the Rose Bowl. In its lead for the story of Brown's victory over Harvard that season, United Press referred to Pollard as "a dusky meteor," which was typical of the references frequently made about black athletes by white sportswriters all the way to World War II. Far more complimentary were the words extended toward Pollard by the black newspapers. One writer noted that the halfback had "given his race a high place in football history through performances of the highest order and at no time of his career has the character of his work been below that of the most finished athlete." For the 1916 season Pollard earned First Team All-America halfback selections from Walter Camp and Frank Menke, along with first- and second-team spots from virtually every other major selector. Pollard was followed by another standout eastern black athlete in Paul Robeson, the future star concert singer and movie actor, who received First Team All-America berths at end for Rutgers in 1917 and 1918.[49]

After World War I there continued to be capable black athletes who were willing to undergo the racial bias and hostilities that came with attending classes and playing football at the predominantly white colleges. Among their ranks can be included players such as Fred "Duke" Slater, an All-America tackle in 1919 and 1921 at Iowa, who was instrumental in the Hawkeyes' undefeated record of the latter season; Brice Taylor of Southern California, named an All-America guard in 1925 and later the head coach at Southern University; and Jack Trice at Iowa State in 1923.[50]

The story of Jack Trice, a member of the Iowa State varsity in 1923 as a sophomore, was particularly tragic and symbolic of the potential risks for any football player of the time. This ongoing personal risk was especially evident for black athletes at the predominantly white universities, where they were frequently singled out for vicious physical attacks by members of opposing teams. In the second half against Minnesota on October 6 of that season, Trice threw a roll block into a group of onrushing Minnesota blockers, but he was knocked onto his back and trampled by the opposing players and forced to leave the game. Doctors at a Minneapolis hospital declared that his injuries were not serious, but when Trice arrived back at Iowa State he was immediately rushed to the university hospital. There it was determined that the young lineman had suffered a broken collarbone and internal injuries. Trice soon developed respiratory problems, yet it was decided that surgery would be too dangerous. On Monday, October 8, he passed away from hemorrhaged lungs and abdominal bleeding.[51]

Despite the black athletes who compiled notable records during the 1920s while playing for white colleges, it was not always without controversy. Southern colleges and universities not only allowed no black players on their intercollegiate teams but also sought to prevent nonwhite athletes from competing against their teams during intersectional games—even when played at northern venues. This practice became known as the "gentlemen's agreement," and it was carried on into the 1950s by some schools. The agreement was intended to maintain racial segregation on the football fields of the United States—at least while southern teams were playing—while supporting a notion of racial hierarchy that identified black athletes as unworthy of competition against white teams.

The so-called gentlemen's agreement came into its widest acceptance by the early 1920s, and it provided that any intercollegiate team (in practice, always northern schools) with black players would hold these athletes out of the games played against white southern schools—specific language covering this even being included in game contracts occasionally. Most northern schools usually went along quietly with this southern-dictated policy, no doubt motivated in great part by the belief that the absence of these players would usually have minimum impact on the game's outcome and the potential financial windfall of attractive intersectional matchups would not be jeopardized.[52]

Disputes over the use of black football players for intercollegiate games was not unique to the period beginning in 1920, as examples of such controversies can be found in earlier football history. In 1904 Yale threatened to break off relations with Harvard over what the *Philadelphia Press* called "the negro question." That season the football roster for Harvard included a black player at end named William Matthews, and as the "Big Game" between the archrivals approached, Coach Edgar Wrightington of Harvard was warned not to use his black player, as it would be considered an affront to the southerners who attended Yale. Yet during the game Matthews was sent in as a substitute, and the angry Yale team, in the words of the reporter for the *Press*, "kicked and hammered" the Harvard substitute "nearly into insensibility."[53]

In the aftermath of Yale's 12-0 win, the *Press* reported that the New Haven school's football coaches had again approached Wrightington and warned him that "no more negroes must be played on Harvard." Interestingly, a short time after the game Matthews wrote a letter to the *Yale Alumni Weekly* in which he denied that Yale players had deliberately attempted to injure him, and he stated that his injuries had been caused by his involvement in several tackles in the midst of Yale's powerful running plays. Rumors quickly spread that Princeton athletic officials had also warned Harvard that football relations would never be resumed between the two schools "until Harvard agreed not to play negroes."[54] The situation resolved itself when Matthews graduated the following spring, while Wrightington was forced out as Harvard's football coach after the 1904 season.

Throughout the 1920s there were a number of high-profile cases of the "gentlemen's agreement" apparently being invoked by southern or mid-South schools for approaching games. Usually, the northern school's athletic officials would deny that any accommodations were being made for the demands of the southerners. During the 1926 season, Colgate's football team included a very good black sophomore halfback named Ray Vaughn. When the Red Raiders tangled with Pittsburgh and Navy on consecutive weekends in 1926, Vaughn, who had appeared in all the earlier games that season, was inexplicably held out of both games, and no mention was made in the game stories of the mainstream newspapers.

Less than a week after the two games, Vaughn told hometown friends that he had been held out against Pitt and Navy because of protests by officials of the two opposition schools. Vaughn said that he had been informed of the protests by Colgate's coach, George Hauser. Quickly, the NAACP stepped in and petitioned the secretary of the navy, Curtis Wilbur, to investigate the charge against the Naval Academy, even as the football coach of the Midshipmen, Bill Ingram, denied that any protest had been made against Vaughn's use. Incredibly, the Navy coach claimed that Colgate officials had notified him that Vaughn would not be making the trip to Annapolis "because the naval academy was rather far south."[55]

In 1929 New York University (NYU) had a standout black quarterback named Dave Myers. Weeks before the Georgia game, when Coach Chick Meehan made it known that his signal caller would not be appearing in the matchup at Yankee Stadium, a major debate broke out over the decision. The mainstream newspapers in New York declared that NYU had obviously consented to honor the gentlemen's agreement for the Georgia game, and they hammered away at the northern school's action.

While NYU officials sought to defuse the embarrassing controversy with a variety of excuses, Meehan was reported as stating, "We did not intend to play Myers when the game was scheduled, and he is not going to play." Just days before the game, NYU finally announced that Myers would be held out because of a shoulder injury reportedly suffered against Georgetown. Although the black press joined in directing criticisms at Meehan and NYU, Myers himself was also the subject of considerable attacks because of his apparent willingness to not speak out against the arrangement. An article in the *Chicago Defender* called upon the black player "to quit making a laughing stock out of his Race. If Meehan refuses to allow him in the Georgia game the entire Race looks for Myers to hand in his uniform and be a man." Myers sat in the grandstand during NYU's 27-19 win over Georgia, whereas black teammate William O'Shields was allowed to sit on the NYU bench.[56]

Even with the willingness of many northern schools to accommodate the gentlemen's agreement, the issue would continue to draw frequent criticisms, and the schools outside the South became increasingly reluctant to publicly acknowledge their participation. In late 1929, at the height of the NYU controversy, stories began circulating that Catholic University of Washington, D.C., had demanded that Duquesne University hold out its star tackle—a black player named Ray Kemp— from an approaching game. In response to an inquiry by the *Pittsburgh Courier*, Duquesne athletic officials moved to quickly deny the allegation. John Halahan, the school's graduate manager of athletics, stated that Duquesne made "no discrimination whatever as to creed or color." Yet the resistance of southern schools to competition against integrated northern football teams would continue until the days after World War II.[57]

Into the Future

When the decade of the 1930s arrived, there was no question that black college football had significantly transformed itself in the years since the end of World War I. New conferences had been organized, and older ones had solidified their memberships, establishing the importance of structure and discipline for black intercollegiate sport. Furthermore, there was no mistaking the improved fundamentals that now characterized much of the play.

Black college football had served as a bonding and uplifting influence for black society during the 1920s, one that provided a sense of belonging for black students and alumni who all too frequently were reminded of the racial inequalities that marked much of the mainstream culture. The black students and black community reveled in the football world that their schools had created by necessity—one that provided all the excitement, glamour, prestige, and social possibilities that were to be found in the mainstream brand of intercollegiate football. Yet college football for the black schools still existed in a clearly segregated sporting world throughout the 1920s and beyond and stood in stark contrast to the story of another ethnic sporting group we will soon examine.

Nevertheless, black college football had been transformed during the 1920s into a structured and publicized intercollegiate sport that increasingly in the future would provide a stage upon which black athletes might demonstrate their skills to the growing world of professional football. Eventually, football's racial barriers in the professional game and at the mainstream universities crumbled in the face of the many talented athletes being produced by an always improving world of black college football. No one in 1930 could have anticipated the days of the late twentieth century when substantial numbers of black players would make up the rosters of America's mainstream college football teams—even in the Southeastern Conference of the Deep South—in the culmination of the transformation brought to college football by black athletes and black intercollegiate sport, which had its origins in the 1920s.

8

LORDS OF THE PRAIRIE

One of the most interesting and significant tales of 1920s college football is the story of the Haskell Indians. Representing the Haskell Institute of Lawrence, Kansas, the centerpiece of the government's Indian educational programs, the football teams from this all-Indian school traveled the length and breadth of the country during the decade. The Haskell teams of the 1920s were in small part a reflection of the transformations taking place within college football during the era, but their story is significant both within football's history and for the study of sport and culture in post–World War I America.

As we have just seen, America's historically black colleges of the 1920s were forced to play intercollegiate football in a very segregated sporting world that was necessitated by the racial attitudes of the country at the time. The Indian athletes from Haskell faced a variety of ethnic biases around the country also, yet there was a major difference in their sporting world—the Haskell football teams were allowed to compete against varsity teams from the predominantly white colleges of the United States. Indeed, on their travels during the 1920s the Haskell football players were allowed to mingle within mainline white society, so they encountered a far different racial experience than did the black college football teams—the two stories providing a clear contrast in America's racial hierarchy of the times.

Yet Haskell's football teams were under constant public scrutiny while traveling around the country, since to many they represented the status of twentieth-century Native American culture. The school's long football journey through the 1920s would demonstrate the seemingly conflicting attitudes within white society toward Native Americans and the government's efforts to assimilate them into the mainstream of American culture.

During the 1920s—at the peak of the Haskell Institute's football history—its teams sought to establish their place in sporting history alongside the famed Carlisle Indian School football teams of pre–World War I days. This little-known part of college football history warrants examination, including the inevitable racial stereotyping that sought to affirm the general public's long-held beliefs regarding Native Americans. Three decades after the tragedy of Wounded Knee, Haskell football teams often played before white spectators who still expected to see the nineteenth-century savages that were being depicted in the popular media of the day.

EARLY HISTORY

The Carlisle School, located in Pennsylvania, had been the focal point of the government's educational programs for the Indian from the time of its opening in 1879. In its earliest years Carlisle had provided just elementary academic training while teaching the students certain basic trades, but as the years passed the curriculum had been expanded, and the Pennsylvania school became the training school for the Indian Service.[1]

Fielding successful athletic teams at Carlisle was seen as an excellent way to publicize the educational opportunities being provided to Native Americans by the government, so a widespread recruiting network was used to ensure that the most athletically talented Indian youth would eventually find their way to the school.[2]

After Carlisle's 1879 founding, federal legislation had been passed in 1882 authorizing the opening of three additional nonreservation boarding schools for Indian students. The schools would be located at Genoa in Nebraska, Chilocco in Oklahoma, and Haskell in Kansas. These schools would be under the direct supervision of the Office of Indian Affairs within the U.S. Department of the Interior.[3] Federal creation of the three nonreservation schools came about after a report from the congressional Committee on Indian Affairs had concluded that such schools would be "the true way to advance civilization and education among the Indian tribes."[4] Historian David Wallace Adams writes that the Indian schools were actually "established for the sole purpose of severing the child's cultural and psychological connection to his native heritage . . . a method of saving Indians by destroying them." George Washington, a former Haskell football player, explained in an interview that the students "drilled just like the military and even the girls wore a uniform. . . . The purpose of this type of system was an attempt to eradicate old tribal loyalties."[5]

Placing Indian children in these boarding schools kept them away from the reservation system and its influences. Students were not allowed to speak in their native languages, while cultural and religious customs also could not be practiced. Historian Robert Berkhofer has written that subsequent events show that "the funding and nature of the White-sponsored native education pointed in the direction of increased subordination and individualization of the Indian."[6]

Against this backdrop, in early 1883 a group of Lawrence citizens donated eight acres of land for the site of the Indian school that would become the Haskell Institute. When the school opened in September 1884, there were just twenty-two students, but within a semester the number had increased to three hundred. The school extended through eighth grade, and the classes initially included English, home economics, mathematics, and industrial training. Located on the east side of Lawrence, the school opened as the "United States Indian Industrial Training School," and in 1887 the name was changed to "the Haskell Institute," in honor of U.S. Representative Dudley C. Haskell of Kansas—a former chairman of the House Committee on Indian Affairs.[7]

By 1904 Haskell had expanded its academic curriculum through the tenth grade while adding vocational training aimed at making the Indian students self-supporting in the outside world. So successful was the training being provided at Haskell that by 1916 a report from the Department of the Interior was calling Haskell's vocational training course the best in the United States.[8]

The Haskell Institute fielded its first football team in 1896, playing a two-game schedule against the University of Kansas and Washburn College. Although Haskell was never more than a junior-college institution during the 1920s—and that status not attained until 1927—its football teams during that period were generally considered to be on a par with mid-level gridiron universities, so putting together representative schedules each season was not a problem. In fact, within just a few years of fielding its first football team Haskell's gridiron schedules would begin to include annual matchups against major universities such as Missouri, Nebraska, Texas, Kansas A&M, Oklahoma, and the Texas Aggies. For the seasons of 1900–1917 Haskell compiled an overall record of 85-68-4 against primarily major college competition. During this same period, Carlisle, with the best Indian athletes, was playing tougher schedules, and the Pennsylvania Indian school piled up an impressive record of 137-62-11.[9]

These outstanding records, against mostly top-flight college opponents, reflected the skill level that Indian youth had always brought to games and recreational activities that were a significant part of their training for adulthood. The organized athletic events conducted by the government's schools provided the young Indian men with an opportunity to establish their reputations for physical prowess while also gathering the respect previously accorded to victory in combat.

Collegiate athletic competition was also viewed by the Indian as a vehicle for affirming their racial superiority. Glenn "Pop" Warner, who coached football at Carlisle for a total of thirteen seasons, later wrote that his Indian players "developed a strong racial spirit rather than a school spirit. . . . When playing against college teams, it was not to them so much the Carlisle School against Pennsylvania or Harvard . . . but it was the Indian against the White Man." Although white sporting society did not generally recognize this fact, the racial stereotyping and ingrained expectations directed toward the Indian athletic teams served to endorse and validate this attitude in the minds of the Indian competitors.[10]

After the United States entered World War I, the Carlisle Indian School was closed in August 1918 and the facility converted for use as a military hospital. Earlier, rumors and accusations concerning the Carlisle School's football program had been growing since the disclosures after the 1912 Olympics of Jim Thorpe's professional baseball playing. When the war ended the government decided that its other Indian education centers were sufficient, so Carlisle was never reopened. The Haskell Institute then quickly became the most athletically prominent of all the government's Indian schools. Previously, the Kansas Indian school had been regarded as substantially inferior to Carlisle on the gridiron, but after the closing of the Pennsylvania school Haskell became the recipient of the top Indian athletes. After years of strict cultural training and discipline, along with the experience gained from playing representative college football schedules, the Haskell teams were ready to step into the spotlight as representatives of Native American culture.[11]

Representing the Race

Haskell played only four games during the 1918 football season because of World War I restrictions and the national influenza epidemic, but when the 1919 gridiron season rolled around the Indian School was ready to tackle an eleven-game schedule that included six away games. Featuring wins over Oklahoma A&M, Kansas A&M, and Xavier, Haskell compiled an 8-2-1 record for 1919, as the Indians featured a speedy, wide-open offensive attack that included plenty of passing.

This style of play would typify the Haskell football teams during the 1920s. Warner explained that this sophisticated offensive play was possible from relatively uneducated players, because "the Indians had a general cunning and a liking for games of all sorts, which made them clever in working strategic plays and tricks, and they delighted greatly in fooling their opponents with clever ruses." Comments about the Indians' football trickery and cunning from Warner and others would appear with frequency in news media reporting throughout the decade, and though usually presented as a compliment, these remarks did much to sustain prevailing attitudes about the Native American personality.[12]

Home games for the Haskell team gave the Indian students a chance to participate in all the traditional rituals of college football. At halftime of the 1919 game against Kansas Wesleyan, Haskell students staged a snake dance across the field. The Indian girls were all wrapped in bright-red striped blankets, which was one of the few trappings suggesting Native American identification and culture that the school administration would allow. Every student had a red blanket, which was usually brought out only for the most festive of occasions. For the government administrators, the red blankets made the Indian appear as a member of a single generic group, or "nationalized" the Indian identity.[13]

Encouraging the participation in nonthreatening athletic-related rituals, such as snake dances and pregame bonfire rallies, also represented an effort to associate the Indian students with an experience that was being shared with their counterparts at the white man's colleges and universities. It was hoped that it would develop "school spirit" among the individual Indian students, along with some of the same life-enduring loyalties that were commonly manifested among white college students.

The close public scrutiny Haskell teams now traveled under was evidenced early, as the team traveled to Cincinnati for the Thanksgiving Day 1919 game against Xavier, and after winning a hard-fought 7-0 decision the Indian players celebrated that evening with a holiday dinner at the Hotel Metropole. The *Cincinnati Enquirer* noted that if the Haskell team returned in the future, "local fans are assured of some classy and sportsmanlike football," while the school newspaper, the *Indian Leader,* commented, "We want to say right here that we were splendidly treated. Everything was done to make us comfortable."[14]

THE PEAK YEARS

For the 1920 season, Haskell had a new football coach in Matty Bell, a recent star player at Centre College in Kentucky who would later move on to become a prominent coach in the Southwest Conference. Joining Bell on the coaching staff at Haskell in 1920 was Frank W. McDonald, who would serve through 1932 as assistant football coach and head coach of the basketball and track teams. In 1920 the Haskell school curriculum still went through only the sophomore year of high school, yet McDonald wrote in his memoir that he was younger than many of the students at the school during the 1920s. The best player on the 1920 team was only in the fourth grade.[15]

September 1921 brought major changes in the educational structure of the Haskell Institute, producing tangible benefits for the athletic programs. That fall the grade levels offered at Haskell were extended through the twelfth grade, so Haskell became the first government-operated Indian school to offer a complete four-year high school course. Coach McDonald wrote that this change had "a tremendous impact on our Athletic Program. We had an influx of young Indian athletes who enrolled at Haskell, who had been attending public high schools." Also in 1921, Haskell launched a two-year normal school program that included teacher training.[16]

The adoption of a full four-year high school curriculum at Haskell in September 1921 was certainly justifiable for political, social, and educational reasons. But the launching of a normal school program at the same time, given Haskell's football accomplishments over much of the following ten years, suggests that the potential benefits to the athletic department may have also been a strong motivation. What-ever the driving forces may have been, in the fall of 1921 Haskell suddenly found itself able to retain its best athletes for up to four additional years, and the *Indian Leader* noted that "many athletes have returned to take advantage of both the aca-demic and athletic privileges. This makes possible a strong team."[17]

It was going to take one season before all the benefits of the academic changes would appear on the football field. Haskell did manage wins over Texas Christian and Tulsa in 1921, while struggling to a 5-4-0 record against a formidable sched-ule that included Notre Dame, Nebraska, and Marquette. The season was notable for one feature that would soon become a staple of the football program—the ex-tended stays away from school—as the Indian team stayed at LaPorte, Indiana, during the week between the games at Milwaukee (Marquette) and South Bend (Notre Dame).[18]

Haskell had a new football coach for the 1922 season in Dick Hanley, as Matty Bell had moved on to Carroll College in Wisconsin. Hanley was a strict discipli-narian, and the Indian gridmen were put through an extremely tough training regimen that produced immediate results, as Haskell fielded a team that was de-scribed as "the fastest, trickiest and the best trained team seen here in years." The Indians posted an 8-2-0 record in 1922 while outscoring the opposition 307 points to 89, but the schedule included only four major opponents. Yet the *Christian Sci-ence Monitor* became one of the first publications to take notice that the Kansas Indian school was carrying on the gridiron traditions of Glenn Warner and Jim Thorpe, commenting, "Haskell Institute has developed a football machine this year which rivals in many ways the teams that the famous Carlisle Indian School turned out in the past."[19]

John Levi, an Arapaho Indian from Oklahoma described by the newspapers as the "huge fullback," was named team captain for 1922 and as a triple-threat back he clearly was the centerpiece of the Indian grid squad. Although he impressed sportswriters everywhere Haskell played, the Indians did not venture east of Cin-cinnati, so Levi was never seen by the influential eastern selectors of the various All-America teams. The high point of the 1922 season came in the last game when the Indians traveled to San Antonio, Texas, and knocked off the rugged Southwest Conference champions from Baylor by a score of 21-20.[20]

With only three lettermen lost from the previous season, Haskell was ready to substantially expand its gridiron horizons during the 1923 season. Featuring the sensational Levi at tailback, the Indians embarked on an ambitious thirteen-game schedule that called for them to play games at Kansas City, Omaha, Minneapo-lis, Tulsa, Indianapolis, Cincinnati, New York City, and Los Angeles, including one stretch of three weeks away from school. Haskell began pursuing far-flung football schedules for strictly financial reasons, as the growing popularity of the colorful

Indian team provided a source of funding that could be capitalized on not only for football expenses but also to help support some of the school's other athletic programs—something that was typical of intercollegiate football after 1918.[21]

The Haskell football team had never played in the East before, where the image of what an Indian should look like had been created, to a great extent, by artists, pulp-fiction writers, and the relatively new motion-picture industry—"the Indian generally depicted as a person of little culture and less language." For their part, the Haskell players and coaches were very much aware of these stereotyped images held by eastern sport fans, as Coach McDonald noted: "In our football trips to Boston, Philadelphia, New York etc, it was essential we have Indian costumes as well as football uniforms. This was because the Eastern public almost demanded seeing Indians as they knew them from pictures and publicity. Naturally our boys didn't wear costumes as street dress but there were times when they would cooperate . . . and pose for the sake of publicity."[22]

Directly opposed to the Indian stereotypes of the movies and pulp literature is a photo taken on Haskell's 1923 trip to the East, which shows a large group of players posing on the front porch of the White House. What we see is a group of well-manicured young men, all dressed in suits, ties, and expensive top coats. It is clear that the school administration fully recognized that the Indian players were on display as representatives of their race, and so were leaving no stone unturned in creating a favorable image for the results of its assimilation efforts. McDonald's comment that the players would occasionally "cooperate" in posing for publicity photos that included racial stereotypes of the Indian, and their general appearance in the White House photo, indicates that the Haskell traveling party hardly regarded themselves as the uneducated savages being portrayed in the movies, yet they were willing to participate in both sides of the conflicting images.[23]

Many historians subscribe to the idea that by the 1920s the government's assimilation plans for the Indian had succeeded in becoming an acceptable concept within the realm of American culture. Frederick E. Hoxie has written that "the redefinition of Indian Assimilation in the early twentieth century reflects a fundamental shift in American social values. . . . In place of the old ideals appeared a new hierarchical view of society that emphasized the coexistence and interaction of diverse groups." Historian Lawrence C. Kelly contends that by the early 1920s, "If [Americans] thought about it at all, they probably concluded that there was no longer any need for a policy toward the Indians."[24]

In a time of increasing sophistication, the stereotypes of the Indian should have no longer been seriously believed by the general populace—being instead replaced by the notion that educated Indians were just another cultural component of the great melting pot that the American population now represented. Yet the newspaper accounts of the Haskell teams' travels carry frequent examples of racially stereotyped comments, while, as McDonald indicated, there clearly existed a consistent expectation that the football team's appearances would be accompanied by popularly held images of the American Indian. Much of the racially suggestive language used by the newspapers in reference to the Haskell football team was repetitive of the experiences of the Carlisle teams in the 1890s and early 1900s.[25]

Haskell opened its 1923 football season with three easy wins against Kansas colleges, as Levi seemed unstoppable while scoring ten touchdowns. The football team then headed to Minneapolis, where a large torchlight rally was held by the nearly five hundred Indians from the region who were in town to attend the game against Minnesota. A visit by the Haskell football team was a major event for nearby Native American communities, and the attendance of large numbers of Indians at the games was a frequent occurrence throughout the 1920s wherever the team was playing in the midwestern and western sections of the country. The following afternoon the great Jim Thorpe himself sat on the Haskell bench during the game, and so provided a symbolic endorsement of the Kansas gridmen as worthy successors to the great Carlisle traditions. After the game—a 13-12 loss for the Indians—the Haskell players were given a reception in one of the ballrooms of the plush Curtis Hotel in Minneapolis.[26]

After the Indians piled up three more wins, the team left on November 11 and headed for New York City to play the Quantico Marines, a service team. A Haskell football team had never before played east of Cincinnati, and the little Indian school from Kansas was virtually unknown to the New York sporting public. Coach McDonald has written of the New York sports editors' complete lack of familiarity with Haskell's football program, and not surprisingly, the Manhattan newspapers were using all the Indian symbolism possible in their pregame write-ups. Typical was the *New York Times*: "There was a time when the cavalry was the country's surest branch of the service when it came to dealing with the Indians, but today the United States Marines will be called out to check the charge of the Red Men."[27]

Before the game, a *New York Times* writer noted that Levi was "a performer who is said to be the equal of the great Jim Thorpe." After watching the Indian's brilliant play against the Marines in the 14-14 tie game, the same reporter wrote that Levi's "performance measured up to the standard set for him in every respect save in his kicking." After meeting all of their financial commitments for the trip to New York, the Haskell team ended up clearing about five thousand dollars on the game. The Indians were invited to return to New York for a game in 1924, but their schedule was already set, so they had to decline the offer. As Coach McDonald later wrote, "The Yankee Stadium game had served its purpose. We were accepted in the former Carlisle area."[28]

After the stopover in Washington, D.C., to visit the nation's capital, the tour moved to Indianapolis for a game with Butler and then on to Cincinnati for a Thanksgiving Day clash with Xavier, before heading back to Kansas after an absence of three weeks. The regular-season schedule for 1923 was closed out with a trip down to Oklahoma in early December to play Tulsa. The Haskell team then stayed over for a few days and defeated Oklahoma Baptist University by a score of 13-0 on December 12, a hastily arranged game that has never been recorded in the football guides and score books.[29]

But Coach Hanley still was not ready to close up the 1923 season, so the Haskell team accepted an offer to travel out to Los Angeles for a Christmas Day matchup against the Olympic Club from San Francisco, an independent team of former college players. The Indian team arrived in California five days before the game and set up training at the Sherman Indian School in Riverside. A *Los Angeles Times* sportswriter could not resist getting in yet another Indian cliché, as he wrote: "The Redskins are in Southern California after the scalps of an indeterminate number of Olympic Club gridders." Yet in the days leading up to the game, Levi and his Indian running mates made a big impression on everyone with their size, speed, and football talent.[30]

On Christmas Day the two teams collided at Washington Park in Los Angeles, and Haskell made a first-quarter touchdown by Levi stand up for a 7-6 win over the Olympic Club. Levi finished the season with a total of 24 touchdowns and 149 points scored, which was enough to earn him First and Second Team All-America backfield spots from some of the major selectors, helped no doubt by playing a game in New York City. The win in Los Angeles closed out Haskell's 1923 season with a record of 11-2-1, after a journey of more than fifteen thousand miles.[31]

Wide-ranging travel in search of lucrative intersectional games had proved feasible from a financial standpoint, but the administration and coaches were not happy about the athletes' extended absences from school. These types of schedules were being pursued only out of a necessity brought about by the lack of suitable football facilities on the Haskell campus.

The football field at Haskell was referred to as the "Gumbo Gridiron" by the staff and students, with the field being extremely hard and with virtually no grass. But worse yet were the crumbling wooden bleachers that could accommodate 350 fans at most. These conditions combined to make it financially and artistically impossible to attract any major college opponents to Lawrence. The 1923 schedule had included four home games, all against small Kansas colleges, while the 1924 slate had three home dates, and 1925 would see the Haskell team playing at home on just one occasion.[32]

Early in 1924 the school administration decided to proceed with a fund-raising program aimed at the construction of a concrete football stadium on campus, and

Coach McDonald was put in charge of the pledge drive. Just before the 1924 season, Coach Hanley spoke at a general assembly in the school auditorium and said that "students and alumni could not expect to see high-class teams which Haskell meets away from home, in games here, until we have suitable grounds and a stadium." The original goal of the drive was to raise $50,000 for the construction of a stadium on the west side of the campus, but McDonald soon recommended that Haskell buy a tract of twelve acres to the north of the school as the site for the new athletic complex.[33]

From the beginning of the fund-raising effort the intent was that all the monies would be raised by donations directly from individual Indians. The raising of funds and the building of the new stadium were more planks in the government's program to establish a feeling of loyalty among the Indian students and alumni for the educational institution that had been provided for them by white society. Extending the fund-raising effort to the former students—most now living back on reservations—resembled to a great extent the funding plans aimed at their alumni by white universities but also was a financial decision aimed at the wealth of many of the Southwest Indians, attained through the discovery of oil and other minerals on reservation lands.

The Haskell administration declared that the stadium was to stand as a symbol of the Indians' "esteem for this great institution, their regard for Haskell athletic teams, and their interest in physical education and love of outdoor games and sports." In April 1924 the first contribution to the stadium campaign was made by U.S. Senator Charles Curtis of Kansas, and within the year a direct-mail solicitation program began producing donations from former Haskell students. By February 1925 approximately $65,000 would be raised, with $56,195 of that total having been received from the 150-member Quapaw Tribe of Oklahoma.[34]

Haskell opened the 1924 season with a pair of easy wins before heading north to Minneapolis for a rematch with Minnesota. The Golden Gophers handed the Indians a 20-0 defeat before more than 20,000 fans, but otherwise the trip was characterized by the colorful proceedings and good feelings usually attendant to college football. Haskell's cheerleader, Alan Shepard, accompanied the team to Minneapolis where he appeared during the game dressed in a complete Indian costume, while at halftime the large crowd was entertained by a band of 25 Indians from nearby reservations who staged a picturesque dance on the field while dressed in traditional Indian ceremonial clothing. After the game the players were honored at a reception in the Curtis Hotel, and Haskell officials would later declare that the treatment received by the Indians in Minneapolis was "the most friendly and thorough that we have ever come in contact with."[35]

Warm receptions such as the ones usually encountered in Minneapolis were a reflection of historian Philip J. Deloria's view that "Americans' embrace of Indian mascots was only part of a broad, early-twentieth-century primitivist nostalgia. . . . Many Americans used a ritualized set of symbols—cowboys, Indians, pioneers—to evoke by-gone American qualities of the frontier era." Hoxie has added, "Native Americans represented virtues the nation risked forgetting in the headlong pursuit of wealth and power." The Haskell football players certainly did not consider themselves mascots, but when their athletic skills were combined with the colorful halftime shows, the total package did provide both a nostalgic and a modern-day experience for the spectators in attendance.[36]

In early November 1924 the Haskell Indians again invaded the East for a pair of games, including a visit to Providence to tangle with a good Brown team in a game that the *Indian Leader* described as "by far the greatest opportunity ever offered a Haskell football team to bring renown to themselves and to their school." Brown University, though not one of the old-line Big Three of eastern football, nevertheless was a school with a long history and, to the Haskell traveling party, one with a clear association with the social, academic, and athletic elite of white society. A game against such a prestigious eastern university, and one with an excellent football team on top of it, was seen as an opportunity for the small Kansas Indian school to further establish itself as the athletic successor to Carlisle.[37]

After a touchdown late in the fourth quarter gave Haskell a thrilling 17-13 win over Brown, the *Providence Journal* described the Indian team as a "fast-running, hard hitting tribe of copper-skinned warriors, led by stalwart . . . John Levi, the modern Jim Thorpe." The *Indian Leader* described the Brown game as "Haskell's greatest victory." Back at the Indian school, when news of the game's outcome had been received, the men of the student body descended on the town of Lawrence and staged a victory parade with all the students wearing their infamous red blankets. When the team returned three days later, another massive parade escorted the players from the Santa Fe station back to the school.[38]

Haskell closed out its 1924 season with a record of 7-2-1 after wins over Butler, Xavier, and Oklahoma Baptist, all on the road. The Oklahoma Baptist game had been hastily scheduled in Muskogee, Oklahoma, in order to generate interest in Haskell's stadium drive among the rich reservation tribes of the area. After the game, members of the Osage Tribe escorted the Haskell players to Hominy, Oklahoma, where they were to be guests at a banquet.

Days before the Muskogee game, Coach McDonald had been approached by a committee of Osage Indians who served as officials of the Hominy Giants, an Indian football team. They sought to hire the four seniors from the Haskell team to play for the Giants against the Fairfax town team in a game scheduled for the day after the Oklahoma Baptist game. Considerable sums of money had been bet on the game by the Indians, and since the Haskell team would still be in Hominy anyway, in the interest of the stadium drive, permission was obtained from the school superintendent to help out the local Indian team.

However, late Sunday morning, the day after the Baptist game, Coach Hanley was approached by a panicked group of officials from the Hominy Giants. The Fairfax team had arrived for the game, but instead of its usual lineup, the Fairfax owners had brought in the entire Kansas City Cowboys semipro team. After some hurried deliberations, Hanley agreed to use the entire Haskell team to represent Hominy against the ringers from Kansas City.

What followed was a rough-and-tumble game, played on a prairie field marked off with lime yard lines. When Levi finally burst into the end zone for a late touchdown, it capped off a come-from-behind win by the Hominy-Haskell team. Unlike the highly publicized 1921 semipro game that had featured players from Illinois and Notre Dame, this game remained relatively unknown for years, so none of the Haskell players were ever declared ineligible for further intercollegiate play. More important, the Haskell Institute now had the unswerving loyalty of the Oklahoma Indians, and McDonald later wrote that "the good-will engendered that day with the recently oil and mineral rich Osage and Quapaw Indians unquestionably built the stadium."[39]

By the summer of 1925 work on the stadium construction had been started. A major element in keeping the cost down was the use of labor provided by male Indian students, especially the young men who lived at the school through the summer break. Very early in the project it had been decided to also construct a major concrete archway at the entrance to the stadium as a memorial to World War I veterans, of which many had been young Indian men. The construction cost of the archway came to approximately $16,000 and was completely funded by the gifts of two wealthy former Haskell students, members of the Quapaw Tribe, Agnes Quapaw-Hoffman and Alice Beaver Hallam. The arch was said to "symbolize the unity among Indian Nations," while the entire stadium project stood as "a testimony of the strength, courage, and unity among the Indian people."[40]

When the 1925 football season rolled around, the Haskell team had to face a grueling thirteen-game schedule without Levi, who had finally used up his eligibility. The Indian gridmen played just one game on their home grounds, and for the rest of the season they traveled from Boston to Los Angeles; Spokane, Washington, to Richmond, Virginia; and points in between. Haskell had a new backfield star in Mayes McLain, who barely had enough Cherokee blood to be called "part-Indian," and who, with his wavy hair, looked more like a handsome Irish movie star. That the small Kansas Indian school now believed it had moved out of the shadow of its famous Pennsylvania predecessor can be seen in a comment by the *Indian Leader* on the prospects for 1925: "The present outlook is for Haskell to make a far greater name than Carlisle ever made in the football world."[41]

14. Archway entrance at the Haskell Institute. Constructed in 1926 as a memorial to the Native Americans lost in World War I, it was completely funded through the donations of two former women students at Haskell. It still stands at the entrance to the football stadium. Author's collection.

Again in 1925, the Indian football team made friends everywhere they traveled. Before Haskell's 10-9 win over Gonzaga at Spokane, an editorial in the *Gonzaga Bulletin* said that the approaching game "betokens a further shattering of hated barriers; of those barriers that completely segregate races." In Richmond the Indian gridmen edged past William and Mary for a 14-13 win, and on that two-week trip the team was accompanied by the school's assistant superintendent, G. E. Peters. In a short article on his travels, Peters wrote of the great praise the players received on all their stops: "It is certainly a credit to Haskell to have a group of students go out into these strange communities and make the good impression our football team has made."[42]

Haskell's brutal 1925 schedule included playing three games in a span of just eight days in late November, and the Indians were described as being "a tired, worn-out, crippled football team." The players were rarely on the school's campus to attend classes, and even the *Indian Leader* took notice of the extended absences:

"Coach Hanley and the Braves made us a little visit the first of the week and then departed to continue their 20,000-mile schedule." After playing a 0-0 tie at Bucknell, the Indian team arrived back at school at noon on Monday and then left for the West Coast the following evening. After the game in Spokane, the Indian team left immediately for the long trip to Dayton, Ohio, to fulfill a date there.[43]

Yet despite their long absences from school and the much better meals and accommodations they received while traveling, the Haskell football players were idolized by the other students of the school—a stark contrast to the situation that had existed at Carlisle in 1914. Occasional items describing the hero worship accorded to the Haskell athletes by many of the younger, grade school–age, students appeared through the years. For the older students the national publicity and the many successes of the football teams created a sense of "belonging" within the intercollegiate athletic community.[44]

After finishing the 1925 season with a record of 9-3-1, the fall of 1926 brought Haskell the greatest football team in school history, along with the dedication of the long-awaited new football stadium, which was expected to launch a new era for the Indian football program. The fund-raising drive had originally targeted $50,000 as the amount needed, but the final cost of the stadium had come in at approximately $185,000. The complex had identical concrete and steel grandstands along the north and south sides of the football field, and each side seated about fifty-five hundred fans.

Coach Hanley had put together an extremely good football team for 1926. Joining McLain in an outstanding Indian backfield was George Levi (a younger brother of former Haskell star John), speedster Elijah Smith, and Louis Colby. Anchoring the line would be a pair of All-America-caliber tackles in Theodore "Tiny" Roebuck and Tom Stidham, along with center Albert Hawley. The 1926 squad included players representing thirteen different tribes. With the new stadium ready, the Haskell team was finally able to play several games on campus, although the schedule still had them traveling to Boston, Cincinnati, Dayton, and San Francisco.

Right from the season opener against a small college opponent, it was clear that this team, and McLain in particular, was something special. Piling up plenty of touchdowns, Haskell stormed through its schedule, including wins over Dayton, Bucknell, Loyola of Chicago, Michigan State, Tulsa, and Xavier. Only a 21-21 tie with an excellent Boston College team, possibly the best team in the East in 1926, marred the string of Haskell victories.[45]

The Bucknell game on October 30, 1926, was played in Lawrence and was the official dedication day for Haskell's beautiful new stadium. The weekend was the occasion for great celebrations, as thousands of Indians converged on Haskell and set up a tent city on the school's grounds, creating a strange scene with their modern cars parked in front of the tents. The long weekend included Indian pa-rades, barbecues, beauty contests, Indian dance demonstrations and exhibitions of horsemanship, while the *Kansas City Star* and other newspapers carried plenty of pictures of Indians wearing ceremonial costumes.[46]

An article appearing in the January 1929 issue of the *American Journal of Sociology* pointed to Haskell's new stadium "as a culmination of the success of winning football teams in developing the Indians' social consciousness and in reducing their inferiority complex," and also as an indication that in the future Native Americans would be active participants in industry, politics, and social affairs. In the official game program, the school's superintendent, Clyde M. Blair, wrote that the new stadium was "evidence of Indian appreciation for the educational oppor-tunities Haskell had been offering the youth of the race." Yet another statement about the school in the game program hinted at the resentment still felt by many: "Its mission is the fitting of young Indian men and women for the problems of life which white civilization has brought to the Indian race."[47]

Hanley accepted an offer for a December 18 postseason game in San Fran-cisco against the unbeaten Hawaii All-Stars, the Pacific Coast club champions, and the Haskell team did its pregame training on the campus of Stanford University. While there the Indians played, and beat, the undefeated and Rose Bowl–bound Stanford team in a scrimmage game. The win over the Hawaii All-Stars closed Haskell's 1926 season with a record of 12-0-1, with McLain scoring 38 touchdowns and tallying 253 points for the season, despite missing two games.[48]

The 1926 season represents the pinnacle of Haskell's football history both on and off the field, and the Kansas Indian school was finally free of the shadows cast by its Carlisle ancestors. But the gridiron fortunes soon turned downward. McLain left to play at the University of Iowa in 1927, but much more serious was the de-parture of Coach Hanley. Haskell's gridiron fortunes had been under his guiding hand since 1922, but during the 1926 season he had announced that he would be leaving to accept the head coach position at Northwestern for 1927.[49]

From an institutional standpoint, Haskell took steps to maintain its football status when in 1927 it added a two-year junior-college program to its curriculum. The academic programs offered included teaching, military science for prospec-tive school disciplinarians, and, most significantly of all for the maintenance of good athletic teams, physical education and athletic training. In studying the gradual evolution of the junior-college programs, historian Loretta Granzer noted, "It seems not improbable that Haskell's football prowess was at least indirectly responsible. . . . Schedules which included games with the country's leading uni-versities and colleges called for an older and more seasoned type of player."[50]

Yet the anticipated benefits from the junior college did not immediately mate-rialize on the football field, as Haskell struggled to records of 5-4-1 and 5-5-0 for the seasons of 1927–1928 under the direction of new head coach, John Thomas. Even more distressing than the team's won-loss record was the continued difficulty in scheduling games on the Haskell campus against major college opponents. At the time of the stadium's dedication it had been the belief of the administration and the students that the football team "should be able to play numerous big home games in years to come." The athletic officials had "promised that the stadium would mean the bringing of many teams of national reputation here to meet the Indians."[51] The stadium had been seen as the final step that would install Haskell football among the big-time programs of the national intercollegiate scene.

Unfortunately, the relative remoteness of Lawrence, Kansas, and the seating capacity of just eleven thousand—considered quite small in the days of the "big-business" stadia—combined to discourage major football schools from making the trip to the Kansas plains. The 1927 Indian team played just three home games, with Loyola of New Orleans representing the only major opponent willing to make the trip to Haskell. Though not playing games on either coast, the Indians still traveled extensively in the midwestern and mideastern sections of the country, and the 1928 schedule included trips to New Orleans and Minneapolis.[52]

When the 1929 football season rolled around, Haskell had a new coach in William "Lone Star" Dietz, and the Indians were about to enter their final years of gridiron glory. Dietz was part Oglala Sioux, and he had played football at Carlisle from 1909 to 1911 before serving as an assistant coach there under Glenn Warner from 1912 to 1914. Dietz had then moved on to the head-coaching job at Washington State University where he led that school's team to the 1916 Rose Bowl game, and after the war years he had moved through a succession of head-coach jobs around the country. With his hiring in 1929, Haskell was now turning back to its Carlisle football heritage for an answer to the current problems.[53]

The 1929 schedule included just two home games among the ten dates, with trips to Pittsburgh and New Orleans highlighting the away games. Before the season opener it had been hinted that the Indians were poised for a comeback season, and the sparkplug for this expected rebound was the last of the great Indian running backs, Louis "Rabbit" Weller. A member of the Caddo Tribe from Oklahoma, Weller was a dazzling breakaway runner with great speed who was also ambidextrous and could pass or punt equally well from either side. Despite Weller nursing an early-season leg injury, Haskell stormed out of the gate with five straight wins before dropping a 19-12 decision to Loyola at New Orleans.

In late November the Indian team traveled to Pittsburgh to take on Duquesne, and while in the Steel City the players were taken to a tour and luncheon at the Westinghouse Company. During the tour the players met two former Haskell gridiron stars, Glenn Tahquette and Peter Davis, who were said to be doing extremely well as Westinghouse employees. It was a clear message that educated Indian men could find rewarding careers within industrial white society and that the segregation of the reservation system was not their only option.

Although school officials were always arranging such affairs for the Indian athletes, by this time in their football history the Haskell traveling parties seldom mentioned the courtesies and warm receptions received on their journeys. Such things had come to be accepted by the Indian students as normal behavior toward them by white society as they traveled. This fact provides further endorsement for the commentaries of Hoxie and Kelly in support of the emergence of cultural pluralism in the 1920s, while also indicating a growing acceptance by the Indians of the potential for assimilation into white society, in spite of the many conflicting events and images that typically surrounded their travels.

Haskell closed out the 1929 campaign with a record of 8-2-0, and after the season Dietz, now being referred to as the "Miracle Man," was signed to a new three-year contract with a substantial increase in salary. Dietz was quoted as attributing his success in 1929 "in large manner to the fact he was an Indian himself and thus had a clear insight into the workings of the Indian mind."[54]

For the 1930 season it seemed as though Haskell was poised for a return to the gridiron glories of the mid-1920s. Once again the Indian football team seemed to be in demand everywhere, and the 1930 schedule called for them to travel more than ten thousand miles, including a trip to Spokane for a game with Gonzaga. Although the schedule had the usual minimum number of home games, Haskell had succeeded in attracting the University of Kansas for a game in the Indians' beautiful stadium. The two schools are located little more than two miles apart, and when Coach McDonald learned that the state university had an open date for 1930, he quickly approached Forrest "Phog" Allen, the Kansas athletic director, with an offer of ten thousand dollars "for taxi fare." The news of the date with the regionally prestigious University of Kansas created considerable excitement on the Haskell campus, and planning began for a festive weekend that would exceed even the stadium dedication weekend back in 1926. McDonald later wrote that "the game with K.U. not only gave us stature by being recognized by the Big Six Conference team, but it was a cinch to be a money-maker for both teams."[55]

Haskell added temporary bleachers to raise its seating capacity to sixteen thousand for the Kansas game, and still it was not enough, as thousands stood in every available space around the stadium. Jim Thorpe and John Levi were brought in to conduct drop-kicking and passing exhibitions, while fireworks and the legendary Indian Eagle Dancers were also part of the halftime festivities. Weller raced 80 yards for a touchdown to give Haskell an early lead, but Kansas, the eventual Big Six champion, came rolling back for a 33-7 victory.[56]

Haskell continued on to post a record of 10-1-0 for the 1930 season, one of its best ever. Weller had another standout campaign, for which he received mention on a number of All-America teams, including Second Team spots on the Hearst and *New York Telegram* mythical elevens. McDonald called Weller "without doubt the greatest broken field runner in the country."[57]

FOOTBALL'S DECLINE

Everything seemed to be looking up for Haskell despite the onset of the Great Depression, as the Indian school was gaining recognition from both academic and athletic standpoints. By 1930 the academic credits earned in the Indian school's junior college were being accepted by the University of Kansas as applying toward bachelor degrees, and Haskell was considered the most advanced within the Indian educational system. From an athletic standpoint, Knute Rockne and Warner had each visited Haskell in 1930 for speaking engagements. Rockne spoke at Haskell's convocation for 1930, during which he gave a "stirring and moving pro-Indian" talk and "referred to the shabby treatment accorded the American Indians." Later that night at a private gathering, Rockne offered Dietz and McDonald a date on Notre Dame's 1932 football schedule, along with a fifteen thousand–dollar guarantee. The Haskell coaches knew that this matchup was way out of the Indian team's class, but when Rockne assured them that he "wasn't about to run up a big score," the offer was quickly accepted. McDonald would later say that in 1930, "to my thinking, the Indian School reached its zenith in recognition."[58]

Yet trouble was in the air for the Haskell football program as the Hoover administration in Washington scrambled to get control of the economy before the 1932 presidential election. By 1931 Haskell "had scaled the heights of athletic glory, had reached the peak of its enrollment and its appropriations," and these accomplishments appeared to be problems for Washington.[59]

With the federal government unable to materially assist the growing ranks of the unemployed, the issue of cultural assimilation for the Indian was no longer something that politically warranted the level of previous expense and exposure. Despite the fact that the government had never provided money for funding of the Haskell football team—a fact not generally known—the newspaper pictures of well-dressed Indian players traveling around the country and living in some of the best hotels could easily become an agent for inflaming the hostility of those individuals who believed that Washington should help the white citizenry first. And so, in the summer of 1931 Haskell received a new superintendent, Dr. R. D. Baldwin. The athletic coaches and faculty expected that the new administrator would be looking to reduce expenses, but none anticipated what was coming.

For starters, Baldwin announced that Haskell was being returned to high school status with the discontinuing of the junior-college program by 1932. Also, during the fall of 1931, teams of inspectors from the Bureau of Indian Affairs began descending upon the school. Haskell had been maintaining two National Guard units, made up of the older Indian students, and the unrest and anger at Washington that was spreading across the country made these quasi Indian-military units an immediate government concern. Quickly, a directive was received from Washington that prohibited the guard units from being stationed at Haskell, action that soon drew considerable criticism, given the many patriotic contributions made by Indian men to the nation's World War I efforts.[60]

In 1931 Haskell finished what proved to be its last football season with college-level players, compiling a record of 5-7-0. With no curriculum beyond high school available, nearly thirty athletes would have to leave Haskell instead of playing for the Indian school in 1932. After the final game of 1931, McDonald, serving as athletic director, was called in to see Baldwin, and the message delivered was that "the players could not be away from class as in the past, and that our [football] schedule should be limited to eight games with the season being completed by Thanksgiving."[61]

The contracts for the football games in the fall of 1932 still had to be fulfilled with what amounted to a high school team. Everywhere the Haskell team traveled in 1932, the pregame publicity contained various forms of apology that emphasized that the two schools had no warning of the approaching academic changes at the Indian school. McDonald, who had always been involved in the publicity work, made it clear that "this would be the last chance to see an Indian team . . . [and] so far as Big Time Football was concerned, we had gone down the same as Carlisle." When McDonald publicly pointed to these affairs as "an example of further persecution of the Indians," his days at Haskell were numbered.[62]

Haskell closed out its 1932 football season with a record of 2-6-1, which was followed by Dietz departing to take over as head coach of the Boston Redskins of the NFL for 1933. Soon after the 1932 football season McDonald was called to a meeting with Baldwin, and after a stormy discussion McDonald was released from his position, bringing to a close his twelve-year career with Haskell's athletic department. Later, in the fall of 1933, Baldwin would take a leave of absence from which he never returned.[63]

The Indian school continued to play football beyond the 1932 season, but quickly the major-school opponents dropped away, leaving Haskell with primarily a localized small-college schedule in the final years. Longtime rivals Creighton, Xavier, and Oklahoma A&M remained loyal the longest, but by 1936 even they were gone from the schedule. Eventually, the financial drain of even a small-college schedule, and the limited pool of players available, was too much, and after the 1938 season Haskell dropped the sport of football.[64]

The government's downsizing of the Haskell Indian School, along with the ultimate elimination of its football program, was both shortsighted and detrimental to the continuance of what had become serious and beneficial attempts at assimilation. The travels of the Haskell football teams, and the exemplary conduct of the Indian athletes, had done much to make the general American populace aware of the progress, potential, and accomplishments being generated by the government's educational programs. The success of the Haskell athletes in moving among white society had potentially opened the doors for future Indian youths to obtain meaningful jobs in American commerce after graduation from college, and so avoid a return to the limitations of the reservation system.

It is ironic that the Haskell football teams had moved freely within the white mainstream of the college sport throughout their existence yet ultimately ended in ruins as a direct result of the racial bias and fears that obviously still existed toward Native Americans in early 1930s America. This tale of Haskell football thus stands in stark contrast to the history of the black colleges, where the gridiron sport was forced to exist in a very segregated world until the day ultimately came when the predominantly white colleges and professional teams could no longer ignore the tidal wave of outstanding black athletes being produced. Taken in total, the government's actions of the early 1930s compromised the outstanding efforts on behalf of Native American education and assimilation by the Haskell football teams of the previous decade—yet the Indian gridmen remain an important part of 1920s college football history.

9

SCANDALS AND DISPUTES

College football's past has been marked by many scandals and disputes, usually revolving around the issues of player eligibility, individual or university sportsmanship attitudes, or the subsidization of athletes. The many transformations within college football during the 1920s contributed to the onset of several nasty athletic disagreements between schools during the decade, and at the heart of all but the most trivial was the driving desire to have a winning football team—or at worst an extremely competitive one.

With the great riches and prestige potentially available in the college football world of the 1920s—not to mention the always-growing hysteria for the sport by students, alumni, and fans—it was no surprise that longtime rivals were frequently at each other's throats or that overzealous outsiders were involved where they should not be. The bitterness was often such that some of the major football schools seemed ready to dissolve long-term traditional rivalries—or even to risk their conference affiliations—in pursuit of the advantages that would help produce a share of the spoils. These affairs did much to fuel the arguments contending that the gridiron game had become far too important in the university community.

The subsidizing of athletes and eligibility disputes had been issues within intercollegiate football since the game's earliest days. In his study of the creation of big-time college sport, historian Ronald Smith wrote that student athletic association groups were formed on most campuses between the 1870s and 1900, their specific purpose being to "provide financial assistance to relieve athletes of the entire expense of their sports." The continued existence of such practices in various forms at schools across the country—ranging from Columbia in the East to Southern Cal in the West—was one of the major discussions in the Carnegie Report of 1929, although its authors noted that "the evils of soliciting and subsidizing athletes" had diminished in scope since the days before World War I.[1]

There had always been competition for the best athletes among those schools that seriously pursued intercollegiate football success, but by the 1920s the construction of the many large on-campus stadiums made some form of recruiting a requisite for most universities. And certainly, the type of high-profile football coach needed to maintain a school's program at the top competitive levels was going to demand the assistance that only subsidization could provide in obtaining outstanding players.

It was also clear during the 1920s that the old-school ideals of amateur athletics were being reshaped consistent with the contemporary expectations for sport that were held by American society. One aspect of athletic relations between most schools that was never going to change, though, was the expectation that there would always be adherence to a spirit of sportsmanship. Although everyone wanted to win on the football field, how that goal was achieved before, during, and after the game was still of prime importance to many in the aftermath of the war.

Many of the disputes between schools became factors in the sport's ongoing transformation throughout the 1920s, yet at the time these developments were certainly not seen as desirable. The situations reviewed in this chapter were the most significant during the decade in helping to shape the beliefs and attitudes about college football among onlookers and contributed greatly to the fueling of efforts by the reform element. Ultimately, the resolution of significant controversies between schools—rather quickly where conference disciplinary action was involved—would prove to be the most prudent course of action for all parties involved. Major college football promised too many potential rewards to allow such disputes to be the final word.[2]

PACIFIC COAST BREAKUP

In 1924 a dispute over athletic eligibility rules for a time threatened to break up the Pacific Coast Conference (PCC), at a time when the far-flung group of schools was aspiring to an equal place among the gridiron elite of the country.

After World War I the football teams from the University of California, under the direction of Coach Andy Smith, had instituted a four-year reign of terror in the PCC from 1920 to 1923. By 1924 Stanford had made clear its intentions of sharing the West Coast's gridiron laurels on a regular basis with the neighboring Golden Bears, the Palo Alto school having constructed a giant new stadium, along with the hiring of Glenn "Pop" Warner, a top-flight football coach with national contacts. Rumors had also been coming out of Los Angeles, telling of alumni efforts to force out the current head football coach of the University of Southern California and to replace him with a high-profile man who would build the Trojans into a national gridiron power.

All three universities had been founded prior to 1900—the University of California the oldest, dating back to 1868—but it was clear that Stanford and Cal, neighboring universities near San Francisco, shared a close athletic and academic bond that did not extend to the University of Southern California. Stanford and California had started their football series in 1892, the annual meeting coming to be known as the "Big Game" on the West Coast in emulation of the traditional eastern matchup between Harvard and Yale. But neither Stanford or Cal chose to establish an ongoing football rivalry with Southern California until shortly before the 1920s.

Football had not been pursued with any seriousness by Southern Cal in the years before World War I, but in 1919 the university hired a new football coach named Elmer "Gus" Henderson, and by 1920 the Trojans were giving more emphasis to the gridiron sport. Southern Cal compiled impressive records between 1920 and 1923, even managing to get an invitation to the 1923 Rose Bowl game, but its schedules during the period were far from distinguished—consisting mostly of small colleges, minor universities, and service teams. The three universities, now referred to by newspapers on the West Coast as the Big Three, had formulated an agreement governing athletic competition among themselves, and during the seasons of 1919–1923 the Trojans played their two San Francisco–area rivals four times each—sweeping all four games from Stanford while giving California three tough battles. By 1923 the obviously improving Southern Cal football program, combined with the rumors about alumni desires for a higher-profile coach, did much to fuel Cal's and Stanford's growing concerns about what was going on in Los Angeles.[3]

Against this background of Southern Cal's growing aspirations, it should have come as no surprise in October 1924 when California protested the eligibility of one of USC's star linemen—Bill Cole—just days before the gridiron matchup between the two schools. Cole was alleged to have accepted two hundred dollars for coaching a schoolboy football team at a Los Angeles–area high school, but while admitting that its star tackle had indeed coached the preps, USC denied that he had received any compensation. At the same time it was learned that USC quarterback Johnny Hawkins was already being investigated over charges of playing professional baseball, while just days before Stanford had questioned the eligibility of three USC freshmen players. It was alleged that Morley Drury—a future All-America halfback—and L. L. Martin both had lacked the necessary twelve units of high school credits required for admission to USC.[4]

When the faculty representatives from the three schools gathered at a quickly scheduled meeting on October 30, 1924, at the Palace Hotel in San Francisco, their meeting lasted several hours, and then the matters in question were passed on to Dr. W. W. Campbell, president of Cal, and Dr. Rufus Von KleinSmid, president of USC. During the meeting of the faculty reps, USC presented documents showing that Bill Cole had in fact been paid two hundred dollars by Santa Ana High School. USC claimed that the payment was not for coaching the prep football team but for working around the grounds of the high school and for using his auto to help drive the Santa Ana players to their games. Martin, one of the three USC frosh charged, was declared ineligible when evidence that he had never finished high school in Berkeley, California, was received, but action on the others was deferred to a vote by members of the PCC. Reportedly, USC had come with some of its own allegations about California players, most notably guard Ray Niswander, who was said to have probably been paid for playing baseball with an American Legion team the previous summer.[5]

When the university presidents considered the facts, Cole was quickly declared ineligible for any further play for USC, and it was announced that the 1924 game between Cal and USC, scheduled for two days later at Berkeley, would be played. But although it was said that the schools had all expressed satisfaction at the results of the conference, there were definitely hard feelings over the charges and countercharges that had been made.[6]

It did not take long for the hostilities to break out again. Just minutes before the kickoff of the game between Southern Cal and California on November 1, newspaper writers in the press box at Cal's Memorial Stadium were given copies of the announcement that Stanford and California had decided to break off all athletic relations with USC. The formal announcement declared that Stanford and Cal officials had "regretfully come to the conclusion that the continuance of athletic relations with the University of Southern California, is not conducive to the best interests of intercollegiate sport."[7]

On the face of it, Stanford's and Cal's severing of athletic relations with USC seemed a rather drastic measure over an athlete having accepted two hundred dollars for an off-campus job and some freshmen athletes, but of course there was much more to it. Not only was there the deep-seated sectional jealousies between the northern and southern parts of the state, but there was also the close academic and athletic relationship that had existed between California and Stanford since 1892, which had always cast Southern Cal into the role of the "poor relation." And most significant of all were the rumors and concerns that had been growing since 1920 over Southern Cal's obvious efforts to become a national football powerhouse.

An unnamed official from one of the northern California schools later told reporters that the case against Cole had been just the final straw in "a series of incidents that have occurred in the relations" between USC and the Stanford-Cal duo. "We have had just one unpleasant experience with USC after another," the official said, "and we feel that when you can't get along with somebody you'd better quit associating with them. . . . USC treated or attempted to treat the whole case as one of Andy Smith's so-called 'smart tricks' to break the morale of the Trojans . . . [and] their answer was a lot of threats to disqualify various California and Stanford players. . . . Our quarrel is . . . with the authorities of the institution, who have, to our notion, countenanced practices not in accordance with the ideals of college athletics."[8]

The timing of the announcement made it impossible to consider any cancellation of the important PCC matchup between California and Southern Cal that day. Both teams came into the game undefeated, with USC considered a strong favorite, but the Golden Bears pulled off a 7-0 upset win that effectively ended any ideas of a conference title for the Trojans. After the totally unexpected announcement Southern Cal officials had no immediate comment, but later that evening the Trojan party had plenty to say. An influential group of San Francisco–area alumni—called "the Trojan Society"—had joined the Southern Cal team for a dinner after the game at the city's plush St. Francis Hotel, and the old grads were more than indignant over the action of the two northern universities. The nearly unanimous sentiment of the alumni group was for canceling the following weekend's scheduled game in Los Angeles against Stanford, whereas the players were about evenly split on the issue, many wanting to give the rugged Stanford outfit "a first-class licking as a farewell."[9]

Only California and Stanford had severed athletic relations with Southern Cal, so effectively the Trojans were still members of the PCC with part of the 1924 football season still to be played. But future scheduling and financial problems were definitely on the horizon for USC athletic teams if they were to remain as members of the conference—competing only against the universities from the Northwest would not be a workable relationship—and a vocal faction of USC students and alumni were ready to see the Trojans drop their affiliation with the PCC. Those individuals advocating a departure from the conference saw Southern Cal's football team competing as an independent, becoming "a sort of western Notre Dame, taking on everybody regardless of size, weight, creed or anything else." Rumors began circulating of efforts to match the Trojans up against Notre Dame for a 1924 postseason game on either Christmas or New Year's Day.[10]

On the morning of November 3, 1924, the USC student executive committee met and decided to cancel the approaching Stanford football game, and later that afternoon a meeting of USC faculty, alumni, and athletic representatives at the Los Angeles Athletic Club gave their unofficial approval to the action. Upon receiving the news, Dr. W. H. Barrow, director of physical education at Stanford, immediately expressed that school's regret over the action taken, indicating that a cancellation of the approaching football game had not been anticipated when the severing of athletic relations was decided upon.[11]

In the official announcement of the Stanford game cancellation, Southern Cal officials stated that their university "had abided by the spirit and letter of the rules and regulations of the Pacific Coast Conference and the triangular agreement." In this statement explaining their position, USC officials also took the opportunity to make reference to the superior and elitist attitudes that it believed were often exhibited by the Cal-Stanford duo, while also aligning the Trojans with those persons that opposed the "professionalism" of intercollegiate sport: "Whereas the honor of the University of Southern California has been assailed, and, whereas the announcement [severing relations] revives an old anti–Southern California feeling . . . and, whereas the conditions resulting from the announcement would make the football game . . . merely a mercenary exhibition devoid of the spirit of intercollegiate sportsmanship and not in accordance with the ideals of the University of Southern California."[12]

With Stanford undefeated and featuring one of college football's greatest players in Ernie Nevers, a near-capacity crowd had been expected for the game at the Los Angeles Coliseum. The decision to cancel the game was clearly going to cost a lot of people a lot of money—starting with an estimated loss of $125,000 by the two universities. The Biltmore Hotel in downtown Los Angeles, which was to have been the official headquarters of the Stanford team, had accepted more than four hundred reservations for the weekend and now expected nearly all of them to be canceled for an estimated loss of $6,000 for the hotel. Meanwhile, the operators of the Coliseum were anticipating a loss of approximately $20,000 because of the game's cancellation. Despite all the controversial events whirling around the Southern Cal football program, the alumni association of Los Angeles held a meeting and produced a unanimous vote of confidence for Coach Gus Henderson and the entire Trojan football team. After the serious public blow to the university's athletic prestige that the action of Cal and Stanford represented, and with all the rumors circulating about the desire to bring in a higher-profile head coach, a vote of confidence was probably the last thing Henderson wanted.[13]

All three schools were very willing to publicly defend their positions, with Stanford repeating the charge that the break was "the result of years of disagreement and wrangling over scholastic standing of athletes, proselyting of athletes, and [a] general 'win at any cost' attitude of USC" and that Southern Cal officials were "defiant and unsympathetic" toward the opinions of California and Stanford. California's statement described its long-growing dissatisfaction with athletic affairs and noted that the relations between itself and Southern Cal had reached the point where "the mutual spirit of criticism has seriously impaired the good will that is essential to good sportsmanship on both sides."[14]

The University of Southern California used considerable space in portraying the actions of California and Stanford as having been based on mere sectional jealousies over the rapid growth in the southern region of the state. After claiming that the "insinuations" made against it had yet to be explained, USC stated that the severing of athletic relations "was based upon what appears to be merely a sectional feeling of the northern against the southern part of the state." USC's statement also said that it was "common knowledge" that for the past four years Cal and Stanford had "looked with amazement at the growth of the University of Southern California and its athletic prowess," and then called attention to the questionable timing of the Cal-Stanford announcement. In fact, Cal and Stanford received considerable criticism over this decision in the newspapers, one columnist describing it as "unsportsmanlike," then continuing on to say that the reason for releasing the announcement at game time was because as game underdogs—and "expecting to be licked"—the California officials did not wish to be accused of taking the action in response to their first loss to USC since 1915.[15]

Faced with the loss of a big payday at the Coliseum the following Saturday, Southern Cal officials scrambled around and came up with a replacement opponent for November 8, 1924—little St. Mary's College from the Oakland Bay area. The little school was aspiring to become the "Notre Dame of the West" among the football-playing Catholic schools, and so had recently hired Edward "Slip" Madigan as its head football coach. The former Notre Dame player had quickly developed the Gaels into a coming football power on the West Coast, and he saw this opportunity to play another of the teams of the prestigious Pacific Coast Conference as a step in the right direction. Besides which, in 1924 Madigan had a top-flight team that featured a pair of dazzling running backs in Red Strader and Ducky Grant, and the Gaels had lost to California after a hard-fought struggle only by a score of 17-7.

Southern Cal clearly did not consider St. Mary's anywhere near the status of Stanford as an opponent and knew their ticket-buying fans would not either. So USC offered to admit two people to the St. Mary's game in exchange for one Stanford ticket, or would exchange one St. Mary's ticket plus one dollar in cash for each Stanford ticket; failing all else, USC would simply issue refunds for any unused Stanford tickets. The Trojan football team was either suffering from all the distractions of the past week, or they simply took St. Mary's too lightly, because the Gaels' twenty-man squad came out and staged a goal-line stand in the game's waning seconds to finish off a stunning 14-10 win over Southern Cal before a crowd of approximately twenty-seven thousand fans at the Coliseum. Meanwhile, Stanford spent the day handing hastily recruited Utah a 30-0 defeat.[16]

When the Pacific Coast Conference held its annual meeting in December 1924 at Portland, there was a complete absence of public discussion about the severing of athletic relations among the three California universities. One of the biggest announcements that came out of the football scheduling sessions was that Southern Cal would be meeting Iowa in a major intersectional game at Los Angeles during the 1925 season. Even though the dispute was not discussed at the PCC meetings, and USC was apparently having no difficulties in filling its athletic schedules without Stanford and Cal, it was clear to everyone that the conference could not exist long-term on a competitive and economic basis with some of the member schools refusing to compete against each other.[17]

Representatives from the three universities began secretly meeting in December 1924, after trustees of Southern Cal reportedly initiated the negotiations by indicating a willingness to address changes being requested by Cal and Stanford. By February 1925 Stanford officials had publicly announced their willingness to resume athletic relations with USC, and when Cal soon after also indicated a willingness to put aside the dispute, it was all but over.[18]

The end of the brief war came in a meeting on the evening of February 18, 1925, in San Francisco, as high-ranking officials from the three universities met and formally agreed to a resumption of athletic relations. In the official statement after the meeting, the universities said that they had "deplored . . . the attitude of friction and antagonism" that had been fostered during the dispute by alumni and other "self-appointed representatives" of the three schools. It was stated that all three universities were now mutually satisfied with the athletic policies and methods of control in place at each school.[19]

There were rumors that Southern Cal had been pressured into agreeing to some personnel moves as a requisite for resolving the dispute. Specifically, observers pointed to the recent announcement that two men, Harold J. Stonier and Warren Bovard, had been removed from their associations with the athletic department at USC. Bovard was the comptroller at USC, and correspondence just a few weeks before the San Francisco agreement shows him actively involved in the secret negotiations to bring Knute Rockne to Southern Cal as the new head coach for 1925—one letter referring to Bovard as the "big power" in USC athletics.[20]

When the 1925 football season rolled around all was well with the athletic relations among the three universities. Southern Cal had a new head football coach in Howard Jones, and the Pacific Coast Conference looked forward to a great year. USC showed that it had no intention of going through another athletic war, as Fay Thomas—captain of the Trojan football team and a star tackle—was declared ineligible for further competition because he had accepted money for playing baseball during the previous summer. California had been unable to open a date on its 1925 football schedule for USC, but on October 17, 1925, Stanford and the Trojans staged a thrilling struggle at the Los Angeles Coliseum before a screaming crowd of more than seventy thousand fans. Those ticket-buying fanatics had been the real reason for ending the Pacific Coast Breakup.[21]

The Iowa Slush Fund Scandal

After the University of Iowa had become a member of the Big Ten Conference in 1899, the Hawkeyes' gridiron fortunes over the next two decades were particularly undistinguished. But all that began to change with the arrival of Howard Jones in 1916, when he assumed the duties of both football coach and athletic director at Iowa.

Jones fielded respectable Iowa football teams from 1918 to 1920, but those seasons were merely the prelude, as the Hawkeyes of 1921 and 1922 produced undefeated campaigns. The 1921 outfit was generally considered the top team in the country, and the Hawkeyes were paced that season by three future College Football Hall of Fame players: Aubrey Devine, Gordon Locke, and Fred "Duke" Slater. Locke would return in 1922 for another All-America campaign, as Iowa notched its second consecutive 7-0-0 record. In fact, the Hawkeyes would eventually register twenty straight victories between November 1920 and October 1923. But Jones left Iowa after the 1923 season, having compiled an overall record of 42-17-1 with the Hawkeyes.[22]

In 1924 the new head coach for Iowa was Bert Ingwersen, a former star player at the University of Illinois who later served as an assistant on the staff of Bob Zuppke. University president Walter A. Jessup of Iowa also named Dr. Paul E. Belting to the position of athletic director and took the further step of placing total responsibility for the school's physical education in Belting's hands. At the same time, Jessup relegated the faculty-staffed Board in Control of Athletics to merely an advisory capacity.[23]

The Big Ten Conference, increasingly concerned with the rumors and occasional evidence of illegal recruiting practices by its member schools, had been one of the first to appoint a full-time commissioner of athletics, hiring Major John Griffith in July 1922. Even before total control of Iowa athletics was turned over to Belting in June 1924, Griffith had written to the new director and described the conference's efforts at curbing illegal recruiting and the "overly enthusiastic" alumni.[24]

Griffith's letter went on to outline his belief that "quite a number" of Iowa alumni had been asked to subscribe to a fund that was being used to help athletes, the money being channeled through local businessmen. Reports had been received that the athletes were not always expected to work for the money they were being paid, and Griffith suggested that such situations were starting to come to the attention of the other athletic directors of the conference.[25]

As the middle years of the decade continued, no further action was taken regarding the rumored Iowa "slush fund," but Griffith continued a constant flow of memos to the athletic directors of the conference on the subject of recruiting practices. Meanwhile, the gridiron fortunes of the Hawkeyes had taken a turn for the worse after Ingwersen produced a decent 6-1-1 overall record in 1924. After conference records of 0-5-0 in 1926 and 1-4-0 in 1927 had relegated Iowa to a position of weakness within the Big Ten, making it difficult to convince conference rivals to travel to Iowa City for football games, the Iowa alumni had seen enough.

By late 1927 Ingwersen and Belting were both being openly criticized around the state, and on January 14, 1928, seventy-five alumni members met in Des Moines, Iowa, and, after an extended debate, passed a set of resolutions condemning the two

15. Mayes McLain of Haskell and Iowa. A bruising fullback who scored a record 38 touchdowns in 1926 for Haskell, he later turned up at the University of Iowa and was involved in the slush fund scandal there in 1929. Author's collection.

university men and demanding Ingwersen's resignation. But that was not all. After accusing President Jessup of ignoring alumni sentiments concerning the football coach, the alumni association requested three permanent positions on the Board in Control of Athletics.[26]

Iowa's gridiron fortunes took an upswing the following autumn, helped in great part by several new players, the foremost being running back Mayes McLain, who had received All-America notice while playing two seasons at the Haskell Institute in 1925 and 1926. Then, on December 8, 1928, at a meeting of the Faculty Eligibility Committee in Chicago, Iowa was shocked to hear that McLain had been declared ineligible for further play, given that he had now played a total of three varsity football seasons between Haskell and Iowa.[27]

Hawkeye athletic officials had believed that the Haskell Institute was considered a preparatory school, which would have allowed McLain two more seasons at Iowa after 1928. But the committee ruling was based on a decision the conference had made back in 1904, in which it declared the Haskell Institute to be "on a basis of athletic equality" with Big Ten universities. Further, the eligibility committee would not indicate whether a protest had been filed against Iowa by other members of the conference.[28]

Everything then began to unravel for the University of Iowa's athletic department, and in particular the football program. Much of the attention directed toward Iowa athletics was a by-product of the animosity created by Paul Belting, the athletic director, who had what was described as "a singular flair for antagonizing people." In late April 1929 President Jessup could no longer resist the continued demands for a shakeup in the athletic department, so he requested Belting's resignation as athletic director. Jessup assured Belting that he could remain at Iowa as the head of physical education for both men and women, and the two men seemed to be in agreement.

Having a change of mind about resigning, Belting returned to Jessup's office the next day only to be advised that the athletic-director position was no longer an option for him, whereupon an angry Belting submitted his written resignation from all positions with the University of Iowa. In his letter Belting outlined the many physical accomplishments made during his five years as athletic director, including the construction of a field house and the new football stadium, which was still in progress. Belting concluded by noting that "continued opposition, dissension, and jealousy have developed over a program that not only has moved so rapidly but also has only educational aims in view." It was later discovered that Belting had removed from his office all the records and files pertaining to his term as athletic director.[29]

It did not take long for the other shoe to fall on the Hawkeyes. On May 25, 1929, the Big Ten's faculty committee met in a special executive session on the campus of Northwestern University and formally suspended athletic relations with Iowa. The university had been charged with violating conference rules against subsidized or paid athletes, although the conference faculty committee declined to make public the names of the players or the specific cases. A presentation of specific evidence had been made by a committee of athletic directors, and it did not take long to figure out who had produced the evidence. Shortly after the announcement of Iowa's suspension, a statement was issued reiterating the principle that "athletic teams of the conference institutions be not composed of hired players." The statement was signed by Amos Alonzo Stagg of Chicago, George Huff of Illinois, and Fielding Yost of Michigan. Many newspapers of the time reported in error that Iowa had actually been expelled from the Big Ten.[30]

A day later, Iowa's faculty representative to the Big Ten, Dr. Louis Pelzer, told reporters that the committee members had been sworn to secrecy as to the proceedings of the meeting. But the professor did hint that one of the principal charges was that a slush fund had been in operation for the benefit of Iowa athletes—saying further that the charges "are true." The news of Iowa's suspension by the conference triggered a campus protest by students and others, and the demonstration proceeded to the homes of Jessup and Belting. The deposed athletic director later claimed that his home had been hit with bricks and other objects throughout the night and that it had been necessary to have Iowa City police disperse the crowd and protect the house.[31]

After visiting Iowa City, Major Griffith delivered a letter on May 31, 1929, to President Jessup, describing in detail all the charges against Iowa. The general violations had been in the recruiting and subsidizing of athletes, and the trail led all the way back to early in the decade. It was charged that prior to 1924, the Faculty Board of Iowa had authorized the diversion of monies made from the sale of student yearbooks into an alumni fund that was to be used for subsidizing athletes. In a meeting with Griffith, Jessup admitted knowing of this practice. In fact, evidence existed that an alumni slush fund had been maintained for many years prior to 1924. Athletes had also been allowed to pay for their tuition charges with notes that were guaranteed by coaches and others, and, not surprisingly, many of them had gone unpaid.[32]

Griffith also described the case of a football player named Tom Stidham, a former standout lineman at Haskell. An Iowa alumnus had arranged Stidham's transportation to Iowa City, where another alumni member met him at the station and drove him out to a fraternity house on the university campus. There the player had a meeting with a Dr. White and a Mr. Williams, during which he was offered seventy-five dollars a month to play football for Iowa. But Stidham had replied that he expected one hundred dollars a month, and that amount is what was eventually paid in checks from Williams. Griffith reported that an alumnus had made arrangements at the business office for payment of Stidham's fees and tuition, the player never making a single payment. What it all came down to was that a group of alumni was actively recruiting and subsidizing athletes for Iowa, obviously with the approval of the university's athletic administration.[33]

Amid all the rumors at the time of Belting's departure, President Jessup had appointed his own investigator to look into the athletic situation, Rufus H. Fitzgerald, the school's director of student services. On June 3, 1929, Fitzgerald wrote to Jessup and documented even further abuses. The alumni fund had been administered prior to 1923 by a Judge Howell, during the tenure of Howard Jones at Iowa. After the judge had passed away, handling of the funds had eventually come down to a Mr. Willis Mercer of Iowa City.[34]

In an interview Mercer disclosed that the fund amounted to about five thousand dollars per year and that the athletes would come to his office and sign notes for the funds, some of which had actually been repaid eventually. Mercer further declared that when the size of the fund had become rather small, Belting, the athletic director, had approached President Jessup about the university becoming more involved with the alumni in the fund's administration. But Jessup had refused to approve "the administering of any fund for which the University was not completely responsible."[35]

Fitzgerald went on to describe the eventual formation of a "Labor Fund" by the alumni, the purpose of which was to promote work for athletes in businesses around the city. Although the alumni contended that most of the athletes actually worked for their money, a notable exception was pointed out in Mayes McLain, who was paid sixty dollars per month for allegedly taking a "real estate census" of Iowa City. This arrangement had become necessary only in McLain's second year at Iowa, since the former Haskell player had been subsidized during the school year of 1927–1928 by funds provided by an alumni group in Chicago.[36]

In July 1929 Jessup appointed a new athletic director, Dr. Edward H. Lauer, previously the director of Iowa's extension division, and then reinstated the faculty's authority over athletics, to be administered by the Board in Control of Athletics. The board proceeded to establish subcommittees for such areas as eligibility and finances, and Iowa set out to gain readmittance to the athletic circles of the Big Ten.[37]

With the suspension of athletic relations between Iowa and the other conference members set to be effective January 1, 1930, everyone had scrambled to fill the Iowa date on their football schedules with other opponents. Although Dr. Lauer eventually put together a very representative 1930 football schedule for Iowa, the difficulties encountered can be seen in a letter from C. L. Brewer, athletic director at Missouri, in which Brewer explains the refusal of a game: "It seems to me that all of our institutions must recognize the actions of sister conferences. . . . I am of the opinion that Missouri would not care to schedule a football game with your institution while it is under suspension. . . . This is said in the spirit of the general good of intercollegiate athletics." Meanwhile, the Board in Control of Athletics maintained an active flow of reports, hearings, and letters, all intended to demonstrate that Iowa had reimplemented "institutional control" over the athletic programs. Yet the board also continued to advance a variety of technicalities while contending that the athletes had really not been at fault, and so did not deserve to be declared ineligible for intercollegiate athletics.[38]

This attitude—which suggested something less than complete repentance by Iowa—was not going to fly with the conference officials, so at the Big Ten meeting in Chicago on December 6–7, 1929, Iowa's request for a reassumption of athletic relations was denied. During the conference meeting Lauer made a presentation during which he attempted to show the changes implemented by Iowa to ensure conformity to Big Ten regulations, but Yost, Stagg, and Huff were not about to let the matter drop, as they hammered away at the new athletic director.[39]

Yost was described as being openly hostile, as the Michigan athletic director objected to many minor points in Lauer's presentation and argued that some of Iowa's athletes must have received improper financial aid. Huff summed up the discussion by declaring that he "was not convinced that Iowa had set her house in order." Lauer later wrote that time and again the directors had made the point that conditions at Iowa were so bad that it was inconceivable that no athletes should be found guilty. When the directors took their vote—Iowa not participating—it was unanimous that the "athletic conditions at Iowa were not satisfactory."[40]

It was clear that Iowa was going to have to conform completely to the demands of the conference officials, so on December 11, 1929, the university's eligibility committee declared all eleven Hawkeye athletes in question to be ineligible for further varsity participation, and so notified the conference committee. For Yost, it still was not good enough. On January 18 the Michigan director wrote to Ohio State's athletic director, L. W. St. John, expressing the opinion that "it would be a great mistake to consider reinstatement of Iowa at present. . . . The Fieseler fund may be closed as stated in Iowa's petition but in my opinion it was opened up somewhere else, at a new stand under a new name."[41]

Yet in the absence of any further specific evidence, the Big Ten faculty committee had heard enough. After a lengthy meeting on February 2, 1930, it was announced that Iowa's athletic suspension had been lifted, and the Hawkeyes could once again compete for Big Ten championships. Much to Iowa's dismay, the conference faculty committee refused to lift the ban on the eleven blacklisted Hawkeye athletes, while also expressing some doubts as to Iowa's ability to keep outside influences from again interfering with athletics.[42]

With the Iowa athletic program restored back within the official confines of the Big Ten Conference, some of the university's backers sought to raise questions about Major Griffith's motivations throughout the recently concluded dispute. Rumors were circulated to the effect that Griffith had "persecuted" Iowa in the performance of his duties as conference commissioner during the scandal, in retaliation for his application for the position of director of athletics at Iowa having been rejected in 1924. Another rumor charged Griffith with "a religious bias" toward the University of Iowa, on the basis of a letter he had written to Belting in January 1928. In that letter, as conference commissioner, Griffith had said that questions were being raised by some concerning what "special reason" a man named Frank Comfort might have for wanting Gus Dorais (a Catholic and former Notre Dame star who was then the head coach at the University of Detroit) as a replacement for Coach Ingwersen at Iowa. In a 1930 letter to Professor Frederic Higbee discussing these attacks on him, Griffith wrote: "I have never felt that a man's religion should be scrutinized relative to the selection of coaches or the makeup of university teams. However . . . I realize that some of our friends accord athletics emotional rather than rational treatment and I am not surprised that my motives have been impugned."[43]

In his memoirs Professor Higbee would later write that three of the conference schools had been found to be about equally guilty of recruiting charges, but Iowa was chosen for disciplinary action because there was more documentary evidence available in its case. Higbee wrote further that the reinstatement of Iowa "did little to improve the attitude of the public and the newspapers toward the conduct of athletics at the University." The only apparent winner from the entire sordid mess was Professor Rufus Fitzgerald, who had conducted the internal investigation for President Jessup. After 1929 Fitzgerald was promoted through several prestigious faculty positions at Iowa until he departed in 1938 to become provost at the University of Pittsburgh. He eventually retired in the 1950s as chancellor of that university.[44]

The Army-Navy Break (1928–1929)

As the decade of the 1920s unfolded, one of college football's biggest rivalries was the one between the U.S. service academies at West Point and Annapolis. Since their first gridiron matchup in 1890, the Army-Navy series had become wildly popular among students, fans, and alumni of the two service academies.

The rivalry was being taken so seriously that the series was interrupted between 1894 and 1898 because of Navy and War Department concerns over the bad feelings the annual game was creating among graduates of the two service academies. After the gridiron series was resumed in 1899 the game was played each season at a neutral site, usually in Philadelphia or New York City, never returning to either of the service-academy campuses except for the World War II seasons of 1942 and 1943.[45]

Except for the period between 1904 and 1907, the two academies had long operated with different eligibility rules for their athletes. The Naval Academy adhered to a guideline that allowed an athlete a total of just three years of varsity collegiate eligibility, while also prohibiting competition at the varsity level until the completion of one year of academic work. Army, on the other hand, considered its cadets eligible for varsity-level competition through all four years of their stay at West Point, even if the athlete had prior years of collegiate experience at other schools. Because of the eligibility rules followed at West Point over the years, Army football teams had been bolstered by many established stars from other schools, most of whom had already played three seasons of college football before entering the military academy. As early as 1903 Navy officials had protested the eligibility of Army players who had already played three seasons of college football.[46]

When the annual football rivalry between the two service academies resumed in 1919 after the war, attendance figures began climbing, eventually reaching a peak figure of 110,000 for the 1926 game that was played at Soldier Field in Chicago. But discontent over the eligibility rules had continued among Navy officials. In an attempt to defuse the controversy, on September 17, 1926, Brigadier General M. B. Stewart, superintendent of West Point, announced that the Army athletic department would be adopting the "one-year rule." This regulation prevented varsity participation until the athlete's second year at the academy, to become effective with the next school year. This new rule did not solve the real problem as far as the Naval Academy was concerned, however.

By June 1927 Naval Academy officials had decided it was time to force the issue, so they announced the formal adoption of the three-year maximum-eligibility rule for their athletes, while further stating that in the future Navy teams would compete only against schools that followed those same eligibility rules. Rumors of a break in football relations between the two service academies had been circulating for weeks before the 1927 game, yet that season's game was the first to be played under a new four-year contract between the two academies, so a break in relations appeared to be only a concern for the distant future.

As tensions between the two academies heightened in early December 1927, sportswriter Westbrook Pegler pointed out that a major irritant to Annapolis officials was the fact that Army's football team had won four and tied two games in their six meetings with Navy between 1922 and 1927. That Navy had won three straight from 1919 to 1921 apparently did not matter. On December 14, 1927, West Point officials announced that no further rule changes would be made with regard to the eligibility of Army cadets for varsity athletics.[47]

In his statement Major General Edwin B. Winans of West Point said that the three-year eligibility rule, and others, was instituted by universities in order to eliminate the migratory or tramp-athlete problem of college sport's earlier years. Winans pointed to the difficulties in securing an appointment to West Point and the strenuous academic curriculum that "operates to preclude the entrance by any young man whose sole objective is athletics." The general then concluded, "The interests of the army are served to best advantage by the present athletic eligibility rules in force at West Point. . . . It would be unjustifiable to make a change detrimental to the athletic training of the army in order to experiment in attaining a temporary parity between the two service institutions."[48]

Regardless of whether the average college football observer was prepared to believe that standout players like Harry Wilson and Chris Cagle had actually encountered any "difficulties" in securing a West Point appointment, the Naval Academy certainly was not buying it. The four-year contract that took effect in 1927 between the two schools was the type described as a "skeleton contract," which meant that for each year of the contract the specific terms were subject to revision by either party. For the 1928 edition of the contract it was Navy's turn to draw up the specific agreement, which normally covered such items as the site of the game and ticket arrangements. When the 1928 game contract arrived at West Point it was found to include the following clause: "It is mutually agreed by the Superintendents . . . that no contestant shall take part in this game on either team who has had three years experience in intercollegiate football . . . to include participation in intercollegiate football while at either academy or any other accredited college or university."[49]

There was no way that Army officials could sign this agreement without dismantling a good part of its football team, and Navy was not going to back down. On December 16, 1927, in New York City, General Winans, superintendent of West Point, announced that he had returned the 1928 contract unsigned and specifically pointed to the eligibility statement in paragraph 14 as the reason. With his statement Winans incorporated the text of his reply that accompanied the unsigned contract back to the superintendent of the Naval Academy, Rear Admiral Louis M. Nulton, including the following: "In view of the statement . . . that rejection of the eligibility feature by the United States Military Academy will be considered as rejection of the proposed contract and that the Naval Academy will consider itself free to schedule another game, I conclude that the authorities of the United States Naval Academy wish to be released from the contract of October, 1926."[50]

The official letter from General Winans had not yet been received at Annapolis when the announcement of the game's apparent cancellation was made in New York City. But despite being surprised at the timing of the West Point release, Naval Academy officials obviously were not surprised that the contract was returned unsigned. The next day Admiral Nulton issued a statement that "the Naval Academy contemplates taking no further steps toward an Army-Navy game in 1928." After noting that seventeen of twenty collegiate conferences had adopted eligibility rules and that eleven of them conformed to the "three-year rule," Nulton confirmed Pegler's theory on the underlying cause of the trouble: "Raising the question of eligibility does not bring into question criticism of ethics. It does, however, bring into question . . . consideration as to whether the contestants are operating under conditions which give each side a sporting chance to win." And just like that the two service academies had severed athletic relations, at least where football competition was involved.[51]

It was clear from the start that government officials in Washington, D.C., did not want to get involved in resolving the dispute. When it was apparent that there would be no quick compromise, both service academies proceeded to schedule other 1928 opponents for their usual game date that was now open—Army to play Stanford, while Navy would be taking on Princeton. When the 1928 football season ended without the annual service gridiron classic being played, some U.S. congressmen did finally speak out on the break in athletic relations.

Representative Hamilton Fish Jr., a former All-America tackle at Harvard, criticized the eligibility rules of West Point and called them "undemocratic and unsportsmanlike," concluding that "Navy is absolutely right in refusing to continue to play West Point." Representative Daniel Britten of Illinois, a member of the House Naval Committee, had earlier said that Army's continued refusal to

adopt the three-year eligibility rule would ultimately result in a severance of relations with West Point by all the major football universities. After pointing to
the many former All-America players who had continued their football careers at
West Point, Britten then attacked Army's claim that these gridiron stars had been
seeking only military careers: "Eighty per cent of its football stars of the past ten
years have resigned from the Army as quickly as possible after graduation. . . .
Did they go through West Point at Government expense for a football career or a
military one?" West Point officials immediately responded to Britten's statistics,
stating that between 1917 and 1927 a total of just eight former football players had
resigned from the military—but Britten's comments had kept alive the idea that
West Point was employing tramp athletes.[52]

For 1929 both service academies again scheduled games with other opponents
for their usual late-season date—Army again playing Stanford while Navy would
meet Dartmouth. In early October 1929 attempts to arrange a postseason game
between the two teams proved unsuccessful, although the *New York Times* was
encouraged enough to print an editorial stating, "Resumption of football relations
between the Military and Naval Academies is now probable." Yet two weeks later,
on October 31, 1929, with the nation reeling from the stock market crash, the *New
York Times* ran a story on page 1 of the newspaper under a headline that read:
"Army-Navy Break in Sports Widens."[53]

The superintendents of the two service academies had traveled to Washington, D.C., in early October for a meeting in the office of General John "Black Jack"
Pershing at the War Department, and after a two-hour meeting no progress had
yet been made in resolving the dispute. Various compromises were offered by Rear
Admiral Samuel S. Robison, including allowing Army to use a four-year rule for
varsity eligibility or playing two years under Navy's rules and then two years under Army's rules on a rotating basis. Yet Major General William R. Smith of West
Point refused to revise Army's eligibility rules, noting that in 1929 West Point had
received more than sixty requests for games from "leading colleges and universities . . . no one of which has asked for the application of the three-year eligibility
rule to West Point." With the highly publicized Carnegie Report on intercollegiate
sport having been released just days earlier, it appeared to be politically unsound
for two of the nation's most prestigious institutions to be continuing a debate over
eligibility practices that seemed to smack of athletic professionalism, yet the break
in sporting relations continued.[54]

By late 1930 the nation's economy was locked in the early stages of the Great
Depression, and conferences and universities everywhere were arranging to play
postseason games for the benefit of unemployment relief funds. An obvious major
fund-raising event would be an Army-Navy game, and bids to host such a matchup
had come from Chicago, New York, and Philadelphia. Army had a November 29

game scheduled with Notre Dame, whereas the Navy team was slated to meet Penn on December 6, but pressure was mounting on the two service academies to set aside their differences and play a charity game. Although the superintendents of the two academies expressed concerns over the weather and field conditions that might be encountered in mid-December, George F. Getz, chairman of the Illinois unemployment relief fund, sent a telegram to President Herbert Hoover in which he claimed that an Army-Navy game in Chicago would generate more than $750,000 in gate receipts. Meanwhile, a delegation of New York officials visited the White House to meet with Hoover about a proposed game in their city.

Yet despite all the pressure for an Army-Navy postseason charity game in 1930, the superintendents of the academies spent another week debating eligibility rules and finding reasons to not play a mid-December game. Finally, the War Department's top brass put an end to the bickering by ordering the two academies to play the charity game at Yankee Stadium in New York City on December 13, 1930, and further debate over eligibility rules was closed. Yankee Stadium was provided rent free with ticket prices scaled from $5 to $10, and the game proved to be a major success, as approximately seventy thousand fans turned out to see Army edge past Navy by a score of 6-0. After the game officials announced that at least $600,000 had been raised for the Salvation Army's unemployment fund.[55]

A year later, in mid-December 1931, the two academy teams again met at Yankee Stadium in a postseason charity football game, Army topping Navy by a score of 17-7 before seventy-five thousand fans. Finally, after seeing the great popularity of the service-game rivalry and realizing that the break in athletic relations was no longer going to be accepted politically in Washington, the two academy superintendents agreed to resume the football series as a regular-season date. On April 20, 1932, General Smith of West Point announced the resumption of football relations between the two academies, noting that "each school agreed to recognize the eligibility standards set by the other." West Point would finally adopt the three-year eligibility rule in 1939.[56]

The Harvard-Princeton Break (1926–1934)

One of the nastiest of all disputes in college football history was that between Harvard and Princeton in the late 1920s. Football results between the two schools since World War I had served only to fuel attitudes of elitism and resentment that were simmering just below the surface. Then, when the student newspapers became a vehicle for public insults, events quickly escalated into a severing of athletic relations between the two universities in 1926.

It was not the first time that a dispute between Harvard and Princeton had resulted in a disruption of their football rivalry. A long-standing disagreement over the use of graduate school students on varsity teams, combined with a history of rough games and hard feelings between their football teams, was enough to bring about the first major break in the gridiron rivalry between Harvard and Princeton after their game of 1896. When the two universities resumed their football series in 1911 it was clear that there had been a change in both athletic and social attitudes on campus since their last meeting. Shortly before that season's game between the two schools, the *Harvard Alumni Bulletin,* with an unmistakably superior attitude, noted that the students on the Cambridge campus did not consider Princeton to have any more athletic prestige than Brown or Dartmouth.

During the early 1920s President A. Lawrence Lowell of Harvard, influenced by the example of athletic competition as practiced by Oxford and Cambridge in England, sought ways to begin trimming back the emphasis on football—regarding Yale as the only real traditional rivalry for Harvard. This effort began to manifest itself in the summer of 1926 with the announcement that Harvard had scheduled football games against Michigan for 1927 and 1928, while dropping Princeton from its slate for those two seasons. Rumors quickly began spreading that Princeton was preparing to sever all athletic relations with Harvard. In fact, in a memo of September 14, 1926, Charles Kennedy, chairman of Princeton's Athletic Control Board, stated that all consideration of the athletic relations between the two schools had been "suspended, pending official conferences to be held later," and that no decisions would be made by Princeton officials until those meetings were held.[57]

Stunned by the uproar over the proposed football series with Michigan, Harvard agreed to a meeting at New Haven on October 6, 1926, with officials from Princeton and Yale. At the conclusion of this conference among the athletic chairmen from the three schools, a statement was issued declaring that the proposed Harvard-Michigan series "was counter to the understanding and practice of the Triple Agreement." It was announced that Harvard had dropped the Michigan game for 1927 and restored the Princeton matchup and that "no change in essential athletic relations . . . is contemplated." The proviso in the Presidents' Agreement that prohibited "long and expensive trips" had been cited in terminating a very successful Princeton-Chicago series in 1922, and it had also been applied to Harvard's desire to play Michigan. The meeting had also considered whether the Presidents' Agreement obligated the three schools to meet annually in football, with no consensus being reached, and William Bingham made it clear that Harvard felt no such obligation.[58]

With Harvard's long-standing conviction that it constituted an American intercollegiate aristocracy with Yale, no one should have expected that the public embarrassment over the Michigan affair would long keep the Crimson football program from continuing in the direction intended by President Lowell.

Accordingly, on October 18, 1926, Harvard's athletic authorities adopted a secret resolution declaring their intention to play only Yale in football every season. Other colleges would be played "only at suitable intervals." As part of the reasoning for this action, the resolution stated that "in recent years the playing of football games against the same colleges every year has tended to keep the excitement of the contests at too high a pitch for too long . . . and has exaggerated the part which intercollegiate rivalry should properly have." Lest anyone accuse Harvard of abandoning the Presidents' Agreement and aspiring to upgrade the overall level of its football opponents, the resolution also emphasized that the Crimson intended to continue honoring "every provision . . . as it has been. We have no intention of withdrawing from that agreement."[59]

Harvard athletic officials had prepared the major resolution three weeks before the 1926 game against Princeton, but its public release was delayed so that the Tiger gridmen would have no more inspiration for the approaching game than they already had. But President Lowell failed to anticipate the latest round of tactless and insulting material about to be published by the Harvard students.

The day of the game, November 6, the fans, alumni, and students flocking to Harvard's Soldier Field could not help noticing the *Harvard Lampoon's* "Princeton Game" number. As usual it contained a substantial amount of insulting material directed at Princeton—the most notorious being a cartoon of two pigs in the middle of a mud puddle, one saying, "Come, brother, let us root for dear old Princeton!" Then for good measure, that day's *Harvard Crimson* newspaper carried an article titled "Bill Roper, Princeton Coach, Dies on Field," with a subheadline that read, "Expires in Arms of Assistants in Last Quarter . . . Held Breath Too Long." When the actual game came to a close with Princeton winning by a score of 12-0, thousands of Tiger fans poured onto the field and easily overran a handful of police while tearing down Harvard's goalposts. What followed was what Joe Vila of the *New York Sun* called "as fine a riot as ever was seen on a college gridiron." Although occasional rough play by Princeton during the game had produced some booing, this desecration of Harvard's football stadium, when mixed in with the insults of the *Lampoon* and the *Crimson*, brought the athletic relations between the two schools to the breaking point.[60]

Harvard officials immediately sought to repair the damage to its patrician image by the student publications, and the Monday after the game a telegram was sent by the *Crimson's* editors to Princeton, claiming that the entire issue carrying the "Roper death" item had been produced by the *Lampoon* staff without the knowledge of the *Crimson* editors. The telegram concluded by stating, "We hope that all Princeton men will remember that the story does not represent Harvard opinion, but rather that of a very small and very tactless group." Lowell sent a letter to President John Hibben of Princeton, wherein the Harvard president said,

"You may imagine how humiliated we feel here by the action of the *Lampoon*. . . . I can only tell you and all Princeton men how badly we feel for the conduct which you all know well is highly repugnant to the sentiment of Harvard men."[61]

It was now common knowledge that the two schools were on the brink of severing athletic relations, and the *New York Times* quoted a Harvard paper editorial that said that "brotherly love and friendly rivalry between the two universities are figments of the imagination. . . . Harvard undergraduates . . . would still like to see Princeton dropped." There was no turning back now, and on November 10, when the Princeton Board of Athletic Control received Harvard's resolution on football scheduling that had been drawn up on October 18, the response was immediate. That same day, after a special meeting in New York of Princeton's Athletic Board, Kennedy sent a telegram to Bingham at Harvard and followed it up with a formal letter, in which the severing of athletic relations between the two schools was announced. In his letter Kennedy wrote, "It is at present impossible to expect, in athletic competition with Harvard, that spirit of cordial good will between the undergraduate bodies of the two universities which should characterize college sport." The response sent to Harvard also stated that "Princeton would never accept the implications of the athletic policy recently adopted by the Harvard committee."[62]

A large part of the problem was that the prevailing thought at Harvard considered Princeton at a lower level, both academically and socially, when compared with the longer-running Harvard-Yale duo. So if President Lowell was to eventually succeed in implementing his athletic vision of an Oxford-Cambridge-style rivalry, while also de-emphasizing football's place in university life, then Princeton's participation had to be scaled back. The *Harvard Crimson* exhibited this attitude of elitism when it described Princeton's "persistent efforts" to continue the Big Three as being essential for maintaining Princeton's own individual prestige, noting that "Princeton has derived no little part of hers [prestige] from the fact that she has long been included in the Big Three." The *Princeton Alumni Weekly* replied to this slur with this comment: "Princeton feels no disproportionate dependence upon triumvirate relationships, and is confident that its contributions have balanced its benefits . . . but if conditions are such as to make impossible good feeling between Harvard and Princeton . . . we see no reason to attempt what would then be the mutually disagreeable task of continuing these athletic relations." The *Daily Princetonian* added, "Princeton by no means feels that it is necessary, at further cost to its dignity, to preserve the Big Three."[63]

Princeton officials and others clearly understood that the events surrounding the 1926 game were not the real cause of the hard feelings between the two schools. Lawrence Perry, writing in the *New York Sun*, suggested that the regional backgrounds of the schools might be part of the equation, with Harvard being greatly influenced by the dominating New England traditions and attitudes that had been ingrained in its administration, faculty, and students. Kenneth Webb of the *New York Herald Tribune* agreed: "Harvard men are natural aristocrats. . . . One of Harvard's Puritan heritages is distrust of externals and the old insistence that man is to be measured only by his inner worth . . . while the extreme attention given to their dress by Princetonians always has aroused Harvard scorn." Webb added, "When all is said and done, there is probably some basis for this mutual scorn felt by the two undergraduate bodies." Robert Harron of the *New York Evening Post* questioned the decorum of Harvard's officials: "If the Harvard elders can treat an old rival in this haughty and unfriendly way, it is harder to blame the youngsters for expressing an identical spirit."[64]

Yale took great pains to remain neutral in the dispute, eventually going so far as entering into "dual" agreements individually with each of the combatant schools—agreements that were basically restatements of the Triple Agreement of 1916 and 1923. Meanwhile, editorial comment in major newspapers and elsewhere made it clear that the general sporting public would not be too distressed over the "wretched controversy," and not too many writers were still in unquestioning awe of the Big Three schools and their football heritage.[65]

The break in athletic relations might have been resolved in a reasonable period of time, but another wedge was driven between the two schools with the publication on January 29, 1927, of an article in *Liberty* magazine by Wynant Davis Hubbard, titled "Dirty Football." Hubbard, a former tackle for Harvard in the 1919–1920 seasons, contended that Princeton football teams were characterized by their dirty, flagrantly rough, and unsportsmanlike play, of which he cited examples of specific plays in games through the early 1920s, including games against teams other than Harvard. Hubbard would later explain that his article "was the outgrowth of a gathering of Harvard men . . . in which it was agreed that talk of dirty football, which had been heard for years, should be brought to the surface. . . . The charges made in the magazine *Liberty* I am ready to prove by affidavit as near as they can be proved."[66]

Predictably, the *Liberty* article brought an immediate flood of denials and commentary. It was quickly made known that President Lowell of Harvard had attempted to prevent publication of the article, having been advised of it in early December, but both *Liberty* and Hubbard ignored his requests. Kennedy, chairman of Princeton's Board of Athletic Control, replied with a statement that said, "The article in the current magazine by Mr. Wynant Davis Hubbard of Harvard is unworthy of answer from Princeton other than by statement that his attack upon the sportsmanship of Princeton football teams . . . is directly contrary to fact and to the testimony of football officials." Coach Roper of Princeton was not nearly as diplomatic as the other officials: "I think that [Hubbard] is a liar and a common dirty one at that; and furthermore, what Harvard thinks now doesn't interest me in the slightest. I have more things to worry about than Harvard now, for we are through with them."[67]

And through with each other they were, as both football programs went their own ways after Bingham, Harvard's director of athletics, publicly stated in March 1927 that until Princeton took the initiative in healing the break in relations there would be no attempts at reconciliation. Finally, by early 1931 the discontent and bitterness had apparently fallen by the wayside with the complete turnover of the student bodies since 1926, along with the departures of the two head football coaches, Arnold Horween and Roper. A meeting between Kennedy and Bingham was held in New York on February 12, 1931, after which it was announced that because of the "complete change of undergraduate sentiment," athletic competition would resume as quickly as schedules could be arranged. Football was excluded from the agreement because of continuing differences on the question of meeting in an annual game.[68]

Yale at last started breaking up the impasse in early 1931, with the announcement that after years of giving Harvard the honored place as the final game on its football schedule, the Bulldogs would now begin rotating Harvard and Princeton in that treasured position, while continuing to meet both schools annually. By not doing so previously, Yale acknowledged that it had "discriminated against Princeton" and that the Tigers were in fact "a legitimate rival on the same basis as Harvard." The *Harvard Crimson* described this announcement as "a bolt from the Blue," but Yale had basically restored Princeton to an equal place in the Big Three athletically, and Harvard did not have much room to continue the break in football relations. At last, on the evening of January 8, 1933, Bingham and Thurston J. Davies, Princeton's acting Athletic Board chairman, announced the resumption of the football rivalry between the two universities, effective with the signing of a two-year contract that would begin with the 1934 game. In making the settlement a little easier for Harvard, Princeton relinquished its insistence on rotating the final-game spot against Yale.[69]

A *New York Times* editorial put a cap on the eight-year dispute between the two longtime rivals: "The regrettable row of 1926 belongs to a past generation of undergraduates. . . . The old tradition of friendly rivalry, the close association in many schools and the longer and closer association of the graduates of the two colleges all make for the good feeling which has gradually been restored."[70]

Conclusion

The college football world of the 1920s experienced many more disputes and scandals than the major cases just examined. The controversies reviewed were unquestionably the most significant on a national scale at the time, as they involved many of the most recognizable universities playing football and received a good deal of publicity in the national media. Yet even more so, these four disputes were symptomatic of the increasing pressures being created within the collegiate sport by some of the transformations it was experiencing during the decade. An increasing number of universities were finding themselves in an athletic world where they had become dependent on the financial rewards and prestige possible from a successful football team, even as they watched in horror as the public reputations of many of the schools were being defined by their gridiron fortunes.

Controversies involving eligibility and recruiting violations, slush funds, sportsmanship, and many other types of issues have continued to play a role within college football throughout the decades ever since the 1920s, often growing in seriousness as the riches at stake in the sport have been magnified through the onset of television and even larger on-campus stadia. Yet the four cases of the 1920s we have examined, along with many others during the decade, were especially notable within the history of college football, as they directly fueled the reform efforts that produced the Carnegie Foundation's study of intercollegiate sport late in the decade. The fact that these types of situations would continue to surface as early as 1930 in the immediate aftermath of the Carnegie Report was a clear signal at the time that the athletic factions were able to survive such disclosures and scandals and would ultimately prove triumphant over academe in the struggle over intercollegiate sport that had reached a fever pitch by the mid-1920s.

10

THE DEBATE OVER REFORM

The final piece in college football's transformation throughout the 1920s proved to be the culmination of a decadelong struggle between the forces of reform and those individuals who supported the gridiron game. The many aspects of change that had fueled the evolution of football into a big-business pursuit were merely preludes to the battle for control of the gridiron sport on university campuses. The eventual outcome would complete the definition of intercollegiate football for the next half century.

The reformers, primarily from the faculty and administrative branches of the university community, sought to return the increasingly commercialized sport of intercollegiate football back to the minor place it had once held in its earliest years within the overall structure of university life. That it was never going to be possible given the substantial financial dependency on football by many universities did not dissuade the reformers from their crusade. In the eyes of the reformers, the manifested evil of the gridiron game was that the educational reputation and worth of a college or university were rapidly coming to be associated with the fortunes of the football team, a situation modern historian John Thelin has described as "debilitating to the entire intellectual atmosphere of the American campus."[1]

Writing of football at the University of Chicago in the 1920s, William McNeill has noted that for the undergraduates, "the worth of the university, in their eyes and in those of most of the citizens of Chicago, was measured mainly by athletic success." This condition was also noted in a Boston College newspaper editorial of the 1920s, which said that "among many people the prowess of the Varsity Team is the measure of an educational institution's worth," while an article in the *New Republic* added that "there is other evidence that the college is becoming in fact, as it has long appeared to the public, a mere appendage to the college sport."[2]

Intending that academic endeavor reign as the central and complete focus in the lives of the undergraduate students—and encouraged by the many controversies and disputes that demonstrated a continued serious decline in the spirit of true amateurism—the reformers attacked such aspects of intercollegiate football as recruiting, alumni influences, paid coaches, and the growing dependence on the revenues being generated. All these issues became prelude to the release of the Carnegie Report in 1929.

EARLY OPPOSITION

Concerns over the enthusiasm of students and alumni for intercollegiate sport were not merely a phenomenon of the 1920s, but had been a factor of university life since early in the history of football. As the gridiron sport rapidly escalated in popularity in the late nineteenth century, the faculties of various institutions— primarily in the East where collegiate football had its origins and first major growth—frequently took actions aimed at prohibiting or restricting the growing role that the game was playing in the lives and emotions of the students. The playing of games by the Big Three schools (Harvard, Princeton, and Yale) in the professionalized metropolitan stadiums of New York City, and the often rowdy conduct of the students in the aftermath of the games, had only increased the concerns of university administrators.[3]

By the turn of the century the overemphasis on college football had spread well into the midwestern states, where the Intercollegiate Conference (the eventual Big Ten) had been formed in 1895 with the intent of controlling the abuses of the idealistic principles of "amateur" sport. It was believed that this new conference structure would place the control of intercollegiate athletics in the hands of the faculty administrators, and thus provide a vehicle among the participating universities for the consistent adherence to regulations that would confine sport to its proper place within the academic community. Professor C. A. Waldo of Purdue University wrote that among the midwestern schools, "teams were becoming a permanent and paid body of men, and the whole thing was rapidly assuming a gladiatorial aspect. . . . Athletics are not the purpose of college life. They are its incident."[4]

Yet the sport of college football continued to escalate in its appeal to both students and nonstudents alike in the first years of the new century, with the continuing faculty opposition being fueled by such signs of overemphasis as the use of professional coaches, a fanaticism for fielding all-conquering teams, and Harvard's building of a large new football stadium in 1903. A growing recognition of the need for an administrative organization that would potentially assist the schools in overseeing intercollegiate sports led to the formation of what eventually became the NCAA in December 1905, although for several years some of the most politically powerful schools declined to become members. By 1906 some major university administrations had used the growing concerns over football's poorly restrained violence as an excuse for suspending intercollegiate play by its students. Among these schools were Stanford, California, and Columbia. When Columbia announced its

dropping of football, Professor Lord, chairman of the committee on student orga-
nizations, said that "the reasons for this action needs no explanation. . . . Only by
such radical action can the university and college life be rid of an obsession which,
it is believed, has become as burdensome to the great mass of students as it has
proved itself harmful to academic standing and dangerous to human life."[5]

In the years immediately before World War I, the dialogue concerning college football's professionalism and overemphasis was widespread. In 1915, Sol
Metzger, sportswriter for the *New York Sun*, published a multipart series in which
he explored the issues of athletic eligibility and the recruiting (or "proselyting") of
high school athletes. Metzger, a former collegiate athlete at the University of Pennsylvania, asserted that the desire to field winning teams was at the root of college
football's many instances of "over-emphasis," while also noting that "many educators believe there is great value in athletic advertising." Metzger wrote of one
college president who had expressed the opinion that "successful football teams
aid in increasing the enrollment." Among his observations in support of football,
Metzger assured critics that intercollegiate athletics had more regulations than
ever for the guidance of athletes and that if collegiate sport was "properly directed
and supervised," there were significant benefits to be realized.[6]

At its 1917 convention the NCAA endorsed Metzger's belief that the tools for
properly administering sport were in place, as the delegates agreed that intercollegiate athletics were currently being conducted "nearer to their ideals than ever
before." The onset of World War I brought a scaling back of most collegiate athletic
programs, and many school officials therefore believed that the theory of true amateur sport had been restored to intercollegiate competition. The NCAA delegates
unanimously endorsed the belief that after the war there would be "no return to
the commercialized systems."[7]

Yet the prevailing sentiment among many observers continued to be that
intercollegiate sport, football in particular, had become far too commercialized to
be cleansed by a temporary cutback in football because of the war effort. An editorial in the *Yale Alumni Weekly* wondered if the prestigious Yale program would
be "willing at least to help lead the way to purer amateurism [with] . . . less of
the trumped-up public spectacle." Before the war, in 1916, a Yale committee report had contended that the need to maintain the "disproportionate salaries demanded by expert coaches" was fueling the growing demands for ever greater
athletic revenues. This demand in turn was producing "many of the perplexing
and disagreeable problems of eligibility," as the coaches sought to field winning
teams that would propagate the box-office bonanzas. The Yale committee suggested that the ultimate solution to the problems of commercialization might
require the discontinuance of paid coaching staffs, and possibly even the aban-
donment of intercollegiate football.[8]

THE STRUGGLE ESCALATES

When college football returned to full-scale operations in the aftermath of the war, it became quickly evident that the popularity and commercial aspects of the sport had not been permanently inhibited, as the prewar reformers had hoped. Those individuals opposed to the growing role of sport within the lives of the undergraduates were quick to again express their concerns. President James R. Angell of Yale, in an address in early 1921 soon after he arrived at the university, declared that he wanted athletics to "not unreasonably invade the time and attentions of the members of the team, and . . . prevent their proper attention to academic work." One month later the Athletic Division of the Intercollegiate Conference on Undergraduate Government held a meeting at MIT to review a wide range of intercollegiate sport issues that included alumni influences, eligibility rules, and the training facilities provided to athletes.[9]

Soon the drumbeat of concern over the commercialization of football began to echo in the public newspaper and magazine forums. In an article in the *New York Times*, writer Robert Kilburn Root leveled the charge that college football had become "an organized, commercialized spectacle, in all essentials as professional as big league baseball." But Root did not particularly see the condition of commercialization as the major issue challenging the universities, but instead whether football was "a salutary influence in college life mentally, physically, and morally." In commenting on Root's concerns, Dr. Stewart Paton of Princeton advanced the theory that "football permanently warps the judgement of the average college man" and that students are taught that "eternal disgrace or dazzling triumph depends on what happens on the successive Saturdays of autumn." Later, John R. Tunis would add that "the religion of football . . . teaches the most ephemeral of values . . . and instead of assisting the undergraduate to distinguish between what is best and what is worthless in life, tends to befuddle his judgement with its hysterical appeals to his emotion and its irrational standards."[10]

The major crowds flocking to college football contests and some of the attendant ceremonies of the students that surrounded the games were primary factors fueling the conception that the undergraduates were being overly distracted by the overemphasis given to the sport. Surprisingly, Walter Camp, one of the longtime supporters of college football, early in the stadium-building boom of the 1920s advanced the suggestion that possibly university officials "have gone too far in the erection of huge bowls and stadiums." Yet here was the dilemma that the universities had placed themselves in—the major source of revenue was greatly needed, but it came only with a price tag that included the frequently fanatical enthusiasms of many undergraduates and alumni.[11]

Some officials from smaller colleges, with virtually nothing to lose in the football debate, and some from the larger eastern football schools, believed that the sport of football belonged within the cloisters of the college environment—far removed from the eyes of the nonacademic public. In his report to the Harvard Overseers in January 1922, President A. Lawrence Lowell of the university noted, "The necessity of maintaining . . . public spectacles attended by thousands of spectators every Saturday of every autumn is certainly not clear; and whether it ought to be maintained . . . is a matter worth consideration."[12]

In an *Atlantic Monthly* article, Dr. Alexander Meiklejohn, a former president of Amherst College, acknowledged that the "external factor" was creating a conflict over the place of sport within the collegiate community. Yet he hastened to add that "it would not be wise or friendly for us to exclude the public from our contests. . . . [I]t would be socially wrong for us to seek such seclusion. The college is, in all essential features, a public institution." But in 1925 Harvard's athletic committee would release a report describing the attentions from outside the campus community as an "undoubtedly undesirable amount of public interest in football," while another advocate of reform, Dr. Karl Wettstone of the University of Dubuque, commented that the old-time college spirit would never return to campuses "until the present evils are wiped out and commercialism in inter-collegiate athletics is given the death blow."[13]

Despite the rhetoric that advocated football strictly for the entertainment and benefit of the students, there was still the issue of the sizable dependence on the box-office revenues for many schools. Indeed, most universities recognized and sought to capitalize upon the relationship between football and devotion to school that existed in the minds of many alumni. Harvard allowed its football team to accept an invitation to the Rose Bowl game at the end of the 1919 season with the specific intent of stimulating the enthusiasm of West Coast alumni for the university's endowment-fund campaign. In 1927 Yale was conducting an endowment drive to raise twenty million dollars, and progress reports published throughout that year consistently included football themes in the cartoons that urged alumni to put the drive over the top. There was no way the universities could have it both ways—keep the large revenues yet play football in a small-scale environment—and sportswriter Lawrence Perry pointed out that, "what all the colleges have got to decide before long . . . is whether incomes from football, together with means to insure such sums, are good and desirable or bad and hence undesirable."[14]

THE ALUMNI ISSUE

Making little headway in the crusade to downsize intercollegiate football, the reformers turned to the abuses within the sport that were brought about by the consuming need to field winning teams. One of the favorite targets was the often inappropriate involvement of alumni in athletic department affairs, which invariably included the illegal recruiting and subsidization of athletes. To a great extent the undergraduates were aware that illegal recruiting was taking place, as a Marquette University newspaper article referred to the "days of 'cash and carry' athletes," when "it is common talk . . . that a high school athlete who is wanted badly has only to sit back and let the colleges bid for his services." In the *New Republic* a faculty member from a major university wrote that "it is practically impossible for a college to have consistently successful football teams unless it bids in the open market for the services of outstanding players in secondary schools."[15]

Financial support for such activities during the 1920s was possible only with the assistance of well-connected alumni or other supporters of the university athletic program, and usually was done with the complicity of someone at the school. One writer, George Owen, attributed football's most serious problems to the alumni: "They have raised the game to its absurd and outrageous importance as an element in collegiate life." Though not as accusatory, sportswriter Grantland Rice noted that "the Old Grads still form most of the football committees, and they still have a lot of power over the football destinies of their university." John Heisman, a prominent football coach, expressed the prevailing belief when he wrote that "the strict tenets of amateurism will be debauched with fierce abandon as long as alumni take an aggressive pride in their colleges, which pride is usually centered in the college's athletics."[16]

At the conference of the Athletic Division of Undergraduate Government in 1921, the involvement of alumni in recruiting athletes was one of the major topics. Although several schools claimed to have no knowledge of alumni involvement within their athletic programs, four schools openly admitted to receiving direct financial support from their alumni for the benefit of athletics. A year later, reacting to mounting concerns by athletic officials over the extent of alumni involvement in the recruiting of players, the Big Ten hired Major John Griffith as its first commissioner in July 1922, with the express purpose of assisting in the interpretation and enforcement of "amateur rules." Griffith soon noted that the interpretation of one of the conference's athletic regulations "practically says that it is desirable for alumni to recruit athletic material from high schools." Acknowledging that "alumni are part of the institution just as much as the faculty," he questioned the potential for abuses of recruiting rules because of this participation. Citing the issue as more important than the growing influence of organized professional football, Griffith suggested that the athletic directors needed to "discourage the raising of slush funds" by the alumni groups.[17]

In April 1924 Griffith sent a memorandum to the athletic directors in which he cited several instances of illegal financial dealings involving athletics and outside groups—yet he expressed a belief "that there is not a great deal of illegitimate recruiting going on in the Western [Big Ten] Conference." Griffith, lacking any real enforcement authority over the athletic affairs of the conference universities, again advanced the suggestion that each athletic director should send a letter to their school's alumni and explain the official opposition to the illegal recruitment of athletes. Yet by early 1925 it was apparent that high school athletes were still being approached with illegal financial incentives by nonuniversity personnel, so Griffith sent a two-page letter to every high school principal in the states that surrounded, or were represented within, the Big Ten Conference. Griffith sketched an overview of the recruiting problems faced by the universities, what the current conference regulations prohibited, and asked the principals to assist by notifying his office "if you know of any illegitimate offers being made to athletes."[18]

Concerns over the often inappropriate and excessive involvement of alumni in the affairs of the football programs and illegal recruiting were two of the major factors that ultimately moved the leaders of the reform element to seek a formal study of intercollegiate sport. Subsequently, in January 1926 the Carnegie Foundation agreed to take on the project, and staffer Howard Savage was assigned to head up a team of five researchers and write the eventual report on their findings. By late 1926 this survey was already well under way, and Griffith had a preliminary discussion with Savage about some of the early findings. The Big Ten commissioner then wrote again to the conference athletic directors and noted that he had recently received many reports of illegitimate recruiting on the part of conference schools, adding that "in practically every situation . . . I have found that there is some key man who is largely responsible for the undue activity on the part of alumni and others." Just six days later Griffith sent out another memorandum on recruiting, noting that "conditions here in this section are not entirely ideal and probably never will be."[19]

Although Griffith stated that university officials were not involved in these affairs, the breaking of the Iowa slush fund scandal in 1929 would prove otherwise. The scandal, which would result in the Big Ten suspending all athletic relations with Iowa, provided endorsement of Heisman's earlier contention that recruiting abuses were "not the secrets of a few. It is absurd to argue that coaches and faculties don't know." Yet Griffith would primarily single out the alumni in the Iowa case, suggesting that a "small group of alumni wished to dominate the Iowa athletic situation and to dictate athletic policies." Despite the forthcoming revelations of the 1929 Carnegie Report, the inappropriate involvement of some alumni members in the recruitment of athletes would continue to plague college football throughout future decades.[20]

The Professional Coaches Dilemma

Another significant aspect of intercollegiate football that attracted the ire of the reform movement during the 1920s was the role and stature of the football coach. In college football's earliest days the formal coaching of a team had been nonexistent at many schools. At the more prominent football schools, such as the Big Three of the East, a degree of coaching was usually provided by former players who would return to campus to work with the team before the biggest games of the season, the team captain handling the chore the rest of the time. The more alumni coaches descending on the campus, the more confusing and unstructured these efforts usually became.

This situation began to change during the 1890s at the most prominent football universities, as the value of expert coaching was recognized in the effort to field winning teams. When Amos Alonzo Stagg was named head football coach at the University of Chicago in 1892, and also given faculty status for his work within the physical education department, it signaled a recognition by some that an athletic coach might have as much value to a school as the faculty members devoted to the academic side of university life.

That notion was never going to gain acceptance within the ranks of the regular faculty, but it did reflect a recognition of what the purpose of intercollegiate football really was: to field winning teams and so spread the name of the university, along with whatever other benefits might accrue. Sport historian Ronald Smith has written that "the professional coaching issue was central to the notion of what individuals believed sport was all about.... The saga of the professional coach does much to explode the myth that there was ever a lengthy period when the amateur spirit pervaded college athletics."[21]

As the 1900s dawned a growing number of universities recognized the tangible benefits that could be obtained with a well-coached football team, and thus the ranks of the full-time, career-oriented coaches grew rapidly with individuals such as Glenn "Pop" Warner, Fielding Yost, John Heisman, Dan McGugin, and Henry Williams. Soon, the idea of the "old grads" coming back to campus to help the football team was considered obsolete and quietly phased out at even the old-line Big Three. As Grantland Rice later wrote, "Today's organization is entirely too efficient for any such harem-scarum coaching methods." This action served to entrench the professional football coach as an essential to fielding winning teams and soon moved legendary sportswriter Casper Whitney to describe such coaches as "the most serious menace of college sport today."[22]

By the 1920s the prominent universities were also financing coaching staffs that included several assistants—much to the annoyance of the academic faculty. In the aftermath of the war, Princeton's Football Committee had made an attempt to reduce the size of its coaching staff, yet this effort met with opposition, as Harvard and Yale were operating with a greater number of coaches. Followers of the Tigers' football program were of the opinion that until its two archrivals reduced their staffs to a minimum, Princeton would be foolishly placing its team under a handicap by unilaterally cutting its coaching staff. This opinion prevailed, as just months later Princeton's Football Committee announced that Coach Bill Roper would be provided all the assistant coaches he needed. In the 1920s Roper would have seven or eight assistant coaches on his staff in the early years of the decade, only cutting back to five and a freshmen coach in 1926 as the clamor against college football's overemphasis neared its peak. The respect that most of the students and alumni might shower on a coach who could consistently deliver winning football teams is evidenced soon after the war in an article in the *Princeton Alumni Weekly* by Donald G. Herring, in which he stated that "the thanks of every Princeton man who loves football are due to Bill Roper and his assistants for the team they developed. . . . Now that we have a coaching system that teaches 'winning football,' let us by all means strive to make it as nearly permanent as we can. I think I voice the hope of every one Princetonian."[23]

As the most successful of the college football coaches became national figures through the prominence of their teams, while the independence and prerogatives for all coaches increased proportionate to the revenue they were producing, the academically oriented reformers seethed with resentment. The salaries awarded to the most prominent of the football coaches at major universities were a particular irritant to most faculty members and served as a continuous source of controversy. Professor Glenn Hoover, writing in the *New Republic* in 1925, summed up the prevailing attitudes of the reformers as he noted that an initial step for addressing many of football's problems would be to "trim the salary and dignity of the professional coach . . . and make him at least a little lower than the university president." Also in 1925, Harvard's Athletic Committee and the American Association of College Professors each proposed that schools return to employing only their graduates as football coaches, the latter group also suggesting term limits of possibly three years for the coaches as a further means of eliminating the high salaries. Another reformer advocated universally making the head football coaches members of the college faculty as a means of enforcing salary controls.[24]

By the end of the 1920s the place of the full-time football coach within the university community had been secured against the reformers. The influence of the prominent coaches was such that writer John Tunis described them as even "more important today than the game" and a "determined opposition to any effort to change or simplify the structure of the game." Tunis also added that the prominent older football coaches considered "the cultural side of university life as something to be endured and regards himself as divorced from any contact therefrom"—yet another irritant to those critics who viewed football as a negative influence on academic life.[25]

The Move for Downsizing

Along with the attacks on alumni and big-time head coaches, there were other proposals advanced by the reformers throughout much of the 1920s—all seeking to restore intercollegiate football to their vision of its proper role within university life. Although several small colleges eventually discontinued their football programs during the decade, reformers considered a more realistic approach of downsizing the sport at the major schools to be a reduction of the annual schedule to just a few games. In late 1925 Harvard's student newspaper, the *Crimson*, published an editorial that advocated a substantial list of reforms aimed at restoring balance between football and the academic side of collegiate life. Among the proposals was one that football schedules include not more than three games for the teams, along with no public sale of tickets for these events. For Harvard, the proposal called for games against Yale and two other opponents—"provided they will agree to adopt a similar plan." But this idea was a student proposal that did not have the endorsement of the university's athletic officials. The graduate manager of Harvard's Athletic Association, Major Fred Moore, discounted the idea of shorter schedules and noted that "the only way to stop interest in collegiate football is either not to play the game at all, substituting some other sport, or to stop the big games on the schedule."[26]

In early December 1925 student delegates from twenty-seven colleges—including representatives from most of the major universities in the Northeast, the Big Three among them—met at Wesleyan University to consider ways of furthering the ultimate purpose of American higher education, which was defined as "the training of the mind." Not surprisingly, one of the major areas addressed was intercollegiate football, and a committee of students recommended that colleges play gridiron schedules of only four games each season, and these games only against teams in their own class and within reasonable traveling distance. The student group anticipated the arguments against lost revenues that were supporting the intercollegiate minor sports, advancing the recommendation that "appropriate taxes on undergraduates would serve instead, if such a step were necessary."[27]

In order to prepare varsity football teams for only a November schedule, the proposal for conducting intramural or class competitions as a means of getting the athletes in shape and selecting the varsity team members was advanced. This "class series" was a system long used by the English universities and appealed to those individuals who cited the Oxford-Cambridge athletic rivalries as the model for true amateur sport. An unsigned article in *Outlook* magazine endorsed the proposals made at the Wesleyan conference, and the writer believed that the abbreviated schedule approach would "stop making Roman holidays for the mob . . . [and] put football back into its original place in the scheme of college things."[28]

The response of the Yale and Harvard student newspapers to the financial shortfalls that would result from abbreviated football schedules was to look to the alumni for endowment funds that would maintain the many athletic programs and facilities that were being supported by football. Expecting the alumni to foot the bill was a clearly unfeasible solution for any large school where football supported the many other athletic teams and sports facilities, along with assisting in paying off the debts from the building of a new stadium. This fact was hinted at by the University of Illinois, which had recently constructed a major new football stadium, where even the student newspaper—the *Daily Illini*—admitted that it had no answers for the dilemma of installing reforms within the football program while still maintaining its benefits to the university. The *Harvard Crimson* acknowledged that so long as the colleges were dependent on the gate receipts from football, there would remain a sufficient reason for continuing the gridiron game in its current format.

At the conclusion of another *Outlook* article that examined the student-oriented reform movement, writer David Reed stated that "the youth of America, which made football, may yet be the saviors of the game." This remark hinted at a smaller-scale reform initiative during the late 1920s—the return of football to student-player control in emulation of the sport in its earliest days, before the advent of professional coaches. Proposing that football be returned to student control was actually just another form of attack on the coaching fraternity and its growing stature within the game. Yet in an article for the *New York Evening Post,* John Tunis described a process for returning scholastic and collegiate sports to the players, "to whom they really belong," while the prominent sportswriter W. O. McGeehan agreed that "this game . . . should be the property of the undergraduates." Others, including Coach T. A. D. Jones of Yale, proposed that football coaches be required to sit in the grandstands during a game with no authority over the play on the field and that control of the teams be returned to the captains.[29]

Not surprisingly, there was considerable opposition to this proposal by most college football coaches. Knute Rockne at Notre Dame described the proposal as being "sponsored by certain types of educators who are jealous of coaches and want to put them completely out of the picture"—an obvious conclusion. Gil Dobie at Cornell defined his opposition in terms of football's technical play, noting, "The movement which purports to give the game back to the boys is being promulgated very largely by those who know little about the intricacies of modern football."[30]

Such points of view from the coaching ranks met with derision from reform advocates such as Tunis, who replied that Dobie's position was a sad commentary on both intercollegiate football and "the educational system" that had allowed the sport to progress to such a state of alleged complexity. Tunis also believed that none of the football coaches in opposition to the issue of player control "were otherwise than entirely bankrupt of ideas about real sport." Yet there was no ignoring that football had progressed substantially in its equipment, styles of play, and complexities and that having some continuity within the schools' programs was essential.[31]

Regardless of whether reformers chose to discount such considerations, the fact was that the organized administration of a college team, both off and on the field, had definitely moved beyond the capabilities of a team captain to handle. Reformers who advocated placing intercollegiate football programs under complete student control failed to consider that many universities were realizing substantial financial benefits from their gridiron programs and were certainly not going to transfer control of the extensive amounts of monies involved, and their economic well-being, to any student athletic committee arrangement. And of possibly greater significance was the need for continuity in alumni affections for the university, as represented by its athletic programs, deemed essential for maintaining any sort of progressive endowment program. Although returning college football to an imagined simpler time seemed like a good idea, by the late 1920s the sport had progressed well beyond the point where such reforms as player control and reduced schedules could be seriously considered by any major university.

FOOTBALL ON THE DEFENSE

For the reform element, the commissioning of the Carnegie Foundation study of intercollegiate athletics in 1926 seemed to be the start of the final and decisive battle in their long-fought war for control over collegiate sport. Yet prominent athletic officials and other supporters of intercollegiate football had not been content to sit passively during the escalating attacks of the early 1920s.

The carefully measured statements of the football faction before the release of the Carnegie Report in 1929 did much to effectively portray intercollegiate sport to the public as a beneficial force, both for the universities and for the youthful population of the nation. Despite some of the obvious instances of overemphasis in college football that were well known to the general sporting public, the rear-guard action throughout the decade by the athletic faction served to create a very complicated and controversial picture of the reformers' position by the time the Carnegie Foundation released its report.

Early Lines of Defense

Intercollegiate football had long had supporters who publicly related the benefits of athletic discipline to the best interests of both the university and the individual. From its earliest days in 1892, the University of Chicago's first president, William Rainey Harper, viewed physical education and intercollegiate competition as integral parts in the life of the university community. However, this belief did not imply that Harper was willing to condone abuses of fair play, sportsmanship, and overemphasis in the name of his football teams. In fact, the University of Chicago was one of the charter organizers of the Western Conference (later the Big Ten) in 1895, an organization formed "to establish and maintain common standards of eligibility and common rules to curb practices which are detrimental to amateur sport or fair and friendly competition."[32]

Ronald Smith has noted the widespread acceptance and support of intercollegiate football during the 1890s by university officials, adding that before 1900 "football . . . was a symbol of college and national virility." And in a 1908 address before a convention of educators, Dr. George Norlin had contended that "athletics are not merely an incidental interest of student life, they are a vital and important element of an institution's educational policy."[33]

In the immediate aftermath of World War I, the defenders of football's place within university life often sought to emphasize the sport's role in forging the national character and commitment that had been essential in the recently completed European conflict. In 1920 General Robert Wood of the U.S. Army stated his belief that "the training that the college men got in their various games was one of the great contributing factors that helped us win the war," while Hamilton Fish, a former Harvard All-America and then U.S. congressman, noted that football "is a great asset to the national health and physical development of our country, and has the advantage of training and democracy of military service." George Marvin of *Outlook* magazine wrote that football provided "intangible benefits in body, mind, and character which have become assets in the morale and fiber of the nation. If British cricket helped win battles for the Empire, football had something to do with Chateau Thierry and the Argonne."[34]

The Defense Settles In

Relating intercollegiate football to the best interests of national preparedness was certainly an effective strategy in the early years after the war, yet defenders of the sport were soon harkening back to the 1890s themes of its spiritual reenforcement and relation to the overall aims and purposes of college life.

Increasingly, the belief in football's place within the diversity of college life became one of the two major lines of defense for the sport throughout the decade and beyond. President Nicholas Murray Butler of Columbia University endorsed this point of view in 1923 when he stated that physical development, sports, and intercollegiate competition all played key roles within university life, while Coach Bill Roper of Princeton added that the "great enthusiasm for athletics is justifiable, because it fills a mighty void in our college and school life." Major Griffith of the Big

Ten lashed out at those reformers who saw no place for athletics within university life, noting that they "believe that the function of education is solely to develop intellectualism and to give cultural advantages to the students." And an editorial in the student newspaper at the University of Detroit pointed out, "Around the game of football is cemented all that is known as college spirit, all that training for loyalty and friendship that is the real basis of an education."[35]

The other major position presented by the defenders of college football stressed the financial significance of the sport to the well-being of the undergraduate population and the university itself. This strategy included support of the "sports for all" programs that provided intramural athletic equipment, facilities, and supervision for the student body at large. Generally, football, with basketball occasionally included, was the only intercollegiate sport that produced any net profits for the colleges at the completion of each school year. With the staggering monetary sums being realized during the 1920s by the major football programs, athletic officials did not hesitate to emphasize that the gridiron sport was covering all the expenses for the schools' intercollegiate teams in addition to subsidizing the intramural programs. In some cases, proceeds from the football programs were also providing for the purchase of additional property and the construction of new campus facilities for the universities. Coach Rockne summed up the position of the sport's defenders when he commented that "football has become the parent, or providing sport of colleges."[36]

At the 1925 NCAA meeting in New York, Griffith presented a paper in which he defended the profit-making aspects of intercollegiate football and noted that in the recent season the colleges had generated an estimated twenty million dollars in profits that would be used to provide larger athletic and physical education programs for millions of students. To those reformers who would eliminate such financial benefits to the universities, Griffith added that "if the practice of making money from amateur athletic sports and of using the profits to promote more athletics for more people is to be condemned, then some means should be devised for financing the school and college physical education work"—meaning that the financial burden would then fall on the school administrations.[37]

Though continuing to press the issues of college football's value and place within the university community, most athletic officials and gridiron coaches were also very much aware of the need to police themselves and the sport as a means of deflecting the criticisms of the reform element. A leading defender of intercollegiate football, and at the same time an advocate for self-policing, was the chairman of the Football Rules Committee, Edward K. Hall. Captain of the Dartmouth football team in 1891, Hall became a prominent business executive with the American Telephone and Telegraph Company and served on the Football Rules Committee for twenty-seven years, from 1905 onward.

In an address to the 1925 American Football Coaches Association, Hall—reflecting the furor over Red Grange's recent defection to professional football that was still current news—defined four aspects of college football that required attention in order to preserve the gridiron game as a fundamentally amateur pursuit: overemphasis in the publicizing of individual players, allowing the encroachment of professional football promoters and coaches onto college campuses before athletes had completed their studies, the overemphasis on fielding winning teams, and the transformation of college football into more of a business than a sport. Hall also noted that athletic officials could deflect some of the criticisms by reducing the sizes of overly large coaching staffs and by eliminating the practices of scouting and sideline coaching. He told the gathered coaches that it was the "friends of the game who are responsible for most of its present troubles," and "it was in their power to bring the game to greater heights than ever or to bring about its complete elimination."[38]

Some of football's prominent head coaches were cognizant of the importance of publicly addressing the legitimate issues of athletic overemphasis. At the 1925 meetings of the American Football Coaches Association and the NCAA, Roper of Princeton, Hugo Bezdek of Penn State, Bob Zuppke of Illinois, and John Wilce of Ohio State were among those coaches advancing formal proposals for various reforms within college football. Unfortunately, most of the reform proposals advanced by various coaches never moved further than the talking stage. Based on some of the activities that were later disclosed, it is problematic that there was any widespread serious interest in reforms among the coaches of the major universities.[39]

In early 1927, after a Big Ten meeting in Chicago that was attended by the university presidents, athletic directors, faculty representatives, and football coaches, the conference announced the adoption of a set of specific regulations concerning the proselyting (recruiting) of high school athletes. The primary intent of the agreement was that "scholarships, loans, and remission of tuition should not be awarded by universities on a basis of athletic skill. . . . [U]nofficial granting of financial aid . . . is unethical."[40]

Griffith stated that he and the Big Ten football coaches had been formulating the new code during the previous three years and that the agreement "merely puts into words ideas we have all had in a gentlemen's agreement and have followed conscientiously." Walter Eckersall of the *Chicago Tribune* noted that the group of Big Ten officials "feels certain it has cleared up one of the bad phases of intercollegiate athletics, something which has been a bone of contention since the conference was organized." Although it may have all looked good in the newspapers, there had been growing suspicions directed toward the athletic affairs of some of the Big Ten schools. When the scandal over the long-running football slush fund at the University of Iowa broke into the news in 1929, it was clear that the earlier pronouncements had carried little or no weight with alumni and many members of the coaching fraternity.[41]

THE HOME STRETCH

The pronouncements of the Big Ten in 1927 were typical of the escalated defense of their sport by the football faction and other supporters in the face of the commissioning of the Carnegie Report in January 1926. Preliminary information on some of the Carnegie findings was already becoming known by late 1926, causing considerable concerns within the athletic community and a fueling of the continued rebuttal of the reformers' attacks.

Of significance for the football faction was the support their game continued to receive from non-athletic-department individuals. At the annual meeting of the NCAA in late December 1925, President Ernest M. Hopkins of Dartmouth presented a paper titled "The Place of Athletics in an Educational Program," during which he defended intercollegiate sports: "Their virtues outweigh their evils, real and imaginary, and . . . they have a desirable place in the American colleges." Grantland Rice was one of football's supporters within the media, and although he believed that the gridiron sport could stand a little less hysteria and overemphasis on winning football teams, he wrote that "football . . . is a building force that in many respects does a magnificent job in the improvement of character and the making of a man."[42]

Many of the prominent coaches within college football also continued to step forward in defense of their sport in the latter years of the decade and to call attention to the pressures they labored under. Rockne was a reluctant supporter of athletic reforms, although he evidenced no hesitation at lashing out publicly at those reformers from the academic community and the popular media who would bring down the intercollegiate gridiron game of which he was a part. In late 1926 Rockne made headlines in sports sections across the country when he declared that "the college professors who hold that football undermines student morale and should be curtailed are simply a symbol for a jealous minority." The prominent coach added, "If football overshadows studies, then it is because the professors are not doing creative teaching." Roper of Princeton and Jones of Yale were two coaches who acknowledged the need for reform within football, but they also believed that "the benefits from the game and its influence on those who play it far outweigh its defects."[43]

Some university administrators were making constructive efforts to encourage the belief that student athletes existed within their athletic departments, such as when Boston University established residential quarters for its football team at Nickerson Field in 1928—a move expected "to improve the men physically but also to provide them more time for study than was possible under former conditions." In order to ensure that the football players were keeping up their studies in this segregated environment, the university appointed a faculty representative, Robert E. Moody of the History Department, to reside at the training quarters. Among his other duties, Professor Moody would obtain regular academic reports on the athletes from the various instructors in the school. President Daniel L. Marsh wrote, "In this way it is hoped to prevent the over-emphasis of athletics at the expense of scholarship and at the same time secure a group of football players who shall be thoroughly representative of the University."[44]

Less than a year before the release of the Carnegie Report, Tunis, writing in *Harper's*, restated his belief that "the attitude of the universities of this country toward football is often hypocritical in the extreme. Certainly their press releases and their statistics of expenditures for football do not square with their protestations that they wish to put an end to the evils which have crept into the game." Yet he also took note of a more realistic attitude toward football that was increasingly becoming evident among undergraduates on many campuses, fostered in large part by the many other extracurricular attractions that the universities offered.[45]

Meanwhile, the *Daily Princetonian* demonstrated that undergraduates could still recognize the charm that often surrounded the gridiron game on a beautiful October afternoon, as it marveled that "beyond all doubt the most gorgeous spectacles in modern America are to be beheld here and there throughout the country on Saturday afternoons during the fall." But by October 1929, neither side of the debate cared what the undergraduates believed.[46]

CONCLUSION

The debate over what reforms intercollegiate football did or did not require, and the impact they would have on the schools, raged on through the 1920s, even as the gridiron sport was in the midst of the various transformations that were in great part fueling the controversy. Both sides had numerous supporters, yet increasingly through the decade the football element appeared to hold the upper hand with the ultimate argument for which the reformers had no good answer: the financial dependence of the schools on the profits that football was generating.

Although everyone, at least publicly, professed to oppose the specific problems of overzealous alumni, overemphasis, and illegal recruiting, as the decade unfolded it became clear that virtually no specific reforms of any substance were going to take effect if the individual schools were left to their own devices. Hence, the reformers turned to the Carnegie Foundation as an organization with the level of political clout within the world of education that might just turn the tide of battle.

All the significant transformations within college football since World War I, and all the verbal warfare over the appropriate place and scale of sport within the university community, had all led to an inevitable showdown that would be realized with the release of the Carnegie Report. The report's findings and the responses to them would ultimately shape in great part the destiny of college football for the rest of the century.

11

THE CARNEGIE REPORT

By the mid-1920s it was clear that no real progress in reforming intercollegiate athletics, football in particular, was going to be realized by merely floating proposals in the news media. In September 1925, Dr. Henry H. Apple, president of Franklin and Marshall College, published an article in which he reviewed various abuses within collegiate sport that were distracting many of the undergraduates from their primary purpose for being in school. Dr. Apple concluded by suggesting that "an investigation might establish that some universities deliberately and officially offer scholarships and other inducements as a reward for athletic ability, especially football."[1]

The proposal by Dr. Apple received immediate public support from the heads of fifteen colleges, although conspicuously absent initially were representatives from any of the major football-playing universities. Dr. A. F. Woods, president of the University of Maryland and the Land Grant College Association, immediately suggested that a coalition of five different educational associations be formed for the purpose of conducting a national investigation into intercollegiate sport. Soon, Dr. W. W. Campbell, president of the University of California, announced that the American Association of University Professors had appointed a committee "to study and report upon the general subject of football abuses in American colleges." Yet just as the reformers realized that such a study could not be entrusted to the university athletic associations, so too was it essential that the envisioned thorough study and subsequent recommendations be prepared by an independent party as a means of blunting the anticipated rebuttals from the football crowd. Dr. Silas Evans, president of Ripon College, advanced the proposal that such an investigation of intercollegiate athletics be financed and conducted by one of the educational foundations, and so, with the agreement of other college heads, a proposal was submitted to the Carnegie Foundation for the Advancement of Teaching.[2]

LAUNCHING THE STUDY

On January 18, 1926, the Carnegie Foundation agreed to take on the study of American intercollegiate athletics. The commission received was for an investigation that would be conducted "with special reference to the effects of athletics on the educational program." The Carnegie Foundation for the Advancement of Teaching, under the direction of President Henry Pritchett, had been regularly active in pursuing such investigations, being especially noted for its study of medical schools in 1910. Howard Savage, a graduate of Tufts and Harvard, was a researcher on the Carnegie staff who had initially taught English at Bryn Mawr College from 1915 to 1923 before joining the foundation. In 1925 Savage had been assigned to investigate athletics at British public schools and universities, and in early 1926 he was placed in charge of the probe into American intercollegiate sport.

A few years earlier the Carnegie Foundation had undertaken a similar study to inquire "into the condition and administration of college athletics," and the report of its findings had been distributed in late 1924. This report had been developed from questionnaires that were returned by just 33 of the universities contacted, and it yielded the usual list of perceived abuses that were alleged to contribute to the commercialization and overemphasis of intercollegiate sport. The study had concluded that "with control of athletic policies and practices entirely in the hands of the president and the faculty . . . many of the evils noted would rapidly disappear."[3]

Initially in 1926, Savage and three other investigators attempted to gather data by means of questionnaires, as was done in 1924. If actual reforms were to be realized from the investigation, it was imperative that there be a broad base of schools participating, that the results from any school be complete and factual, and that those institutions guilty of flagrant abuses be identified for subsequent follow-up. By the spring of 1926 Savage was forced to admit that it was "evident that no trustworthy results could be obtained by a general use of the questionnaire in studying so complex a subject." So the Carnegie Foundation sent five researchers on a lengthy series of on-site visits to 130 colleges and universities in order to gather the material. Initially, the visits to a school ranged between two and six days, but by 1928 they were shortened to a maximum of three days.[4]

It did not take long before word of the findings began to leak out, causing considerable concerns for athletic officials. By late 1926 Griffith was able to obtain what he described as a "sneak" look at some of the preliminary Carnegie findings. In a memorandum to the athletic directors of the Big Ten, the commissioner said, "You can well appreciate that there will be considerable excitement when this report is made public, especially if the names of the institutions are given." Many university athletic officials responded by making certain to evidence every intention of fully cooperating with the researchers. For example, in late 1927, Coach John Wilce of Ohio State extended his stay in New York City after the NCAA convention so that he might meet with Savage, "to give him some of the facts surrounding the . . . athletic situation." Wilce noted that he "considered it worthwhile . . . to make sure that [Savage] had the correct information."[5]

In early 1929 Savage and his team concluded the lengthy investigation, and when the Carnegie Foundation's report was released in October of that year it represented the culmination of the reformers' decadelong struggle to transform college football.

THE CARNEGIE REPORT

On October 24, 1929, after three and a half years and a cost of approximately one hundred thousand dollars, the Carnegie Foundation released its Bulletin no. 23, which was formally titled *American College Athletics.* The 347-page document produced by Savage and his staff concluded that only 28 of the 130 schools studied could be given a clean bill of health in the conduct of their athletic affairs—and only 8 of those institutions were considered to be major football schools. The overall finding of the Carnegie investigators could be summed up in the statement that "intercollegiate athletics as a whole are sordidly commercialized through prevalent recruiting and subsidizing of athletes, and because of their big business aspects are causing a neglect of educational opportunities." The report further noted, "The argument that commercialism in college athletics is merely a reflection of the commercialism of modern life is specious. It is not the affair of the college or the university to reflect modern life."[6]

In his preface to *American College Athletics*, Pritchett, president of the foundation, wrote that the universities were operating "a system of recruiting and subsidizing . . . [that] is demoralizing and corrupt" and that "no college boy training for a major team can have much time for thought or study." Pritchett added that "the blaze of publicity in which the college athlete lives is a demoralizing influence for the boy himself and no less so for his college." Organized sports activities needed to be "brought back to a stage . . . where they do not involve an expenditure of time and money wholly at variance with any ideal of honest study."[7]

American College Athletics contained chapters dealing with a variety of topics within the world of intercollegiate sport. Yet what primarily attracted the attention of athletic reformers, university administrators, and the news media were the scathing indictments of athletic recruiting and subsidization—and most significant, the naming of specific schools that were found to be pursuing these activities. After Pritchett had set the tone in his preface, the researchers proceeded to unfurl page after page that painted intercollegiate sport—football in particular—as an activity that provided little "actual fun" for the undergraduates. Instead, football was cited as a sport that had developed far different values than the ones publicly espoused by the coaching fraternity, noting that "whether from its intrinsic nature as a body-contact game or from the abuses that have grown up to choke it, [football] has bred distrust, suspicion, jealousy, and physical violence." And at the core of this perceived evil was the recruiting and subsidizing of the athletes.[8]

Although the Carnegie researchers conceded that the problem of athletes being recruited for their playing skills had "diminished" in scope over the past twenty-five years, it was charged that "the recruiting of American college athletes, be it active or passive, professional or non-professional, has reached the proportions of nationwide commerce." If true, this situation was clearly counter to the spirit of old-school amateur sport under which much of the academic and reform elements believed American college sport should be operated. And, of particular annoyance, it placed the athlete on a far different level of prestige in relation to the typical struggling undergraduate. The report concluded, "There is no valid reason why even the most worthy athlete should receive any consideration, favor, assistance, or attention that is not available, upon the same terms and with the same readiness, to the general body of undergraduates."[9]

Alumni groups—always ready targets for the reformers—came in for their share of criticism in the discussion of recruiting. The report surprisingly contradicted the prevailing idea that alumni groups were guilty of most of the recruiting efforts—crediting them with handling the job at "only a little over 30%" of the colleges and universities visited. Yet the researchers had also found that "an intensively organized, sometimes subtle, system that may utilize or co-ordinate numbers of agents on or off campus" was being used at a number of the major football schools. And the researchers made clear their finding that any recruiting efforts by alumni groups involved the knowledge and complicity of "some official of the institution or the athletic staff." The accusations were also not directed only at the secular football-playing schools, as Catholic colleges were identified as employing the same types of recruiting networks, and the report noted that "the resulting practices of Catholic institutions have been in general at least as objectionable as those of other colleges and universities."[10]

Not surprisingly, the researchers had also found evidence that alumni groups at a number of major schools were in fact playing substantial roles in deciding how long a coach might last at the school. Despite this fact, the report stated, "Careful consideration of individual instances leads to the conclusion that nowadays the coach who openly teaches his men to win by unfair means is very exceptional," adding a belief that the coach's tenure at a school was becoming less dependent on fielding all-conquering football teams—"a fair winning average" becoming an acceptable state of affairs.[11]

The Carnegie researchers also directed criticisms at the role that the news media played in overinflating the egos and reputations of the individual players through game stories, features, and the proliferating numbers of All-America teams: "The result is a collection of publicity that dilutes an intended honor to the level of ridiculous, and, the country over, included an astonishing number of mediocre players." It was suggested that the excessive publicity being accorded to intercollegiate football was a motivating factor in the widespread recruiting and subsidization of athletes that was taking place.[12]

The writers of the Carnegie Report did include substantial amounts of valuable data on the inner workings of intercollegiate sport, above and beyond the recruiting and subsidization topics. Historian John Thelin has described the report as "an encyclopedic survey of conditions" and written that the Carnegie Report "became the canon that set the standard for reform proposals and policy analyses about the place of intercollegiate sports in American colleges." Author John Watterson has added that the Carnegie Report continues to be "by far the most comprehensive effort to document specific athletic practices and to present a complete picture of college athletics." Although the overall tone of the report portrays college athletics as requiring substantial reforms, Savage and his staff did present their findings in a straightforward manner, with none of the emotionalism that had often characterized the debate over American college football. Savage wrote, "It is far from our intention to imply that no American college or university possesses a well-reasoned athletic policy in the molding of which all of the needs and responsibilities of the institution have been considered."[13]

In what must have been an unwelcome surprise to those reformers who advocated a return to faculty control of intercollegiate sport, the report stated, "Probably more than any other single factor, the operation of faculty control, even at its best, has tended to deprive the undergraduate of that opportunity of maturing under progressively increasing responsibility which an enlightened policy of guidance affords." Yet the researchers did conclude with the general recommendation that the answers were to be found outside the realm of the athletic faction: "The American college must renew within itself the force that will challenge the best intellectual capabilities of the undergraduate. . . . The solution of the problem is . . . not repression, but guidance by college presidents, deans, teachers . . . whose honesty is beyond self-interest or commercialism."[14]

REACTIONS TO THE REPORT

The release of the Carnegie Report in October 1929 certainly created a stir within the world of intercollegiate football and garnered considerable attention within the popular media of the day. Robert Harron of the *New York Evening Post* wrote that college football's skeletons had at last been "yanked out of the closet after years and years of whispering gossip," while John Kieran of the *New York Times* added that "the surprise to those who have been in touch with intercollegiate sports for years is that there should have been any surprise at the findings made public in the report."[15]

Yet despite the satisfaction expressed at the time by the reform faction and the architects of the report, the anticipated return of college athletics to the domain of academe was never realized. Two major factors blunted the impact of the 1929 Carnegie Report: the timing of the report's release and the preliminary ground-work laid out throughout the decade by football's supporters.

When Bulletin no. 23 was publicly released during the final week of October 1929, the timing could not have been any worse. The same day newspapers carried their initial articles on the report's findings, October 24, American society was staggered by news that far overshadowed the disclosures of the collegiate athletic wrongdoings—the continuation of the great Wall Street stock market crash that soon led to the Great Depression that would plague the country for much of the next decade.

On page 1 of most major newspapers of October 24–25 can be found an article on the Carnegie Report's release with a title along the lines of "Proselyting Lid Lifted." But overwhelmingly dominating the front page were headlines that blared out, "Stock Market Has Another Heavy Crash." On October 24, 1929, the New York Stock Exchange lost approximately five billion dollars in capitalization as more than eleven million shares were sold off. The market's "Black Tuesday" had given way to "Black Thursday." After a slight rally the next day, the market took another major tumble on the following Monday, as another five billion dollars vanished in frantic trading. Against this backdrop the Carnegie findings held interest only for the academic reformers—and maybe not even them.[16]

The other significant factor that blunted the report's immediate impact—as if any other factors were necessary—was the measured and effective work of defense that had been done throughout the decade by the supporters of intercollegiate football. Throughout the 1920s the athletic faction had systematically pounded away at the themes of football's importance to the physical preparedness of American youth and the significant financial importance of football-generated income to the well-being of the entire university community. It had also been made clear that much of the athletic department activities were being carried out with the endorsement of university administrations. Even admitting that there were indeed cases of recruiting, subsidization, and overemphasis—usually attributed to misguided alumni—the net effect of this campaign had been to present the media and the general sporting public with a wide-scale picture of a very debatable set of affairs within intercollegiate sport that allowed only the most fanatical reformers to remain in complete opposition. Yet despite the distractions that initially worked against the public effectiveness of the Carnegie findings, there still were immediate and ongoing responses from the various factions that surrounded the controversy over intercollegiate football.

With the appearance of the report the first response of most newspapers was to present an article filled with straightforward excerpts and facts from the lengthy text, while also mentioning specific colleges and universities that had been found to be pursuing organized efforts toward athletic recruiting and subsidization. Quickly, the daily sports pages across the country then followed up with articles of analysis and commentary on the report's findings. Some of the newspaper commentary came in the form of cartoon artwork that poked fun at both sides, such as the drawing by James North in the *Washington Post* that depicts an investigator in a top hat who is examining a college football player through a magnifying glass, while a bag of money labeled "Carnegie Coin" protrudes from the investigator's back pocket. The football player—labeled "College Sports"—is saying in his defense, "But surely, you will give me credit for having a sound mind in a sound body."

Many writers cast a critical eye on the disclosed problems, such as columnist Westbrook Pegler's comment that the report "only points out a typical American state of affairs after all in which high sounding laws are adopted strictly for moralistic display and common practice consistently flaunts them. . . . It is only the pretense and concealment couched in resolutions and agreements of the most elaborate athletic piety, that is immoral." An item in the *New York World* noted: "The comfortable supposition that faculty control and the rules laid down by sectional conferences were keeping college athletics on a sanitary basis melts away under the facts of the report. . . . What is the harm? The essential harm is that the whole spirit which should animate our institutions of higher learning is threatened by the commercialism, materialism and false glory of athletics." In general, the attitude of the printed news media came down more on the side of intercollegiate athletics, some believing their response to be a backlash against the commentary about the newspapers advanced by the Carnegie researchers.[17]

Almost immediately there was a clamor of denials from most of the schools identified in the report as not adhering to the true spirit of amateurism. A writer for the *Chicago Herald-Examiner* noted that "these denials of many of the reported evils are almost a monotone, few educational authorities admitting that the schools . . . have been guilty." The magnitude of the immediate denials issued by many university officials was surprising to some observers—the situation made more complicated by the fact that some college administrators had been given an opportunity to enter their responses and denials of the findings as footnotes in the report. Norman S. Taber, chairman of the athletic council at Brown University, declared of the report: "In part false and in toto so misleading as to make it difficult to believe that the authors could present it as the result of a bona fide survey or that the Carnegie Foundation could allow its name to be attached to it." W. S. Thuerer, the graduate manager at Washington and Jefferson, added, "There is not a word of truth in the report."[18]

Many questioned the objectivity of the report, such as an article in the Ohio State alumni magazine that stated, "In the first place, the investigators seem to have started their survey with a premise prejudicial to intercollegiate athletics. Having undertaken the investigation with a bias, it is quite logical that the commentators should have reached a damning conclusion accordingly." Writing in *Harper's*, even Frank Schoonmaker—who strongly believed that colleges were exploiting their athletes—had to comment, "This writer has never had the opportunity of examining any document less sane and less sympathetic. . . . The decided bias of the Bulletin as a whole can be, I think, quite easily demonstrated." Yet Kieran of the *New York Times* called the report "fairly thorough and apparently unbiased," although he found the generally constructive analysis at odds with the "gloomy tone" and sweeping recommendations made by Pritchett in the preface. Although there was no escaping the validity of many of the charges presented by the report, a prejudicial attitude on the part of the Carnegie researchers did not seem that far afield to many, given Pritchett's hostile opening commentary and the fact that the study had been commissioned by the reform faction.[19]

Reporters sought out student reactions on the campuses at some of the universities cited in the report, and not surprisingly what they discovered in general were widespread attitudes of relative disinterest in the Carnegie Report's findings. Either that or ideas about intercollegiate sport that totally ignored the realities of the schools' significant dependence on the financial benefits being realized. United Press noted that "radical thoughts have been stirred on the campus of important universities of the East" and then disclosed that Princeton students were actually discussing the possibility of "a university in the future with no intercollegiate sports whatsoever." Columbia students were said to be unwilling to decide which sport was more important to their university—football or rowing. More realistic was the comment of a Williams College upperclassman, who summed up the general outlook of the mainstream students toward the gridiron game: "We all back the football team and we want it to win. If it loses that's tough. Yet it is no reason to commit harikari. . . . We try to maintain an accurate balance between the things that are important and the things that are not."[20]

Such "egghead" views of intercollegiate sport as the ones reported from Princeton and Columbia satisfied the general preconceptions of eastern university campuses by others around the country. Although a band of students might be found who actually believed the elimination of intercollegiate sport would solve all the problems, the more general opinion the reporters found on eastern campuses was that a sporting environment consisting strictly of intramural competition was viewed by the students as a "utopian scheme" that was undesirable.

Undergraduate attitudes on midwestern campuses were portrayed as far less radical and leaning more toward an acceptance of the realities of intercollegiate football's significance for major university life. Bert Demby of United Press wrote, "The students seem to have allowed the report to slip out of their minds immediately after it came out . . . because they were excited at the time by the prospects of their team gaining another football victory last Saturday." An upperclassman at Marquette told a reporter that the Carnegie Report "appears as nothing more than an expose which has brought forth facts known by a majority of college students." At Northwestern, a student voiced the opinion that "football has enabled colleges to support all types of athletics and I believe that the spirit of competition it brings about is a fine thing." Right there was a neat summation and acceptance of the fundamental positions that football's defenders had espoused throughout the decade: the character building and physical manliness that supplemented the intellectual side of university life and the financial largess that worked to the benefit of all.[21]

At the NCAA's annual meeting that closed out the year of 1929, the assembled university representatives formally adopted, without a dissenting vote, a statement that expressed an acceptance and appreciation of the Carnegie Report. The delegates resolved to pattern their athletic dealings in accordance with the report's findings—certainly a risky premise given the realities of life within the world of intercollegiate sport. Savage was present at the meeting, and he delivered an address on the Carnegie findings in which he attempted to deflect the initial criticisms of the report, indicating that "up to the present hour we have not been appraised of any inaccuracy in the study as printed, and no one who has charged us with inaccuracy after doing us the honor to read it has substantiated his statements."[22]

Although university officials interested in athletic reforms issued a considerable number of statements in praise of the Carnegie Report, there were also signs that acceptance of the report's findings and recommendations was something less than widespread. General Palmer E. Pierce of West Point, the outgoing NCAA president and a public supporter of the spirit of amateurism, commented that the colleges "must have gate receipts to carry on the athletic program of our colleges"—probably not a surprising position given that West Point was in the middle of a break in relations with the Naval Academy over Army's use of what were essentially tramp athletes. Dr. Charles W. Kennedy of Princeton, the new NCAA president for 1930, disagreed with those reformers who advocated the elimination of paid coaches. Kennedy also did not concur with the overall implication of the report's commentary on the state of intercollegiate sport, stating in defense of athletics: "I don't think that everything in here indicates evidence of dishonesty." Even at the 1929 NCAA meeting, the report from the chairmen of the organization's eight districts indicated that not all the member schools were in agreement with the report's findings.[23]

FOOTBALL GOES ON OFFENSE

Throughout the 1920s the defenders of college football had waged a studied campaign that advanced a belief in the moral, physical, and financial benefits being generated by the gridiron sport. In the aftermath of the Carnegie Report's release, football's supporters basically returned to their measured defense of the game yet, buoyed by the growing disinterest and nonthreatening responses to the report being advanced by many observers, were careful to not advance too far into specific cases cited by the researchers.

This is not to say that some members of the football camp did not express discontent with the report. Major John Griffith of the Big Ten quickly indicated his belief that Savage and the other researchers had been influenced by some of the eastern schools and that among Dr. Pritchett's comments in the preface were indications that the investigation had been started with a "prejudicial" attitude toward intercollegiate sport. Griffith wrote that the report had produced many findings that were "destined to serve a useful purpose," yet he also stated that "Bulletin Twenty-Three is not a true report, since a true report must present both the good and bad features of the institution . . . [and] the report deals almost entirely with defects, and little space is devoted to merits." Bob Zuppke of Illinois, who would continue his defense of intercollegiate sport well into the 1930s, expressed a dislike of the reform element: "Those men who never played the game are always the ones who abolish it or want it abolished. We are going on with football in spite of what these 'indoor drabs' tell us."[24]

Such attitudes toward athletic reformers were fueled in part by some of the conduct of Savage and the Carnegie researchers. Immediately upon the release of the report, Major Griffith wrote to Savage and expressed the Big Ten's intention of eliminating any "subsidized or illegally recruited" athletes and requested Carnegie's list of names of any individuals at Big Ten schools who appeared to fall into that category. Savage's caustic reply noted that "information such as you request is communicated only to the presidents of the colleges and universities cooperating in our study. . . . In practically all cases such information would have been obtainable for such officers in files that were accessible to them." The reply closed with a pointed comment suggesting that Griffith and officials of the Big Ten schools had been less than diligent in their attention to the abuses of amateur ideals within the conference.[25]

Far more serious was the University of Michigan's claim that Carnegie researcher Harold Bentley had secretly removed from its files several letters that seemed to disclose recruiting irregularities. When Michigan requested the return of the letters, Savage indicated that he intended to keep the originals and would send "copies" back to the university. Some university officials claimed that Savage's researchers had indicated that their athletic houses were in order, only to have the report state otherwise.[26]

Despite some of the above situations, the football element's prevailing public attitude toward the Carnegie Report remained one of carefully expressed concerns over any abuses of the amateur ideal, while also continuing to advocate the benefits of intercollegiate sport and its place within university life. In this approach the sport continued to receive support from some among the academic and administrative ranks of the university community, in addition to members of the athletic departments.

Coach Bill Roper of Princeton declared that far too much of the undergraduates' time was being taken up by football practice and that "the best interests of the game are to be served by holding down on the idea of its being an all-year round sport. . . . If this drudgery is not eliminated in the next five years the player will step aside. He wants to play for pleasure and not be driven." Coach Hugo Bezdek of Penn State cited the giving of scholarship help to college athletes as having become the rule rather than the exception by the end of the 1920s, and stated that "if sports are going to interfere with the true object of the school of learning, I say away with sports." Meanwhile, the Reverend Charles L. O'Donnell, president of Notre Dame and a prominent defender of intercollegiate football, stated: "College is not merely a school; it is a life . . . [and] the major emphasis, I affirm, is, as it ought to be on study. But even if it were not, if football interest ran away with one-quarter of the year, then, I say, there are ever so many worse things that could happen. . . . The point of all this is that the game has not got away from the colleges. It has not gone over to some vast, indeterminate, heterogenous mob, known as the general public."[27]

At the December 1929 meeting of the American Association of University Professors, Dean S. V. Sanford of the University of Georgia publicly insisted that "college sports play a leading part in moral education." Among his commentary, Dean Sanford told the gathering of university professors that the solutions to any abuses of existing regulations or the ideals of amateurism were to be found "in whole-hearted co-operation by college presidents and faculties with athletic conferences." This belief in the ability of enforced conference regulations to maintain suitable controls over intercollegiate sport, football in particular, became the ultimate keystone of the gridiron game's defense against its attackers in the post-Carnegie world.[28]

In considering the management of university athletics, Savage had written that "the young men of our colleges over a period of years should be intrusted with an increasing proportion of the responsibility"—a situation that had existed at many schools long before World War I. This unrealistic recommendation for the world of intercollegiate sport in the postwar years brought Griffith's terse reply that "the college undergraduate, for obvious reasons, cannot be expected to employ and discharge coaches or to assume the responsibility of administering a modern athletic department." Further, after the Big Ten athletic directors met in December 1930, the group issued a statement that indicated that although intercollegiate sport remained fundamentally by and for the undergraduates, the universities would continue to define their own administration of sport without the interference of outsiders. Griffith summed up the position of the athletic community in 1930: "Small groups of self-appointed spokesmen and representatives of the alumni have no right to dictate athletic policies. The men who live with the situation should be entrusted with the control of athletics. . . . If athletics do have a rightful place in the college program, they should be administered by the regularly constituted authorities."[29]

And so, in the aftermath of the Carnegie Report, the football community had expressed substantial amounts of appropriate concern for the sport's need to conform to the precepts that were in place for the governance of intercollegiate sport, while also maintaining a proper perspective within the life of the university community. But it was clear that the football coaches and athletic officials had no intention of easily relinquishing their roles and responsibilities, and as time progressed and their positions continued to be strengthened within the university community, they would give less attention to the occasional attacks of reformers in the future.

THE REFORM MOVEMENT STALLS

Immediately after the Carnegie Foundation's publication of Bulletin no. 23, the public response from the reform element appeared rather subdued—influenced no doubt by the obvious attitudes of disinterest and "tell us something new" on the part of the general media and the public. Many of the reformers apparently recognized the difficulties involved in attempting to implement any significant number of the athletic reforms discussed in the Carnegie Report. In an article that appeared in the *New Republic* in November 1929, the author—a professor of English at an eastern university writing under a pseudonym—provided considerable detail on some of the inner workings of the athletic organization at his school, yet concluded with the observation that the faculty was capable of correcting only a portion of the present evils.

In his renowned 1928 *Harper's* article, "The Great God Football," writer John Tunis had expressed the point of view that intercollegiate football was becoming so firmly entrenched that the Carnegie Foundation's eventual report would have relatively little impact on the sport. Instead, Tunis saw the ultimate reform of intercollegiate football as coming from a gradual evolution of undergraduate interest in the many other extracurricular activities available to them. Tunis noted, "It is impossible for anyone to study the colleges of this country, the Eastern universities particularly, without being conscious of the fact that the undergraduate attitude on sports is changing. . . . Some day football may . . . become merely a sport . . . a game which ought not to interfere in any way with the educational program."[30]

Now, in the immediate aftermath of the Carnegie Report, the *Yale Alumni Weekly* joined Tunis in predicting an eventual athletic reformation on eastern campuses and a decline of the fanatical interest in football among undergraduate populations, one that would be brought about by the students' more active participation in physical sports themselves. In response to those individuals who would express concerns over a potential loss of physical preparedness or school loyalties by such an evolution, the article noted that football "still commends itself to the vigorous bodied undergraduate . . . [and] there will still remain a keen interest in developing the best trained intercollegiate crew and football team, but these will not be the whole duty of man." To show that even reformers had a sense of humor, and just might be closet football fans themselves, the week after the Carnegie Report's release James R. Angell, president of Yale, made a speech in Boston during which he said that he would gladly swap the purity credited to Yale by the report "for a couple of good running backs or a pair of great ends."[31]

The immediate challenges to the Carnegie Report by so many university administrators, and the football element's obvious intention to not capitulate to the reformers, made it quickly apparent that no sweeping changes in the operation and administration of college athletics would soon be taking place. And so it was a hollow victory indeed that the report had declared for the football reform movement. This fact became obvious to the more realistic observers during the NCAA meeting held in New York in December 1929. Writer Orlo Robertson of the Associated Press, who began by noting that the Carnegie Report had "shocked the athletic world," commented on the relatively quiet meeting in contrast to some of the affairs of recent years.

After a decadelong clamor for specific changes and reforms within college football that implied the reformers were ready to quickly move to implement their programs, such reorganization proved to be far from reality. In his article Robertson described the NCAA meeting as having "launched a clean-up campaign," but he had to admit that "no definite and sure workable plan" was agreed upon. The best the convention could produce was a statement that urged college presidents to begin "a quiet, earnest effort" to clean up their own institution's athletic affairs, while the delegates also authorized the president of the NCAA to appoint a committee that would draw up "a practical and promising reform program" for presentation at the following year's meeting.[32]

By early 1930 there were some signs of actions aimed at specific reforms. The Reverend John P. McNichols, president of the University of Detroit, announced that he was disbanding the school's Alumni Board of Control that had previously handled Detroit's athletic affairs under his overall direction. In its place McNichols appointed a new "Athletic Advisory Board" that would be administered as a department of the university. To ensure that the faculty would hold a majority voice on the new board, five of the nine members would be from the school's regular teaching body.[33]

Also in early 1930, President Lotus D. Coffman of the University of Minnesota announced that he was prepared to reorganize his institution's athletic organization, and he approached the North Central Association of colleges and secondary schools for guidance on accomplishing this goal. Of course, that group had no more specific ideas for accomplishing athletic reforms than did the NCAA delegates, and so the Carnegie Foundation stepped in and awarded a grant of ten thousand dollars to the North Central Association to assist a committee of four of its officers in "establishing athletic standards for its members." Dr. Harry M. Gage, the president of Coe College and chairman of the North Central's committee on athletics, admitted that he had no definite policy for the future but expressed the belief that the Minnesota "experiment" would serve as the foundation for a permanent system of athletic reforms. It was expected that all the usual reform proposals would be discussed, and newspaper writer Earl Coughlin naively stated, "I do not believe I am exaggerating by asserting that a new era of college athletics is just around the corner." The North Central Association eventually did consider a program of accrediting athletics at the Big Ten schools during the 1930s, but this proposal was quickly dropped in the face of considerable opposition from the universities.[34]

By late 1930, with little specific reform action having been implemented anywhere, President Lawrence Lowell of Harvard wrote to President James Angell of Yale and proposed that the two elite universities take the initiative in defining the "ultimate object of intercollegiate games." Lowell believed that athletics had value as a contributing factor in the moral and physical development of the undergraduates, but he also remained a staunch opponent of the commercialization of sport for the general public. Because he viewed the "constantly recurring spectacular shows" that surrounded each season's college football games as a fundamental "evil," Lowell believed that the number of games each season "should be reduced to the smallest number that would keep up the general interest in athletics." He defined this number as ultimately just one football contest per season, and in this case it would be the Harvard-Yale matchup. Yet Lowell realistically recognized this suggestion would take time to implement—"but our views will ultimately have their effect"—and so he proposed to Angell that their two schools, "by joint agreement," begin "to lessen the number of intercollegiate games played in the autumn."[35]

Although Yale had been one of those schools that had bandied about this idea earlier in the 1920s, by 1930, in the face of the worsening Depression, its administration was desirous of maintaining the cash flow from the football program that had always paid the other bills for the athletic department. In addition, Angell believed that his student body was already evidencing a definite trend "toward a diminishment of excited interest in the intercollegiate contests of the bigger teams and an increased disposition to participate in such sports as give them personal pleasure and satisfaction, without any special reference to public competition." In other words, Yale saw itself already achieving the best of both worlds with respect to the place of intercollegiate sport within the university community, without taking the radical move proposed by Lowell.[36]

Meanwhile, the Carnegie Foundation was interested in documenting and publicizing any reforms that were being implemented in response to its report of 1929, so in late 1930 Savage wrote to a number of universities and requested "any information respecting changes or improvements in regard to athletics . . . that have taken place during the past twelve months." He also noted that "in response to many requests, the Foundation is continuing certain phases of its enquiry concerning American college athletics."[37]

President Angell replied to Savage that Yale's "general athletic conditions . . . have in no essential particular, so far as I am aware, changed since your examination." The Yale president then continued and noted his concern over information given him, "of whose general correctness I find it difficult to doubt, indicating a very unsatisfactory situation in the two more important conferences in the Middle West" and that "the conditions in many of the more important institutions are still far from satisfactory." Savage acknowledged that on a recent trip to the Midwest he too had found the athletic situation in certain schools as "far from satisfactory" but pointed out that "a number of institutions over the country have undertaken sincere and more or less vigorous measures to stamp out practices which do them little credit."[38]

When college administrators gathered in December 1930 for the NCAA Convention in New York, some of the reformers were prepared to resume their attacks on intercollegiate football. President William Mather Lewis of Lafayette blasted away at the commercialization of the gridiron sport during a luncheon speech, stating that "the lack of moderation in the field of athletics, particularly football, has led us away from the ideals of sportsmanship." But the best Dr. Lewis could propose was that student conferences be held over the next few months "to learn the reaction of the students toward sport as now conducted in colleges," while he also advocated the usual "stronger faculty control" as one of the fundamental planks of reform. The inability of the reformers to unify and actually effect any meaningful changes in the athletic programs of major universities was apparent in these warmed-over comments, and headlines like the one in the *New York Times*, "Football Indicted," brought a collective sigh of uninterest in this old news from everyone.[39]

The lack of specific action by the reformers was emphasized by the meeting of the American Football Coaches Association in December 1930, during which the coaches—led by big-time names such as Roper of Princeton and Bezdek of Penn State—were considering and adopting resolutions of specific actions that included such items as restricting postseason games, making spring practice noncompulsory, and defining September 15 as the earliest possible start date for fall football practice. Bezdek advanced an aggressive package of proposals that included fourteen points of change and reform, yet these ideas proved to be too far-ranging for the gathered coaches and so were tabled for future consideration.[40]

As noted earlier, Savage had apparently convinced himself that significant reforms were being effected at many universities, so in late 1930 he had undertaken a smaller-scale follow-up study. When it was released in June 1931 as Bulletin no. 26, titled *Current Developments in American College Sport*, the authors advanced the belief that intercollegiate football was declining in popularity among the public and that many had switched their allegiance to the more skilled game developed by professional football. This new focus was certainly a double-edged sword given the intense hatred directed toward the pro game throughout the 1920s by both the academic and the athletic communities of higher education. Bulletin no. 26 also referred to the football played at the intercollegiate level by 1931 as "the comparatively bungling college match."

Observing the declining attendance figures that were beginning to impact college football in 1930, Savage chose to interpret them as an indication of the eroding enthusiasm for the intercollegiate brand of the game by the sporting public. He believed that "only games played by the most skillful of teams are adjudged worth the high admission charges," apparently failing to recall that the country was now headed toward the depths of the Depression and that only the more affluent citizenry could any longer afford the luxury of spending money on sporting events. Bulletin no. 26 also returned to some of the themes that had been expressed in 1929, including a declaration that concerns of the alumni were irrelevant: "The only valid right an alumnus has respecting college athletics is the right to do his share in seeing that the undergraduate of to-day receives more benefit from the university's athletics . . . than he himself received when he was in college." The Carnegie update even expressed concern for the very future of the intercollegiate brand of football. Yet although Savage might choose to believe that the sport was beginning to move into a decline and away from commercialism, the responses to his 1931 report would make it clear that football reforms were still in the future.[41]

Despite more than a decade of demands and expectations of significant change, by late 1931 the window of opportunity for sweeping reforms in the conduct of intercollegiate football had closed temporarily. Certainly, there would continue to be occasional denunciations of the overemphasis and commercialization within the gridiron sport and talk of needed reforms, but most institutions within the community of higher education were more consumed during the 1930s with concerns for their economic survival in the face of the Great Depression. It would be the post–World War II years of the 1940s and 1950s that would finally witness the implementation of some specific reforms within the world of intercollegiate sport.

The Carnegie Foundation's Bulletin no. 23 had considerable merit in its documenting of many areas within athletic department affairs, and it remains today as the most wide-ranging such study of intercollegiate sport. Unfortunately for the reform element, the timing of the report's release could not have been any more unfortunate, and the reaction of most nonreform observers was typified by the comments of Coach Frank Cavanaugh of Fordham: "Why get excited? The report only tells what everyone already knew."[42]

One might interpret the decadelong battle for control of intercollegiate football, and its apparent outcome by the early 1930s, as the last area resolved within the game's transformation. From a pre–World War I arena, where many believed that college football should be operated under the old European-based concepts of amateur sporting ideals, the game had redefined itself as one that more accurately reflected the American postwar culture that had evolved throughout the 1920s. In a 1931 address Coach Zuppke declared, "The American university in order to be in harmony with life must evolve about something better than the European university. The American university has introduced intercollegiate activities. . . . It has encouraged the spirit of adventure, the spirit of a pioneer that is inherent in the healthy bodies of boys who grow in a nation still filled with oats." In other words, intercollegiate sport was another plank in the shaping of a new nation that was still in the process of defining its full potential, while increasingly severing its ties to outmoded Old World concepts.[43]

And so the world of intercollegiate football would continue on its way through the turmoil of the Depression until the slow economic recoveries of both the United States and sport would begin midway through the 1930s. Until specific conferences, and eventually the NCAA, began to seriously address athletic reforms in the post–World War II years, the commitment of university athletic officials would have to be relied upon for the governance of intercollegiate football.

A comment from the *New York Herald Tribune* best summarized the clamor of responses to the Carnegie Report and defined the prevailing attitude toward intercollegiate sport in its aftermath: "The colleges and intercollegiate sports survived the sad, bad old days, and doubtless will survive these current days, where conditions, according to the report, are better, even tho they are far from perfect."[44]

EPILOGUE

The season of 1930 was the last of college football's golden era, the period of its transformation into the modern gridiron sport that would entertain American fans over the rest of the century. During this final football campaign of the era, gridiron fans were treated to an American sport that seemed to have achieved full maturity in little more than a decade since the close of World War I. Despite the noticeable attendance declines brought on by the advent of the Great Depression—producing a financial pinch on intercollegiate athletic departments—the game of college football clearly had achieved a far more significant place for itself within American culture by 1930.

For those fans unable to attend the games at the new and expanded stadia that dotted college campuses around the country, the 1930 football season nevertheless was an experience available in living rooms everywhere through the impressive game coverage being provided by radio and the newspapers. By 1930 the sports sections of the metropolitan newspapers had achieved an impressive breadth of coverage for college football, featuring substantial stories on the major games, extensive photo layouts of individual players and game action, and a growing body of columns that examined every detail of the intercollegiate sport on a daily basis throughout each autumn. Meanwhile, radio had also grown into a viable commercial outlet, and college football was becoming a fixture of Saturday afternoon radio programming. As early as 1928 an NBC official had estimated a national listening audience of twenty-five million for the radio coverage of the Rose Bowl game by broadcaster Graham McNamee.[1]

Action on the field during the 1930 college football season provided an excellent capstone to the game's era of transformation. The leading teams of the year came primarily from the South, Midwest, and Pacific Coast—a reaffirmation of the shift in power that had taken place during the 1920s. Although the West Coast featured a wide-open struggle for honors that included such powerhouses as St. Mary's, Southern Cal, Stanford, and Washington State, the attention of college football fans was increasingly drawn to the Midwest. Coming off a mythical national championship in 1929, Knute Rockne had perhaps his greatest team at Notre Dame in 1930.

16. Coach Knute Rockne of Notre Dame. He was described by one prominent writer as being primarily responsible for the significant growth of college football during the 1920s. His untimely passing in early 1931 effectively brought to a close the "Golden Age" of the collegiate gridiron game. Courtesy of the Chicago Historical Society [DN-0067774].

Despite featuring such great players as Frank Carideo, Marchmont "Marchy" Schwartz, and Marty Brill, Notre Dame was seriously challenged for regional and national honors in 1930 by Northwestern of the Big Ten Conference. After a season with unprecedented levels of media coverage for college football—and Notre Dame's powerhouse in particular—Rockne's charges settled many of the questions with late-game heroics for victories over Northwestern and Army. In December Notre Dame traveled to Los Angeles and wiped out Howard Jones's Southern Cal team to clinch a second straight national championship. The Fighting Irish were welcomed back to Chicago by a gigantic crowd and parade that surprised even veteran sportswriters.[2]

Intercollegiate football was seemingly at its zenith—its wild growth apparently ready to continue into the foreseeable future, despite the increasing economic woes that plagued the United States. And then, on March 31, 1931, came the stunning news that Rockne was among the eight individuals who had died in an airplane crash on the plains of Kansas. The intercollegiate athletic world, and the sporting world in general, was cast into a state of shock that quickly turned into an immense outpouring of sentiment for the departed football coach.

The immediate coverage of the tragedy overshadowed all other news for a time, and nearly eight thousand mourners jammed South Bend's Union Station when Rockne's body was returned home. Even President Herbert Hoover was moved to declare the accident a "national loss." The blitz of media articles halted only briefly as a relatively simple funeral was held at the church on Notre Dame's campus.

Rockne had served as Notre Dame's head football coach from 1918 through 1930, during which time his team compiled an overall record of 105-12-5 while winning three national championships and one trip to the Rose Bowl. One of the testaments to Rockne's coaching skill was the fact that at the time of his passing there were a reported twenty-three head football coaches around the country who had played for him at Notre Dame. An article in the *New York World-Telegram* described Rockne as "the high priest of the American gridiron," and the *New York Times* added that he was "a sort of god." The *New York Herald Tribune* went almost as far, as it called the Notre Dame mentor "a football genius, a coach who influenced the game more than Walter Camp, Glenn Warner, or any of those great strategists of the past"—the carried-away writer not even deeming the name of Amos Alonzo Stagg worthy of mention with the other two men, all of whom had done as much or more than Rockne for college football.[3]

One of the earlier acclamations of Rockne's coaching prowess had appeared in 1921, when a sportswriter noted that the Notre Dame gridiron mentor "has been proclaimed one of the greatest coaches in the game," and these written declarations only increased in their enthusiasm as the decade progressed. It was no surprise in 1931 when the *New York Times* referred to Rockne as "the most personal symbol of football to most people." Testimonials to Rockne have continued to flow for years after his passing—most from writers who never knew him and have only read the outpourings of the 1920s. Fifty years after the Notre Dame coach's passing, a modern biographer of Rockne, Michael Steele, said of the coach: "There existed a substantial, deep, personal commitment to the values he inculcated in his teams and public speeches." Probably more informed was eastern sportswriter Stanley Woodward, a contemporary of Rockne, who wrote that "in the realm of football he was the dominant figure of his day, a tactician who reached beyond his time, a psychologist and persuader of almost unparalleled ability."[4]

Most of the tributes to Rockne focused on his character, personality, and belief in his sport. A *New York Times* editorial declared, "Rockne believed football was to America man-building what some one said Wellington said of the effect 'the playing fields of Eton' had" for the English during wartime. His close friend Edward "Slip" Madigan of St. Mary's wrote, "There was something about 'Rock' that gnawed at the heartstrings of the people of the nation . . . something that inspired his boys to great heights, something that made him stand for the higher, the cleaner and the better things of life." The flow of written adulation for Rockne seemed endless.[5]

Rockne's personal magnitude and coaching abilities had focused a sizable share of attention on Notre Dame and college football each season throughout the 1920s. Yet the massive number of tributes and testimonies to his greatness was perhaps more than was appropriate, given a football coach who really was no different than many of his counterparts, the Notre Dame coach apparently having little hesitation over such things as manipulating and exploiting sportswriters and other coaches, illegal recruiting, bending the playing rules, or in seeking ways to reduce the academic demands upon his players. Nevertheless, an article in *New Republic* mentioned that "no thesaurus has a longer list of laudatory adjectives than those applied to Knute Rockne," while an entry in *Literary Digest* noted that "not since the death of Rudolph Valentino [a 1920s movie idol] has there been such a high tide of post-mortem hero worship."[6]

Overall, there is no denying Rockne's place within college football history and the significant role he played in the transformation of the sport during the 1920s. His passing provides a logical exclamation point to the end of college football's golden era—its Age of Transformation. Despite the financial woes of the Depression after 1930, the gridiron game settled into what passed at the time as a state of maturity: newspapers, magazines, radio and newsreels offered excellent coverage of college football each week; the stadium-building boom had temporarily provided adequate seating capacities; the most important games continued to attract sizable crowds; the big-business aspects of the game were still very evident; major schools continued intersectional play, while cities in the warm-climate states began to institute postseason bowl games in emulation of the successful Rose Bowl; and the large-scale threat to athletic departments that the Carnegie Report represented had been basically overcome for the time being.

Certainly, at the time of Rockne's tragic passing in March 1931, college football was something far different from the game that had resumed on campuses around the country in the aftermath of World War I. With all the publicity, commercialization, and excitement that surrounded college football by the end of the 1920s—along with the financial significance the sport now held for most of the colleges and universities—there could be no realistic belief that the sport would ever become a true amateur pursuit that existed strictly for the entertainment of the students and faculties within the cloistered world of college campuses.[7]

Intercollegiate football through the 1930s continued to reflect the shift of power that had taken place during the previous decade, teams from the South, Pacific Coast, and Midwest generally representing the top quality of football. Professional football continued to represent a threat in the minds of many of the old-school college coaches, yet in 1934 the intercollegiate sport fundamentally turned toward an acceptance of the Sunday game's existence with the beginning of the College All-Star Game series against the NFL champions, an annual event that helped to ensure pro football's eventual success.

During the 1930s, or shortly thereafter, most of football's longtime prominent coaches who had so staunchly opposed professional football would depart from the college scene—although the sport already had many capable young football coaches already in place or soon to begin their careers. Occasionally, black football players continued to appear on the rosters at the predominantly white universities—including such standout athletes as Joe Lillard at Oregon, Ozzie Simmons at Iowa, Kenny Washington and Jackie Robinson at UCLA, and Brud Holland at Cornell—but the racial barriers and the so-called gentlemen's agreement would not be eradicated from college football until the days after World War II. And Catholic college football would continue its expansion throughout the 1930s, peaking late in the decade with outstanding teams at Fordham, Duquesne, Georgetown, Marquette, Santa Clara, and St. Mary's.

The Carnegie Foundation pursued a follow-up study of college football in 1931, while the Associated Press conducted its own survey and published the results that same year. But the universities, the media, and the general public all had more immediate issues at the time, so the reports passed by in relative anonymity. Coach Bob Zuppke of Illinois—always a defender of football—by 1931 only had to point out that most athletic programs were struggling to survive financially to make the point that charges of overcommercialization could hardly be taken seriously.[8]

A glimpse of the extent to which the major universities were increasingly becoming ready to put aside concerns of commercialization in football can be seen in early 1931, when organizers of the approaching Olympic Games in Los Angeles sent Coach Howard Jones to visit Yale officials. Traveling with no publicity, Jones carried a letter to President James Angell that invited Yale to send its football team to the West Coast to meet Southern Cal in a demonstration football game during the 1932 Olympics. After a lengthy consideration of the invitation by Angell and Yale's athletic officials, the eastern school reluctantly declined the opportunity rather than face the implications their acceptance would have signified. The very fact that Yale officials had to discuss the issue "exhaustively" before declining says much about the strengthened hand athletics was achieving at many schools.[9]

Although the athletic reformers seemed to be temporarily at bay by the 1930s, one of the most shocking events for the college football world would take place after the 1939 season when the University of Chicago terminated its gridiron program. Chicago's football fortunes, slipping for some years before Stagg's departure, tumbled drastically after 1932, and the only logical course should have been the conversion to a small-college level of football competition. Yet this move would have been perceived as a major blow to the university's growing academic prestige, and so President Robert Maynard Hutchins—a longtime opponent of intercollegiate football—pushed through the sport's termination at Chicago.

The reaction of many students, the alumni, and the city's newspapers to this seemingly drastic decision was one of anger and resentment. This hostility would be manifested by the media's virtual ignoring of Chicago's other athletic teams that remained in the Big Ten until 1946. Historian William H. McNeill has written that Chicago's "popular reputation as a place where radical intellect had snuffed out red-blooded, all-American games became an unhappy, half-underground counterpoint to . . . the university's cultural and public roles." McNeill noted the significant damage to Chicago's "town and gown" relationship with the surrounding community—brought about by the dropping of football—and concluded, "The loss for the university was and remains real."[10]

In 1940 Yale declared that it would no longer compete at the big-time level of college football, action also taken by Harvard in 1949. In the fall of 1940 Ogden Miller, director of athletics at Yale, confirmed that the New Haven school was committed to a program of "small time" football, the reformers at the university having at last succeeded at least to that extent. Miller stated that college football was "reaching a peak of emphasis. But there must be a decline or leveling-off." He also added that big-time football's only significant contribution at Yale had been to provide the funds for other athletic programs—a comment that must have stung every former player who had ever worn Yale's blue and white, all the way back to Walter Camp. In 1956 eight of the older Ivy League universities in the East would band together to downsize their football programs—similar to what President Lawrence Lowell of Harvard had envisioned a quarter century earlier.[11]

As the golden era of college football ended in early 1931, the sport stood poised for a future that would eventually bring a level of growth not imagined during the 1920s. It would remain until the 1950s before television would begin to play an ever increasing role in the life of big-time college football, and the major football universities would again be in a position to entertain ideas of expanding their stadia or constructing new arenas, always driven by the need for ever greater revenues from football in order to finance all the other athletic programs—just as the gridiron sport has always done. Yet with another era of major change decades away, college football in 1931 nevertheless remained the modern American sport that had evolved since the end of World War I—a game that would be recognizable to any fan of the late twentieth century. Indeed, the period from 1919 to 1930 had served to radically reshape the sport and lay the groundwork for most of what has transpired within intercollegiate football since that time, and it was truly the game's Age of Transformation.

NOTES

SELECTED BIBLIOGRAPHY

INDEX

NOTES

In this section I have adopted a system of abbreviations for the titling of several of the special collections that were extensively consulted. Following are those abbreviations:

OSUA   Ohio State University Archives: Director of Athletics—Intercollegiate Conference

PUAF   Princeton University Archives: Athletics—Football (1900–1929)

Stagg Papers   University of Chicago Special Collections: Papers of Amos Alonzo Stagg

UADR   University of Notre Dame Archives: Athletic Director's Records, ca. 1909–1929

INTRODUCTION

1. See Allison Danzig and Peter Brandwein, eds., *Sport's Golden Age: A Close-Up of the Fabulous Twenties*. In the foreword to this book, John Kieran, while clearly stating that he was not one who believed that "things were better in every way in the brave days of old," nevertheless wrote that the 1920s "must remain the high water mark in American sports" (ix).

2. John R. Thelin discusses Red Grange as a specific example of the 1920s "college hero turned culture hero" through the publicity of the national media (*Games Colleges Play: Scandal and Reform in Intercollegiate Athletics*, 4–7). Examples of women appearing prominently in advertisements carried in college football game programs during the period can be found in *California-Stanford*, Nov. 20, 1926; *Princeton–Ohio State*, Nov. 3, 1928; *Indiana-Northwestern*, Nov. 16, 1929; and *Yale-Princeton*, Nov. 15, 1930. Examples of illustrations of women on the covers of game programs can be found in *Chicago-Princeton*, Nov. 2, 1929; and *Yale-Princeton*, Nov. 15, 1930. Michael Oriard provides an excellent and comprehensive examination of the print media's treatment of college football and the cultural representations of the gridiron sport during the era, including numerous illustrations (*King Football: Sport and Spectacle in the Golden Age of Radio and Newsreels, Movies and Magazines, the Weekly and the Daily Press*, 23–64, 162–98).

3. Stanley Woodward—a prominent eastern sportswriter—believed that the years in the immediate aftermath of World War II were very comparable to the early 1920s. Woodward cited the large crowds that began to flock to college stadia every Saturday in the late 1940s, as the quality of play was significantly uplifted by the abundance of powerful teams and outstanding players generated by the returning men who had fought during the war (Danzig and Brandwein, *Sport's Golden Age*, 113). Arch Ward, longtime sports editor of the *Chicago Tribune*, offered the period of 1900–1918 as his nomination for college football's greatest era. Of that period Ward wrote: "There was a Golden Age in Middle West football long before the terrific 1920s arrived. . . . No other period is so rich, not only in the midlands, but in any other section of this broad land of ours" (ibid., 131).

4. See Kenneth N. Carlson, *College Football Scorebook*.

5. Gorham Munson, *The Awakening Twenties*, 299. See also a prominent cartoon on postwar released tensions as it related to football, in "One Place Where They Are Not Admitted," *Chicago Tribune*, Oct. 14, 1923, 1. Analogies between the demands of wartime and football were repeated extensively during the 1920s, one example being the comments of William H. Wright in *Outing* magazine: "Football, of all sports, comes nearest to being what the college professors call the moral equivalent of war. The energy, endurance, and wit that go to make soldiers find the most satisfying outlet on the gridiron in time of peace" ("Come On, Yale!"). Yet this comparison did not mean that the postwar undergraduates were willing to undergo any sort of organized military drills on their university campuses. In the fall of 1919 an effort was made to establish a Reserve Officer's Training Corp at Washington and Lee University, and this attempt "was met with such marked indifference, not to say hostility . . . [that] the War Department found it necessary very shortly to disband the organization" (Carter N. Bealer, "A Distinguished Exception," 521). Historian Frank F. Stephens has written of similar opposition efforts at the University of Missouri during the 1920s, noting that "there was agitation in student bodies throughout the entire country against military education in colleges" during the decade (*A History of the University of Missouri*, 507).

6. Stanley Coben, *Rebellion Against Victorianism: The Impetus for Cultural Change in 1920s America*, 49. For discussions of the evolving American culture, see Frank Freidel and Alan Brinkley, *America in the Twentieth Century*, 147–79; and Frederick Lewis Allen, *The Big Change: America Transforms Itself, 1900–1950*. Historian Preston William Slosson has noted that by 1928 the ownership of a car was no longer "a class distinction" (*The Great Crusade and After, 1914–1928*, 220).

7. Freidel and Brinkley, *Twentieth Century*, 180. In 1922, historian Somnia Vana observed that "the plain truth is that neither in college nor out, do the majority of students have a deep and consuming interest in learning. The affections of the average college graduate centre in his fraternity or club" ("College Education: An Inquest").

8. For examples of good overviews of Walter Camp's career in football, see Bruce Stewart, "Walter C. Camp: The Father of American Football"; and Camp's obituary article in the *New York Times*, Mar. 15, 1925.

9. Grantland Rice is one sportswriter of the 1920s who was usually guilty of such flowery prose, yet historian Michael R. Steele has written that "Rice's views . . . evince the enthusiastic romanticism of the golden age of the twenties. Rice's prose unabashedly argues for the idealized spirit that infused collegiate football of the period. . . . Rice [was] in that group of sports personalities who preferred the legends and the myths, who held that collegiate football was an honorable force in the lives of the young" (*Knute Rockne: A Bio-Bibliography*, 179–80). Overall, sports coverage in the printed media increased by 50 percent between 1900 and 1920, and then more than doubled during the decade of the 1920s (Oriard, *King Football*, 25).

10. "Millions Listen in on Rose Festival," *New York Times*, 3 Jan. 1928. Although the 1920 (WTAW in College Station, Texas) and 1921 (KDKA in Pittsburgh) football games are usually cited as being the first ever broadcast on radio, it should be recognized that an experimental station at the University of Minnesota (9X1-WLB) carried a wireless account of a game in 1912 (Ronald Smith letter to author, 3 Aug. 1998).

11. Francis Wallace, "This Football Business," 10; Grantland Rice, "Not in the Rules."

12. Michael Parrish has written that the explosion of exciting football heroes during the 1920s could not have come at a worse time for many in higher education: "Administrators had long struggled to raise their institutions' academic stature. . . . Now they faced clamorous alumni who demanded a bigger football stadium, a more famous coach, and a scholarship for the high school quarterback prospect" (*Anxious Decades: America in Prosperity and Depression, 1920–1941*, 172–73).

13. "College Football." In discussing the approaching Harvard game in 1919, an editorial in the Princeton student newspaper noted that "the importance of the game cannot be overestimated in its effect on undergraduate life, on the prestige of the University, and on the present Endowment campaign" ("To-Day," *Daily Princetonian*, Nov. 8, 1919).

14. A. Lawrence Lowell to James R. Angell, Oct. 25, 1930; Angell to Lowell, Oct. 28, 1930, President Angell Papers, Box 26, Folder 283, Yale University Archives.

15. John R. Tunis, "The Great God Football," 743; Tunis, "Football on the Wane?" 744. A column in *Outlook* magazine noted that, "To-day football, particularly intercollegiate football, has become a great public spectacle. It is to America what the bull-fight has been to Spain and what throwing Christians to the lions used to be in old Rome" ("Football under Fire").

1. SHAPING NATIONAL PARITY

1. Bernie McCarty, *All-America: The Complete Roster of Football's Heroes.* For informative overviews of college football's pre-1900 era, see Parke H. Davis, *Football: The American Intercollegiate Game*, 51–118; Allison Danzig, *The History of American Football: Its Great Teams, Players, and Coaches*, 6–29; Ronald A. Smith, *Sports and Freedom: The Rise of Big-Time College Athletics*, 67–98; and Mark F. Bernstein, *Football: The Ivy League Origins of an American Obsession*, 10–65.

2. James R. Shortridge, *The Middle West: Its Meaning in American Culture*, 9; Walter McCornack, "Football Comparisons," an unattributed 1905 newspaper article in the Walter Camp Papers, Yale University Archives.

3. Carlson, *College Football Scorebook*, 424; A. A. Stagg, "Stagg Would Help Out Eastern Football," an unattributed newspaper article of Dec. 11, 1904, in the Camp Papers, Yale University Archives.

4. "Eastern Football Has No Champion," a Dec. 1919 *New York Times* article reprinted in *CFRA Bulletin* (June–July 1989): 15–18.

5. Carlson, *College Football Scorebook*; Nathaniel J. Hasenfus, *Athletics at Boston College*, 229–30; *Heights* (Boston College newspaper), Oct. 15, 1920, 1. Frank Cavanaugh was typical of the excellent breed of football coaches who were showing up around the country and developing outstanding collegiate teams and players.

6. *New York Times*, Nov. 25, Dec. 16, 17, 18, 1919. At the time of his hiring as Yale's football coach for 1920, T. A. D. Jones was general manager of the Ames Shipbuilding and Drydock Company in Seattle. The company's owners, Yale men, allowed Jones a three-month leave of absence to serve as an unpaid head football coach at Yale in 1920, but Jones decided to stay on at Yale through 1927 ("Tad Jones First and Only Choice," *New York Evening Post*, Jan. 18, 1920).

7. "Tigers Humbled by West Virginia," *New York Times*, Nov. 2, 1919.

8. Donald Grant Herring Sr., *40 Years of Football*, 206, 295–96; Morris A. Bealle, *The History of Football at Harvard, 1874–1948*, 455.

9. Clifton N. McArthur to Walter Camp, Nov. 17, 24, 1919, Box 16, Folder 443, Camp Papers, Yale University Archives; Walter Camp, "The All-America Team"; McCarty, *All-America*, 46.

10. "College Football Teams of the Eastern Section as Ranked for 1920 Season," Dec. 1920 *New York Times* article reprinted in *CFRA Bulletin* (Apr.–May 1990): 15–19. Walter Camp and Parke Davis were two prominent football observers who also placed Princeton at the top of the nation's teams for 1920.

11. "Centre Conquers Harvard, 6 to 0," *New York Times*, Oct. 30, 1921; "Centre Stops Harvard Crew," *Joliet Evening Herald-News*, Oct. 30, 1921. Centre College featured three-time All-America Bo McMillin at quarterback for the seasons of 1919–1921, and during his career the Praying Colonels

compiled an overall record of 27-3-0 (Deke Houlgate, *The Football Thesaurus: 77 Years on the American Gridiron*, 37).

12. Ken Rappoport, *Wake Up the Echoes*, 101; E. C. Patterson, "Collier's All-Western Conference Eleven."

13. "Penn State Rated Best Team in East," *New York Times*, Dec. 4, 1921. Lawrence Perry published his national rankings for 1921 in a wire-service column that appeared in many newspapers around the country, including the *Joliet Evening Herald-News* on Dec. 9, 1921.

14. "Princeton Eleven Is Leader in 1922," *New York Times*, Dec. 3, 1922.

15. L. L. Little, "Football's Biggest Year," 147; Albert Britt, "Football on Eastern Gridirons," 154; "Where Does Yale Get It?" *Chicago Tribune*, Dec. 5, 1922.

16. "Review of 1923 Football Season," *Joliet Evening Herald-News*, Dec. 7, 1923.

17. Murray Sperber, *Shake Down the Thunder: The Creation of Notre Dame Football*, 178–79; Danzig and Brandwein, *Sport's Golden Age*, 125. California wrapped up its fifth consecutive undefeated season in 1924 with a 14-0 win over unbeaten Penn and dealt yet another blow to eastern football's prestige.

18. Brick Morse, *California Football History*, 125; McCarty, *All-America*, 269; Jack James, "California Varsity Is Greatest," an unattributed newspaper article, Oct. 10, 1920, St. Mary's Football Scrapbook, 1918–1922, St. Mary's College Archives.

19. Morse, *California Football History*, 128.

20. Danzig and Brandwein, *Sport's Golden Age*, 160–61.

21. Details of the meetings with Howard Jones and the extending of a Rose Bowl invitation to Iowa can be found in wire-service stories such as *Joliet Evening Herald-News*, Nov. 20, 21, 1921. See also Howard Roberts, *The Big Nine: The Story of Football in the Western Conference*, 244; S. Dan Brodie, *66 Years on the California Gridiron, 1882–1948*, 142; Morse, *California Football History*, 133; and Herb Michelson and Dave Newhouse, *Rose Bowl Football since 1902*, 50–53.

22. Robert DeRoos, "Remaking a National Sport"; Warren Bovard to Knute Rockne, telegram dated Jan. 15, 1925, and letter dated Jan. 27, 1925, Box 8, Folder 179, UADR; Elmer Henderson to Rockne, Feb. 20, 1925, Box 13, Folder 66, UADR. The USC affair was just one of many occasions when Rockne was enticed with job offers from other universities. Less than one year after the attempt to leave for USC, Rockne agreed to terms with Columbia University, and the school's Committee on Athletics even issued an official announcement that he would be taking over their football program for 1926. Rockne's backing out of the Columbia negotiations, and the resulting charges and counter-charges, was probably the most uncomplimentary of all these affairs for the Notre Dame coach. An overview on the attempts by Columbia to hire Rockne can be found in the *New York Times*, Dec. 12, 13, 15, 19, 1925. For other such events involving Rockne, see also "Events Point to Rockne as Iowa Coach," *Chicago Tribune*, Mar. 23, 1924; Dick Lamb and Bert McGrane, *75 Years with the Fighting Hawk-eyes*, 85–88; and L. W. St. John to Athletic Board, Jan. 16, 1929, Folder "Director of Athletics–Athletic Board 1928–29," OSUA.

23. Allison Danzig, "Players of the Game: Howard Jones," *New York Times*, Nov. 24, 1931; Ray Schmidt, "Kaer and 1926 USC," *College Football Historical Society* 8, no. 2 (Feb. 1995): 13–17; and Schmidt, "The Forgotten Trojans," *College Football Historical Society* 3, no. 1 (Nov. 1989): 6–10.

24. George Kirksey, "Sketches of Football Coaches," *Dallas Morning News*, Sept. 12, 1926; Walter Eckersall, "Intersectional Grid Games to Grow in Favor," *Chicago Tribune*, Oct. 29, 1920.

25. Andrew Doyle, "Causes Won, Not Lost: College Football and the Modernization of the American South," 231–35; Zipp Newman, *The Impact of Southern Football*, 65–66; Danzig and Brandwein, *Sport's Golden Age*, 157.

26. Keith Dunnavant, *Coach: The Life of Paul "Bear" Bryant*, 36; Doyle, "Causes Won, Not Lost," 231.

27. The first published All-America team appeared in 1889—attributed to the authorship of Caspar Whitney and Walter Camp—and until 1898 the selections were drawn exclusively from the ranks of eastern schools. Gerald Gems has written that in the early years the two selectors were highlighting football as a "sustainer of the capitalist status quo" and that they were reinforcing "the perception of elite eastern leadership" in American culture and commerce—which in Camp's case was a position that continued right into the 1920s (*For Pride, Profit, and Patriarchy: Football and the Incorporation of American Cultural Values*, 21).

28. McCarty, *All-America*; "Westward the Star of Football Takes Its Course."

29. Walter Eckersall, "Score 21 to 21: Story of Game," *Chicago Tribune*, Nov. 28, 1926. Using the mathematical rating system of Professor Frank G. Dickinson that provided the national rankings used to award the Rissman National Trophy from 1924 to 1930, and then the Knute Rockne Memorial Trophy from 1931 to 1940, along with the Associated Press national rankings that began in 1936, the following post-1924 seasons through 1948 produced Big Three teams rated among the nation's Top Ten: 1927 (Yale, no. 5), 1931 (Harvard, no. 7; Yale, no. 8), 1933 (Princeton, no. 7), 1935 (Princeton, no. 3), and 1937 (Yale, no. 6) (Dr. L. H. Baker, *Football: Facts and Figures*, 639–43).

30. Alan J. Gould, "Thirty Million Viewed Grid Game of 1928," *Joliet Evening Herald-News*, Dec. 3, 1928; Danzig and Brandwein, *Sport's Golden Age*, 158; "Football Post-Mortem Finds Zuppke at Best."

31. "Crowley Analyzes Football Season," *New York Times*, Nov. 28, 1927; Fielding Yost, "Across the Gridiron," *Joliet Evening Herald-News*, Nov. 1, 1928.

32. Hugh MacNair Kahler, "Football Team Defeats Yale by Narrow Margin," *Princeton Alumni Weekly*, Nov. 19, 1926; *Daily Princetonian*, Nov. 7, 1927. For information on the "Triple Agreement" governing athletic competition by the Harvard-Princeton-Yale trio, see, for example, *Constitution and By-laws Governing Athletics in Yale University*, a 1928 booklet issued by the Yale University Athletic Association, Box 23, Angell Presidential Records: 1921–1937, Yale University Archives. Apparently, not all athletic officials believed that strict adherence to the Triple Agreement was mandatory. There was considerable discussion at a 1923 meeting of the Big Three university presidents over the "embarrassment" occasioned by Harvard graduate treasurer Moore's "overt implication that the agreement was not taken seriously at Harvard and would not be followed unless they found it convenient" (statement contained in "Memorandum on the New York Conference with Presidents Lowell and Hibben, Jan. 10, 1923," Box 30, Folder 331, ibid.).

33. Bealle, *Football at Harvard*, 266.

34. "The Downhearted at Yale," *New York Times*, Nov. 3, 1926; "Yale Organ Defends Jones," *New York Times*, Nov. 12, 1926; "Tad Jones Resigns, Will Finish Season," *New York Times*, Sept. 7, 1927.

35. Slosson, *Great Crusade*, 274; "Big Three History Ends," *Daily Princetonian*, Nov. 20, 1926; James Isaminger, "Crimson Gains First Yale Win since 1922," *Philadelphia Inquirer*, Nov. 25, 1928; Dan McGugin, "Georgia Won Real Prize," *New Orleans Times-Picayune*, Oct. 14, 1930. See also Bernstein, *Football*, 113–47, for a review of the postwar period to 1930 among the eight schools that eventually formed the "Ivy League."

36. Tunis, "Football on the Wane?" 748.

37. Parrish, *Anxious Decades*, 172.

2. Rise of the Intersectionals

1. In stating that there was very limited playing of intersectional games in the seasons prior to World War I, I have excluded the Carlisle Indians in considering the number of such matchups. The football team from the Carlisle Institute in Pennsylvania was a nomadic outfit that perpetually played

on the road, and pregame articles did not often tout them as a visiting team from the East. The same situation is found in the 1920s with the touring of the team from the Haskell Indian School.

2. Looking to another contest as the most significant in the rise of intersectional football, Michael Oriard has described the 1921 game between Centre and Harvard as "the decisive event in launching the age of intersectionalism" (*King Football*, 75). Gerald Gems also cites the significance of the Harvard-Centre game in his excellent chapter on intersectional play in *Pride, Profit, and Patriarchy*, 151–81.

3. One sportswriter acknowledged the demand for an upgrading of the traditional nonconference schedules: "The trend of modern football is decidedly against the old-time schedules where a lot of soft spots were picked to put the team on edge for one or two final games. . . . Some may hold out for a time, but the football fan may look for better and better schedules as time goes by" ("Intersectional Football Will Help the Game," an uncredited and undated 1920 newspaper clipping from the Camp Papers, Yale University Archives).

4. *Los Angeles Times*, Nov. 28, 1920; "Nebraskans Bring Team of Veterans," *New York Times*, Nov. 2, 1920; Walter Eckersall, "Intersectional Grid Games to Grow in Favor," *Chicago Tribune*, Oct. 29, 1920; *New York Times*, Dec. 25, 1920; "Intersectional Football Will Help the Game," an uncredited and undated 1920 newspaper clipping from the Camp Papers, Yale University Archives.

5. Camp, "The All-America Team"; William France Anderson Jr., interview conducted during 1929 Christmas holidays with A. A. Stagg, Box 110, Folder 6, Stagg Papers.

6. Walter Eckersall, "Stagg Molding Grid Plans," *Chicago Tribune*, Sept. 20, 1920; Eckersall, "Maroon-Tiger Struggle Draws Grid World Eye," *Chicago Tribune*, Oct. 27, 1922; "East Holds Intersectional Grid Honors," *New Orleans Times-Picayune*, Nov. 18, 1925. Michael Oriard has described the 1920s as a time when "sectional comparisons and intersectional games became the primary theme in national football reporting" (*King Football*, 65).

7. George Trevor, "When the Twain Meet," 224, 237; *New York Times*, Sept. 29, 1929.

8. Eckersall, "Maroon-Tiger Struggle Draws Grid World"; "Princeton Undergrads Celebrate," *New York Times*, Oct. 29, 1922; "Tiger Special Leaves," *Chicago Tribune*, Oct. 27, 1922; Hugh Fullerton, "Tiger-Maroon Grid Tilt Sets Chicago Afire," *Chicago Tribune*, Oct. 28, 1922.

9. "Princeton Undergrads Celebrate."

10. Donald Grant Herring, "The Outlook for 1922," *Princeton Alumni Weekly*, Oct. 4, 1922.

11. W. A. Jessup telegram to J. R. Angell, Nov. 25, 1922, and Angell to Jessup, Nov. 27, 1922, Box 30, Folder 332, Yale Football-Angell, Yale University Archives. The exact share of the gate receipts realized by Princeton from the 1922 game in Chicago was reported by Stagg as $44,587.98 (Stagg to Thomas W. Cloney, Nov. 1, 1922, Box 42, Folder 7, Stagg Papers).

12. Herring, "The Outlook for 1922"; Dr. J. E. Raycroft to Stagg, Nov. 11, 1922; Stagg to Raycroft, Nov. 21, 1922, Box 42, Folder 8, Stagg Papers; Roberts, *Big Nine*, 244. The Stagg Papers contain several examples of the correspondence the Chicago coach received with encouragement to continue the Princeton series. See, for example, Ernest Quantrell to Stagg, Dec. 5, 1922, Box 20, Folder 5, Stagg Papers.

13. Robin Lester, *Stagg's University: The Rise, Decline, and Fall of Big-Time Football at Chicago*, 117; Stagg to Cloney, Nov. 1, 1922, Box 42, Folder 7; Stagg to Raycroft, Nov. 21, 1922, Box 42, Folder 8, Stagg Papers.

14. Lester, *Stagg's University*, 119; Len Elliott, *One Hundred Years of Princeton Football*, 41.

15. *New York Times*, Sept. 19, 1926; "Chicago Willing to Raise $100,000," *New York Times*, Dec. 19, 1925; "More Than a Football Game," *Chicago Herald and Examiner*, Dec. 3, 1925; "500,000 Fail to Get Army-Navy Tickets," *New York Times*, Nov. 13, 1926; "$10 and $15 Is the Price Set," *New York Times*, Oct. 22, 1926; "Series Trip to Chicago Costs," *New York Times*, Nov. 28, 1926. Sample accounts of major intersectional games on the West Coast can be found in the *Los Angeles Times*, Dec. 9, 26, 1924, Jan. 2, Nov. 22, 1925.

16. "Rockne Will Bring His Touring Irish to Coast," *Los Angeles Times*, Nov. 6, 1924; "Knute Rockne Says Contest to Be Played," *Los Angeles Times*, Nov. 7, 1924; "Rockne Team Will Refuse U.S.C. Game," *San Francisco Examiner*, Nov. 26, 1924.

17. Rockne to Paul J. Schissler, Dec. 9, 1925, Box 19, Folder 67, UADR; "The Profits," *Chicago Tribune*, Nov. 27, 1927; Steele, *Knute Rockne*, 39; *New York Times*, Feb. 13, 1929, Nov. 3, 1928. The Southern California series was not the only intersectional box-office bonanza for Notre Dame during the 1920s. The seasons of 1926–1930 produced an average attendance of more than 79,000 per game for the annual matchups against Army. Notre Dame's 1928 game with Navy attracted an estimated 122,000 fans to Soldier Field, and sportswriter Alan Gould described it as "the greatest gridiron spectacle American football has ever known" (*Joliet Evening Herald-News*, Oct. 14, 1928).

18. *Los Angeles Times*, Nov. 15, 1920, Nov. 2, 23, 1921; "Abandons Hope for Game," *New York Times*, Nov. 23, 1921; "Notre Dame Only Foe Left for Coast Team," *Chicago Tribune*, Nov. 29, 1921; "Centre to Cavort in San Diego," *Los Angeles Times*, Nov. 20, 1921; *Los Angeles Times*, Nov. 23, 1921. "East vs. West Battle in Air," *Los Angeles Times*, Nov. 24, 1921; "Notre Dame–Centre Game Is Off Again," *New York Times*, Dec. 13, 1921. The Centre College team was widely celebrated on its travels in 1921. Typical was its stopover in St. Louis on the way west to San Diego, where the Kentucky Society of that city escorted the team to the Terminal Hotel for a festive breakfast. One reporter described the Centre team as the "sensations of the gridiron game" ("Centre College Men Pay Visit," *St. Louis Star*, Dec. 17, 1921).

19. *Los Angeles Times*, Nov. 16, 1925.

20. George Brown Tindall, *A History of the South*, 69–71. See also John Sayle Watterson, *College Football: History, Spectacle, Controversy*, 183. For discussions of the linkage between college football and regional social prestige, see Oriard, *King Football*, 76–82; and Doyle, "Causes Won, Not Lost," 231–35.

21. William McG. Keefe, "Viewing the News," *New Orleans Times-Picayune*, Sept. 29, Oct. 27, 1925; Jack Gallagher, "Florida Seeking Big Tilt," *Los Angeles Times*, Nov. 22, 1925; Marty Mule, *Sugar Bowl: The First Fifty Years*, 6–7.

22. Wallace, "This Football Business," 11; Charles L. Bruce, "Arranging a University Football Schedule," *Varsity News* (University of Detroit student newspaper), Holiday Number, 1923–1924, 9.

23. Wallace, "This Football Business," 11.

24. Ibid.

25. Ibid.

26. Ibid; Robert W. Maxwell, "Quaker State Eleven Seldom Plays at Home," *Los Angeles Times*, Nov. 23, 1921.

27. "Western Grid Teams Face Much Travel," *Joliet Evening Herald-News*, Oct. 7, 1928; "Coast Grid Teams Strong on Touring," *Joliet Evening Herald-News*, Sept. 26, 1929; Grantland Rice, "Coaches to the Depot." In justifying the Yale football team's trip to the University of Georgia in 1929 for the dedication of its stadium, the Annual Report of Yale's Athletic Board explained, "These temporary departures represent no basic change of basic policy. . . . Such games . . . are those of long pre-determined regular schedules where the determining factor is not accidental rivalry for intersectional athletic supremacy but a settled community of academic interests and friendly regard" (George H. Nettleton, "Athletic Board of Control Annual Report, 1928–1929," Box 25, Folder 270, Angell Presidential Records, 1921–1937, Yale University Archives).

28. Norman E. Brown, "Travel Helps Grid Players, Coach Avers," *Joliet Evening Herald-News*, Oct. 3, 1928. Promoters often used the "education" approach in attempting to lure teams into long-distance travels, such as the invitation to Stagg for a trip to Los Angeles for a 1923 game (Herbert M. Harwood to Stagg, Nov. 18, 1922; Stagg to Harwood, Dec. 9, 1922, Box 42, Folder 8, Stagg Papers).

29. "Yost Roasts Late Games," *Los Angeles Times*, Jan. 5, 1925; Art Cohn, "Zuppke Gives Grid Views," *Long Beach Press-Telegram*, Aug. 7, 1928; "Notre Dame Head Deplores Its Football Fame," *New York Times*, Feb. 13, 1929.

30. "Detroit Whips Tulane Eleven," *Varsity News*, Dec. 8, 1920, 2; "West vs. East," *New York Evening Post*, May 22, 1920; John Heisman, "What's the Matter with Football," *New Orleans Times-Picayune*, Nov. 21, 1922; Kieran, *New York Times*, Sept. 29, 1929; Michael Oriard, "Home Teams."

3. Stadium Building and the Days of Big Business

1. Historian Robin Lester has also taken note of the commitment for the future generated by the building of large stadia, writing that the "building boom across the country provided the most graphic evidence of the enlargement of place that American football enjoyed . . . [and] ensured that the institutions would attempt to increase America's commitment to the game" (*Stagg's University*, 127).

2. Philip J. Lowry, "College Green Gridirons," *College Football Historical Society* 4 (Feb. 1991): 13–15; John M. Carroll, *Red Grange and the Rise of Modern Football*, 60; "Franklin Field," *University of Pennsylvania Media Guide* (1980); "Rome's Colosseum Outdone by Our Football Bowls," *New York Times*, Nov. 5, 1922; Toni Ginnetti, "Dyche Gets New Name," *Chicago Sun-Times*, May 29, 1997; Tom Laue, "Memorial Stadium: An Illini Institution," *Daily Illini*, Oct. 21, 1967.

3. "Palmer Stadium"; *New York Times*, Nov. 5, 1922.

4. Patrick B. Miller, "Athletes in Academe: College Sports and American Culture, 1850–1920" (Ph.D. diss., Univ. of California at Berkeley, 1987), 475–76.

5. "Football as Our Greatest Popular Spectacle," 52; "Rome's Colosseum Outdone." Social historian Frederick Allen has written that "the war had pulled millions of young men and women out of their accustomed environments and given them a taste of freedom . . . [B]y 1920 the rebellion against puritanism and stuffiness was widely visible, and it gained impetus as the decade progressed" (*Big Change*, 134).

6. Allen, *Big Change*, 123–24; *The Memorial Union and Stadium*, a booklet supplement to the *University of Missouri Bulletin* 24, no. 29 (Oct. 10, 1923), found in the Stadium file at the University of Missouri Archives.

7. Allen, *Big Change*, 138; Clark C. Spence, *The Sinews of American Capitalism: An Economic History*, 253–54.

8. Leland M. Roth, *A Concise History of American Architecture*, 235, 250; Wayne Andrews, *Architecture, Ambition, and Americans: A Social History of American Architecture*, 257.

9. Gavin Hadden, "Stadium Design," a paper presented to the New York Section of the American Society of Civil Engineers, May 20, 1925, reprinted in booklet *Stadium Design*, found in Box 20, Folder 8, Stagg Papers. Hadden, based in New York City, was one of the most active architects involved in the building of football stadiums in the 1920s. James H. Forsythe, "The Stadium—Construction and Design," *Minnesota Memorial Stadium Dedication Day Program*, 15 Nov. 1924. For examples of the behind-the-scenes maneuvers to land stadium-building contracts, see letters exchanged between Dr. R. N. Blackwell, the Southern Methodist athletic business manager, and Knute Rockne dated Nov. 21, 28, Dec. 21, 1929, Box 8, Folder 163, UADR. Also see James Carmody, "Believe It or Not," *Notre Dame Scholastic*, Oct. 3, 1930, 49.

10. John Griffith, "Correlation Between Growth in Attendance at Football Games and Growth in Student Attendance," report to Directors of Western Conference, Mar. 18, 1926, Commissioner Memoranda, 1922–1926, OSUA. Of great significance is the fact that the percentage of the country's population between the ages of eighteen and twenty-one that was enrolled in college increased from just 4 percent in 1900 to more than 12 percent by 1930.

11. "A Stadium for Notre Dame," *Notre Dame Scholastic,* Nov. 22, 1919, 139; Sperber, *Shake Down the Thunder,* 88.

12. "Build the Stadium," *South Bend News-Times,* Oct. 28, 1923.

13. John Bechtold, "The House That Rockne Built," *Notre Dame Scholastic,* Dec. 2, 1960, 34; "Trustees Move to Rush Stadium at Notre Dame," *Chicago Herald and Examiner,* Nov. 17, 1927; "Stadium at Notre Dame," *New York Times,* Nov. 17, 1927; Mike Bynum, ed., *Pop Warner: Football's Greatest Teacher,* 179.

14. Sperber, *Shake Down the Thunder,* 270; Rockne to P. E. Evans, Oct. 23, 1928, Box 11, Folder 96, UADR; "Notre Dame Head Deplores Its Football Fame," *New York Times,* Feb. 13, 1929.

15. Lester, *Stagg's University,* 24, 105; "Report of Alonzo Stagg Jr. on Additional Seating on Stagg Field for Football Season 1922," undated memorandum, Box 20, Folder 5, Stagg Papers; Stagg to W. S. Harman, Feb. 8, 1923, Box 20, Folder 5, Stagg Papers.

16. "Chicago Eleven to Use City Stadium," *New York Times,* Nov. 29, 1922; "Chicago to Build Stadium," *New York Times,* Nov. 8, 1924; A. A. Stagg Jr. to Henry S. Thompson, 12 Dec. 1927, Box 20, Folder 10, Stagg Papers. The great expansion of the seating capacity on the limited property of Stagg Field was made possible by shifting the direction of the football field from north and south to east and west. Retaining the permanent grandstand on the west end, the construction added a new concrete and steel north grandstand with seating for 17,000 along with 31,000 temporary seats that were spread wherever possible around all sides of the field, resulting in a total seating capacity of 58,000. Robin Lester has provided an excellent overview of the expansion of Stagg Field and the subsequent decline in revenues (*Stagg's University,* 128–33).

17. Joseph R. Hickey, "Stanford Stadium Becomes Reality," *San Francisco Chronicle,* Nov. 6, 1921; Roxanne Nilan and Karen Bartholomew, "Rivalry and Entrepreneurship Mark 1921 Construction."

18. See the extensive wire-service article on the expansion of Franklin Field in *Joliet Evening Herald-News,* Oct. 8, 1922; *The Ohio Stadium,* undated booklet published by Ohio State University, most likely in 1922, p. 7, located in folder "Stadium Fund Raising, 1919–1922," OSUA; Brodie, *66 Years,* 152; *The Story of the Stadium,* undated booklet published by the University of Illinois, most likely in 1921, located in "Illinois Stadium" file, University of Illinois Archives. Also see lengthy wire-service article about Illinois Stadium in *Joliet Evening Herald-News,* Oct. 16, 1924. The University of Pennsylvania would expand its Franklin Field again in 1926 with the addition of an upper deck, which raised the stadium's seating capacity to 83,500. See "Franklin Field," in *University of Pennsylvania Media Guide (1980);* and letter of Ernest B. Cozens to Stagg, June 24, 1926, Box 85, Folder 2, Stagg Papers.

19. John Richard Behee, *Fielding Yost's Legacy,* 138, 168; "Capacity of Yale Bowl Not to be Increased, Says Mendell," *New York Times,* Nov. 27, 1921; *Joliet Evening Herald-News,* Nov. 28, 1921. Many of the smaller, primarily private universities also got in on the stadium-building boom but on a more modest scale. Included are such schools as Detroit (1921), Vanderbilt (1922), Columbia (1923), West Point (1924), Cornell (1924), Pittsburgh (1925), Lafayette (1926), and North Carolina (1927).

20. "Yale Rejects Plan for Enlarged Bowl," *New York Times,* Dec. 16, 1923; Hadden, "Stadium Design," 11.

21. "Changes at Polo Grounds," *New York Times,* Oct. 27, 1920.

22. "Vast Stadium Awaits Inaugural Throngs," *Los Angeles Times,* Oct. 8, 1922; "The Rose Bowl," *UCLA Game Program,* Nov. 4, 2000, 99; Steven A. Riess, "Power Without Authority: Los Angeles' Elites and the Construction of the Coliseum"; Paul Gapp, "Soldier Field: 54 Years of Spectacles," *Chicago Tribune,* Feb. 28, 1978; "Chicago Soon to Seat 280,000 in 3 Stadia," *New York Times,* Dec. 1, 1927.

23. "Rome's Colosseum Outdone."

24. James E. Pollard, *Ohio State Athletics, 1879–1959,* 123; Walter Camp, "What Happened to Football in 1922"; "Answers Criticisms of Football's Trend," *New York Times,* Dec. 28, 1925; "Football as Spectacle," 52.

25. Dr. J. W. Wilce, "The Stadium—an Editorial," *Ohio State University Monthly*, Oct. 1922, 9; "Football as Spectacle," 56.

26. "A Campaign of Opportunity, Not Importunity," subscription blank form for the University of Missouri's stadium fund-raising, 1924, Box "Physical Plant—Campus Buildings," Folder "Memorial Union and Stadium," University of Missouri Archives; Stagg to Harold Swift, Dec. 4, 1924, Box 20, Folder 6, Stagg Papers; "The Stadium," *University of Minnesota Dedication Program*, Nov. 15, 1924, 15; "Memorial Stadium; An Illini Institution," *Daily Illini*, Oct. 21, 1967; *The Ohio Stadium*, undated booklet, p. 5, Folder "Stadium Fund Raising, 1919–1922," OSUA.

27. "Rome's Colosseum Outdone"; Joseph R. Hickey, "Stanford Stadium Becomes Reality," *San Francisco Chronicle*, Nov. 6, 1921; Stagg to Swift, Dec. 4, 1924, Box 20, Folder 6, Stagg Papers. For Stagg's ideas on a new stadium appealing to the public, see Stagg to William S. Harman, Jan. 31, 1922, Box 20, Folder 5; to Swift, Dec. 4, 1924, Folder 6; and to Ernest E. Quantrell, Dec. 9, 1922, Folder 5, Stagg Papers.

28. Charles M. Steele to H. R. Caraway, Apr. 12, 1924, Box 20, Folder 7; Quantrell to Stagg, Dec. 5, 1922, Folder 5, Stagg Papers; "Law Building and Stadium Completed."

29. *The Ohio Stadium*, p. 11, in folder "Stadium Fund Raising, 1919–1922" in OSUA; "Baker Field to Be Ready in the Fall," *New York Times*, Dec. 27, 1922; "New York Assured of Bigger Football," *New York Times*, Oct. 15, 1919; "Detroit Team Again Honored," *Varsity News*, Dec. 7, 1921, 4. Examples of football stadia serving as venues for noncollegiate affairs include Marquette University hosting the golden jubilee celebration of the Archdiocese of Milwaukee in 1925; Stagg Field in Chicago hosting an alternate Olympic event in 1932; and the University of Detroit hosting a pageant in honor of the 150th anniversary of the nation's founding. See letter of Sept. 2, 1925 to Knights Templar committee in "Univ. A-1.1 Series 3," Box 1, Folder "Athletics," in Marquette University Archives; "Stadium Scene of Archdiocese Golden Jubilee," *Marquette Tribune*, Oct. 1, 1925, 2; Gapp, "Soldier Field"; and "Dorais Picks Line-Up," *Varsity News*, May 6, 1926, 2.

30. "Chicago Students Want No Stadium," *New York Times*, Nov. 24, 1922; "Chicago Eleven to Use City Stadium."

31. The first quote on President Kinley's view of Illinois stadium as "a link" to Greek civilization is from Carroll, *Red Grange*, 61. Kinley's quote is from the fund-raising booklet *The Story of the Stadium*, unnumbered pages and undated but most likely 1921, found in the football papers at the University of Illinois Archives.

32. *Yale Alumni Weekly*, May 24, 1912, copy of article is in folder "Stadium: Fund Raising, 1919–1922," OSUA.

33. *The Story of the Stadium*, in football papers at the University of Illinois Archives; Nilan and Bartholomew, "Rivalry and Entrepreneurship," 2; *The Ohio Stadium*, 13, folder "Stadium, Fund Raising, 1919–1922," OSUA; "New Issue" (announcement for University of Iowa Stadium bonds), Mar. 15, 1929, File "Kinnick Stadium," University of Iowa Archives, Iowa City; Joe Doyle, "Rockne Was Father of Stadium," *South Bend Tribune*, undated article in "Stadium" file at University of Notre Dame Archives; "The Michigan Stadium Story," in *University of Michigan Football Media Guide (2000)*, 386.

34. Pollard, *Ohio State Athletics*, 119–24; "Secretary's Report to Stadium Executive Committee," Jan. 1, 1922, Folder "Stadium, Fund Raising 1919–1922," OSUA; letter from President William O. Thompson to "Students on the Campus," Jan. 5, 1922, Folder "Stadium, Fund Raising, 1919–1922," OSUA.

35. Sperber, *Shake Down the Thunder*, 333; "$275,000 Football Stadium Is Gift to North Carolina," *New York Times*, Nov. 14, 1926.

36. Basic information on the construction of Nebraska's new stadium in Richard D. Loosbrock, review of "Give Till It Hurts: Financing Memorial Stadium," by Michele Fagan, *Journal of Sport History*

26, no. 3 (Fall 1999): 631; Irving Weber, "UI Stadium," *Iowa City Press-Citizen*, Oct. 20, 1984, and also his "Hawkeye Flashback," unsourced newspaper article, Oct. 13, 1995, University of Iowa Archives; "The Michigan Stadium Story," in *University of Michigan Football Media Guide (2000)*, 386.

37. "First Unit of Memorial Stadium to Be Ready"; Stephens, *History of Missouri*, 560–62; undated and untitled memorandum on Missouri athletic department's funding crisis, found in UW 4/30/2, Box 4F8, Folder "Vice-President for Administrative Affairs General Files," University of Missouri Archives. The actual cost of the construction projects fluctuated widely, influenced greatly by not only the seating capacity desired but also various design features of the stadium such as the number of ramps and walkways, the depth to which the playing field was to be excavated below ground level, and so on. Some examples of costs expressed on a per-seat basis include Stanford at $3.50 per seat in 1921, eventually raised to $6.50 per seat after major additions and improvements in 1927; Northwestern—considered to be excessively expensive—at $40 per seat; Iowa at $11.70 per seat; and Michigan at $10.50 per seat (Nilan and Bartholomew, "Rivalry and Entrepreneurship," 1, 6; Blackwell to Rockne, Nov. 21, 1929, and Rockne to Blackwell, Nov. 28, 1929, Box 8, Folder 163, UADR; Weber, "Hawkeye Flashback").

38. Thelin, *Games Colleges Play*, 33. For information on student enrollments, see Freidel and Brinkley, *Twentieth Century*, 179; and John L. Griffith, "Memorandum to Directors of Athletics," Folder "Commissioner Memoranda, 1922–26," OSUA.

39. "Record Year for Conference Teams," *New York Times*, Nov. 25, 1921; "Football in Midwest Now Real Industry," *Joliet Evening Herald-News*, Oct. 24, 1922. The extent of the lost incomes was seen when it was disclosed that the 1922 Chicago-Princeton game, played at Chicago's 31,000-seat Stagg Field, drew more than 100,000 ticket applications, each calling for at least two tickets.

40. "Comparative Statement of Net Incomes from Football of the Conference Universities (1923–1929)," Box 84, Folder 7, Stagg Papers.

41. "Many Records Set in Football Season," *New York Times*, Dec. 7, 1924; "10,000,000 Attend 1924 Grid Games," *Chicago Herald and Examiner*, Dec. 1, 1924; "East Trails West in College Football Crowds," *Chicago Tribune*, Dec. 3, 1924; "A Gain of Two Million Saw College Football Contests," *New York Times*, Nov. 30, 1925. Red Grange was generally considered to be college football's greatest drawing card during his final season at Illinois, as his Big Ten team played before approximately 371,000 fans in 1925, or an average of more than 46,300 per game. The profit figure from Big Ten football in 1925 was reported in "Million Dollar Profit Shown by Western Football," *Joliet Evening Herald-News*, Oct. 9, 1926.

42. Joseph S. Rogers, "Losing Opportunity of Seeing Big Encounters," *Philadelphia Inquirer*, Oct. 27, 1923; Allison Danzig, "Football Outgrows Stadiums," *New York Times*, Oct. 17, 1926.

43. "Comment on Current Events," *New York Times*, Nov. 24, 1924; "Football Has Always Been Storm Center," *Joliet Evening Herald-News*, Dec. 7, 1923; "Football in Midwest Now Real Industry"; *Joliet Evening Herald-News*, Oct. 24, 1922 (item on Big Ten schools taking newspaper ads to advise fans of ticket unavailability); Danzig, "Football Outgrows Stadiums." Fans lucky enough to obtain valuable tickets for the traditional rivalry game between California and Stanford were offered the opportunity to buy "rain insurance" for the 1921 meeting. For just fifty cents a fan could protect his investment, and in case of rain "the purchase price [will] be refunded if desired" (*Joliet Evening Herald-News*, Nov. 14, 1921).

44. *Ohio State University Monthly*, Oct. 1920; *New York Times*, Oct. 20, 1922; *Princeton Alumni Weekly*, Oct. 4, 1922.

45. "Viewing the News," *New Orleans Times-Picayune*, Oct. 28, 1925; Ernest B. Cozens to Stagg, June 24, 1926, Box 85, Folder 2, Stagg Papers; *New York Times*, Oct. 22, 1926; *Army-Navy Official Program*, Nov. 27, 1926; *Princeton Alumni Weekly*, Sept. 27, 1929; *Yale-Army Official Program*, Oct. 26, 1929; *South Bend Tribune*, Sept. 14, 1996.

46. Walter Camp, "Wise Commercialism Will Win."

47. E. K. Hall, "Report of American Intercollegiate Football Rules Committee, Dec. 1924," Box 50, Folder 12, Stagg Papers; Danzig, "Football Outgrows Stadiums"; *Statement to Subscribers: The Ohio Stadium Fund,* a pamphlet distributed by the Ohio State athletic department in Columbus, Ohio, newspapers, Jan. 21, 1923, copy in folder "Athletic Board, 1913–1928," OSUA; John L. Griffith, "Studies and Investigations, August 1922 to June 1925," June 3, 1925, Box 85, Folder 1, Stagg Papers; *New York Times,* Oct. 16, 1929. Reports detailing the extent of college football's support of the other varsity sports can easily be located in newspapers throughout the decade.

48. "Big Ten Sports Get $100,000 in Taxes," *New York Times,* Dec. 19, 1926; Fielding Yost, "Grid Profits Defended by Coach Yost," *Joliet Evening Herald-News,* Dec. 18, 1927; "Ohio State Football to Pay for Athletic Plan," *New York Times,* Nov. 3, 1928; *Joliet Evening Herald-News,* Dec. 9, 1928; Wallace, "This Football Business," 170.

49. Tunis, "The Great God Football," 749; *Statement to Subscribers: The Ohio Stadium Fund.*

50. Tunis, "The Great God Football," 749.

51. "$30,000,000 Was Paid for 1926 Football," *New York Times,* Dec. 3, 1926; "Football Receipts for 1926," an unsigned report found in Box 85, Folder 3, Stagg Papers. An attendance figure of 90,437 fans, far in excess of the seating capacity, was reported for the Ohio State–Michigan game at Columbus, Ohio, in 1926. The actual attendance could not be determined, as standing room had been sold for every conceivable space in the stadium, while gate crashers also climbed over the fences to get in. The reported attendance figure "was chosen arbitrarily" at a meeting in St. John's office (Pollard, *Ohio State Athletics,* 145).

52. Curley Grieve, "Sports Parade," *San Francisco Examiner,* Nov. 15, 1932.

53. Comments and reports concerning gambling and drinking by fans attending Big Ten games can be found in John L. Griffith, "Studies and Investigations, August 1922 to June 1925," memorandum to conference directors dated June 3, 1925, Box 85, Folder 1, Stagg Papers; and "Coaches Urge Football Fans to Stop Drinking, Gambling," *Joliet Evening Herald-News,* Sept. 26, 1926.

54. Alan J. Gould, "30,000,000 See College Grid Tilts," *Chicago Herald and Examiner,* Nov. 28, 1927; "30,000,000 Attended Football," *New York Times,* Nov. 28, 1927; Gould, "Thirty Million Viewed Grid Games," *Joliet Evening Herald-News,* Dec. 3, 1928.

55. "Comparative Total Receipts of All Big Ten Universities, 1923–1929," undated report, Box 84, Folder 7, Stagg Papers (Big Ten football receipts); "Sportsmania in the Colleges: Pro and Con"; "Football Revenue $1,000,000 at Yale," *New York Times,* Nov. 1, 1929; Rappoport, *Wake Up the Echoes,* 145 (Notre Dame figures); *Joliet Evening Herald-News,* Dec. 3, 1928 (Navy game attendance); "Sportsmania" (quote from *New York World*). When Yale's football revenue figure topped $1 million in 1927, the Athletic Association was still destined to end the school year of 1927–1928 with a total deficit of just over $40,000 as a result of football's supporting of the university's non-revenue-producing sports ("Yale University Athletic Association Financial Statement: June 30, 1925 to Feb. 28, 1926," Box 23, Folder "Athletic Association Financial Statements," Angell Presidential Records, 1921–1937, Yale University Archives).

56. *Joliet Evening Herald-News,* 3 Nov. 1929; *New York Times,* 21 Dec. 1929; Danzig and Brandwein, *Sport's Golden Age,* 129.

57. J. F. Steiner, "1921–1930 Attendance and Revenue Study for President's Research Committee," undated, Box 114, Folder 5, Harold Higgins Swift Papers, University of Chicago Archives.

58. "Football Is Hit by Decreased Attendance," *New York Times,* Dec. 5, 1930; "Letting the Air Out of College Football." John Watterson cites a decline of 25 percent in college football's attendance figures between 1929 and 1933, based on a survey by collegiate officials, a figure that seems understated if the University of Chicago's estimated figures developed in 1930 are reasonably accurate (*College Football,*

177). The Chicago figures appear to be closer to the mark for 1930, based on football's national attendance figures that were being reported at the beginning of the 1920s (Steiner, "1921–1930 Attendance and Revenue Study," Swift Papers).

59. John Kieran, "Wrestling with Big Football Problems," *New York Times*, Dec. 5, 1930; George Trevor, "Football Feuds."

60. "Coach Rockne Finds Football Not Commercialized Enough," *New York Times*, Dec. 17, 1930; Douglas P. Haikell, "Football as Big Business."

61. "Football's New Czar," 58.

62. Wallace, "This Football Business," 170.

4. Opposing Organized Pro Football

1. John Griffith, "Professionalism in Collegiate Athletics," undated memorandum, Commissioner Correspondence, 1922–29, OSUA. See Amos Alonzo Stagg, *Touchdown!* 294, and W. W. Roper, *Football, Today and Tomorrow*, 139, for examples of professional football being described as a "parasitical" outgrowth of the college game.

2. Beau Riffenburgh, *The Official NFL Encyclopedia*, 9; Keith McClellan, *The Sunday Game: At the Dawn of Professional Football*, 3. For discussions of the early days of professional football's evolution, see Roger Treat, *The Encyclopedia of Football*, 19–20; and McClellan, *Sunday Game*, 3–28.

3. *Constitution and By-laws Governing Athletics in Yale University* (New Haven: Yale Athletic Association, 1928), 43.

4. "Meeting of the Amateur Athletic Association," *Sporting Life*, Dec. 2, 1916.

5. Joe Ziemba, *When Football Was Football: The Chicago Cardinals and the Birth of the NFL*, 69; Treat, *The Encyclopedia of Football*, 20–29; Stagg to E. K. Hall, Mar. 1, 1920, Box 50, Folder 8, Stagg Papers; "Sunday Football Illegal," *New York Times*, Oct. 7, 1919.

6. Stagg to Hall, Mar. 1, 1920; see also Hall's letter to Stagg on Feb. 2, 1920, in which the rules chairman writes of Dartmouth having just "disqualified" two students for having played professionally after the football season was over (Box 50, Folder 8, Stagg Papers). "Big Ten Makes Grid Numbers a Requirement," *Chicago Tribune*, Dec. 5, 1920; "Coaches Hostile to Pro Football," *New York Times*, Dec. 28, 1921.

7. "Walter Camp Supporter of Pro Football," *Chicago Tribune*, Dec. 5, 1920; "Independent Football Flourishing This Year," *Los Angeles Times*, Nov. 24, 1921.

8. "Football Pros Show Green Bay the Door," *Chicago Tribune*, Jan. 29, 1922; Sperber, *Shake Down the Thunder*, 121; "Mohardt Admits Playing with Legion," *Chicago Daily News*, Feb. 3, 1922. Despite all the controversy, when the 1922 NFL season rolled around, Green Bay was back in the league.

9. *Chicago Daily News*, Jan. 28, Feb. 3, 1922; president of Friars Club to captain of Rose Poly Varsity Football Team, Dec. 12, 1916; W. P. Dudley to M. Hartong, Feb. 26, 1921, Box 24, Folder 9, Stagg Papers.

10. *Chicago Daily News*, Jan. 28, 1922; McClellan, *Sunday Game*, 11; Treat, *The Encyclopedia of Football*, 20; *Chicago Daily News*, Feb. 2, 1922; *Chicago Tribune*, Feb 2, 3, 1922; Sperber, *Shake Down the Thunder*, 121; Steele, *Knute Rockne*, 172.

11. *New York Times*, Jan. 29, 1922; *Chicago Tribune*, Jan. 30, 1922; *New York Times*, Jan. 31, 1922; *Chicago Daily News*, Jan. 30, 1922; *Champaign News-Gazette*, Aug. 29, 1937.

12. Stagg to Harold Nicely, Mar. 8, 1922, Box 42, Folder 9, Stagg Papers; *Chicago Evening American*, Jan. 31, Feb. 1, 1922.

13. Raymond Schmidt, "Major John Griffith," *College Football Historical Society* 13 (Feb. 2000): 1–3; "Press Release," July 26, 1922, Commissioner Correspondence, 1922–1929, OSUA.

14. Griffith, "Professionalism in Collegiate Athletics," undated memorandum, Commissioner Correspondence, 1922–1929, OSUA.

15. "Open Letter to All Friends of College Football," press release, Oct. 26, 1923, Box 109, Folder 11, Stagg Papers. See the *New York Times*, Nov. 2, 1923, which reprinted much of Stagg's letter under the banner story headline "Pro Elevens Hurt Sport, Says Stagg." See also Boston College's *Heights*, Dec. 1, 1923, p. 3, for an example of how college newspaper writers lifted entire sections of Stagg's letter and dropped them into the middle of their articles. For the letter sent by Big Ten directors to their student newspapers, see Athletic Directors, "Professional Football," Nov. 4, 1923, in folder "Professionalism, 1923," OSUA.

16. Herbert Reed, "DeGranging Football." See also cartoon in *Dallas Morning News*, Nov. 30, 1923.

17. See "The Visit of M. A. Romney," Nov. 8, 1923; "The Visit of R. T. Halladay," Nov. 12, 1923; and "The Visit of John B. Hurlburt," Nov. 13, 1923; all three of these memos on the meetings of the former players with Stagg can be found in Box 24, Folder 9, Stagg Papers.

18. Oriard, "Home Teams," 474. For an example of the continuing opposition to professional football led by Big Ten commissioner Griffith, see "Athletics in the Minor Colleges," Griffith memorandum, Jan. 20, 1925, "Commissioner Memoranda, 1922–1926," OSUA.

19. "Pro Football Gains Favor with Fandom," *Joliet Evening Herald-News*, Nov. 30, 1925; Carroll, *Red Grange*, 99; McClellan, *Sunday Game*, 18; "For Professional Football," *Chicago Tribune*, Oct. 2, 1925.

20. Grantland Rice, "The Pigskin Ballyhoo."

21. "Pro Football," *Joliet Evening Herald-News*, Nov. 30, 1925; "Pro Football Chief Gives Views on Game," *Chicago Daily News*, Dec. 8, 1925; "Football: The Frankenstein of Athletics," 56–58.

22. Ray Schmidt, "Red Grange of Wheaton," *College Football Historical Society* 4 (May 1991): 11–13; McCarty, *All-America*, 65, 76; Carroll, *Red Grange*, 57; "Pro Promoters Rumored After Captain Grange," Nov. 12, 1925, article from unknown newspaper in the University of Illinois Archives; "Football Hero Put on Carpet," *Los Angeles Times*, Nov. 18, 1925; "Grange Has Passed Threshold," *New Orleans Times-Picayune*, Oct. 21, 1925.

23. Memorandum from Stagg Jr. to Stagg, Nov. 19, 1925, Box 24, Folder 5, Stagg Papers. In the memorandum Stagg Jr. repeats comments about the contradiction in Grange's wearing an expensive raccoon coat while his family was reported to be living under difficult financial conditions in Wheaton.

24. "Red Grange Runs to Fame in Final Game," *New Orleans Times-Picayune*, Nov. 22, 1925; "Grange Signs with Chicago Bears Grid Team," *Joliet Evening Herald-News*, Nov. 23, 24, 1925.

25. Parrish, *Anxious Decades*, 173.

26. Reed, "DeGranging Football," 102; J. D. McKee, "Red's Decision," *Cleveland Plain Dealer*, Nov. 23, 1925; "The Case of Grange," *Heights*, Dec. 1, 1925, 2; "Red and I Are Still Friends," *Kansas City Journal*, Feb. 6, 1926. Although Zuppke professed lifelong beliefs in amateur sport, there were occasional instances that raised questions about his position. In a memorandum dictated by Stagg in 1925, the Chicago coach complained that "Zuppke for instance has helped professional football by attending games and sitting on the bench among the players" ("Comments on Professional Football, 1925," an undated memorandum, Box 24, Folder 9, Stagg Papers).

27. "An Open Market for Galloping Ghosts," 508; "Pro Football Gains Favor," *Joliet Evening Herald-News*, Nov. 30, 1925; W. O. McGeehan, "Down the Line," *New York Herald Tribune*, Nov. 24, 1925.

28. *New Orleans Times-Picayune*, Jan. 12, 1926; "It's Do or Die for Coach, Not School," *Chicago Tribune*, Dec. 15, 1929; McGeehan, "Down the Line"; "More Than a Football Game," *Chicago Herald and Examiner*, Dec. 3, 1925.

29. Ziemba, *When Football Was Football*, 117. Michael Oriard believes that Grange's turning professional did not motivate any long-running gradual development of the public consciousness and interest in pro football but rather was an event that foretold how professional football would eventually become the dominant version of the gridiron sport in the 1960s ("Home Teams," 483).

30. "Griffith of Big Ten Fears Pro Football," *New York Times*, Oct. 13, 1925; "Amateur Sport Due to Topple," *Los Angeles Times*, Nov. 25, 1925; Reed, "DeGranging Football," 103; "American Coaches Bar Pro Brethren," *New York Times*, Dec. 29, 1925. Griffith noted the possible financial ramifications on the intercollegiate game when he said that "if the sport becomes highly professionalized . . . twenty-five years from now these beautiful stadiums that we are building will be no more useful than the ruined stadiums in Aries, Rome or Athens" ("Griffith of Big Ten Fears Pro Football").

31. "Englewood Players Confess," *Chicago American*, Dec. 15, 1925; "Pros' Version of Grid Tangle," *Chicago Tribune*, Dec. 17, 1925; James Crusinberry, "Engage under False Names Against Cards," *Chicago Tribune*, Dec. 16, 1925; Harry Neily, "Claim Boys Victims of Folz," *Chicago American*, Dec. 16, 1925; Everett Swanson, "4 Englewood Youths Admit Playing Cards," *Chicago Herald and Examiner*, Dec. 16, 1925; Everett Swanson, "League Prexy to Investigate Use of Preps," *Chicago Herald and Examiner*, Dec. 17, 1925; Guy High, "Cardinal Owner to Assist in Clearing Boys," *Chicago American*, Dec. 17, 1925; James Crusinberry, "Folz Takes All Blame, O'Brien Admits Fault," *Chicago Tribune*, Dec. 17, 1925; Crusinberry, "Board Fixes Full Penalty on Four Boys," *Chicago Tribune*, Dec. 24, 1925; W. V. Morgenstern, "4 Who Played Against Cards Get No Mercy," *Chicago Herald and Examiner*, Dec. 24, 1925.

32. "NCAA to War on Pro Football," *New York Times*, Dec. 16, 1925; "Central Board Hands Off on Pro Official Problem," *New York Evening Post*, Oct. 21, 1926.

33. "American Coaches Bar Pro Brethren"; "Missouri Schools Rap Pro Football," *New York Times*, Dec. 6, 1925; Keats Speed to Big Ten athletic directors, undated, 1926, Box 85, Folder 2, Stagg Papers.

34. "Pro Officials Ask College Star Ban," *New York Times*, Dec. 27, 1925; Carroll, *Red Grange*, 104; Ziemba, *When Football Was Football*, 140.

35. "Football's New Czar," 54.

36. Glenn E. Hoover, "College Football."

37. "Poor Professional Football"; Stagg, *Touchdown!* 294–95; Reed, "DeGranging Football," 103.

38. Roper, *Football, Today and Tomorrow*, 140, 154; Art Cohn, "Pro Football Lacks Spirit of College Grid Game," uncredited clipping, Aug. 6, 1928, Box 8, Bob Zuppke Papers, University of Illinois Archives; Reed, "DeGranging Football," 102.

39. Rice, "The Pigskin Ballyhoo"; "The College Game," *Heights*, Dec. 1, 1928. For contrasting coverage of pro football by college newspapers, see "Hagerty Stars in Professional Game," *Hoya*, Oct. 16, 1929; and "Red and Lavvie Star in Pro Game," *Marquette Tribune*, Oct. 13, 1927, 12.

40. Roper, *Football, Today and Tomorrow*, 151. For examples of growth in college enrollment figures, see Griffith to directors of Western Conference, Mar. 18, 1926, "Commissioner Memoranda, 1922–1926," OSUA; and Coben, *Rebellion Against Victorianism*.

41. Stagg would remain a foe of professional sports well beyond the 1920s. Years later, in his introduction to a Japanese-published book on athletic training, Stagg wrote that professional athletics were "seriously impairing ideal results" in American athletics and exerting "an exaggerated importance and undue influence upon the youth of the United States" (introduction to unknown book title [Japan: H. Okabe, n.d.], found in Box 110, Folder 8, Stagg Papers). The temporary truce between the leaders of college and pro football would come to an end in the 1960s with their battles over the potential riches from television. See Ronald A. Smith, *Play-by-Play: Radio, Television, and Big-Time College Sport*, 92–102.

5. Advances on the Gridiron

1. Watterson, *College Football*, 103–7. In addition to Watterson's review of the 1906 rules revisions, see also Danzig, *American Football*, 31.

2. Percy D. Haughton, "Fifty Year Struggle Is Told by Haughton," *Dallas Morning News*, Nov. 11, 1922; Watterson, *College Football*, 110–11, 121–28.

3. E. K. Hall, "Report of the American Intercollegiate Football Rules Committee (1920)," Box 50, Folder 8, Stagg Papers; *Joliet Evening Herald-News*, Oct. 21, 1921; Walter Camp, "Annual Review of the Season," in *Spalding's Official Intercollegiate Football Guide, 1922*, 9.

4. Donald Grant Herring, "Football," *Princeton Alumni Weekly*, Nov. 26, 1919; Camp, "What Happened," 28.

5. Charles D. Daly, *American Football*, 30–31, 35, 56–57, 135.

6. Camp, "What Happened," 13; Camp, "Wise Commercialism Will Win"; Camp, "Walter Camp Reviews 1923 Football," 20–28.

7. William Abbott, "West Superior in Football," *Joliet Evening Herald-News*, Oct. 31, 1924. See also "What's Wrong with Harvard System?" *Joliet Evening Herald-News*, Nov. 8, 1925.

8. William Abbott, "West Superior in Football," *Joliet Evening Herald-News*, Oct. 31, 1924; Herbert Reed, "1925 Football a Game That Dazzles"; Reed, "Football Lessons of 1924"; William France Anderson Jr., "Interview with Coach Amos Alonzo Stagg," an unpublished interview, Christmas Holidays 1929, Box 110, Folder 6, Stagg Papers.

9. Reed, "1925 Football"; Grantland Rice, "Fast Work"; Camp, "Walter Camp's Sports Page."

10. "West Coast Style Is More Daring, Says Glenn Warner," *New Orleans Times-Picayune*, Nov. 22, 1925.

11. Glenn S. Warner, "Western Heads Termed More Progressive," *San Francisco Examiner*, Oct. 2, 1927.

12. "It's a Far Cry from Red Grange to Heffelfinger"; Fielding Yost, "Yost Explains Grid Lure," *Joliet Evening Herald-News*, Oct. 18, 1927.

13. W. W. Roper, "Football from the Grand Stand," 13, 16; Roper, *Football, Today and Tomorrow*, 14.

14. Anderson, "Interview with Coach Amos Alonzo Stagg," Box 110, Folder 6, Stagg Papers; Danzig, *American Football*, 222–23; Russell J. Newland, "Warner Devises New Formation," *Joliet Evening Herald-News*, Nov. 19, 1928; Danzig, *American Football*, 56 (Stanley Woodward quote from 1930 *New York Herald Tribune*).

15. Howard Jones and Alfred F. Wesson, *Football for the Fan*, 44; *San Francisco Examiner*, Oct. 26, 1930.

16. "Pennsylvania to Offer New Grid Attack," *Joliet Evening Herald-News*, Sept. 4, 1929; "Illinois Now Uses System Exclusively," *Philadelphia Inquirer*, Nov. 20, 1928; "New Plays Add Color to Dixie Football Games," *Joliet Evening Herald-News*, Nov. 13, 1927.

17. Danzig, *American Football*, 61; Watterson, *College Football*, 32.

18. Danzig, *American Football*, 62.

19. Parke H. Davis, "Fifty Years of Intercollegiate Foot Ball," in *Spalding's Official Intercollegiate Football Guide, 1926*, 19; Danzig, *American Football*, 59–62; unpublished Stagg interview by William France Anderson Jr., Dec. 1929, Box 110, Folder 6, Stagg Papers.

20. *New York Evening Post*, Oct. 24, 1921. For a little extra deception against Princeton, the Chicago backfield used another confusing maneuver in which "a few seconds before a play was launched, the trio would leap in the air and whirl once, coming down right in their tracks. Immediately following the acrobatic feat the ball would be snapped." Every time this movement took place, the heads of the Princeton linemen would all come up, so they were off balance when Chicago's line charge hit them (*Philadelphia Inquirer*, Oct. 25, 1921).

21. Daly to Rockne, Nov. 15, 1921, Box 6, Folder 60, UADR.

22. Zuppke to Stagg, Feb. 14, 1922, Box 51, Folder 12, Stagg Papers.

23. Stagg, "The More Important Changes in the Rules," an undated memorandum on the 1922 rule changes, Box 54, Folder 6, Stagg Papers.

24. Ibid. For examples of the analysis and study of shift formations, see "Notre Dame's Winning Formation," *Joliet Evening Herald-News*, Oct. 26, 1923; and Reed, "Football Lessons of 1924."

25. "Penn State Downed by Georgia Tech," *New York Times*, Oct. 11, 1925; "Illini Shift Is Held Marvel," *Joliet Evening Herald-News*, Nov. 7, 1926.

26. "Zuppke Will Open War on Shift Plays," *Joliet Evening Herald-News*, Nov. 21, 1926; "Yost Criticizes Shift Play," *Joliet Evening Herald-News*, Nov. 11, 1926; "Football Rule Changes Fail to Hurt Game," *Joliet Evening Herald-News*, Oct. 18, 1927.

27. Sperber, *Shake Down the Thunder*, 213, 244, 246; *New York Times*, Nov. 23, 1926 (Zuppke quote).

28. "Shift Is Barred by Big Ten Heads," *New York Times*, Nov. 27, 1926; "Big Ten Will Bar Shift Play," *Joliet Evening Herald-News*, Nov. 28, 1926; *New York Times*, Nov. 23, 1926.

29. "Officials to Endorse Four Rule Changes," *Chicago Defender*, Jan. 1, 1927; "Shift Play Curbed under New Ruling," *New York Times*, Dec. 30, 1926.

30. Rockne to Hall, Feb. 28, 1927, Box 13, Folder 10, UADR. In his letter, Rockne refers to the "Lily Whites" on a couple of occasions, a sarcastic reference to Big Ten coaches who he believed were hypocritical in their reform efforts.

31. Hall to Rockne, Mar. 3, 1927, ibid.; Hall, "Report of American Intercollegiate Football Rules Committee for 1927," Box 50, Folder 14, Stagg Papers.

32. Hall to Rockne, Mar. 12, 1927, Box 13, Folder 10, UADR; Francis Wallace in Rappoport, *Wake Up the Echoes*, 77 (information on Rockne's switch to heavier and stronger linemen and backs in 1927); "Football Rule Changes Fail to Hurt Game," *Joliet Evening Herald-News*, Oct. 18, 1927; Rockne to Edward "Slip" Madigan, May 16, 1930, Madigan Collection, St. Mary's University Archives, Moraga, Calif.

33. "Rockne Says He Can Win Minus Shift," *New Orleans Times-Picayune*, Oct. 28, 1930.

34. Sport historian James Mark Purcell relates the similarities of 1920s passing statistics and their meaning to the numbers of the late 1930s in "Gerry Mann," *College Football Historical Society* 2, no. 4 (Aug. 1989): 7; and "Spears and Vandy: Excitement in 1927," *College Football Historical Society* 2, no. 1 (Nov. 1988): 5.

35. Watterson, *College Football*, 103–4. See commentary on the 1906 version of the forward pass in Neilson Poe, "The Forward Pass."

36. Stagg, "Evolution of Forward Passes in 1906," a memorandum dictated Aug. 13, 1930, Box 110, Folder 8, Stagg Papers. Stagg's statement that he had diagrammed sixty-four different pass patterns in 1906 is taken from his letter of Jan. 31, 1952, which is quoted in Danzig, *American Football*, 37. See coverage of the Chicago-Illinois game in *Chicago Tribune*, Nov. 18, 1906; and *Chicago Inter-Ocean*, Nov. 18, 1906. See also Ray Schmidt, "Walter the Second," *College Football Historical Society* 2, no. 3 (May 1989): 3–6.

37. Danzig, *American Football*, 34–36. Quotes from John E. Wray are from *St. Louis Post-Dispatch* article of Nov. 20, 1927, which was reprinted as "Local Sport Authority Corrects Parke Davis," *Varsity Breeze*, Nov. 23, 1927. In writing of the contributions by the St. Louis University coach to the evolution of the forward pass, Wray noted, "No man in history did more for modern football than Cochems, and no man ever received less credit."

38. Danzig, *American Football*, 38. The quotes from Warner and the *Chicago Tribune* can be found in Schmidt, "Walter the Second," 5.

39. Parke H. Davis, "Twenty Years of Forward Passes," *Spalding's Official Intercollegiate Football Guide, 1927*, 11.

40. Poe, "The Forward Pass"; Danzig, *American Football*, 35–36; Arthur Daley, "Sports of the Times," *New York Times*, Aug. 1, 1971; William Sprackling, "To the Editor," *New York Times*, Aug. 29, 1971.

41. An excellent overview of the 1910 battles over college football's rules can be found in Watterson, *College Football*, 120–30. The forward pass would continue to be attacked even after the rules battles of 1910. At the close of the 1911 season, Edward R. Bushnell, as eastern newspaperman, wrote a blistering article that claimed Princeton had won the mythical Big Three title for 1911 without resorting to any use of the forward pass and that the Tigers' coaches had discarded pass plays after coming to "the conclusion that it was utterly useless." The sportswriter also contended that "the abolition of the forward pass would not change the game in any important respect" ("Pass a Hindrance Instead of a Help," an uncredited 1911 newspaper article found in the Camp Papers, Yale University Archives).

42. Walter Eckersall, "Forward Passes Win for Michigan," *Chicago Tribune*, Nov. 20, 1910; "Wolverines Capture Football Crown of West from Gophers," *Chicago Inter-Ocean*, Nov. 20, 1910. A later writer, Ivan N. Kaye, has pointed to the 1910 Michigan-Minnesota game as one of the early influences in college football's growing use of the forward pass as a tactical weapon rather than merely one of desperation (*Good Clean Violence: A History of College Football*, 62–64).

43. "Notre Dame's Open Play Amazes Army," *New York Times*, Nov. 2, 1913; Sperber, *Shake Down the Thunder*, 39–40. Sperber quotes Coach Jesse Harper of Notre Dame as stating that he "had used the forward pass a great deal at Wabash [College] before going to Notre Dame." Notre Dame completed thirteen of seventeen pass attempts for 243 yards against Army in 1913. See also Sol Metzger, "Great Clash Between Army and Navy: Pass Won for West Point Eleven, Says Metzger," *New York Tribune*, Nov. 30, 1913.

44. Herbert Reed, "Football Lessons of the Year"; "Football in 1916." See also Bob Royce, "The Passing Game, 1914," *College Football Historical Society* 9, no. 4 (Aug. 1996): 11.

45. Examples of Princeton passing statistics can be found in *Daily Princetonian*, Nov. 3, 10, 17, 1919; "Notre Dame Is Victor," *Chicago Herald and Examiner*, Nov. 23, 1919 (for a typical example of George Gipp's passing exploits); Rube Samuelsen, *The Rose Bowl Game*, 36–40. Ohio State's Hoge Workman demonstrated his passing talents in the Buckeyes' important come-from-behind 13-7 victory over Wisconsin in 1920, described by sportswriter W. D. Richardson as a "brilliant exhibition of forward passing—an exhibition which perhaps has never been equaled" (*Chicago Tribune*, Oct. 24, 1920). See also Dr. John W. Wilce, "Supreme Football Strategies," *New Orleans Times-Picayune*, Nov. 25, 1924.

46. Poe, "The Forward Pass," 682.

47. Camp, "The All-America Team"; Robert W. Maxwell, "Forward Pass Is More Prominent Than Ever," *Los Angeles Times*, 2 Nov. 1921; *New York Times*, 4 Dec. 1921.

48. Donald Grant Herring, "Athletics," *Princeton Alumni Weekly*, Nov. 1, 1922, 102; "Football's Biggest Year," 150; *New York Times*, Dec. 4, 1921. Researchers can easily locate examples of game statistics and commentary that illustrate the widespread growth of the forward-passing attack through all regions of the country during the period 1919–1922. The 1921 Fordham team in New York City was considered to have a very impressive passing game under the direction of Coach Joe DuMoe. One newspaper story referred to DuMoe as the "father of the long forward pass offense," referring to his play as a standout passer while at Syracuse (undated and unidentified newspaper clipping found in *Football Scrapbook, 1921*, Fordham University Archives, New York City). An example of western passing trends can be seen in Vic Klee, "Saints Seek Defense for Pass Game," unidentified newspaper article, Oct. 27, 1922, found in *Football Scrapbook, 1922–1924*, St. Mary's University Archives, Moraga, Calif.

49. Percy D. Haughton, *Football and How to Watch It*, 146, 162; Daly, *American Football*, 132, 134; Camp, "What Happened," 28.

50. The evolving defensive strategies being used to combat the forward pass and the increased deception by the offensive backfields are discussed to some extent in Camp, "Camp Reviews 1923 Football," 20; and H. G. Salsinger, "Football Strategy," 20, 41.

51. *Princeton Alumni Weekly,* Nov. 16, 1921; *Daily Princetonian,* Nov. 15, 1926; *Notre Dame Scholastic,* Oct. 1923; Harry Cross, "Princeton Crushes Harvard," *New York Times,* Nov. 8, 1925; Robert F. Kelley, "Holy Cross Passes Beat Harvard," *New York Times,* Oct. 10, 1926.

52. "Forward Passing Is Favorite Dish for Midshipmen," *New Orleans Times-Picayune,* Oct. 22, 1922; Samuelson, *The Rose Bowl Game,* 272; Grantland Rice, "Oberlander Star as Dartmouth Swamps Cornell," *New York Herald Tribune,* Nov. 7, 1925; Allison Danzig, "Dartmouth Makes West Football Mad," *New York Times,* Nov. 14, 1925. See also "Dartmouth Rush Beats Harvard," *Kansas City Star,* Oct. 25, 1925.

53. For examples of the expanded use of the forward pass in the Big Ten, see *Iowa Alumnus,* Oct. 1, 15, 1923; *Minneapolis Tribune,* Nov. 4, 18, 1923; and Ray Schmidt, "Red Grange of Wheaton," *College Football Historical Society* 4, no. 3 (May 1991): 11–13. Benny Friedman of Michigan was regularly in the area of twenty pass attempts per game. For a sampling of items on Friedman, see *Dallas Morning News,* Oct. 26, 1924; *Kansas City Star,* Oct. 11, Nov. 1, 1925; *Joliet Evening Herald-News,* Nov. 15, 27, 1925; and *Chicago Tribune,* Oct. 3, 1926.

54. William Abbott, "Forward Passes Deciding Factor in Big Games," *Joliet Evening Herald-News,* Oct. 23, 1924; "Military Students' Failure at Aerial Game Proves Costly," *Minneapolis Tribune,* Oct. 14, 1923; *Notre Dame Scholastic,* 1924–1925; "Rockne Team Wins, 40 to 19," *Los Angeles Times,* Nov. 30, 1924; *Oakland Tribune,* Oct. 13, 1924; Ray Schmidt, "St. Mary's 1924 Mystery Game," *College Football Historical Society* 7, no. 3 (May 1994): 1–4; "St. Louis U. Wins," *Chicago Herald and Examiner,* Oct. 19, 1924.

55. *Missouri Alumnus,* Oct., Nov. 1920, Nov. 1924; *Notre Dame Scholastic,* 1924–1925; *St. Louis Globe-Democrat,* Oct. 10, 1926; *Missouri Student,* Oct. 26, 1926; *Columbia Missourian,* Oct. 11, 18, Nov. 8, 1926; *Kansas City Star,* Oct. 18, 1926.

56. For examples of passing statistics in 1925 southern football, see *Atlanta Constitution,* Oct. 18, Nov. 15, 27, 1925.

57. Danzig, *American Football,* 261; Kern Tips, *Football—Texas Style: An Illustrated History of the Southwest Conference,* 31; Joe Utay, "Southwestern Conference," in *Spalding's Official Intercollegiate Football Guide, 1924,* 79.

58. Camp, "Annual Review of the Season," in *Spalding's Official Intercollegiate Football Guide, 1925,* 21; *Dallas Morning News,* Oct. 26, 1924, Nov. 16, 23, 28, 1926; William B. Ruggles, "Sewanee Springs Threat with Air Attack," *Dallas Morning News,* Oct. 12, 1924. At the University of Oklahoma during the seasons of 1914–1915, Coach Bennie Owen installed a wide-open aerial attack that frequently included nearly thirty pass attempts a game, and the Sooners registered a whopping twenty-five touchdown passes in 1914. For detailed descriptions of Owen's 1914–1915 seasons, see Harold Keith, *Oklahoma Kickoff,* 276–314.

59. Purcell, "Gerry Mann," 7. For examples of statistics demonstrating SMU's struggling passing attack in 1925, see *Dallas Morning News,* Nov. 8, 15, 1925. Despite the near standoff between the SMU and Missouri aerial attacks, a Kansas City sportswriter, apparently impressed by SMU's pregame publicity, noted that "until today the forward pass of the [Missouri] Tigers had been feared by every team that opposed them, yet tonight the Tigers know pass formations they never dreamed existed" ("Hold the Tigers to a Tie," *Kansas City Star,* Oct. 17, 1926). See also "Mustangs Play Aerial Game," *Missouri Student,* Oct. 12, 1926. James Mark Purcell compiled the offensive statistics for the 1926 SMU team that showed Mann completing 42 of 114 pass attempts for 843 yards and 11 touchdowns, while as a team SMU completed 59 of 149 passes for 1,154 yards and averaged 144.2 yards per game passing and 210.4 yards rushing ("Gerry Mann," 4–7).

60. *Dallas Daily Times Herald,* Nov. 26, Oct. 24, 1926; *Dallas Morning News,* Oct. 3, 1926. The SWC received a surprise in a 1926 intersectional game when Kansas A&M (now Kansas State) completed

eleven of twenty passes for 142 yards on the way to defeating Texas, which attempted seventeen of its own aerials. For details on the 1927 Vanderbilt season, see Purcell, "Spears and Vandy," 1–5.

61. For detailed accounts of the 1928 SMU-Army game, see Allison Danzig, "Army Wins, 14 to 13," *New York Times*, Oct. 7, 1928; and George White, "S.M.U. First to Score," *Dallas Morning News*, Oct. 7, 1928.

62. *Missouri Alumnus*, Dec. 1928; Cas Adams, "Looking Them Over," *Ram*, Dec. 7, 1928.

63. Danzig and Brandwein, *Sport's Golden Age*, 144–45.

64. Tips, *Football—Texas Style*, 31; Danzig, *American Football*, 45–46. The week of the SMU-Army game in 1928 also saw plenty of mention of the forward pass in other region's of the country, including Fielding Yost's own syndicated article on the aerial game in which he stated that "forward passing has been an integral part of football play in the central west for many years" (*Joliet Evening Herald-News*, Nov. 1, 1928).

65. "Football or Baseball the National Game?" 61; Reed, "Football Lessons of 1924," 498; Abbott, "Forward Passes Deciding Factor."

66. "The New Order in Football Playing"; "Calls Forward Pass Evil," *New York Times*, Dec. 16, 1924; "Coaches See Need for Altering Pass," *New York Times*, Dec. 19, 1924.

67. W. V. Morgenstern, "East-West Clash over Play," *Chicago Herald and Examiner*, Dec. 25, 1924; "Zuppke and Rockne Back Forward Pass," *New York Times*, Dec. 25, 1924.

68. "Report of E. K. Hall, Chairman American Intercollegiate Football Rules Committee for the Year 1926," Box 50, Folder 13, Stagg Papers; W. O. McGeehan, "Down the Line," *New York Herald Tribune*, Mar. 22, 1926.

69. Stagg, "The New Five Yard Restriction to the Forward Pass Rule," undated memorandum; Bill Alexander to Stagg, Apr. 27, 1926; Yost to Stagg, Apr. 26, 1926, Box 51, Folder 14, Stagg Papers; "Majority Is Dissatisfied with Penalty," *New York Times*, Nov. 23, 1926. The eastern coaches were not satisfied with the initial version of the 5-yard-penalty rule on incomplete passes, and at their annual meeting in late 1926 a further change, never adopted into the rules, was proposed whereby the second incomplete pass in the same series of downs would result in possession of the football going over to the defensive team ("Officials to Endorse Changes").

70. Roper, *Football, Today and Tomorrow*, 68; Herbert Reed, "Nassau's Football Uprising." By late in the decade Stagg's Chicago teams were not regarded as among the leading passers, yet in 1927 the Maroons produced their first win over Penn, and a sportswriter noted, "Stagg's backfield aces passed and passed and passed until the bewildered Pennsylvanians became dizzy under the barrage" (Charles W. Dunkley, "Stagg Springs Surprise to Beat Penn," *Joliet Evening Herald-News*, Oct. 23, 1927). In 1929 the Maroons exceeded even this mark, as they completed eighteen of thirty-five pass attempts for a whopping 305 yards on the way to a 26-6 win over Washington ("Chicago Ruins Huskies," *Los Angeles Times*, Nov. 24, 1929).

71. "Football, Quo Vadis?"

6. Searching for the Notre Dame Experience

1. Carlson, *College Football Scorebook*; Houlgate, *Football Thesaurus*; James Whalen Sr., *Gridiron Greats Now Gone: The Heyday of 19 Former Consensus Top-20 College Football Programs*; *Fordham Today: On the Eve of the Sesquicentennial*, 7; Randy Andrada, *They Did It Every Time: The Saga of the Saint Mary's Gaels*, 18–20.

2. "Notre Dame's Open Play Amazes Army," *New York Times*, Nov. 2, 1913.

3. Charles R. Morris, *American Catholic*, 158–59. In 1926 the number of Roman Catholics in the United States was placed at 18,608,003, with the total U.S. population estimated to be 117,399,000 (Leo Rosten, ed., *Religions of America: Ferment and Faith in an Age of Crisis*, 442–46). See also Mark S. Massa,

Catholics and American Culture: Fulton Sheen, Dorothy Day, and the Notre Dame Football Team, 201; and Chester Gillis, *Roman Catholicism in America*, 71, 220. Gillis is one of the many sociologists who has identified American Catholics of the 1920s as a "culture within a culture."

4. Gerald R. Gems, "The Prep Bowl: Football and Religious Acculturation in Chicago, 1927–1963," 284, 293; Massa, *Catholics and American Culture*, 218; Herman J. Muller, *The University of Detroit, 1877–1977: A Centennial History*, ix.

5. "Loyola to Build Own Stadium," *New Orleans Times-Picayune*, Nov. 19, 1922; "University Owes Debt to Its Athletes," *Marquette Tribune*, Oct. 1, 1925; "St. Louis U. to Begin Work on Athletic Field," *St. Louis Times*, Nov. 25, 1929.

6. Jack James, "Found—a Man Who Finds Sport Page Does College a Whole Lot of Good," *San Francisco Call-Bulletin*, undated 1920 article, in *Football Scrapbook, 1918–1922*, St. Mary's College Archives; letter from presidents of St. Mary's and Santa Clara to the pastors of the Bay Area Diocese, Oct. 1922 (not specifically dated), Box 230, Folder "Football 1922," Madigan Collection, ibid.

7. "The Catholic Spirit," *Varsity Breeze*, Oct. 24, 1924, 4; letter from presidents of St. Mary's and Santa Clara to the pastors of the Bay Area, Oct. 1922 (not specifically dated), Box 230, Folder "Football 1922," Madigan Collection, St. Mary's College Archives.

8. Sperber, *Shake Down the Thunder*, 242.

9. Charles F. Donovan, David R. Dunigan, and Paul A. Fitzgerald, *History of Boston College: From the Beginnings to 1990*, 27, 139; *Boston Saturday Evening Transcript*, Oct. 30, 1915.

10. Jack Falla, *Till the Echoes Ring Again: A Pictorial History of Boston College Sports*, 15; Hasenfus, *Athletics at Boston College*, 18; *Ram*, Nov. 5, 1926. By 1928 the St. Louis University student publication was noting the poor attendance figures at Sportsman's Park, describing crowds of just three and four thousand (*Archive 1929* [St. Louis University yearbook], 175). See also *St. Louis Star*, Sept. 10, 1922. The 1923 Fordham–Holy Cross game attracted attendance of just three thousand to cavernous Yankee Stadium ("Holy Cross Trims Fordham," uncredited 1923 New York newspaper clipping in *Fordham Football Scrapbooks*, Fordham University Archives).

11. "Georgetown to Have Athletic Stadium," *Hoya*, Dec. 15, 1921; Muller, *University of Detroit*, 130. Original designs for the University of Detroit's new football stadium called for a seating capacity of seventy-five thousand, and the student newspaper pointed out that the new facility would exceed the size of the University of Michigan's Ferry Field and would be rivaled only by the stadia at Harvard and Yale. But these plans were quickly scaled back to a more realistic twenty thousand ("Detroit Team Again Honored," *Varsity News*, Dec. 7, 1921).

12. James F. Foley, "Hilltop Sport Mirror," *Marquette Tribune*, Nov. 11, 1926; "Stadium Scene of Archdiocese Golden Jubilee," *Marquette Tribune*, Oct. 1, 1925, 2; "Dorais Picks Line-Up," *Varsity News*, May 6, 1926, 2.

13. Muller, *University of Detroit*, 127–29.

14. Gems, "Prep Bowl," 286; Lester, *Stagg's University*, 261. Murray Sperber is among those individuals who have cited Chicago's decision concerning the Carlisle game as indicative of an anti–Notre Dame position (*Shake Down the Thunder*, 44, 132, 339).

15. Sperber, *Shake Down the Thunder*, 159–61; Walter Eckersall, "Nebraska Wins Over Notre Dame," *Chicago Tribune*, Oct. 24, 1915; "Varsity Plays Wonderful Game," *Notre Dame Scholastic*, Oct. 30, 1915, 124–27; Sperber, *Shake Down the Thunder*, 200–202, 292.

16. "Through the Eagle's Eye," *Heights*, Oct. 4, 1923; Carlson, *College Football Scorebook*, 904–5; "Marquette-Wisconsin Football Game Off," *Marquette Tribune*, Dec. 9, 1926.

17. John L. Griffith to Professor F. G. Higbee, Mar. 10, 1930, Athletics Box 1, Folder "Athletics Board of Control Correspondence Concerning 1929–30 Controversy," University of Iowa Archives.

18. Gems, "Prep Bowl," 295. See also Edward Madigan to Jack Coffey, June 22, 1933, Box 230, Folder "Fordham," Madigan Collection, St. Mary's College Archives.

19. "Jesuit Colleges Hold Athletic Conference," *Ram*, Jan. 6, 1922, 3. An example of the Jesuit Conference meetings is seen in 1921 when they considered the "universal migratory rule" that called for abolishing all athletic eligibility for any athlete transferring after having competed for his original college—the four schools deciding against this more extreme measure.

20. Hasenfus, *Athletics at Boston College*, 101. An example of the coverage of a mythical Jesuit Conference football pennant race can be found in Bill Daly, "Sportitorial," *Hoya*, Nov. 3, 10, 1921. The *Hoya* issue of Dec. 8, 1921, contains a cartoon of a Georgetown man sitting atop a world that is labeled "Jesuit Champions," while the accompanying article mentions that the *New York Tribune* had rated Georgetown as the number-seven team nationally. Examples of team standings and mythical Jesuit Conference champions being declared can be found in *Ram*, Dec. 5, 1924, Nov. 6, Dec. 4, 1925; *Heights*, Dec. 10, 1920, Nov. 11, 1923; and *Hoya*, Oct. 27, Nov. 24, 1921, Dec. 1, 1927. Examples of all-conference teams being selected from the Jesuit universities can be found in *Heights*, Dec. 14, 1922; and *Ram*, Dec. 12, 1924, Dec. 11, 1925, Dec. 10, 1926, Dec. 2, 1927, Dec. 7, 1928.

21. "Athletic Association Publishes Letter Game," *Ram*, Oct. 17, 1924, 4; "1927 Banner Year for Eagle Teams," *Heights*, Dec. 13, 1927, 4. The disagreement over visiting-team guarantees is described in a letter from Rev. William Eulin, president of Boston College, to Georgetown (Eulin to Rev. John Creeden, S.J., Dec. 14, 1923, Sports Box 3, Folder "Football, 1888–1940," Georgetown University Archives).

22. In 1929, the Fordham newspaper, always a leader in publicizing the mythical Jesuit Conference, did not select an all-conference football team but instead named an All-Metropolitan grid squad from the New York–area universities (Bill Lynch, "Looking Them Over," *Ram*, Dec. 6, 1929, 4). This change not only was in keeping with the public de-emphasis of the Jesuit school rivalries but also signaled Fordham's aggressive move into the scheduling of primarily secular-university football teams that would extend until World War II.

23. *Discover Marquette*; Houlgate, *Football Thesaurus*, 121; Raphael N. Hamilton, *The Story of Marquette University*, 114–18, 219–21; *Marquette University: Stadium Dedication*, booklet issued on Oct. 18, 1924.

24. "Holy Cross and Marquette Plan Football Game," *Marquette Tribune*, Oct. 14, 1926, 1; Fred Montiegel, "Hilltop Sport Mirror," *Marquette Tribune*, Nov. 10, 1927.

25. Joseph W. Berg, "Hilltop Sport Mirror," *Marquette Tribune*, Nov. 8, 1928, 10; "Hilltop Sport Mirror," *Marquette Tribune*, Dec. 13, 1928; Whalen, *Gridiron Greats*, 237–57.

26. Muller, *University of Detroit*, 1; Houlgate, *Football Thesaurus*, 58–59.

27. Muller, *University of Detroit*, 131, 153; "East's Critics Rate Titans as Leaders," *Varsity News*, Nov. 22, 1927, 1; "Titans Rated High," *Varsity News*, Dec. 7, 1927, 3; Whalen, *Gridiron Greats*, 120–29; *Varsity News*, Nov. 21, Dec. 5, 1928. A set of telegrams related to the battle over Dorais between Detroit and Gonzaga, dated Mar. 8, Dec. 3, 1924 (2), and Jan. 2, 1925, is found in the Dorais File, Folder 3, University of Detroit Archives.

28. "Saint Louis University," an unpublished memorandum history of the university approved by the Executive Board, Feb. 14, 1962, St. Louis University Archives; Christy Walsh, *College Football and All America Review*, 697–99.

29. Dent McSkimming, "Blue and White Secures Sportsman's Park," *St. Louis Globe-Democrat*, Sept. 22, 1919; "O'Rourke Will Take Charge of St. Louis Eleven," uncredited Aug. 1921 newspaper article found in *Saint Louis University Historical Scrapbooks*, Reel 1, St. Louis University Archives. Examples of the declarations of the new era for St. Louis athletics can be found in *The Archive: Being the Saint Louis University Year Book* of 1922 (p. 202) and 1923 (p. 268). Discussion of the 1922 Notre Dame game can be found in the *St. Louis Star* and *St. Louis Times* of Oct. 11, 1922.

30. *St. Louis Globe-Democrat*, Jan. 28, 1923; Walsh, *College Football*, 698. Coverage of Robert Mathews and his rapid departure from St. Louis can be found in the *St. Louis Post*, *St. Louis Star*, and *St. Louis Times* of Dec. 16, 1927; and *Varsity Breeze*, Dec. 21, 1927.

31. "Anderson, New Billikin Football Coach," *St. Louis Globe-Democrat*, Mar. 13, 1928; *The Archive (1928)*, 174; Walsh, *College Football*, 697–99; Whalen, *Gridiron Greats*, 276–77.

32. "The College History," in *Catalog of Courses: St. Mary's College of California* (Moraga, Calif.: St. Mary's, 2000), 1–2; Walsh, *College Football*, 702.

33. The turmoil during the 1920 season at St. Mary's is documented in the aftermath of the Cal game in a series of undated *San Francisco Call-Bulletin* newspaper clippings found in *St. Mary's Football Scrapbook, 1918–1922*, St. Mary's College Archives, concluding with "Schedule for Rest of Year Cancelled," on Oct. 15, 1920. Madigan's hiring with a three-year contract is described in *San Francisco Call-Bulletin*, Jan. 9, 1921.

34. *San Francisco Call-Bulletin*, Jan. 9, 1921; "Secret Practice for St. Mary's," an uncredited and undated 1921 newspaper clipping in *St. Mary's Football Scrapbook, 1918–1922*, St. Mary's College Archives. Madigan's early efforts in the spring of 1921 are reviewed in Vincent V. Foley, "Athletics," in *The Collegian*, an undated 1921 school newspaper article in Box 230, Folder "Football 1921," Madigan Collection, St. Mary's College Archives.

35. "Notre Dame Game Off," uncredited 1921 newspaper clipping in *St. Mary's Football Scrapbook, 1918–1922*, which also includes uncredited clippings concerning the alumni kickoff luncheon and the institution of a football training table.

36. Walsh, *College Football*, 703–4; *Los Angeles Times*, Nov. 7, 8, 1924; J. F. Coffey to Madigan, Dec. 7, 1929, Madigan Collection, St. Mary's College Archives; Frank Schoonmaker, "Pity the Poor Athlete"; Sperber, *Shake Down the Thunder*, 257. The Madigan Collection at the St. Mary's Archives contains a file of memorabilia, itineraries, and advertisements for many of the trips to New York to play Fordham.

37. Wallace, "This Football Business," 169; Carlson, *College Football Scorebook*, 557; McCarty, *All-America*, 275.

38. Massa, *Catholics and American Culture*, 203–4; "Rockne's Wonder-Teams Built on Notre Dame Men's Virility," *Notre Dame Scholastic* (1924–1925): 222–24; Massa, *Catholics and American Culture*, 206.

39. Rockne to Madigan, Sept. 9, 1930, Box 230, Madigan Collection, St. Mary's Archives; Rockne to R. M. Waldron, Jan. 24, 1924, Sports Box 3, Folder "Football, 1888–1940," Georgetown University Archives; Madigan to Rockne, Jan. 15, 1921, Box 15, Folder 110, UADR; telegrams between Dorais and John B. Scallen, Dec. 3, 1924, Jan. 2, 1925, Dorais File, Folder 3, University of Detroit Archives.

40. Rockne to Madigan, May 16, 1930, Box 230, Madigan Collection, St. Mary's Archives.

41. "Anderson, New Billikin Coach"; letter signed "Some of the Professors" to Charles E. Dorais, Apr. 24, 1933; James Hamilton to Dorais, Oct. 21, 1934, Dorais File, Folder 1, University of Detroit Archives.

42. The longtime ban on playing other Catholic schools was temporarily lifted in 1951 when Notre Dame played the University of Detroit, but the South Bend school would not play another parochial opponent again until Boston College in 1975 (Carlson, *College Football Scorebook*, 555–57).

43. "ND-Tiger Football Game Possible," *Varsity News*, Oct. 6, 1920. "No Game with Notre Dame," *Varsity News*, Oct. 13, 1920, and similar articles on Dec. 15, 1920, Dec. 7, 1921; Charles L. Bruce, "Arranging a University Football Schedule," *Varsity News*, Holiday Number, 1923–1924, 9; R. J. Ducote to Rockne, Sept. 11, 1924, Box 15, Folder 8, UADR. Concerning St. Mary's attempts at scheduling Notre Dame, see George T. Cameron to Rev. Archbishop Edward Hanna, Feb. 20, 1930, Box 229; and Rockne to Madigan, Feb. 26, 1930, Folder "Games," Madigan Collection, St. Mary's College Archives. Examples of the ongoing attempts to get Georgetown a game with Notre Dame can be found in letters from Lou

Little to Rockne dated Oct. 29, 1925, Jan. 31, Oct. 4, 1927, Sept. 27, 1928, Box 14, Folders 159–60, UADR. Examples of Rockne's wide-ranging rejection excuses to Georgetown can be found in letters from Rockne to Little dated Oct. 26, 1926, Feb. 4, Oct. 1, 7, 1927, Box 14, Folders 159–60, UADR. Telegrams, Little to Rockne and the reply, Nov. 16, 1926, Box 14, Folder 159, UADR. The request to hire a former Notre Dame player at Columbia is in Rockne to Little, Dec. 24, 1929, Box 14, Folder 160, UADR.

44. Sperber, *Shake Down the Thunder*, 99, 129, 256–57; Jesuit Conference managers of athletics to graduate manager of athletics, Notre Dame, May 18, 1927, Box 14, Folder 160, UADR. In responding to an inquiry from a newspaper reporter with the *South Bend Tribune* early in the 1930s, Madigan replied, "We comply with every rule of the Pacific Coast Conference in regard to all matters, including academic, athletic and business relationship. . . . Furthermore, [the athletes] must maintain a scholastic standing superior to that established by the Pacific Coast Conference in order to compete on St. Mary's teams" (Madigan to E. J. Meeham, Dec. 21, 1933, Box 228, Folder "M," Madigan Collection, St. Mary's College Archives).

45. Shortly after Anderson was named as Rockne's successor, Madigan wrote, "I think I express the attitude of every Notre Dame man when I say . . . we are working harder with you than ever that the enviable prestige that Rock built in his school and in his men shall not perish" (Madigan to Anderson, Apr. 29, 1931). The secret sharing of scouting information is seen in Anderson to Madigan, Sept. 14, 29, 1931. All three letters are in the Madigan Collection, St. Mary's Archives. A small indication of the critical feelings about Rockne by secular-school coaches is seen in Stagg's "Memorandum of Conversation with Judge Walter P. Steffen," Dec. 13, 1928, Box 24, Folder 6, Stagg Papers. Murray Sperber also discusses the antagonism directed toward Notre Dame by the Big Ten at some length in his *Shake Down the Thunder*.

46. Charles J. Deane, S.J., to Father McGinley, Mar. 20, 1949, Football File, Fordham University Archives; Robert Francis Mahoney, "Gargan Outlines His Athletic Policy," *Ram*, Dec. 9, 1921; "One Year Rule for Fordham Athletics," uncredited 1922 newspaper clipping, *Fordham Football Scrapbook, 1922*, Fordham University Archives; Seward A. Simons to Rockne, Dec. 14, 1921, Box 6, Folder 96, UADR; Father Edward J. Ryan, S.J., to James Hagerty, Nov. 13, 1922, Box 230, Folder "Football 1922," Madigan Collection, St. Mary's College Archives.

47. Roger Kiley to Rockne, Aug. 15, 1929, Box 14, Folder 71, UADR; Rockne to Kiley, July 25, 1929, Box 14, Folder 71, UADR; Rockne to Kiley, Apr. 9, 1929, ibid., Folder 70. An example of the controversy that sometimes arose over the recruiting by Catholic colleges is seen in 1925, when Loyola of New Orleans withdrew from the Southern Intercollegiate Athletic Association in a dispute over the eligibility of three football players who had transferred in from other schools (*New Orleans Times-Picayune*, Oct. 2, 29, 1925).

48. Rev. William Devlin, S.J., to Rev. J. N. Dinand, S.J., June 20, 1925, Box 5, Folder 11, Devlin Papers, Boston College Archives.

49. Dinand to Devlin, June 23, 1925; Devlin to Dinand, June 24, 1925, ibid.

50. "Subsidies at Hilltop Denied by Lou Little," *Washington Post*, Oct. 24, 1929; Little to Father Rector (W. Coleman Nevils, S.J.), May 4, 1929, Box 3, File "Sports: Football 1888–1940," Georgetown University Archives.

51. "Lou Little Resigns Position at Hilltop," *Hoya*, Dec. 11, 1929; Morris A. Bealle, *The Georgetown Hoyas*, 136. The agreement to pay Little 10 percent of the annual net profits from football is contained in a memorandum by Rev. Vincent McDonough, S.J., June 11, 1926, Box 3, File "Sports: Football 1888–1940," Georgetown University Archives. See also Little to Nevils, Sept. 22, 1929; and an undated late-1929 letter from Little to Nevils, both found in ibid. Examples of Little's denials of receiving offers to leave Georgetown can be seen in *Washington Post*, Jan. 28, 1929; and *Washington Star*, Dec. 3, 1929.

52. E. A. Batchelor, "Personal and Confidential," *Detroit Saturday Night*, Nov. 30, 1929, and "Extract from Speech of Rev. John P. McNichols at Alumni Banquet, 1930," are found in Father J. P. McNichols File, Folder 2, University of Detroit Archives.

53. Albon Holden, "Football Is Abolished at Loyola," *Chicago Herald and Examiner*, Dec. 5, 1930; "Loyola U. Drops Intercollegiate Football Play," *Chicago Evening Post*, Dec. 5, 1930; "Public Appeal Overdone, Says School Leader," *Chicago Tribune*, Dec. 5, 1930; *Chicago Daily News*, Dec. 5, 1930.

54. Morris, *American Catholic*, 270.

7. Black College Football: A Separate Gridiron World

1. Oriard, *King Football*, 324. See also Patrick Miller, "To 'Bring the Race along Rapidly': Sport, Student Culture, and Educational Mission at Historically Black Colleges During the Interwar Years." Valuable information on the organization of black colleges and universities into conferences may be found in Edwin Bancroft Henderson, *The Negro in Sports*, 238–68.

2. Kenneth Estell, ed., *The African-American Almanac*, 29–32; Robin D. G. Kelley and Earl Lewis, eds., *To Make Our World Anew: A History of African Americans*, 406; W. E. B. DuBois, "Opinion" (1926). William Slosson, a historian from the period, has written that "the economic situation of the American Negro improved during and after the World War. Though due in part to the competitive bidding of field and factory for his services, the improvement came even more from the spread of education" (*Great Crusade*, 261).

3. Estell, *The African-American Almanac*, 29–32; Charles M. Christian, with the assistance of Sari J. Bennett, *Black Saga: The African American Experience*, 317, 325, 328.

4. The earliest documented football games between black colleges have been discussed in several works, including Ocania Chalk, *Black College Sport*, 197–99; Michael Hurd, *Black College Football, 1892–1992: One Hundred Years of History, Education, and Pride*, 27–31; and Roger B. Saylor, *Historically Black Colleges Football Teams Record Book, 1892–1999*, 1. The need for a thoroughly researched history of football as played by the historically black colleges is one of the major challenges still facing modern sport historians.

5. A brief amount of information concerning the organization of the first two black athletic conferences is found in Chalk, *Black College Sport*, 222; Hurd, *Black College Football*, 145, 149; and Saylor, *Historically Black Colleges*, 1.

6. In 1914 Howard edged past Hampton by a score of 6-0 in a game that was described by a sportswriter as "another story of a team with open football overcoming a powerful opponent with straight football. Hampton's chief plays were a mass play through center and . . . as soon as Howard had mastered these two they were helpless." This statement could easily have referred to the transformation of offensive play that was taking place in white college football of the East and Midwest during the same period. The importance of capable coaching was also becoming widely recognized among the black colleges during the same period; Howard's win over Fisk University in 1916 prompted one sportswriter to take note of the Washington team being the "best coached team" that had appeared in the mid-South to that time. Another writer specifically credited the outstanding team at Wilberforce in 1915 to the work of Coach Peterson. *Indianapolis Freeman*, 19 Dec. 1914; "Defeated but Not Disgraced," *Indianapolis Freeman*, 2 Dec. 1916; "Fisk Ties Wilberforce," *Indianapolis Freeman*, 13 Nov. 1915. Historian Gerald Gems has taken note of the improving sport at the historically black colleges prior to World War I, citing the *Chicago Defender*'s claim that the game had become an "obsession" for these schools—including the trustees, alumni, faculty, and women—as early as 1910 (*Pride, Profit, and Patriarchy*, 117).

7. Lincoln University was mentioned as one of those schools ready to field a football team that featured bigger, faster, and stronger players, while Hampton showed itself ready to begin more fully exploiting the use of the passing game and the open style of play (*Indianapolis Freeman*, 15 Nov. 1919; Chalk, *Black College Sport*, 226–27). An account of the Tuskegee forfeit to Morehouse over a dispute can be found in the *Indianapolis Freeman*, Nov. 22, 1919.

8. W. E. B. DuBois, "Opinion" (1920). Historian Patrick Miller has described the various rituals surrounding black college football games as being "significant in cultural terms." The social rituals provided black undergraduates with a sense of "belonging" within the overall American collegiate world through the sharing of various football traditions, while for black society in general they afforded an opportunity to stage events that were increasingly interpreted as a mark of higher education and culture within civilized American society ("To 'Bring the Race along Rapidly,'" 119). Gems is another who has contended that the "parallel sporting culture" constructed by African Americans provided them with "some sense of inclusion in the mainstream sporting activities" and an opportunity to dispel "notions of inferiority" (*Pride, Profit, and Patriarchy*, 113, 115).

9. P. Bernard Young Jr., "Morehouse-Bluefield Game Will Draw Record Crowd," *Chicago Defender*, Nov. 17, 1928. In 1924 the *Pittsburgh Courier* provided a list of dos and don'ts for fans of black college football who were attending the big games. Among them were, "Don't wait until the last minute to purchase your tickets; Don't rush the gates, get in line; and Don't flash large sums of money in a crowd" (Ganaway, "Don'ts-for-Football-Games," *Pittsburgh Courier*, Nov. 1, 1924). See also Chester L. Washington, "Norfolk All Het Up," *Pittsburgh Courier*, Oct. 25, 1924.

10. "Defeated but Not Disgraced"; *Pittsburgh Courier*, Nov. 29, 1924. Before the 1924 Howard-Lincoln game at Washington, D.C., being played at the city's major league stadium, William Nunn wrote of the "air of enthusiasm and excitement pervading the very heart of things. . . . [T]he flash and flare of college enthusiasm is manifest in all quarters of the historic old city. . . . All is expectancy; all savors of the feverish pleasure of witnessing a fair struggle on the football grid. . . . The hotels are filled" ("Nation's Capitol [*sic*] All Agog as 30th Annual Classic Looms," *Pittsburgh Courier*, Nov. 29, 1924). See also *Indianapolis Freeman*, Dec. 6, 1919; and *Pittsburgh Courier*, Nov. 14, 1925.

11. Richard H. Cook Jr., "Cotton Scores Two Panther Tallies," *Pittsburgh Courier*, Oct. 19, 1929; Chalk, *Black College Sport*, 232; "Walker Is Another Red Grange, Claim," *Pittsburgh Courier*, Nov. 8, 1924; "Post-Season Contest in Atlanta," *Chicago Defender*, Nov. 26, 1927.

12. W. Rollo Wilson, "Eastern Snapshots," *Pittsburgh Courier*, Oct. 25, 1924; William G. Nunn, "Ritchie's Field Goal Gives Wilberforce 3-2 Victory," *Pittsburgh Courier*, Dec. 4, 1926.

13. The forfeited game by Hampton is described in the *Indianapolis Freeman*, Dec. 11, 1920. The controversy leading to Lincoln's forfeit against Virginia Union in 1921 is described in Frank Young, "Sport Editorial: Poor Officials," *Chicago Defender*, Nov. 26, 1921. Descriptions of the Wilberforce incident can be found in "Savoy Helps Howard Win Grid Debate," *Chicago Defender*, Nov. 12, 1927.

14. "Two Students Suspended for Unwarranted Attack," *Chicago Defender*, Nov. 13, 1926. Referee Campbell's claims of bribery attempts and displayed weapons by Simmons's followers were supported by the other game officials. It should probably not be surprising to learn that the Louisville, Kentucky, school dropped football after the 1930 season ("Referee Has His Side of Controversy," *Chicago Defender*, Nov. 27, 1926).

15. "Alabama State President Rushes to Protect Coach," *Chicago Defender*, Nov. 19, 1927.

16. "Fay Says," *Chicago Defender*, Dec. 15, 1928. Examples of Young's editorials on football controversies can be seen in the *Chicago Defender*, Nov. 26, 1921, Nov. 11, 25, 1922. An example of conference actions intended to improve the sportsmanship attending black college football can be seen in 1927, when the Colored Intercollegiate Athletic Association adopted a league rule that declared any school

forfeiting a football game to be immediately ineligible for the conference championship (Charles H. Williams, "C.I.A.A. Takes Drastic Action," *Chicago Defender*, Dec. 17, 1927).

17. "Sport Editorial: Poor Officials," *Chicago Defender*, Nov. 26, 1921. Early on, Young of the *Defender* was a consistent voice in expressing concerns over the financial impact that the many disputes and game forfeits might have on black college athletic programs. See "Fay Says: Poor Sportsmanship," *Chicago Defender*, Nov. 11, 1922; and "Fay Says," *Chicago Defender*, 25 Nov. 1922.

18. Young, "Real Truth of Disputed Pass in Wilberforce Game with Howard," *Chicago Defender*, Jan. 2, 1926; "Fay Says," *Chicago Defender*, Dec. 15, 1928.

19. "Howard Making Progress," *Indianapolis Freeman*, Nov. 1, 1924.

20. Miller, "To 'Bring the Race along Rapidly,'" 126–27.

21. The controversy over Howard using an ineligible player is covered very well in the *Chicago Defender* of Dec. 29, 1924; and "Lincoln Will Uphold C.I.A.A. Ruling," *Pittsburgh Courier*, Dec. 27, 1924.

22. "Lincoln Will Uphold C.I.A.A. Ruling"; *Chicago Defender*, Dec. 20, 1924. After Howard's resignation from the CIAA in December 1924, the conference then inducted North Carolina A&T into the vacated membership slot.

23. Miller, "To 'Bring the Race along Rapidly,'" 127.

24. Christian, *Black Saga*, 339; Louis R. Lautier, "Fraternities Played a Part in Defeat," *Chicago Defender*, 12 Dec. 1925; Hurd, *Black College Football*, 164.

25. Lincoln's athletic association quickly responded with the school's willingness to "endeavor to arrive at an amiable agreement," and in fact the Pennsylvania university was readmitted to the CIAA after a meeting on Nov. 4, 1926 (Charles Williams, "Howard Balks on Joining C.I.A.A.," *Chicago Defender*, Dec. 18, 1926).

26. Louis R. Lautier, "Washington Eleven Accused of Lying Down," *Chicago Defender*, Oct. 8, 1927; Chalk, *Black College Sport*, 245.

27. Lautier, "Washington Eleven Accused"; Lautier, "Strikers at Howard Face Prexy's Rule," *Chicago Defender*, Oct. 15, 1927; "Howard Grid Men Turn Out for Practice," *Chicago Defender*, Oct. 22, 1927; Lautier, "Strikers at Howard." Although *Crisis* magazine occasionally gave some attention to student discontent in nonathletic areas, it is interesting to note that no coverage was provided in 1927 for the football affair at Howard. In his report on the 1927 season for *Crisis*, Paul Jones wrote only that "in the early weeks of the season morale was at low tide, and the team could not muster that fighting spirit which wins football games" ("Foot Ball in Negro Colleges, 1927").

28. Lautier, "Howard University Prexy for Clean Sport," *Chicago Defender*, Nov. 2, 1929; "18th Annual C.I.A.A. Meet Makes Awards," *Chicago Defender*, Dec. 15, 1928. The controversy over football at Howard University hit the coaches also, with Louis Watson leaving after the 1927 season and Charley West departing after serving as head coach in 1928.

29. Wilson, "Howard Loses Again, Student Unrest Grows," *Pittsburgh Courier*, 2 Nov. 1929. An article in the *Amsterdam News* contended that President Johnson's actions toward the Howard football team had been motivated by a fear of disclosures that might be in the forthcoming Carnegie Report. A discussion of the *Amsterdam News* article of Nov. 22, 1929, is found in Chalk, *Black College Sport*, 252. See also Saylor, *Historically Black Colleges*, 42.

30. *Amsterdam News*, Nov. 22, 1929.

31. Edwin B. Henderson, *Messenger*, June 1925, 234. The Henderson quote on the circulation of black newspapers can also be found in Patrick Miller and David K. Wiggins, eds., *Sport and the Color Line: Black Athletes and Race Relations in Twentieth-Century America*, 274.

32. Young, "Fay Says," *Chicago Defender*, Dec. 15, 1928. An example of the expanded and professional coverage provided for black college football can be seen for the Thanksgiving Day games in

1928, when the *Pittsburgh Courier* had bylined, and well-written, pregame and game reports for three big matchups (*Pittsburgh Courier*, Dec. 1, 1928).

33. Young, "Fay Says," *Chicago Defender*, Dec. 17, 1927.

34. Wilson, "Hampton, Lincoln Await Zero Hour," *Pittsburgh Courier*, Nov. 2, 1929; Wilson, "Sports Shorts," *Pittsburgh Courier*, Nov. 16, 1929.

35. Oriard, *King Football*, 327.

36. "Southern College Elevens Open Football Season," *Chicago Defender*, Oct. 8, 1921; "Wilberforce May Stop Roger Williams," *Chicago Defender*, Oct. 22, 1921; Young, "We Live to Learn," *Chicago Defender*, Nov. 12, 1921; Robert Butler, "Wilberforce Downs Roger Williams," *Chicago Defender*, Nov. 12, 1921; "Roger Williams U. Takes Wilberforce into Camp," *Chicago Tribune*, Nov. 7, 1921. Pregame ticket sales for the 1921 Wilberforce–Roger Williams game were generally available through outlets located in Chicago's South Side black communities. One article mentioned, "Tickets are on sale at all drug stores operated by the Race." It was reported that the proceeds from the game would go to the endowment funds of the two colleges—Wilberforce a Methodist school and Roger Williams having Baptist backing. See pregame dispatches in *Chicago Defender*, Oct. 22, 29, Nov. 5, 1921.

37. *Chicago Defender*, Oct. 19, 1929; "Prairie View to Play Wiley at Dallas Fair," *Chicago Defender*, Jan. 12, 1929.

38. "Negro Football Teams Play Today," *New Orleans Times-Picayune*, Dec. 13, 1924. Examples of notes on separate seating and ticket-sales locations for white spectators can be found in "Negro Teams Play at Fair Monday," *Dallas Morning News*, Oct. 18, 1925; and Young, "Paul Quinn and Wiley Ready," *Chicago Defender*, Nov. 21, 1925.

39. "Wilberforce–West Virginia Clash at Columbus Turkey Day," *Chicago Defender*, Nov. 7, 1925. Paul W. L. Jones of *Crisis* magazine was one of the sportswriters calling for more intersectional play among the black college football teams: "Certainly they would awaken keener competition, bring about changes in styles of play and introduce new methods, thus making the game more attractive to fans and spectators" ("Foot Ball in Negro Colleges in 1924").

40. Young, "Sport Editorial," *Chicago Defender*, Nov. 19, 1921; Young, "Howard Must Bolster Up to Win from Lincoln," *Chicago Defender*, Nov. 25, 1922; "Football Classic Is Insured," *Chicago Defender*, Nov. 25, 1922; *Pittsburgh Courier*, Nov. 16, Dec. 7, 1929. See also Wilson, "Sports Shorts," *Pittsburgh Courier*, Nov. 9, 1929, and "Howard to Meet Lincoln U.," *Chicago Defender*, Nov. 22, 1930.

41. *Indianapolis Freeman*, Nov. 8, 1919; "Pollard and Bird Coach Lincoln," *Chicago Defender*, Oct. 9, 1920; "Pollard Explains," *Chicago Defender*, Dec. 18, 1920.

42. "Here Is Another All-Southern Team," *Chicago Defender*, Dec. 29, 1923; Hurd, *Black College Football*, 161, 164; "Fay Names All-Americans," *Chicago Defender*, Dec. 19, 1925; C. L. Abbott, "All-Southern 1925 Elevens Are Selected," *Chicago Defender*, Dec. 12, 1925; Young, "Ben Stevenson Leads Mates in Victory," *Chicago Defender*, Nov. 12, 1927.

43. "Meet Lincoln Lions in South vs. North Battle," *Chicago Defender*, Oct. 29, 1927; "Stevenson Stars as Booker T's Win," *Chicago Defender*, Nov. 5, 1927; Eric Roberts, "Dixie Doings," *Chicago Defender*, Nov. 12, 1927.

44. Jones, "Foot Ball in Negro Colleges in 1925," 221–22; Abbott, "Football in South Given Once Over," *Chicago Defender*, Dec. 25, 1926; "Brice Taylor Starts Work at Claflin," *Chicago Defender*, Sept. 17, 1927; "Brice Taylor at Southern U.," *Chicago Defender*, Sept. 15, 1928; "Lincoln University Heads Discharge Coach Morrison," *Chicago Defender*, Nov. 17, 1928. The next year Jones led off his report on the 1926 season by calling it the "greatest year in the history of Negro college foot ball" ("Foot Ball in Negro Colleges in 1926"). Historian David Wiggins has noted that Henderson of the *Messenger* was another who consistently stressed the need for conferences and emphasized "the importance of organizational

structure and administrative oversight" in responding to many of the problems that had plagued black intercollegiate sport through the early 1920s (Miller and Wiggins, *Color Line*, 274).

45. J. B. Simms, "Wilberforce and West Va. Tie," *Chicago Defender*, Dec. 8, 1928; "Bluefield in 129 to 0 Victory," *Chicago Defender*, Nov. 24, 1928; "Wiley and Bluefield to Meet," *Chicago Defender*, Dec. 8, 1928; "Wildcats Toss Hat in Ring," *Pittsburgh Courier*, Dec. 15, 1928.

46. Washington, "Howard Ties Blues in Bitter Battle," *Pittsburgh Courier*, Nov. 10, 1928.

47. "Football Is Fatal to Star of Claflin U.," *Chicago Defender*, Dec. 17, 1921; "Howard at Wilberforce," *Chicago Defender*, Nov. 1, 1924; "Sam Carline Breaks Neck in Scrimmage," *Chicago Defender*, Oct. 1, 1927.

48. Bob Royce, "All America Bill Lewis," *College Football Historical Society* 2, no. 4 (Aug. 1989): 8–9; McCarty, *All-America*, 3.

49. McCarty, *All-America*, 38; "Pollard Making Football History," *Indianapolis Freeman*, Dec. 9, 1916. Michigan State's backfield in 1918 included halfback Harry Graves—later head football coach for many years at Wilberforce—who scored the winning touchdown in the Spartans' 13-7 win over a Notre Dame team that included George Gipp ("Michigan Aggies Earn Win," *Chicago Tribune*, Nov. 17, 1918).

50. McCarty, *All-America*, 46, 52. Robert Francis was a black player who logged substantial playing time at end and tackle for the University of California in the 1925 and 1926 seasons. An article in the black media implied that Francis had initially been held out of action at Cal because of his race by Coach Andy Smith and was promoted to the varsity only when Nibs Price took over the head coaching position ("University of California Is Promoting Colored Star," *Pittsburgh Courier*, Nov. 6, 1926; Morse, *California Football History*, 150, 155). See also "Michigan State Has Negro Star," *Pittsburgh Courier*, Nov. 8, 1924; *Pittsburgh Courier*, Nov. 7, 1925; "Brilliant Brown Back," *Pittsburgh Courier*, Oct. 26, 1929; and "Star Ohio State Tackle," *Pittsburgh Courier*, Nov. 16, 1929.

51. "Who Was Jack Trice?" *Iowa State Football Media Guide* (1997): 236.

52. Charles H. Martin, "Racial Change and 'Big-Time' College Football in Georgia: The Age of Segregation, 1892–1957." Martin has also identified the postseason football bowl games that were initiated in the South during the 1930s as major advocates of the ideology of white supremacy and insistent upon the application of the gentlemen's agreement for their events ("Integrating New Year's Day: The Racial Politics of College Bowl Games in the American South").

53. "Yale Threatens to Drop Harvard for Using Negro," *Philadelphia Press*, Nov. 22, 1904.

54. Ibid.; "Negro Player Not Attacked," an uncredited newspaper article of Dec. 10, 1904, found in the Camp Papers, Yale University Archives.

55. "Pitt and Navy Bar Colored Grid Star," *Pittsburgh Courier*, Oct. 30, 1926. "Football Stirs Two Rival Camps," an Associated Press dispatch in the *Joliet Evening Herald-News*, Oct. 29, 1926. Typical accounts in the mainstream press of Colgate's two 1926 games in which Ray Vaughn did not appear can be found in the *New York Times* of Oct. 17, 24, 1926. At the end of the 1926 season Vaughn received his varsity letter, and he would continue on to also play for Colgate during the seasons of 1927 and 1928 ("Colgate Awards Football Letters," *New York Times*, Dec. 11, 1926).

56. "Prejudice Will Keep N.Y.U. Star Out of Ga. Game," *Chicago Defender*, Oct. 26, 1929; "Yellow Label on Football Player When He Dodges Issue," *Chicago Defender*, Nov. 2, 1929; "Meyers Lost During Game with Georgia," *Chicago Defender*, Nov. 16, 1929. An extensive examination of the Myers incident can be found in Martin, "Racial Change," 540–44.

57. "No Discrimination at Duquesne University," *Pittsburgh Courier*, Nov. 9, 1929. During the following season of 1930, Ray Kemp and the Duquesne team traveled to Chicago for a matchup against Loyola University. While in Chicago, the collegiate team stayed at the prestigious Edgewater Beach Hotel, and Kemp was allowed to stay there without any reported incidents ("Pittsburgh Eleven vs.

Loyola," *Chicago Defender*, Oct. 11, 1930). In one of his books, Henderson of the *Messenger* devotes an entire chapter to short overviews of the football careers of many black athletes who played at predominantly white colleges (*The Negro in Sports*, 86–126).

8. Lords of the Prairie

1. John S. Steckbeck, *Fabulous Redmen: The Carlisle Indians and Their Famous Football Teams*, 5. See also Francis Paul Prucha, *The Great Father: The United States and the American Indians*, 234–37. Prucha says that for Carlisle, playing colleges such as Harvard, Cornell, and Pennsylvania left the impression that the Indian school was at a comparable academic level, when in fact it was basically a grammar school. In college football's early days it was common for teams from four-year institutions to regularly schedule noncollege opposition. In 1904 the Big Ten formally endorsed the continued play of its schools against Haskell when it declared that the Indian school was "on a basis of athletic equality" with the conference's schools (*Joliet Evening Herald-News*, Dec. 9, 1928).

2. David Wallace Adams, *Education for Extinction: American Indians and the Boarding School Experience, 1875–1928*, 184–85. Adams writes that founder Richard Pratt saw Carlisle's successful football teams as winning support for the idea that "Indians, if given the opportunity, were capable of competing with whites not only on the football field but in society as well."

3. Loretta Mary Granzer, "Indian Education at Haskell Institute, 1884–1937" (master's thesis, Univ. of Nebraska, 1937), 1, 8.

4. "Report of Committee on Indian Affairs," *Congressional Record*, 47 Cong., 1881, 1st sess., 6152–53. See also Granzer, "Indian Education at Haskell," 15.

5. "Book Review: The Earth Shall Weep," *Chicago Tribune*, May 23, 1999; Adams, *Education for Extinction*, x, 97, 118–19; Robert W. Wheeler, *Jim Thorpe: World's Greatest Athlete*, 15.

6. *Self-Study Report, 1997/1998: In Preparation for Visit by North Central Association* (Lawrence: Haskell Indian Nations University, 1998), 5; Robert F. Berkhofer Jr., *The White Man's Indian: Images of the American Indian from Columbus to the Present*, 155, 171.

7. Granzer, "Indian Education at Haskell," 1, 18, 20–21; *Self-Study Report, 1997/98*, 4.

8. *Self-Study Report, 1997/98*, 4; Granzer, "Indian Education at Haskell," 103–4; Prucha, *Great Father*, 284; Adams, *Education for Extinction*, 154; Granzer, "Indian Education at Haskell," 114, 156–57. For a discussion of the evolution of Indian educational programs in the early 1900s, with emphasis on vocational training, see Frederick E. Hoxie, *A Final Promise: The Campaign to Assimilate the Indians, 1880–1920*, 190–207.

9. Houlgate, *Football Thesaurus*, 86; Steckbeck, *Fabulous Redmen*, 133.

10. William K. Powers, *Indians of the Northern Plains*, 183; "Differences Between Red and White Football Material." David Adams has written that football to the Indian players was a "ritualistic replay of frontier conflict" and was about "another time and space"—about history and myth—and that Indian-white football was "deep play" (*Education for Extinction*, 188–90).

11. Steckbeck, *Fabulous Redmen*, 6–7, 51–52; Frank W. McDonald, "Unusual Background for Beer Distributor" (unpublished memoir in Haskell Archives, 1976), 10. Today, the Carlisle facility serves as a school within the U.S. military's War College system.

12. Houlgate, *Football Thesaurus*, 86; *Indian Leader*, Oct. 17, 1919; *Literary Digest*, Dec. 11, 1920, 79. One of the most glaring examples of racially stereotyped commentary concerning the Indian personality is to be found in a 1926 *Boston Globe* cartoon that shows a vicious-looking Indian with a tomahawk about to scalp an eagle (the Boston College mascot). The eagle is saying, "That's just like an Indian—to sneak right up from behind" (*Boston Sunday Globe*, Nov. 14, 1926).

13. *Indian Leader,* Oct. 31, 1919. For a discussion of changing the Indian students' clothing, length of hair, and names, as part of the assault on tribal identities, see Adams, *Education for Extinction,* 103–8.

14. *Cincinnati Enquirer,* Nov. 28, 1919; *Indian Leader,* Dec. 5, 1919.

15. *Indian Leader,* Sept. 10, 1920; McDonald, "Unusual Background," 7.

16. Granzer, "Indian Education at Haskell," 159; McDonald, "Unusual Background," 8; Prucha, *Great Father,* 285; Granzer, "Indian Education at Haskell," 165, 168.

17. *Indian Leader,* Sept. 23, 1921. Haskell officials had to regularly address allegations of recruiting and a lack of eligibility rules: "The Haskell football authorities state that there is an impression out that the school runs its football on a semi-professional basis. This is denied" (*Wichita Eagle,* Sept. 25, 1926). Though perhaps not openly recruiting athletes, it was well known that the Kansas Indian school was always looking for top athletes, as indicated by this student newspaper item: "The athletic department at Haskell is always glad to receive information regarding good football material that might be interested in Haskell as a school" (*Indian Leader,* Nov. 14, 1924).

18. *Indian Leader,* Nov. 11, 25, 1921. In 1921, on the football team's first-ever extended stay away from school, it is significant that the *Indian Leader* carried no reports of the players doing anything other than practicing football.

19. *Indian Leader,* Sept. 29, Oct. 13, Nov. 24, Dec. 29, 1922.

20. "Indian Athletic Hall of Fame Biographical Sheet—John Levi," Hall of Fame files that are maintained in the Haskell Archives; *Indian Leader,* 15 Dec. 1922. A sportswriter wrote the following description of Levi in 1923: "Levi is a star of no mean attributes. There probably is not a faster back of his weight, 190 pounds, on American collegiate gridirons today. . . . With his speed he combines a shifty, sidestepping style of running" (Hubert M. Dustin, "Minnesota Is Rushed by Indians," *Minneapolis Tribune,* Oct. 14, 1923).

21. McDonald, "Unusual Background," 11.

22. Berkhofer, *White Man's Indian,* 101–3; McDonald, "Unusual Background," 41.

23. "Football with a Haskell War Whoop."

24. Hoxie, *Final Promise,* 241; Lawrence C. Kelly, *The Assault on Assimilation: John Collier and the Origins of Indian Policy Reform,* 141; Berkhofer, *White Man's Indian,* 176.

25. The racial stereotyping that typified so much of the newspaper coverage of Carlisle's football teams is effectively discussed at length in Michael Oriard, *Reading Football: How the Popular Press Created an American Spectacle,* 229–47.

26. *Indian Leader,* Sept. 28, Oct. 5, 12, 19, 1923.

27. *Indian Leader,* Nov. 9, 16, 23, 1923; *New York Times,* Nov. 17, 1923; McDonald, "Unusual Background," 41. For a complete discussion of the pregame activities concerning finances and publicity for the game in New York against the Quantico Marines, see Frank W. McDonald, *John Levi of Haskell,* 19–26.

28. *New York Times,* Nov. 17, 18, 1923; *Indian Leader,* Nov. 23, 1923; McDonald, *John Levi of Haskell,* 26, 28.

29. *Indian Leader,* Nov. 30, Dec. 7, 14, 1923.

30. *Los Angeles Times,* Dec. 21, 22, 1923.

31. *Los Angeles Times,* Dec. 26, 1923; Houlgate, *Football Thesaurus,* 86; McCarty, *All-America,* 63.

32. *Indian Leader,* Sept. 26, 1924, Sept. 18, 1925.

33. McDonald, *John Levi of Haskell,* 31; *Indian Leader,* Sept. 19, 1924; McDonald, "Unusual Background," 10.

34. *Supplement to Indian Leader,* May 8, 1925.

35. *Indian Leader,* Oct. 3, 10, 17, 1924.

36. Philip J. Deloria, "Mascots and Other Public Appropriations of Indians," in *Encyclopedia of North American Indians*, 359–60; Adams, *Education for Extinction*, 187; Hoxie, *Final Promise*, 99. Evidence that games against Haskell did take on an aspect of frontier nostalgia for some can be seen in the following from the University of Detroit's student newspaper: "Custer's Massacre was avenged last Saturday when the Haskell Indians attempted to ambush the Titans. They returned to the reservation much sadder and wiser tribesmen" (William Harrington, "Titans Trample Tawny Tribes," *Varsity News*, Nov. 9, 1927).

37. *Indian Leader*, Nov. 7, 14, 1924.

38. *Indian Leader*, Nov. 14, 1924; "Haskell's Greatest Victory," *Catalog of Haskell Institute, Supplement to Indian Leader* (May 8, 1925), 41–42.

39. *Indian Leader*, Nov. 28, 1924; *Haskell Annual* (1925 yearbook), 75; McDonald, *John Levi of Haskell*, 40–45; *Kansas City Star Magazine*, Sept. 20, 1970. Prucha explains of the Osage Indians: "Largely destitute at the time of their removal, they were located by chance on lands of tremendous riches in oil and gas resources, and they became probably the richest class of people in the world" (*Great Father*, 308).

40. McDonald, "Unusual Background," 10; "The History Behind the Haskell Arch and Stadium" (Haskell fund-raising flyer, 1998), Haskell Archives; *Supplement to Indian Leader*, May 8, 1925; *Indian Leader*, Oct. 29, 1926, 5; *Lawrence Journal-World*, Feb. 19, 1925; "Haskell-Bucknell" game program, Oct. 30, 1926, 12, copy in Haskell Archives.

41. *Indian Leader*, Sept. 18, 1925; "Indian Athletic Hall of Fame Biographical Sheet—Mayes McLain"; *Catalog of Haskell Institute*, May 8, 1925, 44.

42. *Indian Leader*, Nov. 6, Dec. 4, 1925.

43. *Indian Leader*, Oct. 23, Dec. 4, 1925.

44. Adams, *Education for Extinction*, 324.

45. *Des Moines Sunday Register*, Mar. 20, 1983 (the final construction cost of the stadium, from an interview with McDonald); . Granzer, "Indian Education at Haskell," 173; *Cincinnati Enquirer*, Oct. 16, Nov. 26, 1926; *Dayton Daily News*, Oct. 15–17, 1926; *Dayton Journal*, Oct. 15–17, 1926; *Wichita Eagle*, Sept. 25, 1926; *Lawrence Journal-World*, Sept. 11–Dec. 30, 1926; *Boston Sunday Globe*, Nov. 13, 14, 1926.

46. *Indian Leader*, Oct. 29, 1926; *Kansas City Star*, Oct. 31, 1926.

47. Granzer, "Indian Education at Haskell," 174; "Haskell-Bucknell" game program, Oct. 30, 1926, 21.

48. *San Francisco Chronicle*, Dec. 12–19, 1926; *Lawrence Journal-World*, Dec. 18, 19, 1926; "Review of the Season," in *Haskell Annual* (1927 yearbook); "1926 Haskell Figures," *College Football Historical Society* 2 (May 1989): 6. For a detailed account of the 1926 Haskell football season see also Ray Schmidt, "Princes of the Prairies," *College Football Historical Society* 2 (Feb. 1989): 2–8.

49. *Lawrence Journal-World*, Nov. 27, 1926.

50. Granzer, "Indian Education at Haskell," 168.

51. Houlgate, *Football Thesaurus*, 86; *Indian Leader*, Oct. 29, 1926; "Haskell-Bucknell" game program, Oct. 30, 1926, 42.

52. *Indian Leader*, Sept. 23, Oct. 28, Nov. 18, 1927.

53. John Hibner, "Lone Star Dietz," *College Football Historical Society* 1 (Aug. 1988): 1–4.

54. *Indian Leader*, Sept. 13, 1929, 5; Dec. 6, 1929, 4; Dec. 13, 1929, 7; Dec. 27, 1929, 3; "Indian Athletic Hall of Fame Biographical Sheet—Louie Weller"; Houlgate, *Football Thesaurus*, 86–87.

55. *Indian Leader*, Dec. 27, 1929, 3; McDonald, "Unusual Background," 12–14.

56. *Kansas City Star*, Oct. 11, 1930.

57. Houlgate, *Football Thesaurus*, 86; McCarty, *All-America*, 104–7; McDonald, "Unusual Background," 15.

58. Granzer, "Indian Education at Haskell," 171; McDonald, "Unusual Background," 14, 16–18.

59. Granzer, "Indian Education at Haskell," 193. In 1931 Haskell reached an enrollment of 1,236 students (ibid., 184).

60. McDonald, "Unusual Background," 21, 24; Granzer, "Indian Education at Haskell," 171, 193.

61. McDonald, "Unusual Background," 25–26.

62. Ibid., 25–28, 33.

63. Ibid.

64. Houlgate, *Football Thesaurus*, 86–87.

9. Scandals and Disputes

1. Smith, *Sports and Freedom*, 119; Howard J. Savage et al., *American College Athletics*, 225.

2. The Carnegie Report provided specific information on slush-fund amounts at various schools in its discussion of the practice (Howard J. Savage et al., *American College Athletics*, 259). See also John Watterson's discussions on recruiting and subsidizing practices in *College Football*, 158–69.

3. Carlson, *College Football Scorebook*, 700–701.

4. "Coast Big Three in Row over Pros," *Chicago Tribune*, Oct. 30, 1924; *Los Angeles Times*, Oct. 30, 1924.

5. *Los Angeles Times*, Oct. 31, 1924.

6. Ibid.

7. "Collegians Disagree," *Los Angeles Times*, Nov. 2, 1924.

8. Ibid.

9. Ibid.

10. *Los Angeles Times*, Nov. 3, 1924.

11. "Trojan Council Calls Off Game," *Los Angeles Times*, Nov. 4, 1924.

12. Ibid.

13. Ibid.

14. "California, Stanford and U.S.C. Present Their Case," *Los Angeles Times*, Nov. 5, 1924.

15. Ibid.; Bill Henry, "Observations," *Los Angeles Times*, Nov. 5, 1924.

16. "Oakland Team to Show Here," *Los Angeles Times*, Nov. 5, 1924; "Card Tickets Good Saturday," *Los Angeles Times*, Nov. 5, 1924; Ray Schmidt, "St. Mary's 1924 Mystery Game," *College Football Historical Society* 7 (May 1994): 1–4.

17. "Hawkeyes Coming for Big Game," *Los Angeles Times*, Dec. 12, 1924.

18. Harry B. Smith, "Peace for Colleges," *Los Angeles Times*, Feb. 19, 1925.

19. Ibid.

20. W. B. Bovard to Rockne, Jan. 15, 27, 1925, Box 8, Folder 179, UADR. One of the rumors mentioned at the time of the dispute's settlement was that Gus Henderson's "retirement" as head football coach at USC, already public knowledge by February 1925, had been one of the conditions imposed by Cal and Stanford for resuming athletic relations. It was definitely not true, as Henderson's contract was bought out by Bovard to clear the head coaching spot for Rockne, a hiring that never took place. See Henderson to Rockne, Feb. 20, 1925, Box 13, Folder 66, UADR; and Smith, "Peace for Colleges."

21. "Grid Captain Is Ruled Out," *Los Angeles Times*, Sept. 22, 1925; Paul Lowry, "Grid Spectacle Keeps 70,000 Fans in Frenzy," *Los Angeles Times*, Oct. 18, 1925.

22. David L. Porter, ed., *Biographical Dictionary of American Sports: Football*, s.v. "Jones, Howard Harding"; Carlson, *College Football Scorebook*, 325.

23. Frederic G. Higbee, "Faculty Memoirs: F. G. Higbee" (unpublished memoir in University of Iowa Archives, 1958), 1–3.

24. Lamb and McGrane, *75 Years*, 100–101.

25. Ibid.

26. *Mason City Globe-Gazette*, Jan. 16, 1928.

27. *Joliet Evening Herald-News*, Dec. 9, 1928.

28. Ibid.

29. Higbee, "Faculty Memoirs," 1–3; Paul Belting to Walter Jessup, Apr. 26, 1929, Athletics: Box 2, Folder "Athletic Situation, 1928–29," University of Iowa Archives.

30. *Cedar Rapids Gazette and Republican*, May 26, 1929.

31. *Cedar Rapids Gazette and Republican*, May 27, 1929; Lamb and McGrane, *75 Years*, 106.

32. John L. Griffith to Jessup, May 31, 1929, Athletics: Box 1, Folder "Athletic Board of Control Correspondence Concerning 1929–30 Controversy," University of Iowa Archives.

33. Ibid.

34. Rufus H. Fitzgerald to Jessup, June 3, 1929, Athletics: Box 2, Folder "Athletic Situation, 1928–29," University of Iowa Archives.

35. Ibid.

36. Ibid.

37. Higbee, "Faculty Memoirs," 1–3; Lamb and McGrane, *75 Years*, 111.

38. See Athletics: Box 1, Folder "Athletics Board of Control Correspondence Concerning 1929–30 Controversy," University of Iowa Archives, for letters from Secretary-Board in Control to Griffith, Oct. 10, 1929; and Frederic G. Higbee to the Directors and Officers of the Alumni Association, Dec. 14, 1929, for examples of Iowa's attempts to avoid suspending specific athletes, along with the final acknowledgment that the university must bow to the "higher authority of the Conference" (C. L. Brewer to Higbee, Jan. 3, 1930, ibid.). See also Lamb and McGrane, *75 Years*, 114, for examples of the many technicalities advanced by Iowa officials.

39. Edward Lauer, "Memorandum on Big Ten Meeting," in *Board in Control of Athletics: Minutes of Meeting, 1929–1934*, 33–35, in University of Iowa Archives.

40. Ibid.

41. Unsigned memorandum, Jan. 10, 1930, Athletics: Box 1, Folder "Athletics Board of Control Correspondence Concerning 1929–30 Controversy," University of Iowa Archives; Yost to L. W. St. John, Jan. 18, 1930, Folder "Intercollegiate Conference: Iowa Controversy: 1929–1920," OSUA.

42. *Cedar Rapids Gazette and Republican*, Feb. 3, 1930; "The Ineligibility of Certain Iowa Athletes," an unsigned and undated memorandum in Athletics: Box 1, Folder "Athletics Board of Control Correspondence Concerning 1929–30 Controversy," University of Iowa Archives. The unsigned memorandum was apparently written in early 1930, and the four-page document does an excellent job of outlining the various actions taken by the Iowa Board of Control in attempting to gain reinstatement to the conference.

43. Griffith to Higbee, Mar. 10, 1930, Athletics: Box 1, Folder "Athletics Board of Control Correspondence Concerning 1929–30 Controversy," University of Iowa Archives.

44. Higbee, "Faculty Memoirs," 5, 17; "Faculty File: Rufus H. Fitzgerald," University of Iowa Archives. With other Big Ten schools being considered equally guilty of recruiting practices—the Carnegie Report leaving Illinois and Chicago as the only two schools unmentioned for violations—later writers have expressed the commonly held perception of 1930 that "Iowa was made the scapegoat paying for the sins of all conference schools" (Lamb and McGrane, *75 Years*, 134).

45. Jack Clary, *Army vs. Navy: Seventy Years of Football Rivalry*, 29, 319.

46. Ibid., 97–98.

47. Ibid., 322–23; *New York Times*, Sept. 18, 1926; *New Orleans Times-Picayune*, Nov. 15, 1927; Clary, *Army vs. Navy*, 98; *Kansas City Star*, Dec. 4, 1927; *New York Times*, Dec. 15, 1927. The *New York Times* carried the complete text of the statement issued by Major General Williams, completely spelling out West Point's position on the debate.

48. *New York Times*, Dec. 15, 1927.

49. *New York Times*, Dec. 17, 1927.

50. Ibid.

51. *New York Times*, Dec. 18, 1927. See also *Joliet Evening Herald-News*, Dec. 18, 1927, for an example of the basic Associated Press dispatch on the break in relations between the two academies.

52. *New York Times*, Dec. 20, 1928; Dec. 27, 28, 1928.

53. *New York Times*, Oct. 8, 18, 1929.

54. *New York Times*, Oct. 31, 1929.

55. *Chicago Herald and Examiner*, Nov. 5, 1930; *New Orleans Times-Picayune*, Nov. 7, 1930; *New York Times*, Nov. 8, 1930; *New Orleans Times-Picayune*, Nov. 11, 14, 1930; *New York Times*, Dec. 14, 1930.

56. Clary, *Army vs. Navy*, 102–3, 107–11, 134; Tim Cohane, *Gridiron Grenadiers*, 188, 192–93.

57. Jay Dunn, *The Tigers of Princeton: Old Nassau Football*, 69, 95; Marcia G. Synnott, "The Big Three and the Harvard-Princeton Football Break, 1926–1934," 190; *Princeton Herald*, Aug. 20, 1926; "Charles Kennedy Memo," Sept. 14, 1926, Box 86, PUAF. George Trevor wrote that "Harvard is working toward the day when intramural sports will replace inter-collegiate contests, the annual Yale game remaining the only outside contact" ("Football Feuds"). For another review of this controversy, see also Bernstein, *Football*, 136–40, 155–56.

58. Undated memo by Charles Kennedy, Box 86, PUAF; "Princeton and Harvard," *Harvard Alumni Bulletin*, Nov. 18, 1926, 201–2.

59. "Princeton and Harvard," *Harvard Alumni Bulletin*, Nov. 18, 1926, 201–2.

60. *Harvard Lampoon*, Nov. 3, 1926; *Harvard Crimson*, Nov. 6, 1926; "Setting the Pace," *New York Sun*, Nov. 8, 1926.

61. *Daily Princetonian*, Nov. 9, 1926; "Princeton and Harvard," *Harvard Alumni Bulletin*, Nov. 18, 1926, 203. The *Alumni Bulletin* article notes that the *Lampoon* staff members, obviously stunned by the reaction to their articles, sent a letter of apology to the *Daily Princetonian* in which they stated, "The *Lampoon* in its latest issue was guilty of a breach of good taste which has not the support of Harvard authorities or graduates. . . . It was certainly not our intention that the quips in the *Lampoon* should carry the weight which has been attached to them by its readers" ("Princeton and Harvard," 204).

62. "Slurs in *Lampoon* Stir Princeton Men," *New York Times*, Nov. 8, 1926; Kennedy to William Bingham, Nov. 10, 1926, Box 85, PUAF; *Joliet Evening Herald-News*, Nov. 11, 1926.

63. "Princeton and Harvard," 204; "Harvard and Princeton?" *Princeton Alumni Weekly*, Nov. 12, 19, 1926.

64. "Princeton Severs Athletic Relations with Harvard," *Princeton Alumni Weekly*, Nov. 19, 1926, 245; Lawrence Perry, "For the Game's Sake," *New York Sun*, Nov. 10, 1926; Kenneth Webb, "The Harvard-Princeton Row," *New York Herald Tribune*, Dec. 5, 1926; "Leaving Big Three," *New York Evening Post*, Nov. 11, 1926.

65. "Yale Men Regard Break as Tragedy," *New York Sun*, Nov. 11, 1926; "Yale Men Offer Aid in Pacifying Rivals," *New York Times*, Nov. 19, 1926; "Princeton-Yale Athletic Agreement," *Yale-Princeton Game Program*, Nov. 12, 1927, 18. For examples of the general media commentary on the "ridiculous situation," see "Gentlemen and Scholars and Football," *New York Times*, Nov. 12, 1926; and "The Big Fight," *New York Daily News*, Nov. 12, 1926.

66. Wynant Davis Hubbard, "Dirty Football: A Former Harvard Player Tells Why His University Broke Relations with Princeton," 38, 43–44; "Hubbard Renews Football Attack," *New York Sun,* Jan. 26, 1927.

67. "Lowell Opposed Hubbard Attack on Princeton," *New York Tribune,* Jan. 25, 1927; "Lowell Attempted to Stop Hubbard," *New York Times,* 25 Jan. 1927; "Football Men Deny Rough Play by Princeton," *New York Herald Tribune,* Jan. 24, 1927; "Officials in Harvard Games Discredit Published Charges," *Princeton Alumni Weekly,* Feb. 4, 1927, 487.

68. "Princeton Must Act First," *New York Times,* Mar. 11, 1927; "Princeton Peace Voted at Harvard," *New York Times,* Jan. 21, 1931; "Princeton-Harvard Resume Relations," *New York Times,* Feb. 14, 1931.

69. "Reshuffling Football's Ancient and Honorable Triple Alliance"; "Grid Relations Between Harvard and Princeton to Be Renewed," *Daily Princetonian,* Jan. 9, 1933.

70. "A Happy Truce," an undated *New York Times* editorial reprinted in the *Daily Princetonian,* Jan. 11, 1933.

10. The Debate over Reform

1. Thelin, *Games Colleges Play,* 23. Writing of the 1920s, Thelin has noted that "American college sports programs' expenses, crowds, and public appeal had long departed from the Oxford-Cambridge model of genuine amateur sports by and for students" (24).

2. William H. McNeill, *Hutchins' University: A Memoir of the University of Chicago, 1929–1950,* 8; "Football Frenzy," *Heights,* Nov. 6, 1928, 2; Hoover, "College Football," 257.

3. For a good review of early faculty resistance to the growth of intercollegiate sport, see Smith, *Sports and Freedom,* 118, 120.

4. Mervin D. Hyman and Gordon S. White Jr., *Big Ten Football: Its Life and Times, Great Coaches, Players, and Games,* 24–26; C. A. Waldo, "Regulation of Athletics—What Next?"

5. Smith, *Sports and Freedom,* 202; "First to Abolish Game," article from unknown newspaper, Nov. 24, 1905, found in Camp Papers, Yale University Archives.

6. Sol Metzger, "College Athletes and the Problem of Professionalism," *New York Sun,* Dec. 12, 1915.

7. "College Athletics Near Ideal System," *New York Times,* Dec. 31, 1917.

8. Ibid.; George F. Gundelfinger, *The Decay of Bulldogism: Secret Chapters in Yale Football History,* 37 (quote from *Yale Alumni Weekly* of Nov. 11, 1917); "Money and College Athletics."

9. Minutes from the Apr. 15–16, 1921, meeting at MIT are found in Fred J. Bell, "Report of the Proceedings in the Athletic Division of the Intercollegiate Conference on Undergraduate Government," an undated report in "Athletic Board: 1913–1928," OSUA.

10. "College Football Reform," *New York Times,* Oct. 26, 1924; "Too Much Football," *New York Times,* Nov. 27, 1923; "Reforming Football," *New York Times,* Nov. 30, 1926; Tunis, "The Great God Football," 746.

11. "Football: Frankenstein of Athletics," 52.

12. Quote from report of President A. Lawrence Lowell of Harvard is found in Gundelfinger, *Decay of Bulldogism,* 68. Later in the 1920s, with student interest in football beginning to decline at many of the traditional eastern schools, some would point to the noncloistered environment as being responsible. An editorial in the Boston College student newspaper noted that "the so-called college spirit . . . is becoming an unknown quantity at many of the great universities of America. The students feel all at sea among the great throngs of outsiders who swarm to the games" ("Football Frenzy," *Heights,* Nov. 6, 1928). See also *Yale News,* Nov. 16, 1925; and "Yale Spirit Waning," *New York Times,* Dec. 11, 1926.

13. Alexander Meiklejohn, "What Are College Games For?" 668; "Football Reforms Urged by Harvard," *New York Times,* Oct. 23, 1925; Dr. Karl Wettstone, *Dubuque's Stand Against Commercialized Athletics,* July 1925, a pamphlet concerning Dubuque's discontinuance of intercollegiate sport, Box 123, Stagg Papers.

14. Gundelfinger, *Decay of Bulldogism,* 195–97 (illustrations of Yale's use of football themes in its 1927 endowment drive); Lawrence Perry, "For the Game's Sake," *Sandusky (Ohio) Register,* Dec. 18, 1923.

15. James F. Foley, "Hilltop Sport Mirror," *Marquette Tribune,* Sept. 30, 1926, 10; Raymond L. Summers, "The Football Business," 319.

16. "Football Is Denounced by a Star," *New York Times,* Nov. 7, 1925; Grantland Rice, "The Gang's All Here"; John W. Heisman, "Their Weight in Gold." Heisman was often identified by reformers as one of the coaches contributing to football's overemphasis. This opinion was solidified in early 1929 when it was disclosed that in a letter to Coach H. C. Byrd of Maryland, Heisman had proposed that a national college champion be determined by a four-team playoff each season ("Four-Team Tourney to Decide U.S. Football Title Proposed," *New York Times,* Jan. 16, 1929).

17. Bell, "Intercollegiate Conference on Undergraduate Government," 3. See also Stevens Institute's President Alex Humphreys to President Charles W. Lyons, June 28, 1926, Box 3, Folder "Sports: Football 1888–1940," Georgetown University Archives; and "Football Scholarships," *New York World,* Jan. 23, 1927. "Conference Director's Meeting Minutes," June 1, 1922, Box 84, Folder 5, Stagg Papers; Ray Schmidt, "Major John Griffith," *College Football Historical Society* 13, no. 2 (Feb. 2000): 1–3. Details on the sharing of Griffith's expenses by the Big Ten schools, and the difficulties in calculating and collecting the amounts due from each member school, can be seen in N. A. Kellogg to Stagg, Jan. 26, July 3, 1923, Box 84, Folder 6; and John Griffith to Stagg, Oct. 24, 1924, Box 84, Folder 8, Stagg Papers. Griffith to L. W. St. John, Apr. 5, 1923, "Intercollegiate Conference Commissioner: Correspondence 1922–29," OSUA.

18. Griffith to Directors of Athletics of the Intercollegiate Conference, 1 Apr. 1924, "Intercollegiate Conference Commissioner Memoranda: 1922–26," OSUA. A copy of Griffith's May 25, 1925, letter to the high school principals can be found in "Intercollegiate Conference Commissioner Memoranda: 1922–26," OSUA.

19. Griffith to Directors of Athletics of the Western Conference, Sept. 23, 1926, "Intercollegiate Conference Commissioner Memoranda: 1926–29," OSUA; Griffith to Athletic Directors, Sept. 29, 1926, "Intercollegiate Conference Commissioner Memoranda: 1926–29," OSUA.

20. Griffith to Walter A. Jessup, May 31, 1929, Athletics Box 1, Folder "Athletics Board of Control Correspondence Concerning 1929–30 Controversy," University of Iowa Archives; Heisman, "Their Weight in Gold."

21. Smith, *Sports and Freedom,* 147, 162.

22. Rice, "The Gang's All Here"; Smith, *Sports and Freedom,* 148.

23. Donald Grant Herring, "The Princeton Season in Review," *Princeton Alumni Weekly,* Dec. 3, 1919, Jan. 7, 1920; *Princeton Alumni Weekly,* Nov. 3, 1920, Nov. 22, 1922, Sept. 24, 1926; Herring, "The Princeton Season Reviewed," *Princeton Alumni Weekly,* Nov. 24, 1920. See also Lou Young, "Touchdown Technic"; 28; and "Coaching, a Profession," *New York Times,* Aug. 28, 1924.

24. Hoover, "College Football," 257; "Football Reforms Urged by Harvard," *New York Times,* Oct. 23, 1925; "Shall Intercollegiate Football Be Abolished?" 68; "Wants Coaches Picked From Alumni Ranks," *New York Times,* Dec. 29, 1925.

25. John R. Tunis, "Whose Game Is It?" 424–25.

26. "Shall Football Be Abolished?" 69–71; "Harvard Paper Urges Three-Game Schedule," *New York Times,* Dec. 1, 1925; "Moore Criticizes Curtailment," *New York Times,* Dec. 9, 1925. Hamilton Holt, president of Rollins College in Florida, wrote that the major problem for college football was "the timidity

and laxity of college authorities in enforcing the standards they set." Holt also believed that dropping football was not the answer to the problems of over-emphasis and commercialization ("An Appeal to College Presidents," May 3, 1927, Box 85, Folder 3, Stagg Papers). See also Wettstone, *Dubuque's Stand Against Commercialized College Athletics*, 5, 19, 23.

27. "Football Reforms Urged by Students," *New York Times*, Dec. 7, 1925.

28. "Yelping Alumni," 23. See also "Revaluing Football," *New York Times*, Dec. 3, 1925. A variation on the "class series" proposal came from A. A. Stagg in 1925 and 1926. At the conference meeting in both years, the Chicago coach unsuccessfully suggested that Big Ten schools limit the selection of their football teams to students in their junior and senior years (Stagg to L. W. St. John, May 25, 1926, "Athletic Director's Correspondence: 1912–1956 [Folder 2 of 2]," OSUA.

29. "Harvard Paper Urges Three-Game Schedule," *New York Times*, Dec. 1, 1925; David P. Reed, "Is College Football Doomed?" The *New York Evening Post* article by Tunis, titled "Player Control," was reprinted in its entirety in the *Hoya*, Oct. 23, 1929. "Football Reform Urged by Students," *New York Times*, 7 Dec. 1925; Tunis, "Whose Game Is It?" 425, 437.

30. Tunis, "Whose Game Is It?" 440.

31. Ibid.

32. Lester, *Stagg's University*, 17–19; Roberts, *Big Nine*, 14.

33. Ronald Smith has also noted that by the close of the nineteenth century, "football . . . could provide the proof that colleges as institutions, as well as college men, were virile," and that college presidents "generally praised" the sport "for fostering manly virtues" (*Sports and Freedom*, 96–97). The quote from Dr. Norlin's address before the College and High School Section of the Colorado State Teachers' Association in 1908 was found in the *Colorado School Journal* (Feb. 1909), copy of article in Box 123, Stagg Papers.

34. The quote from General Wood was repeated in a speech by Bill Roper, Princeton's football coach, in an address to the university's National Alumni Association meeting in Chicago in October 1922 ("The Value of College Athletics: Address by William W. Roper," *Princeton Alumni Weekly*, Nov. 8, 1922, 123). Hamilton Fish Jr., "In Defense of Modern Football"; George Marvin, "The Big Business of Football," 184. For additional examples of endorsements for the relationship between intercollegiate football and the demands of active military life, see "The Friendly Fight," *New York Times*, Oct. 19, 1919, and a quote from President Lotus D. Coffman of the University of Minnesota in "Football or Baseball the National Game?" 66.

35. "Strikes at Critics of College Sports," *New York Times*, Dec. 7, 1923; "The Value of College Athletics," *Princeton Alumni Weekly*, 123; "The Growth of Football," a memo from John Griffith to the Big Ten Directors of Athletics, Dec. 18, 1924, Folder "Commissioner, Memoranda 1922–1926," OSUA. Shortly after being appointed Big Ten commissioner, Griffith explained to *Outlook* magazine, "The evils which threaten our inter-collegiate athletics are gambling, professionalism, distrust and enmities which sometimes arise over the contests and a willingness to violate the rules" (Griffith letter to Newton Fuessle of *Outlook* magazine, Aug. 10, 1922, Folder "Commissioner, Correspondence 1922–29," OSUA). See also Paul Belting, "Physical Education at Iowa," *Iowa Alumnus*, Oct. 20, 1924, 64–65. "Collegiate Competition," *Varsity News*, Dec. 4, 8, 15, 1920.

36. "Praises Football as College Sport," *New York Times*, Dec. 10, 1923; "Football Receipts Support 16 Other Sports at Penn," *New York Times*, Dec. 21, 1924; "Two of 15 Sports Paid Way at Penn," *New York Times*, Dec. 11, 1926; "$801,258 Received for Sports at Yale," *New York Times*, Dec. 4, 1925; "Rockne Hits at Opponents of Football," *Joliet Evening Herald-News*, Sept. 25, 1926.

37. Excerpts from Griffith's paper to the 1925 NCAA convention are found in "College Officials to Meet This Week," *New York Times*, Dec. 27, 1925. See also Haikell, "Football as Big Business," 245; and the editorials entitled "College Athletics," *New Haven (Conn.) Union*, Jan. 2, 1925, and "Colleges and

Athletics," *Reno (Nev.) Gazette,* Jan. 10, 1925, which were both reprinted and distributed by Griffith of the Big Ten and are found in Folder "Commissioner Memoranda: 1922–26," OSUA.

38. "E. K. Hall, 62, Dead: Leader in Football," *New York Times,* Nov. 11, 1932. A version of the Associated Press obituary is "Hall, Executive Head of College Football," *San Francisco Examiner,* Nov. 11, 1932. E. K. Hall, "Report of American Intercollegiate Football Rules Committee," Dec. 1922, Box 50, Folder 10, Stagg Papers; "American Coaches Bar Pro Brethren," *New York Times,* Dec. 29, 1925.

39. Ibid.; "Colleges Deplore Games for Profit," *New York Times,* Dec. 31, 1925.

40. Among other things, the Big Ten Conference presidents and athletic officials agreed that it was not legitimate for athletic directors and coaches to initiate correspondence, distribute literature, or conduct interviews for the purpose of seeking athletes or to request students or alumni to do so. It was also agreed that "athletes will be compelled to sign a sworn statement to the effect they have not violated a single phase of the recommendation" (Walter Eckersall, "Bar Gifts and Scholarships for Athletes," *Chicago Tribune,* Jan. 29, 1927).

41. Fred A. Hayner, "New Code to Abolish Sport Proselyting," *Chicago Daily News,* Jan. 27, 1927; Eckersall, "Bar Gifts and Scholarships." Other conferences and groupings of schools were also making public declarations of their opposition to athletic recruiting during the late 1920s. See "Football as the 'Goat' of College Sports."

42. Information on preliminary findings by the Carnegie investigators is in Griffith to Athletic Directors, Sept. 29, 1926, Folder "Commissioner Memoranda: 1926–1929," OSUA. "Colleges Deplore Games for Profit," *New York Times,* Dec. 31, 1925; "How Football Fosters Fair Play and Clean Living," 58; Grantland Rice, "The Spoil-Sports."

43. "Rockne Hits at Opponents of Football," *Joliet Evening Herald-News,* Sept. 25, 1926; *New York Times,* Dec. 8, 1925; Roper, *Football, Today and Tomorrow,* 137; Tad Jones, "Let Football Alone," 81–83; "Tad Jones Defends Game," *New York Times,* Dec. 8, 1925. Examples of student publications supporting football's place in university life can be found in Charles L. Bruce, "Arranging a University Football Schedule," *Varsity News,* Holiday Number 1923–1924, 9; and the introduction to the "Athletics" section, in *The Archive: Being the Saint Louis University Year Book (1929).*

44. Letter from Daniel L. Marsh to Professors and Instructors of Members of the Football Squad, Oct. 9, 1928, found in "Reggie Brown Notebook Collection," Notebook no. 6, Joyce Sports Research Collection, University of Notre Dame.

45. Tunis, "The Great God Football," 750.

46. "The Season," *Daily Princetonian,* Nov. 7, 1927.

11. THE CARNEGIE REPORT

1. "Shall Football Be Abolished?" 68.

2. "Athletic Life in School Needs Housecleaning," *Los Angeles Times,* Sept. 20, 1925; "Shall Football Be Abolished?" 68.

3. "Athletic Life in School Needs Housecleaning"; Watterson, *College Football,* 159–60. A summary of the findings on collegiate sport as contained in the 18th annual report of the President of the Carnegie Foundation for the Advancement of Teaching was distributed to the Big Ten athletic directors with a cover letter on Sept. 20, 1924 by John L. Griffith, and a copy can be found in "Commissioner Memoranda: 1922–26," OSUA.

4. Savage et al., *American College Athletics,* 4.

5. Griffith to Athletic Directors, Sept. 29, 1926, "Commissioner Memoranda 1926–1929," OSUA; John Wilce to L. W. St. John, Jan. 12, 1928, "Record of Proceedings and the Official Minutes of the 1927–28 meetings of Athletic Board," OSUA.

6. The statement of the overall findings of the Carnegie Report is found in "The Athletic Probe," *Princeton Alumni Weekly,* Nov. 1, 1929, 156; Savage et al., *American College Athletics,* 308.

7. Savage et al., *American College Athletics,* xiv–xv.

8. Ibid., 107, 197.

9. Ibid., 225, 240, 265.

10. Ibid., 228, 237, 239, 264.

11. Ibid., 164–71, 186.

12. Ibid., 273–77.

13. Thelin, *Games Colleges Play,* 13, 22, and 25; Watterson, *College Football,* 176; Savage et al., *American College Athletics,* 80.

14. Ibid., 306–7, 309–10.

15. "The Big Scrimmage over College Football," 58; John Kieran, "Sports of the Times," *New York Times,* Oct. 25, 1929.

16. Examples of the typical stories on the release of the Carnegie Report can be found in any sizable community's daily newspaper. Representative of the United Press wire service release is "Proselyting Lid Lifted," *Ventura County Star,* Oct. 24, 1929. Coverage of the major losses incurred on the New York Stock Exchange is ongoing in any newspaper dated from Oct. 23, 1929 onward.

17. *Washington Post,* Oct. 26, 1929; Walter Trumbull, "Gridiron Probe Findings Give Food for Thought," *Washington Star,* Oct. 26, 1929; Westbrook Pegler, "Carnegie Probe Seems to Be a Waste of Time," *Chicago Tribune,* Oct. 25, 1929; "Big Scrimmage" (quotation from the *New York World* article); John B. Fullen, "Carnegie Report Is Expected to Have Beneficial Effect," *Ohio State University Monthly* (Nov. 1929): 55–56; "The Press and College Sports," *New York Times,* Oct. 26, 1929.

18. "False, Untrue, Misleading, Is General Word," *Chicago Herald and Examiner,* Oct. 25, 1929; "Big Scrimmage," 66; "Sports Study Stirs Furor in Colleges," *New York Times,* Oct. 25, 1929; "The Athletic Probe," *Princeton Alumni Weekly,* Nov. 1, 1929, 156; United Press dispatch titled "U.S.C. Denies Sports Charge," *Ventura County Star,* Oct. 24, 1929.

19. Fullen, "Carnegie Report;" Schoonmaker, "Pity the Poor Athlete," 686; Kieran, "Sports of the Times," *New York Times,* Oct. 25, 1929.

20. Versions of the United Press articles on eastern student reactions can be found in Morris DeHaven Tracy, "Radical Thoughts Arise over Sports Subsidizing," *Ventura County Star,* Oct. 29, 1929; and Tracy, "New England Schools Seek Carnegie Charge Panacea," *Ventura County Star,* Nov. 2, 1929.

21. Bert Demby, "Mid-West Colleges Take Carnegie Report Calmly," *Ventura County Star,* Oct. 31, 1929.

22. Arthur J. Daley, "N.C.A.A. Endorses Carnegie Report," *New York Times,* Jan. 2, 1930. In early 1930, the Big Ten's athletic directors met and this time they began to adopt some agreements aimed at the problem of recruiting—the widely publicized agreements adopted in January 1927 apparently having fallen by the wayside (John L. Griffith, "Minutes of the Meeting of the Directors of the Intercollegiate Conference," Dec. 6–7, 1929, Box 85, Folder 8, Stagg Papers; Griffith, "Minutes of the Meeting of the Directors of Athletics," Mar. 7–8, 1930, Box 86, Folder 2, Stagg Papers).

23. Daley, "N.C.A.A. Endorses Carnegie Report." See also Griffith, "Summary of the Discussion of the Athletic Directors," Dec. 5, 1930, Box 86, Folder 2, Stagg Papers.

24. Griffith to L. W. St. John, Nov. 6, 1929, "Intercollegiate Conference Commissioner: Correspondence, 1929–1931," OSUA; Griffith to Directors of Athletics of the Intercollegiate Conference, Nov. 26, 1929, "Intercollegiate Conference Commissioner Memoranda: 1929–1933," OSUA; Griffith, "The Carnegie Reports," 325; "Zuppke Attacks Football Enemies," an unattributed newspaper article found in Box 8, Zuppke File, University of Illinois Archives.

25. Griffith to Savage, Oct. 29, 1929; Savage to Griffith, Nov. 1, 1929, "Intercollegiate Conference Reports: Carnegie 1929–1930," OSUA.

26. There is a discussion of the Carnegie findings related to Michigan athletics and the stolen correspondence in Behee, *Fielding Yost's Legacy*, 107–10. "U.S.C. Denies Sports Charge," a United Press story in the *Ventura County Star*, Oct. 24, 1929. USC claimed that researcher Harold Bentley had stated to university officials that they ran, "a very efficient athletic system and that he found nothing off color or out of the way." Considering USC's difficulties with Stanford and California just a few years earlier over allegations of illegal recruiting and subsidization, such a statement should have been questioned by any university official ("Sports Study Stirs Furor in Colleges," *New York Times*, Oct. 25, 1929).

27. "Football Is Now Being Overemphasized," *New Orleans Times-Picayune*, Oct. 16, 1930; Robert F. Kelley, "Roper at Princeton Luncheon," *New York Times*, Oct. 16, 1930; "Roper Sees Decline Ahead for Football," *New York Times*, Dec. 21, 1930; "Bezdek Assails College Sports as Harming Boys," *New York Herald Tribune*, Dec. 17, 1929; Reverend Charles L. O'Donnell, "This Football Phenomenon," 39–40. Amos Alonzo Stagg defended the holding of spring football practice, but added that, "at Chicago, we put no pressure on anybody to take spring football. . . . The revolt against spring practice comes mainly from the attempt to conduct it with much of the strenuosity of the regular football season and because of the application of pressure . . . to force letter men and substitutes to turn out for practice" (Stagg to Ralph Cannon, Aug. 18, 1930, Box 110, Folder 8, Stagg Papers).

28. "College Athletics under Fire at Convention of Professors," an uncredited newspaper clipping dated Dec. 28, 1929, in *Football Scrapbook, 1929–30*, Fordham University Archives. In respect to the Big Ten's disciplinary action of 1929 against Iowa, Missouri refused to schedule a football game for 1930 against the Hawkeyes, and C. L. Brewer, Missouri's athletic director, wrote: "I feel that the most important principle of intercollegiate athletics is involved and that . . . regulations imposed by conferences are our greatest safe-guards in the conduct of intercollegiate athletics" (Brewer to Higbee, Jan. 3, 1930, Athletics Box 1, Folder "Correspondence Concerning 1929–1930 Controversy," University of Iowa Archives).

29. Griffith, "The Carnegie Reports," 327; Griffith, "Summary of the Discussion of the Athletic Directors," Dec. 5, 1930, Box 86, Folder 2, Stagg Papers.

30. Summers, "The Football Business"; "Buying Football Players," *New York Times*, Nov. 5, 1929 (commentary on the Summers article); Tunis, "The Great God Football."

31. "Yale Weekly Predicts Decline of Football," *New York Times*, Oct. 25, 1929. The *Ventura County Star*, Oct. 31, 1929, was one of the newspapers carrying the short United Press dispatch on Angell's speech.

32. Orlo L. Robertson, "Reform Board Is Appointed," *Los Angeles Times*, Jan. 2, 1930.

33. "Speech to University of Detroit Alumni Banquet by Reverend John P. McNichols," 1930, File "Fr. McNichols, President," Folder 2, University of Detroit Archives.

34. Earl Coughlin, "New Era in Intercollegiate Athletics Seen on Horizon," *Cedar Rapids Sunday Gazette and Republican*, Feb. 2, 1930; Watterson, *College Football*, 235. Watterson also presents an excellent review of the North Central's attempt at athletic administration during the early 1950s (272–75).

35. Lowell to Angell, Oct. 25, 1930, Box 26, Folder 283, Angell Papers, Yale University Archives.

36. Angell to Savage, Oct. 25, 1930, ibid., Box 25, Folder 278.

37. Savage to Angell, Oct. 24, 1930, ibid.

38. Angell to Savage, Oct. 25, 1930; Savage to Angell, Oct. 28, 1930, ibid.

39. Robert F. Kelley, "Lafayette's Head Indicts Football," *New York Times*, Dec. 30, 1930.

40. Ibid.

41. "Gridiron Probe Findings Give Food for Thought," *Washington Star*, Oct. 26, 1929; Thelin, *Games Colleges Play*, 38–39. For a general overview of Bulletin no. 26, see "Letting the Air Out." In the immediate aftermath of the release of Bulletin no. 23 in October 1929, attendance at college games

experienced no identifiable decline from their decadelong popularity. It was only when the 1930 season rolled around that the economic woes of the Depression became measurable in college football's attendance, Watterson noting that football attendance ultimately declined 25 percent between 1929 and 1933 (*College Football*, 177).

42. Watterson, *College Football*, 175–76; "Grid Charge Causes Talk," *Ventura County Star*, Oct. 25, 1929; Clarence E. Cason, "The Football Hero Rebels," 491.

43. "Address by Bob Zuppke to 1931 NEA Sports Meeting in Detroit," Zuppke File, Box 1, University of Illinois Archives. See also "Football," *Varsity News*, Oct. 23, 1929, 2; and Griffith, "The Carnegie Reports," 325.

44. Griffith, "Education for Character and for World Peace," an address before the South Dakota State Teachers Association, 26 Nov. 1929, "Intercollegiate Conference Commissioner Correspondence: 1922–29," OSUA; "Big Scrimmage." An excellent analysis of the Carnegie Report's historical significance for sport can be found in Watterson, *College Football*, 175–76.

Epilogue

1. "Millions Listen in on Rose Festival," *New York Times*, 3 Jan. 1928. The growing financial problems for intercollegiate sport were clearly being documented in the public media by late 1930, and private acknowledgments of this reality can be found in letters of the time between athletic officials. One such example came from Amos Alonzo Stagg of the University of Chicago, who in early 1931 noted that his athletic department had suffered deficits during the two previous football seasons as gross receipts declined to less than one-half of previous levels (Stagg to Parke Davis, Apr. 29, 1931, Box 2, Folder 1, Stagg Papers).

2. Baker, *Football: Facts and Figures*, 639–43; McCarty, *All-America*, 108–11; Earl Gustkey, "Rockne's Last Game," *Los Angeles Times*, Dec. 6, 1990.

3. "What of Football Without Rockne?"; "Rock Is of the Ages"; "Rockne: Maker of Men, Idol of Boys." Michael Oriard took note of the five biographies of Rockne written in the aftermath of his 1931 passing, and commented that such writings joined the many newspaper and magazine articles in "collectively transforming Rockne from a shrewd and charismatic football coach into the mythic spirit of college football itself" (*King Football*, 130).

4. *Joliet Evening Herald-News*, Nov. 14, 1921; "A Symbol of Football," *New York Times*, Apr. 2, 1931; Steele, *Knute Rockne*, 47; Danzig and Brandwein, *Sport's Golden Age*, 125 (Woodward quote).

5. "A Symbol of Football," *New York Times*, Apr. 2, 1931; Edward P. Madigan, "Knute Rockne: A Great Man Passes."

6. "Rock Is of the Ages"; "A Symbol of Football," *New York Times*, Apr. 2, 1931, 26; "Rockne."

7. I have chosen to delimit college football's "Age of Transformation" with Knute Rockne's passing because of the significant role he played in the gridiron game's glory days of the 1920s, and also because of the somber mood that had already settled onto the sport by early 1931. A notable sportswriter of the time, Allison Danzig, wrote, "Rockne became the most publicized coach in the entire history of football. . . . More than anyone else, this flat-nosed, bald-headed dynamo from Norway was responsible for the tremendous boom that intercollegiate football enjoyed in the twenties" (*American Football*, 233). See also "Rockne's Record Impressive One," *New York Times*, Dec. 26, 1924.

8. "Zuppke Defends Football Despite Carnegie Reports," an unattributed 1931 newspaper article in Box 8, Zuppke File, University of Illinois Archives. For a review of the College All-Star Game series and its role in helping to popularize pro football, see Raymond Schmidt, *Football's Stars of Summer: A History of the College All-Star Football Game Series of 1934–1976*.

9. In his letter to Angell, William Garland, president of the Tenth Olympiade Committee, indicated the great respect that the eastern Big Three still commanded: "Having decided upon the game it was the most logical and easiest thing imaginable for our Committee to hope that Yale University would provided one of the teams." In Angell's reply it was clear that Yale officials had reluctantly reached their decision, and he noted that, "I only regret that it seems to us so impossible to reach any other decision." Garland to Angell, Jan. 30, 1931; Angell to Garland, Feb. 5, 1931, Box 26, Folder 283, Angell Papers, Yale University Archives.

10. McNeill, *Hutchins' University*, 97. The University of Chicago eventually returned to intercollegiate football in 1968 at the NCAA Division III level (small college).

11. Gene Ward, "Yale Will Go 'Small-Time' on Gridiron," *San Francisco Chronicle*, Oct. 15, 1940. Contrary to the comments by Ogden Miller of Yale, the significant role college football has continued to play in university life has been endorsed periodically throughout the sport's history, examples in more modern times being University of Missouri historian Frank F. Stephens's comment that the sport is "a necessary part of student life" (*History of Missouri*, 559), while Oriard has noted that football is "not an adjunct to higher education but a fundamental aspect of it" (*King Football*, 366).

SELECTED BIBLIOGRAPHY

During the course of researching intercollegiate football for the period of 1919–1930, I consulted numerous books dealing with the history of the game, along with others that related to various aspects of American social history for the time. Also of great benefit to my studies were the many articles on the sport that appeared in the popular periodicals of the period, in newspapers, and in student and alumni publications at many of the universities visited.

BOOKS AND ARTICLES

Adams, David Wallace. *Education for Extinction: American Indians and the Boarding School Experience, 1875–1928*. Lawrence: Univ. Press of Kansas, 1995.

Allen, Frederick Lewis. *The Big Change: America Transforms Itself, 1900–1950*. New York: Harper and Brothers, 1952.

Andrada, Randy. *They Did It Every Time: The Saga of the Saint Mary's Gaels*. Self-published, 1987.

Andrews, Wayne. *Architecture, Ambition, and Americans: A Social History of American Architecture*. New York: Free Press, 1978.

Baker, Dr. L. H. *Football: Facts and Figures*. New York: Farrar and Rinehart, 1945.

Bealer, Carter N. "A Distinguished Exception." *Freeman* 7 (Aug. 8, 1923): 521.

Bealle, Morris A. *The Georgetown Hoyas*. Washington, D.C.: Columbia Publishing, 1947.

———. *The History of Football at Harvard, 1874–1948*. Washington, D.C.: Columbia Publishing, 1948.

Behee, John Richard. *Fielding Yost's Legacy*. Ann Arbor: Uhlrich's Books, 1971.

Berkhofer, Robert F., Jr. *The White Man's Indian: Images of the American Indian from Columbus to the Present*. New York: Alfred A. Knopf, 1978.

Bernstein, Mark F. *Football: The Ivy League Origins of an American Obsession*. Philadelphia: Univ. of Pennsylvania Press, 2001.

"The Big Scrimmage over College Football." *Literary Digest*, Nov. 9, 1929, 58–70.

Britt, Albert. "Football on Eastern Gridirons." *Outing*, Jan. 1922, 154–57.

Brodie, S. Dan. *66 Years on the California Gridiron, 1882–1948*. Oakland: Olympic Publishing, 1949.

Bynum, Mike, ed. *Pop Warner: Football's Greatest Teacher*. Washington, D.C.: Gridiron Football Properties, 1993.

Camp, Walter. "The All-America Team." *Collier's*, Dec. 13, 1919, 8.

———. "Walter Camp Reviews 1923 Football." *Collier's,* Dec. 15, 1923, 20.

———. "Walter Camp's Sports Page," *Collier's,* Dec. 1, 1923.

———. "What Happened to Football in 1922." *Collier's,* Dec. 23, 1922, 13.

———. "Wise Commercialism Will Win." *Collier's,* Dec. 1, 1923.

Carlson, Kenneth N. *College Football Scorebook.* Lynnwood, Wash.: Rain Belt Publications, 1984.

Carroll, John M. *Red Grange and the Rise of Modern Football.* Urbana: Univ. of Illinois Press, 1999.

Cason, Clarence E. "The Football Hero Rebels." *Nation,* Oct. 30, 1929, 490–91.

Chalk, Ocania. *Black College Sport.* New York: Dodd, Mead, 1976.

Christian, Charles M., with the assistance of Sari J. Bennett. *Black Saga: The African American Experience.* Boston: Houghton Mifflin, 1995.

Clary, Jack. *Army vs. Navy: Seventy Years of Football Rivalry.* New York: Ronald Press, 1965.

Coben, Stanley. *Rebellion Against Victorianism: The Impetus for Cultural Change in 1920s America.* New York: Oxford Univ. Press, 1991.

Cohane, Tim. *Gridiron Grenadiers.* New York: G. P. Putnam's Sons, 1948.

"College Football." *New Republic,* Oct. 19, 1927, 224–26.

Daly, Charles D. *American Football.* New York: Harper and Brothers, 1921.

Danzig, Allison. *The History of American Football: Its Great Teams, Players, and Coaches.* Englewood Cliffs, N.J.: Prentice-Hall, 1956.

Danzig, Allison, and Peter Brandwein, eds. *Sport's Golden Age: A Close-Up of the Fabulous Twenties.* New York: Harper and Brothers, 1948.

Davis, Parke H. *Football: The American Intercollegiate Game.* New York: Charles Scribner's Sons, 1912.

Deloria, Philip J. "Mascots and Other Public Appropriations of Indians." In *Encyclopedia of North American Indians,* edited by Frederick E. Hoxie, 359–60. Boston: Houghton Mifflin, 1996.

DeRoos, Robert. "Remaking a National Sport." *Stanford Observer* (Mar.–Apr. 1994), 14.

"Differences Between Red and White Football Material." *Literary Digest,* Dec. 11, 1920, 78.

Discover Marquette. Milwaukee: Marquette Univ., 1998.

Donovan, Charles F., David R. Dunigan, and Paul A. Fitzgerald. *History of Boston College: From the Beginnings to 1990.* Chestnut Hill: Univ. Press of Boston College, 1990.

Doyle, Andrew. "Causes Won, Not Lost: College Football and the Modernization of the American South." *International Journal of the History of Sport* 11 (Aug. 1994): 231–51.

DuBois, W. E. B. "Opinion." *Crisis,* Nov. 1920, 15.

———. "Opinion." *Crisis,* Aug. 1926, 163.

Dunn, Jay. *The Tigers of Princeton: Old Nassau Football.* Huntsville, Ala.: Strode Publishers, 1977.

Dunnavant, Keith. *Coach: The Life of Paul "Bear" Bryant.* New York: Simon and Schuster, 1996.

Elliott, Len. *One Hundred Years of Princeton Football.* Princeton: Princeton Athletic News, 1969.

Estell, Kenneth, ed. *The African-American Almanac.* 6th ed. Detroit: Gale Research, 1994.

Falla, Jack. *Till the Echoes Ring Again: A Pictorial History of Boston College Sports*. Lexington, Mass.: Stephen Greene Press, 1982.

"First Unit of Memorial Stadium to Be Ready." *Missouri Alumnus* 14, no. 2 (Oct. 1925): 35.

Fish, Hamilton, Jr. "In Defense of Modern Football." *Saturday Evening Post*, Dec. 19, 1925, 118.

"Football: The Frankenstein of Athletics." *Literary Digest*, Dec. 1, 1923, 52–59.

"Football, Quo Vadis?" *Outlook*, Jan. 14, 1925, 52–53.

"Football as Our Greatest Popular Spectacle." *Literary Digest*, Dec. 2, 1922, 52–57.

"Football as the `Goat' of College Sports." *Literary Digest*, Jan. 15, 1927, 80–81.

"Football in 1916." *Outing*, Jan. 1917, 475–80.

"Football or Baseball the National Game?" *Literary Digest*, Dec. 6, 1924, 61–66.

"Football Post-Mortem Finds Zuppke at Best." *Magazine Sigma Chi* (Jan.–Feb. 1930): 63.

"Football's Biggest Year." *Outing*, Jan. 1923, 149–51, 175.

"Football's New Czar." *Literary Digest*, Mar. 27, 1926, 54–58.

"Football under Fire." *Outlook*, Dec. 16, 1925.

"Football with a Haskell War Whoop." *Kansas City Star Magazine*, Sept. 20, 1970, 10.

Fordham Today: On the Eve of the Sesquicentennial. New York: Fordham Univ., 1988.

Freidel, Frank, and Alan Brinkley. *America in the Twentieth Century*. 5th ed. New York: Alfred A. Knopf, 1982.

Gems, Gerald R. *For Pride, Profit, and Patriarchy: Football and the Incorporation of American Cultural Values*. Lanham, Md.: Scarecrow Press, 2000.

———. "The Prep Bowl: Football and Religious Acculturation in Chicago, 1927–1963." *Journal of Sport History* 23, no. 3 (Fall 1996): 284–302.

Gillis, Chester. *Roman Catholicism in America*. New York: Columbia Univ. Press, 1999.

Griffith, John. "The Carnegie Reports." *Journal of Higher Education* 1 (June 1930): 325–29.

Gundelfinger, George F. *The Decay of Bulldogism: Secret Chapters in Yale Football History*. Sewickley, Penn.: New Fraternity, 1930.

Haikell, Douglas P. "Football as Big Business." *New Republic*, Jan. 19, 1927, 244–45.

Hamilton, Raphael N. *The Story of Marquette University*. Milwaukee: Marquette Univ. Press, 1953.

Hasenfus, Nathaniel J. *Athletics at Boston College*. Vol. 1, *Football and Hockey*. Worcester: Heffernan Press, 1943.

Haughton, Percy D. *Football and How to Watch It*. Boston: Marshall Jones, 1922.

Heisman, John W. "Their Weight in Gold." *Collier's*, Nov. 24, 1928, 28.

Henderson, Edwin Bancroft. *The Negro in Sports*. Washington, D.C.: Associated Publishers, 1939.

Herring, Donald Grant, Sr. *40 Years of Football*. New York: Carlyle House, 1940.

Hoover, Glenn E. "College Football." *New Republic*, Apr. 14, 1926, 257–58.

Houlgate, Deke. *The Football Thesaurus: 77 Years on the American Gridiron*. Los Angeles: Nash-U-Nal Publishing, 1946.

"How Football Fosters Fair Play and Clean Living." *Literary Digest*, Oct. 31, 1925, 57–58.

Hoxie, Frederick E. *A Final Promise: The Campaign to Assimilate the Indians, 1880–1920*. Lincoln: Univ. of Nebraska Press, 1984.

Hubbard, Wynant Davis. "Dirty Football: A Former Harvard Player Tells Why His University Broke Relations with Princeton." *Liberty,* Jan. 29, 1927, 38, 43–44.

Hurd, Michael. *Black College Football, 1892–1992: One Hundred Years of History, Education, and Pride.* 2d ed. Virginia Beach: Donning, 1998.

Hyman, Mervin D., and Gordon S. White Jr. *Big Ten Football: Its Life and Times, Great Coaches, Players, and Games.* New York: Macmillan, 1977.

"It's a Far Cry from Red Grange to Heffelfinger." *Literary Digest,* Oct. 31, 1925, 55–56.

Jones, Howard H., and Alfred F. Wesson. *Football for the Fan.* Los Angeles: Times-Mirror Press, 1929.

Jones, Paul. "Foot Ball in Negro Colleges in 1924." *Crisis,* Feb. 1925, 172.

———. "Foot Ball in Negro Colleges in 1925." *Crisis,* Mar. 1926, 221–24.

———. "Foot Ball in Negro Colleges in 1926." *Crisis,* Mar. 1927, 7.

———. "Foot Ball in Negro Colleges, 1927." *Crisis,* Feb. 1928, 45.

Jones, Tad. "Let Football Alone." *Outlook,* Sept. 21, 1927, 81–83.

Kaye, Ivan N. *Good Clean Violence: A History of College Football.* Philadelphia: Lippincott, 1973.

Keith, Harold. *Oklahoma Kickoff.* Norman: Univ. of Oklahoma Press, 1978.

Kelley, Robin D. G., and Earl Lewis, eds. *To Make Our World Anew: A History of African Americans.* New York: Oxford Univ. Press, 2000.

Kelly, Lawrence C. *The Assault on Assimilation: John Collier and the Origins of Indian Policy Reform.* Albuquerque: Univ. of New Mexico Press, 1983.

Lamb, Dick, and Bert McGrane. *75 Years with the Fighting Hawkeyes.* Iowa City: Univ. of Iowa Athletic Department, 1964.

"Law Building and Stadium Completed." *Notre Dame Alumnus,* Sept. 1930, 4.

Lester, Robin. *Stagg's University: The Rise, Decline, and Fall of Big-Time Football at Chicago.* Urbana: Univ. of Illinois Press, 1995.

"Letting the Air Out of College Football." *Literary Digest,* June 27, 1931, 40–41.

Little, L. L. "Football's Biggest Year." *Outing,* Jan. 1923, 147.

Madigan, Edward P. "Knute Rockne: A Great Man Passes." *College Forum,* May 1931, 4.

Martin, Charles H. "Integrating New Year's Day: The Racial Politics of College Bowl Games in the American South." *Journal of Sport History* 24 (Fall 1997): 360.

———. "Racial Change and `Big-Time' College Football in Georgia: The Age of Segregation, 1892–1957." *Georgia Historical Quarterly* 80 (Fall 1996): 532–62.

Marvin, George. "The Big Business of Football." *Outlook,* Oct. 3, 1923, 183–87.

Massa, Mark S. *Catholics and American Culture: Fulton Sheen, Dorothy Day, and the Notre Dame Football Team.* New York: Crossroad Publishing, 1999.

McCarty, Bernie. *All-America: The Complete Roster of Football's Heroes.* Vol. 1, *1889–1945.* University Park, Ill.: Self-published, 1991.

McClellan, Keith. *The Sunday Game: At the Dawn of Professional Football.* Akron, Ohio: Univ. of Akron Press, 1998.

McDonald, Frank W. *John Levi of Haskell.* Lawrence, Kan.: World, 1972.

McNeill, William H. *Hutchins' University: A Memoir of the University of Chicago, 1929–1950.* Chicago: Univ. of Chicago Press, 1991.

Meiklejohn, Alexander. "What Are College Games For?" *Atlantic Monthly,* Nov. 1922, 663–71.

Michelson, Herb, and Dave Newhouse. *Rose Bowl Football since 1902.* New York: Stein and Day, 1977.

Miller, Patrick. "To `Bring the Race along Rapidly': Sport, Student Culture, and Educational Mission at Historically Black Colleges During the Interwar Years." *History of Education Quarterly* 35, no. 2 (Summer 1995): 111–33.

Miller, Patrick, and David K. Wiggins, eds. *Sport and the Color Line: Black Athletes and Race Relations in Twentieth-Century America.* New York: Routledge, 2004.

"Money and College Athletics." *Nation,* Oct. 12, 1916, 339–40.

Morris, Charles R. *American Catholic.* New York: Times Books, 1997.

Morse, Brick. *California Football History.* Berkeley: Gillick Press, 1937.

Mule, Marty. *Sugar Bowl: The First Fifty Years.* Birmingham, Ala.: Oxmoor House, 1983.

Muller, Herman J. *The University of Detroit, 1877–1977: A Centennial History.* Detroit: Univ. of Detroit, 1976.

Munson, Gorham. *The Awakening Twenties.* Baton Rouge: Louisiana State Univ. Press, 1985.

Newman, Zipp. *The Impact of Southern Football.* Montgomery, Ala.: Morros-Bell Publishing, 1969.

"The New Order in Football Playing." *Literary Digest,* Jan. 15, 1921, 58–59.

Nilan, Roxanne, and Karen Bartholomew. "Rivalry and Entrepreneurship Mark 1921 Construction." *Stanford Historical Society Newsletter* 9, no. 1 (Autumn 1984): 1–7.

O'Donnell, Reverend Charles L. "This Football Phenomenon." *Notre Dame Alumnus* 9, no. 2 (Oct. 1930): 39–41.

"An Open Market for Galloping Ghosts." *Outlook,* Dec. 2, 1925, 507–8.

Oriard, Michael. "Home Teams." *South Atlantic Quarterly* 95 (Spring 1996): 471–500.

———. *King Football: Sport and Spectacle in the Golden Age of Radio and Newsreels, Movies and Magazines, the Weekly and the Daily Press.* Chapel Hill: Univ. of North Carolina Press, 2001.

———. *Reading Football: How the Popular Press Created an American Spectacle.* Chapel Hill: Univ. of North Carolina Press, 1993.

"Palmer Stadium." *Princeton Athletic News* (Fall 1996): 62.

Parrish, Michael E. *Anxious Decades: America in Prosperity and Depression, 1920–1941.* New York: W. W. Norton, 1992.

Patterson, E. C. "Collier's All-Western Conference Eleven." *Collier's,* Dec. 11, 1920, 13.

Poe, Neilson. "The Forward Pass." *Leslie's Illustrated Weekly,* Nov. 12, 1921, 662–63, 682.

Pollard, James E. *Ohio State Athletics, 1879–1959.* Columbus: Ohio State University, 1959.

"Poor Professional Football." *Outlook,* Oct. 27, 1926, 262.

Porter, David L., ed. *Biographical Dictionary of American Sports: Football.* New York: Greenwood Press, 1987.

Powers, William K. *Indians of the Northern Plains.* New York: G. P. Putnam's Sons, 1969.

Prucha, Francis Paul. *The Great Father: The United States and the American Indians.* Lincoln: Univ. of Nebraska Press, 1986.

Rappoport, Ken. *Wake Up the Echoes.* Huntsville, Ala.: Strode Publishers, 1984.

Reed, David P. "Is College Football Doomed?" *Outlook,* Dec. 23, 1925, 627–28.

Reed, Herbert. "DeGranging Football." *Outlook,* Jan. 20, 1926, 102–4.

———. "Football Lessons of 1924." *Outlook,* Nov. 26, 1924, 498–501.

———. "Football Lessons of the Year." *Outing,* Jan. 1915, 504–8.

———. "Nassau's Football Uprising." *Outlook and Independent,* Dec. 5, 1928, 1288–89.

———. "1925 Football a Game That Dazzles," *Outlook,* Nov. 4, 1925, 348–50.

"Reshuffling Football's Ancient and Honorable Triple Alliance." *Literary Digest,* Mar. 7, 1931, 40.

Rice, Grantland. "Coaches to the Depot." *Collier's,* Sept. 28, 1929, 11.

———. "Fast Work," *Collier's,* Nov. 30, 1929, 21.

———. "The Gang's All Here." *Collier's* Nov. 7, 1925, 15.

———. "Not in the Rules." *Collier's,* Dec. 29, 1928, 17.

———. "The Pigskin Ballyhoo." *Collier's,* Sept. 18, 1926, 20.

———. "The Spoil-Sports." *Collier's,* Dec. 18, 1926, 10.

Riess, Steven A. "Power Without Authority: Los Angeles' Elites and the Construction of the Coliseum." *Journal of Sport History* 8, no. 1 (Spring 1981): 50–65.

Riffenburgh, Beau. *The Official NFL Encyclopedia.* New York: New American Library, 1986.

Roberts, Howard. *The Big Nine: The Story of Football in the Western Conference.* New York: G. P. Putnam's Sons, 1948.

"Rock Is of the Ages." *New Republic,* Apr. 15, 1931, 220–22.

"Rockne: Maker of Men, Idol of Boys." *Literary Digest,* Apr. 18, 1931, 29.

Roper, W. W. *Football, Today and Tomorrow.* New York: Duffield, 1927.

———. "Football from the Grand Stand." *Collier's,* Nov. 6, 1920, 13, 16.

Rosten, Leo, ed. *Religions of America: Ferment and Faith in an Age of Crisis.* New York: Simon and Schuster, 1975.

Roth, Leland M. *A Concise History of American Architecture.* New York: Harper and Row, 1979.

Salsinger, H. G. "Football Strategy." *American Boy,* Oct. 1923, 20–21, 41.

Samuelsen, Rube. *The Rose Bowl Game.* Garden City, N.Y.: Doubleday, 1951.

Savage, Howard J., with Harold W. Bentley, John T. McGovern, and Dean F. Smiley, M.D. *American College Athletics.* Bulletin no. 23. New York: Carnegie Foundation for the Advancement of Teaching, 1929.

Saylor, Roger B. *Historically Black Colleges Football Teams Record Book, 1892–1999.* Hobe Sound, Fla.: Self-published, 2000.

Schmidt, Raymond. *Football's Stars of Summer: A History of the College All-Star Football Game Series of 1934–1976.* Lanham, Md.: Scarecrow Press, 2001.

Schoonmaker, Frank. "Pity the Poor Athlete." *Harper's Monthly Magazine,* Nov. 1930, 685–91.

"Shall Intercollegiate Football Be Abolished?" *Literary Digest,* Oct. 10, 1925, 68–76.

Shortridge, James R. *The Middle West: Its Meaning in American Culture.* Lawrence: Univ. Press of Kansas, 1989.

Slosson, Preston William. *The Great Crusade and After, 1914–1928.* New York: Macmillan, 1930.

Smith, Ronald A. *Play-by-Play: Radio, Television, and Big-Time College Sport.* Baltimore: Johns Hopkins Univ. Press, 2001.

———. *Sports and Freedom: The Rise of Big-Time College Athletics.* New York: Oxford Univ. Press, 1988.

Spalding's Official Intercollegiate Football Guide. New York: American Sports Publishing, 1920–1931.

Spence, Clark C. *The Sinews of American Capitalism: An Economic History.* New York: Hill and Wang, 1964.

Sperber, Murray. *Shake Down the Thunder: The Creation of Notre Dame Football.* New York: Henry Holt, 1993.

"Sportsmania in the Colleges: Pro and Con." *Literary Digest,* Dec. 8, 1928, 54.

Stagg, Amos Alonzo, as told to Wesley Winans Stout. *Touchdown!* New York: Longman's, Green, 1927.

Steckbeck, John S. *Fabulous Redmen: The Carlisle Indians and Their Famous Football Teams.* Harrisburg, Penn.: J. Horace McFarland, 1951.

Steele, Michael R. *Knute Rockne: A Bio-Bibliography.* Westport, Conn.: Greenwood Press, 1983.

Stephens, Frank F. *A History of the University of Missouri.* Columbia: Univ. of Missouri Press, 1962.

Stewart, Bruce. "Walter C. Camp: The Father of American Football." *American Football Quarterly* 2 (2nd Quarter, 1996): 79–81.

Summers, Raymond L. "The Football Business." *New Republic,* Nov. 6, 1929, 319–22.

Synnott, Marcia G. "The Big Three and the Harvard-Princeton Football Break, 1926–1934." *Journal of Sport History* 3 (Summer 1976): 188–202.

Thelin, John R. *Games Colleges Play: Scandal and Reform in Intercollegiate Athletics.* Baltimore: Johns Hopkins Univ. Press, 1996.

Tindall, George Brown. *A History of the South.* Vol. 10, *The Emergence of the New South.* Baton Rouge: Louisiana State Univ. Press and the Littlefield Fund for Southern History, 1967.

Tips, Kern. *Football—Texas Style: An Illustrated History of the Southwest Conference.* Garden City, N.Y.: Doubleday, 1964.

Treat, Roger. *The Encyclopedia of Football.* 13th rev. ed. New York: A. S. Barnes, 1975.

Trevor, George. "Football Feuds." *Outlook and Independent,* Nov. 19, 1930, 464.

———. "When the Twain Meet." *Outlook and Independent,* Feb. 5, 1930, 224, 237.

Tunis, John R. "Football on the Wane?" *Harper's Monthly Magazine,* Nov. 1929, 744–54.

———. "The Great God Football." *Harper's Monthly Magazine,* Nov. 1928, 742–52.

———. "Whose Game Is It?" *Outlook and Independent,* Nov. 13, 1929, 424–25, 437, 440.

Vana, Somnia. "College Education: An Inquest." *Freeman* 4 (Feb. 22, 1922): 563.

Waldo, C. A. "Regulation of Athletics—What Next?" *School Review* 11 (May 1903): 305–6.

Wallace, Francis. "This Football Business." *Saturday Evening Post,* Sept. 28, 1929, 10–11, 168, 170.

Walsh, Christy, ed. *College Football and All America Review.* Hollywood: House-Warven Publishers, 1951.

Watterson, John Sayle. *College Football: History, Spectacle, Controversy.* Baltimore: Johns Hopkins Univ. Press, 2000.

"Westward the Star of Football Takes Its Course." *Literary Digest,* Jan. 15, 1927, 66.

Whalen, James, Sr. *Gridiron Greats Now Gone: The Heyday of 19 Former Consensus Top-20 College Football Programs.* Jefferson, N.C.: McFarland, 1991.

"What of Football Without Rockne?" *Literary Digest,* Apr. 11, 1931, 7.

Wheeler, Robert W. *Jim Thorpe: World's Greatest Athlete.* Norman: Univ. of Oklahoma Press, 1983.

Wright, William H. "Come On, Yale!" *Outing,* Nov. 1919, 94.

"Yelping Alumni." *Outlook,* Jan. 6, 1926, 22–23.

Young, Lou. "Touchdown Technic." *Saturday Evening Post,* Nov. 9, 1929, 28.

Ziemba, Joe. *When Football Was Football: The Chicago Cardinals and the Birth of the NFL.* Chicago: Triumph Books, 1999.

NEWSPAPERS

Amsterdam News

Atlanta Constitution

Boston Saturday Evening Transcript

Boston Sunday Globe

Cedar Rapids Gazette and Republican

Champaign (Ill.) News-Gazette

Chicago American

Chicago Daily News

Chicago Defender

Chicago Evening American

Chicago Evening Post

Chicago Herald and Examiner

Chicago Inter-Ocean

Chicago Sun-Times

Chicago Tribune

Cincinnati Enquirer

Cleveland Plain Dealer

Collegian (St. Mary's College)

Columbia Missourian

Daily Illini

Daily Princetonian

Dallas Daily Times-Herald

Dallas Morning News

Dayton Daily News

Dayton Journal

Des Moines Register

Harvard Alumni Bulletin

Harvard Crimson

Harvard Lampoon

Heights (Boston College)

Hoya (Georgetown Univ.)

Indianapolis Freeman

Indian Leader (Haskell Indian School, Lawrence, Kans.)

Iowa City Press-Citizen

Joliet (Ill.) Evening Herald News

Kansas City Journal

Kansas City Star

Lawrence (Kans.) Journal-World

Long Beach (Calif.) Press-Telegram

Los Angeles Times

Marquette (Wisc.) Tribune

Mason City (Iowa) Globe-Gazette

Minneapolis Tribune

Missouri Student

New Orleans Times-Picayune

New York Daily News

New York Evening Post

New York Herald Tribune

New York Sun

New York Times

New York Tribune

New York World

New York World-Telegram

Notre Dame Scholastic

Oakland Tribune

Ohio State University Monthly

Philadelphia Inquirer

Philadelphia Press

Pittsburgh Courier

Princeton Alumni Weekly

Princeton Herald

Ram (Fordham Univ.)

Sandusky (Ohio) Register

San Francisco Call-Bulletin

San Francisco Chronicle

San Francisco Examiner

South Bend News-Times

South Bend Tribune

Sporting Life

St. Louis Globe-Democrat

St. Louis Star
St. Louis Times
Varsity Breeze (St. Louis Univ.)
Varsity News (Univ. of Detroit)
Ventura County (Calif.) Star
Washington Post
Washington Star
Wichita (Kans.) Eagle
Yale Alumni Weekly

INDEX

Abbott, William, 85, 105

Adams, David Wallace, 155, 272n. 10

All-America selections, 21–22, 220, 247n. 27

Alumni coaching, 9, 206

Alumni loyalties: as affected by football, 43, 61; and new stadiums, 48–49; and school's progress and prestige, 47

Alumni relations, 127, 204

Amateur ideals: and alumni involvement, 204; and effects of World War I, 201; and spirit of competition, 80; support for, 76; and threats to continued relevance, 72, 75–76, 80–81

American Football Coaches Association: and actions toward reforms, 213, 232; and opposition to professional football, 65, 78; and opposition to shift plays, 92

Anderson, Eddie, 88

Anderson, Hartley (Hunk), 119, 123

Angell, James R., 30, 202, 229, 231

Army (U.S. Military Academy): and the Navy dispute, 188–92; rivalry with Navy, 31–32

Attendance: and cause of declining figures, 60; figures and revenues, 54–55, 58, 59–60; and problems from growth, 58–59

Automobiles and highways: as stimulus to popularity, 41

Berkhofer, Robert, 155

Big business: and end of Golden Era, 59; factors contributing to image of, 62; and football's need for, 61; legacy of 1920s, 39, 61

Big Ten Conference: attendance and revenue, 54–55, 59; and competitive balance, 13; enrollments and population growth, 43; and the forward pass, 101; and gambling, 59; and hiring first athletic commissioner, 69; and intent in forming, 200, 211; and interest in intersectionals, 31; and the Iowa scandal, 181–88; and opposition to long trips, 30; and opposition to professional football, 65, 69–70; and reform actions, 213, 228, 281n. 40, 282n. 22; and rejected Rose Bowl bid, 17; and the shift formation, 92; and shortage of tickets, 55

Big Three (Harvard, Princeton, and Yale): and early prestige, 8, 9; and the forward pass, 96; and the Harvard-Princeton dispute, 192–97; and intersectional games, 26, 31, 35; and opposition to professional football, 64; Presidents' Agreement, 10, 12, 30, 46; and signs of approaching parity, 10–11; and style of play criticisms, 11, 83, 100; and support for continued significance, 23–24; and threats to tradition, 29–30

Black college football: and big city games, 143–45; cultural significance of, 268n. 8; and dangers of play, 147–49; and discrimination toward writers, 142–43; first game, 132; and game disputes, 135–36; and game officials, 137; and media coverage, 135, 141–43; national champions of, 146–47; and quality of play, 146–47; and schedules, 133; and social events, 134–35, 152

Black colleges: growth of enrollments, 132

Black football players: at predominantly white schools, 148–52

Boston College, 10–11, 80, 111, 114, 127–28

Boston University, 214–15